Frommer's

Jamaica

3rd Edition

by Darwin Porter & Danforth Prince

Here's what the critics say about Frommer's:

"Amazingly easy to use. Very portable, very complete."
—*Booklist*

"Detailed, accurate, and easy-to-read information for all price ranges."
—*Glamour Magazine*

"Hotel information is close to encyclopedic."
—*Des Moines Sunday Register*

"Frommer's Guides have a way of giving you a real feel for a place."
—*Knight Ridder Newspapers*

WILEY

Wiley Publishing, Inc.

About the Author

As a team of veteran travel writers, **Darwin Porter** and **Danforth Prince** have produced numerous titles for Frommer's, including best-selling guides to Italy, France, the Caribbean, England, and Germany. Porter, a former bureau chief of *The Miami Herald,* is also a Hollywood biographer; his most recent releases are *The Secret Life of Humphrey Bogart* and *Katharine the Great,* a close-up of the private life of the late Katharine Hepburn. Prince was formerly employed by the Paris bureau of the *New York Times,* and is currently the president of Blood Moon Productions and other media-related firms.

Published by:

Wiley Publishing, Inc.

111 River St.
Hoboken, NJ 07030-5774

ISBN 0-7645-7064-1

Editor: Stephen Bassman
Production Editor: M. Faunette Johnston
Cartographer: Elizabeth Puhl
Photo Editor: Richard Fox
Production by Wiley Indianapolis Composition Services

Front cover photo: Colorfully dressed woman on beach
Back cover photo: School of Sergeant Majors

For information on our other products and services or to obtain technical support, please contact our Customer Care Department within the U.S. at 800/762-2974, outside the U.S. at 317/572-3993 or fax 317/572-4002.

Wiley also publishes its books in a variety of electronic formats. Some content that appears in print may not be available in electronic formats.

Manufactured in the United States of America

5   4   3   2   1

Contents

(8) Kingston & the Blue Mountains   191

Appendix: Jamaica in Depth   218

Index   237

List of Maps

An Invitation to the Reader

In researching this book, we discovered many wonderful places—hotels, restaurants, shops, and more. We're sure you'll find others. Please tell us about them, so we can share the information with your fellow travelers in upcoming editions. If you were disappointed with a recommendation, we'd love to know that, too. Please write to:

Frommer's Jamaica, 3rd Edition
Wiley Publishing, Inc. • 111 River St. • Hoboken, NJ 07030-5774

An Additional Note

Please be advised that travel information is subject to change at any time—and this is especially true of prices. We therefore suggest that you write or call ahead for confirmation when making your travel plans. The authors, editors, and publisher cannot be held responsible for the experiences of readers while traveling. Your safety is important to us, however, so we encourage you to stay alert and be aware of your surroundings. Keep a close eye on cameras, purses, and wallets, all favorite targets of thieves and pickpockets.

Other Great Guides for Your Trip:

Frommer's Caribbean
Frommer's Caribbean Ports of Call
Frommer's Caribbean from $70 a Day
Caribbean For Dummies
Frommer's Virgin Islands
Frommer's Portable Aruba
Frommer's Dominican Republic
Frommer's Puerto Rico
Frommer's Cuba

Frommer's Star Ratings, Icons & Abbreviations

Every hotel, restaurant, and attraction listing in this guide has been ranked for quality, value, service, amenities, and special features using a **star-rating system**. In country, state, and regional guides, we also rate towns and regions to help you narrow down your choices and budget your time accordingly. Hotels and restaurants are rated on a scale of zero (recommended) to three stars (exceptional). Attractions, shopping, nightlife, towns, and regions are rated according to the following scale: zero stars (recommended), one star (highly recommended), two stars (very highly recommended), and three stars (must-see).

In addition to the star-rating system, we also use **eight feature icons** that point you to the great deals, in-the-know advice, and unique experiences that separate travelers from tourists. Throughout the book, look for:

Finds	Special finds—those places only insiders know about
Fun Fact	Fun facts—details that make travelers more informed and their trips more fun
Kids	Best bets for kids and advice for the whole family
Moments	Special moments—those experiences that memories are made of
Overrated	Places or experiences not worth your time or money
Tips	Insider tips—great ways to save time and money
Value	Great values—where to get the best deals
Warning	Warning—traveler's advisories are usually in effect

The following **abbreviations** are used for credit cards:

AE	American Express	DISC	Discover	V	Visa
DC	Diners Club	MC	MasterCard		

Frommers.com

Now that you have the guidebook to a great trip, visit our website at **www.frommers.com** for travel information on more than 3,000 destinations. With features updated regularly, we give you instant access to the most current trip-planning information available. At Frommers.com, you'll also find the best prices on airfares, accommodations, and car rentals—and you can even book travel online through our travel booking partners. At Frommers.com, you'll also find the following:

- Online updates to our most popular guidebooks
- Vacation sweepstakes and contest giveaways
- Newsletter highlighting the hottest travel trends
- Online travel message boards with featured travel discussions

What's New in Jamaica

The most volatile country in the Caribbean continues to explode with change. Here is a preview of just some of the new developments.

PLANNING A TRIP In August Jamaica comes alive with the pulsating sounds of reggae presented at week-long music extravaganzas. The biggest and best of these has been relaunched as **Reggae Summerfest,** taking place in August (dates vary) at Montego Bay, the leading resort on the island. During the same month an equally compelling festival, the **Reggae Sunfest,** also takes place at Mo Bay. Featured performers include some of the biggest names in reggae, especially Ziggy Marley, son of the late reggae king, Bob Marley. See p. 65.

MONTEGO BAY The old Jack Tar resort, familiar to thousands of visitors, has reincarnated itself as **Montego Beach Resort,** 2 Gloucester Ave. (© **800/858-2258** or 876/952-4340). The 1.3-hectare (3¼-acre) beachfront resort attracts everyone from families to honeymooners, most of whom live in their bathing suits. See p. 59.

NEGRIL This hedonistic resort has seen the opening of a small and intimate inn, **Idle Awhile Resort,** Norman Manley Boulevard (© **877/243-5352**), right on a choice strip of white sand along Seven Mile Beach. You can choose from a double with spacious deluxe bedroom or a junior suite. Everyone from families to loving couples are coddled in luxury here. You can even hire a cook for only $15 a day.

Still new but much larger is **Fun Holiday Beach Resort,** Norman Manley Boulevard (© **876/957-9688**), also on choice sands along the fabled Seven Mile Beach. It offers comfortably furnished and spacious bedrooms, the most desirable accommodations opening onto the ocean. Reggae music and an intriguing beachfront restaurant are part of the charm of this new addition to the Negril hotel scene.

The latest addition is the largest of all the new resorts: **Beaches Sandy Bay,** Norman Manley Boulevard (© **800/BEACHES** or 876/957-5100), an ocean-bordering resort spread across 2.4 hectares (6 acres), opening onto a white-sand beach. Unlike many of the couples-only resorts of Negril, this one is open to singles, couples, and families, the latter finding a nursery and a kids camp a particular attraction. See p. 103.

THE SOUTH COAST Along the emerging southern coastline of Jamaica, **Mar Blue Domicil,** Treasure Beach (© 876/840-5772), has opened to great success even though the stylish little place has only four guest rooms. The complex opens onto the sea with to-die-for balconies and rather stylish, though comparatively simple, furnishings. For such a small place, the restaurant is top-notch—you might want to reserve a table even if you're not a guest. See p. 126.

OCHO RIOS In the northern resort of Ocho Rios, the famous old all-inclusive Ciboney has renewed itself as the **Grand Sport Villa Golf Resort & Spa,** Main Street, St. Ann (© 876/974-1027). Much improved, this lush resort stands on 18 hectares (45 acres) of tropical gardens, with its own white-sand beach. See p. 141.

PORT ANTONIO   A real pocket of posh has opened in this North Coast resort, **Chateau en Exotica,** San San Estate (© 561/793-7257). It contains only three accommodations, but what delightful ones they are, worthy of being called a fantasy retreat. This small and exclusive resort stands on a 2-hectare (5-acre) private estate with lots of white-sand beaches close at hand.

Driving east of Port Antonio you reach Morant Bay and the new **Whispering Bamboo Cove Resort,** 105 Crystal Dr. (© 876/982-1788), which is the ultimate retreat, lying close to the Botanical and Mineral Springs in Bath. This is a little-visited area along the coast of Jamaica and perfect for nature-loving escapists. See p. 189.

KINGSTON   The dining sensation of the capital of Jamaica is **Redbones the Blues Café,** 21 Braemar Ave. (© 876/978-6091). Its Jamaican cuisine is among the finest in the area. The flamboyantly decorated former Spanish colonial setting provides such a glamorous setting you'd want to dine here even if the food weren't as good as it is. See p. 198.

The Best of Jamaica

Most visitors already have a mental picture of Jamaica before they arrive: its boisterous culture of reggae and Rastafarianism; its white-sand beaches; and its lush foliage, rivers, mountains, and clear waterfalls. Jamaica's art and cuisine are also remarkable.

Yet Jamaica's appealing aspects have to be weighed against its poverty, crime, and racial tensions, the legacy of colonial rule and subsequent political upheavals.

So, should you go? By all means. Just be prudent and cautious. The island has fine hotels and savory food. It's well geared to heterosexual couples who come to tie the knot or celebrate a honeymoon. And Jamaica boasts the best golf courses in the West Indies, some of the finest diving waters in the world, and good river rafting. In this chapter we'll lay out our favorite places and experiences.

1 The Best Beaches

- **Doctor's Cave Beach** (Montego Bay): This 8km (5-mile) stretch of white sand made "Mo Bay" a tourist destination. Waters are placid and crystal clear, and there are changing rooms and a beach bar. This one is a family favorite. See p. 72.
- **Cornwall Beach** (Montego Bay): Although it's often crowded, this beach is covered with soft, white, sugary sand. The water is clean and warm, and it's a good spot to take the family. But "higglers"— vendors—will aggressively hawk anything from jewelry to drugs. See p. 72.
- **Seven Mile Beach** (Negril): This beach stretches 11km (7 miles) along the west coast. These golden sands are fine for families, though there are several (sectioned-off) nudist patches where guests bare all. See p. 93.
- **Treasure Beach** (South Coast): Tired of fighting the crowds? Head for this beach on the dry, sunny South Coast. The undertow can be dangerous, so swimming is tricky. But crashing waves make it one of the most dramatic beach-scapes in Jamaica. See p. 124.
- **Boston Bay Beach** (Port Antonio): It's known not only for its white sands and clear waters, but also for the great jerk-pork stands. This beach has the biggest waves in Jamaica, and you can rent surf-boards and even get a lesson. See p. 176.

2 The Best Watersports Outfitters

- **North Coast Marine Sports** (Montego Bay; © 876/953-2211): Offering the best scuba diving in Montego Bay, this staff of instructors knows some great spots to dive among coral reefs. See p. 74.

Jamaica

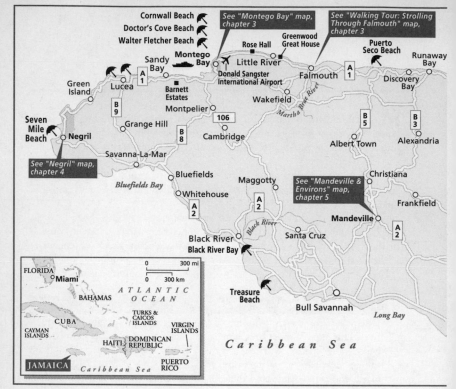

Cornwall Beach
Doctor's Cove Beach
Walter Fletcher Beach

See "Montego Bay" map, chapter 3

See "Walking Tour: Strolling Through Falmouth" map, chapter 3

Greenwood
Great House

Rose Hall

Puerto
Seco Beach

Runaway
Bay

Montego
Bay

Sandy
Bay

Little River

Falmouth

Discovery
Bay

Green
Island

Lucea

Donald Sangster
International Airport

Barnett
Estates

Wakefield

Montpelier

106

Seven
Mile
Beach

Negril

Grange Hill

Cambridge

Albert Town

Alexandria

Savanna-La-Mar

See "Negril" map, chapter 4

Bluefields

Christiana

Bluefields Bay

Maggotty

See "Mandeville & Environs" map, chapter 5

Whitehouse

Frankfield

Mandeville

Black River
Black River Bay

Santa Cruz

FLORIDA

Miami

ATLANTIC
OCEAN

0   300 mi
0   300 km

Treasure
Beach

Bull Savannah

Long Bay

BAHAMAS

CUBA

TURKS &
CAICOS
ISLANDS

VIRGIN
ISLANDS

Caribbean Sea

CAYMAN
ISLANDS

HAITI

DOMINICAN
REPUBLIC

JAMAICA   Caribbean Sea

PUERTO
RICO

- **Negril Scuba Centre** (Negril; ℭ **800/818-2963** in the U.S., or 876/957-9641): This is the best-equipped dive facility in Negril, with a very professional staff. See p. 113.
- **Jamaqua Dive Center** (Runaway Bay; ℭ **876/973-4845**): Its slogan

is "We Be Divin'," and this outfitter takes you to some of the best dive sites along the northern coast. Equipment can be rented on-site, and offerings range from one-tank dives to six-boat packages. See p. 158.

3 The Best Golf Courses

- **White Witch of Rose Hall Golf Course** (Montego Bay; (ℭ **876/ 953-2204**): This is the newest Jamaican golf course and one of the most spectacular, set on 80 hectares (200 acres) of lush greenery. See p. 74.
- **Wyndham Rose Hall Golf & Beach Resort** (Montego Bay;

ℭ **876/953-2650**): This has been called one of the top courses in the world. It's a challenging seaside and mountain course. The 14th hole passes a waterfall. See p. 74.

- **Tryall Club Jamaica** (Montego Bay; ℭ **876/956-5660**): Jamaica's finest course, this is the site of the

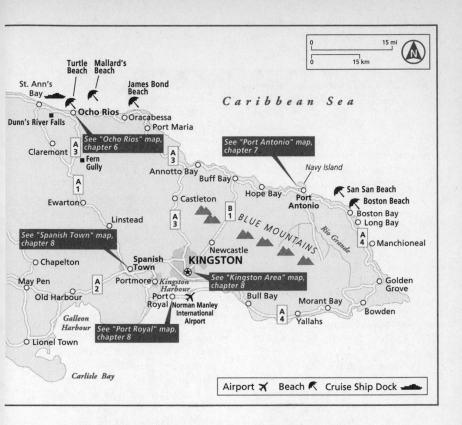

annual Johnnie Walker World Championship. Wind direction can change suddenly, making the course even harder. See p. 57.

- **Half Moon Golf, Tennis & Beach Club** (Montego Bay; **876/953-2211**): A top island course, Half Moon features well-manicured and interestingly shaped greens, but it's not as challenging as the one at Tryall. See p. 56.
- **Sandals Golf & Country Club** (Ocho Rios; ℂ **876/975-0119**): This course is known for panoramic vistas, rolling terrain, and lush vegetation. Sandals guests play for free. See p. 147.

4 The Best Tennis Facilities

- **Half Moon Golf, Tennis & Beach Club** (Montego Bay; ℂ **876/953-2211**): This is Jamaica's best tennis—13 state-of-the-art courts, 7 of which are lit for night games. See p. 56.
- **Wyndham Rose Hall Golf & Beach Resort** (Montego Bay; ℂ **876/953-2650**): This resort has six hard-surface courts, all lit at night. Hotel guests play free. See p. 74.
- **Tryall Club Jamaica** (Montego Bay; ℂ **876/956-5660**): Tryall has nine superb hard-surface courts, three of which are lit for night play. See p. 57.

- **Grand Sport Villa Golf Resort & Spa** (Ocho Rios; ℂ **876/974-1027**): This resort offers three clay and three hard-surface courts, all lit at night. Twice-a-day clinics are offered for beginners as well as advanced players. See p. 147.

5 The Best Natural Attractions

- **Martha Brae's Rafters Village** (Montego Bay; ℂ **876/952-0889**): Martha Brae's Rafters Village offers the best river-rafting experience in and around this popular resort. You sit on a raised dais on bamboo logs and watch the river scenery unfold. See p. 75.
- **The Black River** (South Coast): You can explore what feels like real Tarzan country, with mangrove trees and crocodiles in the wild, on an outing with **South Coast Safaris** (ℂ **876/965-2513**). Lots of wild things grow in these swamps, and birders delight in the bird life. See "The South Coast," on p. 123.
- **Green Grotto Caves** (Discovery Bay; ℂ **876/973-2841**). These limestone caves were once used to hide runaway slaves. They're a world of stalagmites and stalactites, with seemingly endless chambers and eerie Grotto Lake, which you can visit in a boat. See p. 149.
- **Somerset Falls** (Port Antonio): Waters from the Daniels River race down a deep gorge through a rainforest. Flowering vines, waterfalls, and foaming cascades form a lush backdrop. You can swim in the deep rock pools. See p. 185.
- **Rafting on the Rio Grande** (Port Antonio; ℂ **876/913-5434**): Shades of Errol Flynn, this is the grandest rafting experience in Jamaica. The rafts are propelled by bamboo poles. See p. 178.
- **Exploring the Blue Mountains** (outside Kingston; ℂ **876/960-6685**): This is one of the biggest, wildest, and greenest parks in the Caribbean, ideal for exploring. You must hike 5 to 6 hours through thick vegetation (hearing amazing birdsong on the way) to reach the summit. See p. 213.

6 The Best Honeymoon Resorts

- **Sandals** (Montego Bay, Negril, and Ocho Rios; ℂ **800/SANDALS** in the U.S.): These resorts pride themselves on fun, food, and drink, laid out in abundance and all paid for in advance—no tips or bills here. Staff members bring heroic amounts of community spirit and enthusiasm to weddings. All the properties are high-quality, but Sandals Royal Caribbean at Montego Bay and Sandals Dunn's River at Ocho Rios are probably the best in the chain. See p. 65, 106, and 142.
- **Half Moon Golf, Tennis & Beach Club** (Montego Bay; ℂ **876/953-2211**): This resort offers honeymooners deluxe oceanview rooms and cottages fronting a near-perfect crescent-shaped beach. There are lots of activities, too, such as aerobics, tennis, swimming, and, most definitely, golf. See p. 56.
- **Jake's** (Treasure Beach; ℂ **800/OUTPOST**): Funky and idiosyncratic, this is a really offbeat choice for a honeymoon where no one will find you. Set on a remote rocky beach, the place is small and personal. See p. 125.

• **Jamaica Inn** (Ocho Rios; 📞 **800/470-6975** in the U.S., or 876/974-2514): Winston Churchill slept in a suite here; if you can't afford that suite, there are plenty of other classy rooms fine for honeymooners. The resort opens onto a private cove with powdery champagne-colored sand and maintains a British colonial aura of formality. See p. 135.

• **Grand Sport Villa Golf Resort & Spa** (Ocho Rios; 📞 **876/974-1027**): The honeymoon villas at this stately, plantation-style spa and resort are perfect private retreats for newlyweds. Each has a private attendant and pool. Guests are pampered with massages, pedicures, and manicures. The resort is all-inclusive, and there's a range of sports facilities. See p. 141.

• **Blue Lagoon Villas** (Port Antonio; 📞 **800/237-3237**): A favorite with movie stars visiting "off the record," this pocket of posh is pure luxury: Each plush villa comes with a dedicated chef, housekeeper, and butler. Break out your wallet. See p. 166.

• **Sans Souci Resort & Spa** (Ocho Rios; 📞 **800/448-7702** in the U.S., or 876/994-1206): Sink into one of the whirlpool tubs in the elegant marble bathrooms here— with your newly acquired spouse, of course—and the day is yours. This is a far classier joint than the Sandals properties. An on-site spa and clothing-optional beach are also alluring for many couples. See p. 143.

• **Breezes Runaway Bay** (Runaway Bay; 📞 **800/GO-SUPER** or 876/973-4820): Ten kilometers (6 miles) west of Ocho Rios, this all-inclusive hotel re-creates the South Seas on Jamaican soil. It's stylish, with luxurious accommodations and good food. Activities include reggae classes. See p. 155.

7 The Best Family-Friendly Resorts

• **Beaches Boscobel Resort & Golf Club** (Boscobel Beach; 📞 **888/BEACHES**): On a sandy beach 16km (10 miles) east of Ocho Rios, this property is more geared to families than any other hotel on the north shore. See p. 139.

• **FDR Pebbles** (Trelawny, near Montego Bay; 📞 **888/FDR-KIDS** or 876/617-2500): This new hotel caters mainly to families with one or two children, though larger groups can be accommodated. There's a host of activities, and you're even assigned a woman to assist with housekeeping and babysitting. See p. 63.

• **Coyaba** (Mahoe Bay, Little River, Montego Bay; 📞 **877/232-3224** in the U.S., or 876/953-9150): With a graceful British colonial atmosphere, this small all-inclusive resort offers children 11 and under a 50% discount. The oceanfront location is intimate and inviting, with a lovely strip of sandy beach. There's a nanny service to keep little ones fed and entertained. See p. 58.

• **Beaches Negril** (Negril; 📞 **800/BEACHES** in the U.S., or 876/957-9270): Opened in 1997, this is the family-oriented wing of the Sandals chain. A roster of child and teen activities awaits youngsters on grounds studded with palms and sea grapes, adjacent to a sandy beach. There's even a restaurant for "children only." See p. 102.

• **Franklyn D. Resort** (Runaway Bay; 📞 **888/FDR-KIDS** in the U.S., or 876/973-4592): This is a North Coast family favorite. All meals and activities are included in the price; you're housed in Mediterranean-style villas, and a personal attendant takes care of cooking, cleaning, and child care. Lots of programs keep the kids

entertained. A Kiddies' Centre features everything from computers to arts and crafts. See p. 157.

8 The Best Places to Get Away from It All

• **Lethe Estate** (Montego Bay; ☎ **876/956-4920**): Found 16km (10 miles) inland, away from the beach-loving hordes, this elite retreat occupies the grounds of a 61-hectare (150-acre) banana plantation. Inspired by some of the great houses in the area, it was opened to the public in 1996. Bedrooms evoke Jamaica under British colonial rule. See p. 86.

• **Rockhouse** (Negril; ☎ **876/957-4373**): It's like living on the west coast of Africa. You stay in a thatch-roofed villa in Negril's West Inn and sleep in an old-fashioned bed under mosquito netting. It's a splendid getaway if you don't mind climbing down ladders carved into the sea cliffs. Open-air showers cool you off—and let you put on a show for the fish. See p. 101.

• **Treasure Beach Hotel** (South Coast; ☎ **876/965-0110**): On a lush hillside above a sandy South Coast beach, this is a place where

no one will ever find you. It hardly competes with Jamaica's megaresorts, but it does offer tranquillity and a laid-back feel. Bedrooms are in a series of outlying cottages, all offering complete privacy. It's cheap, too. See p. 126.

• **Noël Coward's Blue Harbour** (Port Maria; ☎ **876/725-0289**): The 1950s retreat of Noël Coward, this is where the playwright and composer entertained the rich and famous of his day. Today it's rented whole or in part to paying guests who appreciate its funky nostalgia. See p. 138.

• **Strawberry Hill** (Blue Mountains; ☎ **800/OUTPOST** or 876/944-8400): This highland retreat has been called "a home-away-from-home for five-star Robinson Crusoes." Perched 930m (3,100 ft.) above the sea, it's our favorite lodging in eastern Jamaica. Set in a well-planted garden, the cottage complex is a memorable, lush retreat. See p. 213.

9 The Best All-Inclusives

• **Sandals Montego Bay** (Montego Bay; ☎ **800/SANDALS** in the U.S., or 876/952-5510): This is a honeymoon haven despite a nearby airport of zooming jets. Everything's included, even the notorious toga parties; this place is for couples who want to have a good time. Guests tend to be extroverted and gregarious, and eat and drink their money's worth. We think it's outclassed by better resorts at Ocho Rios, but many vacationers seem to prefer this location. See p. 65.

• **Breezes Montego Bay** (Montego Bay; ☎ **876/940-1150**): This five-story SuperClub complex calls itself "a sandbox for your inner child" and is the only major hotel built on Doctor's Cave Beach. From intimate cabins to lavish suites, you can live it up in various styles and price ranges. See p. 63.

• **Grand Sport Villa Golf Resort & Spa** (Ocho Rios; ☎ **800/BEACHES** in the U.S., or 876/974-1027): This 18-hectare (45-acre) resort is one of the top all-inclusives in the Ocho Rios area. The lodgings consist of one-, two-, and three-bedroom villas, each with its own pool and fully equipped kitchen. The dining choices are the best of any of the competing resorts. It's not directly on the beach, but there's a beauty spa and a health-and-fitness center. See p. 141.

- **Royal Plantation Spa & Golf Resort** (Ocho Rios; 888/48-ROYAL or 876/974-5601): Less than 3km (2 miles) east of Ocho Rios, the main house of this recently renovated all-inclusive resort evokes an antebellum Southern mansion. Among its luxurious touches is the finest hotel spa on the North Coast. See p. 142.
- **Couples Ocho Rios** (Ocho Rios; ℂ 800/268-7537 in the U.S., or 876/975-4271): "Any man and woman in love" are pampered and coddled here; the resort even offers its own private island where couples can bask in the buff. It's more upscale and, we think, classier than either of the Sandals resorts in the Ocho Rios area. Accommodations are top quality, and the food is among the best in the area: Four restaurants serve widely varied cuisine. See p. 140.
- **Hedonism III** (Runaway Bay; ℂ 877/GO-SUPER or 876/973-4100): Serene and isolated, this all-inclusive is the most fun-oriented hotel on the North Coast. It rents rooms to both singles and couples over age 15. There are two good beaches: one where you can wear your suit, and another that's au naturel. See p. 157.

10 The Best Restaurants

- **Sugar Mill Restaurant** (Montego Bay; ℂ 876/953-2314): Located in the Half Moon Club, this is the top restaurant in Montego Bay. The chef's smoked marlin is without equal, and he makes the island's best Jamaican-style bouillabaisse. Guests dine by candlelight indoors or on an open terrace. See p. 68.
- **Norma's** (Negril; ℂ 876/957-4041): Widely acclaimed as Jamaica's finest woman chef, Kingston's Norman Shirley has now brought her recipes to Negril's Sea Splash Resort. The Jamaican and international food here is the finest on Seven Mile Beach, and Norma gets the best produce from local vendors. See p. 107.
- **Redbones the Blues Café** (Kingston; ℂ 876/978-6091): In a former Spanish colonial house, one of the most elegant restaurants on the island is the setting for a refined Jamaican cuisine of artful preparation and unexpected flavors. Ever had shrimp, lobster, and salmon in a creamy coconut sauce? See p. 198.
- **Rockhouse Restaurant** (Negril; ℂ 876/957-4373): Perched above a rocky inlet, this restaurant serves terrific cuisine, such as smoked marlin and peppered pork with yams. See p. 108.
- **Bloomfield Great House** (Mandeville; ℂ 876/962-7130): Once part of a coffee plantation, this restaurant today serves one of the island's best-orchestrated menus—everything from smoked marlin with black caviar to the best pasta dishes in this part of Jamaica. See p. 130.
- **Evita's Italian Restaurant** (Ocho Rios; ℂ 876/974-2333): Evita (actually Eva Myers) is a local culinary star, devoting at least half her menu to pastas. Her recipes range from the north to the south of

Italy. Try snapper stuffed with crabmeat or lobster and scampi in buttery white-cream sauce—all washed down with a good Italian wine. See p. 144.

- **Mille Fleurs** (Port Antonio; ☎ 876/993-7267): In the Hotel Mocking Bird Hill, this restaurant is terraced and perched 180m (600 ft.) above sea level with panoramic views. People come here for the delectable food, which have been praised by *Gourmet* magazine. Opt for coconut-and-garlic soup or the fish with a spicy mango-and-shrimp sauce. See p. 173.
- **Norma's on the Terrace** (Kingston; ☎ 876/968-5488): Kingston's Norma Shirley, the island's foremost female restaurateur, serves up a nouvelle Jamaican cuisine without equal in the area. Try such Jamaican specialties as chowder with crabmeat, shrimp, conch, and lobster, or grilled smoked pork loin in a teriyaki-and-ginger sauce. See p. 198.
- **Day-O Plantation Restaurant** (Montego Bay; ☎ 876/952-1825): On the site of the 19th-century Barnett Plantation—a house that sugar built—this fine restaurant, serving a refined international and Jamaican cuisine, is often a venue for singing and other entertainment. Jamaican spices and herbs permeate all dishes. See p. 67.
- **Strawberry Hill** (Kingston; ☎ 876/944-8400): This is one of the best modern Jamaican restaurants, tucked in the Blue Mountains. Even if you don't stay at this exclusive resort, try grilled fish with jerk mango or grilled shrimp with fresh cilantro in its restaurant. See p. 214.

11 The Best Romantic Experiences

- **Reach Falls** (Manchioneal): East of Port Antonio, this is one of the oft-photographed beauty spots of the Caribbean. Visitors enter a virgin rainforest for a cooling dip and perhaps some nude love-making under the watery cascades. See p. 182.
- **Goldeneye** (Oracabessa; ☎ 800/688-7678): An intimate and romantic retreat east of Ocho Rios, this is our favorite spot in Jamaica for a tryst with your own "secret agent." This is where then-owner Ian Fleming created the character 007, James Bond. Rock stars and other celebs often seek it out. See p. 140.
- **The Blue Lagoon** (Port Antonio; ☎ 876/993-8491): Another beauty spot, this is where teenage Brooke Shields swam nude in the film of the same name. You can have the same experience in an enchanted pool fed by a natural amphitheater. The water, 56m (186 ft.) deep at its deepest point, is said to have aphrodisiac powers—which you'll have to determine for yourself. See p. 166.
- **Bloomfield Great House** (Mandeville; ☎ 876/962-7130): If you should ever grow nostalgic for the Jamaica that used to be, plan a dinner at this historic house set on 2 hectares (5 acres) of beautiful landscaping. After a drink on the old-fashioned veranda, enjoy an elegantly presented and good-tasting meal in a colonial setting of long ago. See p. 130.
- **YS Falls** (Black River): The best place to escape for a romantic picnic is along the coast east of Negril. Three kilometers (2 miles) north of the port of Black River,

in a "Me Tarzan, You Jane" setting, you can actually swing from an overhead vine or a jungle rope

into cooling ponds made by the waterfall. See p. 123.

12 The Best Shopping Buys

- **Art:** Its paintings may never rival those of the finest Haitian artists, but Jamaica is at least the second-best center for art in the Caribbean. Prices are still reasonable, too, even when the artist has a certain renown. Although paintings are sold all over the island, the finest art is found in Kingston at either the **Frame Centre Gallery** or the **Mutual Life Gallery,** the two leading display showcases for the best of the island's artistic talent. See p. 205.
- **Handicrafts:** Crafts come in many forms, ranging from alabaster and woodcarvings to weavings. But quality is highly variable. Any outlet of **Things Jamaican,** including the one in Montego Bay (© **876/952-5605**) has a good assortment of crafts, as does **Harmony Hall** outside Ocho Rios on the North Coast. See p. 149.
- **Fashions:** Many artisans in Jamaica produce quality resort wear; Jamaican women are known as good seamstresses, and they often make quite passable copies of the works of top designers at a fraction of the original's price. Some of the best resort wear is found at **Caribatik Island Fabrics** (Rock Wharf on the Luminous Lagoon; © **876/954-3314**).
- **Jewelry and Watches:** Some watches at various outlets in Jamaica sell for 20% to 40% off stateside prices. Be sure to buy from a reliable dealer, not vendors hustling so-called gold Rolex watches. Jamaican gemstones include coral agate and black coral, and many fashionable pieces are made from these stones; quality handmade necklaces are sold nearly everywhere.

13 The Best After-Dark Fun

- **Time 'n' Place** (Falmouth, east of Montego Bay; © **876/954-4371**): A raffish beach bar built of driftwood, this place looks as though it might blow away in the next storm. The setting is so authentic that many fashion magazines, including *Vogue,* have used it for background shots. The bartender makes the island's best daiquiris. See p. 82.
- **Mingles** (Kingston; © **876/929-9000**): In the Courtleigh Hotel, this is one of the best places—and the safest—to be after dark in the capital of Jamaica. Filled with Jamaican youth, it is both a bar and a dance club, with uniformed
- bartenders and the constant beat of reggae, pop, and soca. See p. 206.
- **Jamaic'N Me Crazy** (Ocho Rios; © **876/974-2201**): The most popular club in this resort area, this hotspot may have the best lighting and sound system on the island. In winter the aura is virtually that of a New York club, so don't come for an authentic Jamaican experience. See p. 154.
- **Hedonism II** (Negril; © **876/957-5200**): For the hottest night at this resort, don your toga and head for the most notorious all-inclusive resort in Jamaica, a place known for its wild and raunchy

parties. If you aren't already a guest, you'll have to purchase a night pass for $75, entitling you to all the food and drink you can consume. See p. 105.

- **Margueritaville Sports Bar & Grill** (Montego Bay; © 876/952-4777): If you're macho, or at least grow hair on your chest, head for the most popular sports bar in Jamaica. Overlooking the sea, across from the Coral Cliff Hotel, this hangout also serves the best margaritas on the island and features the best sports broadcasts on satellite TV. See p. 70.

Planning Your Trip to Jamaica

This chapter will give you all the nuts-and-bolts information about your trip to Jamaica—what you need to do before leaving home. We'll answer questions such as when to go, how to get the best airfare or package deal, what to take along, and what documents you'll need. In case you're not sure where in Jamaica you want to go, we begin with a rundown of the various options.

1 Jamaica in Brief

Most casual visitors to Jamaica pick a resort without paying much attention to its location on the island. That is particularly true for guests who prefer to spend most of their time at an all-inclusive resort, venturing out only occasionally to shop or see some of the local sights. Even so, knowing a bit about the different areas of Jamaica can help you find the perfect resort for you.

Most travelers who visit Kingston do so for business reasons, although for the true Jamaican culture buff, it offers the most museums, the best galleries, and some great historic sights. It also has more nightlife than most of the top resorts, ranging from jazz and reggae clubs to upscale supper clubs and English theater. But you don't come here for beaches.

Port Antonio is for the elite traveler who wants to escape the mass package tours of Ocho Rios or Montego Bay. Come here for some good beaches, plus great river rafting, scuba diving, and snorkeling.

To the west, Ocho Rios features some of the grandest and most traditional resorts in Jamaica, as well as some of the leading Sandals properties. But it doesn't have the best beaches, shops, or scenic attractions.

Nonetheless, if you're resort-oriented, this might be your choice.

The grande dame of Jamaica is Montego Bay, which boasts four of the poshest resorts in the Caribbean. Although we prefer the beaches of Negril, those of Montego Bay are equally fine (if crowded in winter). Shopping here is superb for Jamaica; nightlife is surprisingly lackluster.

Negril's great beaches are for hedonists and families.

The South Coast is for back-road adventurers. Chances are you'll overlook the inland city of Mandeville, although it's a good day trip from Negril or the South Coast.

MONTEGO BAY

This is the number-one destination for all of Jamaica, appealing to the widest possible range of visitors. "Mo Bay," as it's known, has the best golf in the West Indies, and four of the grandest resorts on the island; the duty-free shopping here is great. This is about as far from rural Jamaica as you can get: The tourist dollar drives its economy. But it also boasts several attractions in its environs, including former great houses of plantations, decaying old towns such as Falmouth, and daylong adventures into remote Maroon Country.

NEGRIL

Situated near Jamaica's relatively arid western tip, Negril enjoys a reputation as the nudist center of the West Indies, with a kind of gently provocative do-as-you-please attitude. Its **Seven Mile Beach** is one of the longest uninterrupted stretches of sand in the Caribbean. Other than that beach, its laidback lifestyle, and wild parties, there isn't much here. Outside the megaresorts, restaurants here tend to be locally run dives; amusing, but rarely the place for first-class cuisine.

THE SOUTH COAST

The little-visited South Coast, lying east of Negril along the A2 (the road to Kingston), is undiscovered Jamaica—although it's becoming better known all the time. Contrary to the island's lush, tropical image, this area is dry and arid. Hotels are few and far between, and they are frequently of the mom-and-pop persuasion. The chief draw here is **Treasure Beach,** tucked away on the secluded coast.

MANDEVILLE

Located in south-central Jamaica, Mandeville is the country's highest-altitude town and is built in a style strongly influenced by the British. It is now the center of the island's noted coffee cultivation; a sense of slow-paced colonial charm remains a trademark of the town.

THE NORTH COAST

This region's primary natural attractions include its steeply sloping terrain, the setting for panoramic public gardens and dramatic waterfalls.

Set on a deep-water harbor easily able to accommodate cruise ships, **Ocho Rios** boasts a dense concentration of resort hotels and other vacation spots. It runs a very distant second to Mo Bay in its appeal, although its hinterlands do contain a number of Jamaica's premier attractions, including the overrun Dunn's River Falls. It also can't compete with Mo Bay in beaches or nightlife. What it does offer, however, are some of the grandest resorts in the Caribbean.

Directly west of Ocho Rios is the satellite town of **Runaway Bay,** which boasts a handful of resorts opening onto some good beaches and has the distinct advantage of not being as overrun with tourists as much of Ocho Rios.

The hub of verdant eastern Jamaica, **Port Antonio** still basks in nostalgia. Frequently photographed for its Victorian/Caribbean architecture, it is a refreshing change of pace from touristy Negril, Ocho Rios, and Montego Bay. Beaches such as San San are among the most alluring in the country, and this is also a base for exploring some of the major attractions in Jamaica's hinterlands, including rafting on the Rio Grande River.

KINGSTON & SPANISH TOWN

Located on the southeast coast, **Kingston** is Jamaica's capital, largest city, and principal port. It's a cosmopolitan city with approximately 750,000 residents in its metropolitan area and serves as the country's economic, cultural, and government center. Residents proudly call it the world's reggae capital, as well. The city's northern district, New Kingston, consists mostly of high-rises, modern buildings, business hotels, and upscale homes. There are, however, extensive poverty-stricken areas as well, and it's not the safest city to visit.

Nevertheless, Kingston could make for a fascinating 1-day visit; it has more cultural attractions, including the National Gallery, than anywhere else on the island.

Nearby are the remains of **Port Royal,** once an infamous lair of pirates and renegades. Twenty minutes west of Kingston by car is **Spanish Town,** a slow-paced village containing the Cathedral of St. James.

THE BLUE MOUNTAINS

A land of soaring peaks and deep valleys with luxuriant vegetation, the Blue Mountain range rises to the north of Kingston. Mountain roads wind and dip, and they are in bad repair, so don't try to visit on your own: It's easy to get lost. However, travel agents in Kingston can book you into tours throughout this region of coffee plantations and rum factories. Maintained by the government, the prime part of the mountain range is the 192-acre Blue Mountain–John Crow Mountain National Park.

2 Visitor Information

TOURIST OFFICES

Before you go, you can get information from the **Jamaica Tourist Board** at 1320 S. Dixie Hwy., Suite 1101, **Coral Gables, FL** 33146 (© **800/233-4582** or 305/665-0557).

In Canada contact the office in **Toronto** at 303 Eglinton Ave. E., Suite 200, Toronto, ON M4P IL3 (© **800/ 465-2624** or 416/482-7850). Brits can contact the **London** office: 1–2 Prince Consort Rd., London SW7 2BZ (© 020/7224-0505; www.visitjamaica. com).

INFO ON THE WEB

The Internet is a great source of travel information. Jamaica is on the Internet at **www.jamaicatravel.com**. In addition, **Yahoo** (www.yahoo.com), **Excite** (www.excite.com), **Lycos** (www.lycos. com), **Infoseek** (www.infoseek.com), and the other major Internet indexing sites all have subcategories for travel, country/regional information, and culture—click on all three for links to travel-related websites.

Other good clearinghouse sites for information are **Microsoft Expedia** (www.expedia.com), **Travelocity** (www. travelocity.com), and **Travelweb** (www. travelweb.com).

You might also check out "The Unofficial Website on Jamaica" (**www. jamaicans.com),** the best all-around site, with some good pointers, cultural tidbits, a patois primer, and plenty of humor. This is one of the few Jamaica Web pages that isn't either a blatant ad or just somebody's home page with a few vacation pictures.

TRAVEL AGENTS

Travel agents can save you plenty of time and money by steering you toward the best package deals, hunting down the best airfare for your route, and arranging for cruises and rental cars. Airlines have cut commissions, though, and most agents have to charge a service fee to hold the bottom line. Agents don't get the same rates from all hotels—many have special deals with particular hotels that they do a lot of business with. So if one agent turns you down on a hotel, another may still be able to get you a room, and at a different price. In the worst instances, unscrupulous agents will offer you only travel options that bag them the juiciest commissions. Shop around and ask hard questions—use this book to become an informed consumer.

If you decide to use a travel agent, make sure the agent is a member of the **American Society of Travel Agents (ASTA),** 1101 King St., Alexandria, VA 22314 (© **703/739- 8739;** www.astanet.com). If you send a self-addressed stamped envelope, ASTA will mail you the free booklet *Avoiding Travel Problems.* If you get poor service from an ASTA agent, you can write to the **ASTA Consumer Affairs Department** at the address and phone number above.

You may also want to contact the U.S. State Department for background bulletins, which supply up-to-date information on crime, health concerns, import restrictions, and other travel matters. Write the **Superintendent of Documents, U.S. Government Printing Office,** Washington, DC 20402 (© **202/512-1800**).

DESTINATION: JAMAICA— RED ALERT CHECKLIST

- If you purchased traveler's checks, have you recorded the check numbers and stored the documentation separately from the checks?
- Did you pack your camera and an extra set of camera batteries, and purchase enough film? If you packed film in your checked baggage, did you invest in protective pouches to shield film from airport X-rays?
- Do you have a safe, accessible place to store money?

- Did you bring your ID cards that could entitle you to discounts, such as AAA and AARP cards, student IDs, and so on?
- Did you bring emergency drug prescriptions and extra glasses and/or contact lenses?
- Do you have your credit card PINs?
- If you have an E-ticket, do you have documentation?
- Did you leave a copy of your itinerary with someone at home?
- Did you check to see if any travel advisories have been issued by the U.S. State Department (http:// travel.state.gov/travel_warnings. html) regarding Jamaica?
- Do you have the address and phone number of your country's embassy with you?

3 Entry Requirements & Customs

ENTRY REQUIREMENTS

DOCUMENTS U.S. and Canada residents do not need passports but must have proof of citizenship (or permanent residency) and a return or ongoing ticket. A passport is the best bet, but an original birth certificate (or a certified copy) plus photo ID will usually suffice. Do check on the latest entry requirements before you travel, as the rules can change. Our advice is to always bring a passport when you're going to another country.

Other visitors, including British citizens, need passports that are good for a maximum stay of 6 months.

Immigration cards are given to visitors at the airport arrivals desks. Hold on to yours because you will need to surrender the document to Jamaican Customs when you leave the country.

For information on how to get a passport, go to the "Fast Facts" section of this chapter—the websites listed provide downloadable passport applications as well as the current fees for processing passport applications. For an up-to-date country-by-country listing of passport requirements around the world, go to the "Foreign Entry Requirement" Web page of the U.S. State Department at **http://travel. state.gov/foreignentryreqs.html**.

CUSTOMS

WHAT YOU CAN BRING INTO JAMAICA Many small island nations in the Caribbean let you go through Customs without a thorough check: Jamaica is an exception. The Jamaican government is concerned about drug running and smuggling more than most other island nations. Therefore, your luggage may get a more thorough check in Jamaica than it would elsewhere.

You can bring in 2 liters of alcohol, plus 2 cartons of cigarettes. You're allowed to bring in some duty-free goods, but there's potential confusion here. You're not supposed to bring in an "inordinate" amount of such goods; local Customs officials have great leeway interpreting what's meant by "inordinate." So limit your import of duty-free goods to avoid paying a big import tax.

Tips   Passports

Allow plenty of time before your trip to apply for a passport; processing normally takes 3 weeks but can take longer during busy periods (especially spring). And keep in mind that if you need a passport in a hurry, you'll pay a higher processing fee. When traveling, safeguard your passport in an inconspicuous, inaccessible place like a money belt and keep a copy of the critical pages with your passport number in a separate place. If you lose your passport, visit the nearest consulate of your native country as soon as possible for a replacement.

WHAT YOU CAN TAKE HOME

U.S. Customs   Returning U.S. citizens who have been away for 48 hours or more are allowed to bring back, once every 30 days, $600 worth of merchandise duty-free. You'll be charged a flat rate of 10% duty on the next $1,000 worth of purchases. Be sure to have your receipts handy. On gifts, the duty-free limit is $100. You cannot bring fresh foodstuffs into the United States; canned foods, however, are allowed.

Joint Customs declarations are possible for members of a family traveling together.

Collect receipts for all purchases made abroad. You must also declare on your Customs form the nature and value of all gifts received during your stay abroad. It's prudent to carry proof that you purchased expensive cameras or jewelry on the U.S. mainland. If you purchased such an item during an earlier trip abroad, you should carry proof that you have previously paid Customs duty on the item.

Sometimes merchants suggest a false receipt to undervalue your purchase. *Be warned:* You could be involved in a sting operation—the merchant might be an informer for U.S. Customs.

If you use any medication that contains controlled substances or requires injection, carry an original prescription or a note from your doctor.

For more specifics, write to the **U.S. Customs Service**, 1301 Constitution Ave., P.O. Box 7407, Washington, DC 20044 (© **202/354-1000;** www. customs.ustreas.gov), and request the free pamphlet *Know Before You Go.*

U.K. Customs   U.K. citizens returning from a non-E.U. country such as one of the Caribbean nations have a Customs allowance of 200 cigarettes; 50 cigars; 250 grams of smoking tobacco; 2 liters of still table wine; 1 liter of spirits or strong liqueurs (over 22% alcohol volume); 2 liters of fortified wine, sparkling wine, or other liqueurs; 60 cubic centimeters (ml) perfume; 250 cubic centimeters (ml) toilet water; and £145 worth of all other goods, including gifts and souvenirs. People under 17 cannot have the tobacco or alcohol allowance. For more information, contact **HM Customs & Excise,** Passenger Enquiry Point, Second Floor Wayfarer House, Great South West Road, Feltham, Middlesex, TW14 8NP (© **0845/ 010-9000** or 020/8929-0152 from outside the U.K.; www.hmce.gov.uk).

Canadian Customs   For a clear summary of Canadian rules, write for the booklet *I Declare,* issued by the **Canadian Customs & Revenue Agency,** 2265 St. Laurent Blvd., Ottawa, ON K1G 4KE (© **800/461-9999** or 204/983-3500; www.ccra-adrc.gc.ca). Canada allows its citizens a C$750 exemption, and you're allowed to bring back duty-free 200 cigarettes, 2.2 pounds of tobacco, 40 imperial ounces of liquor, and 50 cigars. In addition, you're allowed to mail gifts to Canada from abroad at the rate of C$60 a day, provided they're unsolicited and don't contain alcohol or tobacco (write on the package "Unsolicited gift, under $60 value"). All valuables should be declared on the Y-38 form before departure from Canada, including serial numbers of valuables you already own, such as expensive foreign cameras. *Note:* The C$750 exemption can be used only once a year and only after an absence of 7 days.

Australian Customs The duty-free allowance in Australia is A$400 or, for those under 18, A$200. Personal property mailed back from Jamaica should be marked "Australian goods returned" to avoid paying duty. Upon returning to Australia, citizens can bring in 250 cigarettes or 250 grams of loose tobacco, and 1,125 milliliters of alcohol. If you're returning with valuable goods you already own, such as foreign-made cameras, you should file form B263. A helpful brochure, available from Australian consulates or Customs offices, is *Know Before You Go.* For

more information, contact **Australian Customs Services,** GPO Box 8, Sydney NSW 2001 (© **1300/362-263;** www.customs.gov.au).

New Zealand Customs The duty-free allowance for New Zealand is NZ$700. Citizens over 17 can bring in 200 cigarettes, or 50 cigars, or 250 grams of tobacco (or a mixture of all three if their combined weight does not exceed 250g); plus 4.5 liters of wine and beer, or 1.125 liters of liquor. New Zealand currency does not carry import or export restrictions. When you leave New Zealand, you should fill out a certificate of export, listing the valuables you are taking out of the country; that way, you can bring them back without paying duty. Most questions are answered in a free pamphlet available at New Zealand consulates and Customs offices: *New Zealand Customs Guide for Travellers, Notice no. 4.* For more information, contact **New Zealand Customs,** 17–21 Whitmore St., Box 2218, Wellington (© **04/ 473-6099** or 0800/428-786; www. customs.govt.nz).

4 Money

Jamaica has its own dollar, far less valuable than the U.S. dollar. In all exchanges, *determine which dollar unit is being quoted in the price.* Otherwise, it's possible you could get cheated— badly—in a financial transaction.

All the major resorts and first-class restaurants quote prices in U.S. dollars, so many visitors can go through their entire trip without the bother of converting their currency into Jamaican dollars. But it's still prudent to carry some Jamaican dollars: For some transactions, such as a drink of coconut water from a roadside vendor, prices are only quoted in Jamaican dollars.

If you have Jamaican dollars left over at the end of your trip, you'll need to show exchange receipts from a bank or other official bureau for the

local dollars you purchased. This is a rather cumbersome process. Exchange only the amount of Jamaican money you think you'll actually need.

Note: Prices in this guide quoted in Jamaican dollars are for *general guidance.* The Jamaican dollar sometimes fluctuates wildly. In general, it has been in a long decline against the Yankee dollar since the early 1990s.

All Jamaican cities and most large towns on the island have banks with a **foreign exchange bureau.** If you're heading into the remote countryside, make sure you have solved your cash problem before setting out. Banks give far better exchange rates than your hotel will.

Because of inadequate ATMs, **traveler's checks** are still a popular means

Currency Exchange Rates

Jamaican $	US $	UK £	CAN $
1	2¢	1p	2¢
5	8¢	4p	11¢
10	16¢	9p	22¢
20	32¢	18p	44¢
50	80¢	44p	1.10
100	1.60	89p	2.20
500	8.00	4.44	11.00
1000	16.00	8.90	22.00
10,000	160.00	88.90	220.00

of currency to take to Jamaica. They are widely accepted, but you should always inquire about the fee before cashing them. Sometimes there's a high surcharge, which can vary from place to place.

Relying on **ATMs** is a bit risky in Jamaica. Most banks in cities such as Kingston and Montego Bay have 24-hour ATMs in secure booths. You are, however, given Jamaican dollars—not U.S. dollars—at these machines. *Always try to use ATMs during regular business hours.* There are frequent muggings of visitors who use ATMs at night in Jamaica.

Be aware that many Frommer's readers have written to describe their frustration with the island's ATMs. It's best to ask your local bank how effective your ATM card will be in Jamaica before you depart. Failing all else, we've found branches of **Scotiabank** work best with North American ATM cards.

CURRENCY

The unit of currency in Jamaica is the Jamaican dollar, with the same symbol as the U.S. dollar, "$." There is no fixed rate of exchange for the Jamaican dollar; it is traded publicly and is subject to market fluctuations.

Visitors to Jamaica can pay for any goods in U.S. dollars, *but be careful.* Always insist on knowing whether a price is quoted in Jamaican or U.S. dollars.

In this guide we quote some prices in both Jamaican and U.S. dollars, though for the most part U.S. dollars are listed alone because the Jamaican dollar tends to fluctuate. U.S. dollar values give a better indication of costs. Prices given in Jamaican dollars are indicated by "J$"; all other prices are in U.S. dollars.

(This chart assumes the following conversion ratios, each of which was in effect at the time of its compilation: J$:US$=.016; J$:£=.00889; J$:CAN $=.022.)

There are Bank of Jamaica **exchange bureaus** at both international airports (Montego Bay and Kingston), at cruise-ship piers, and in most hotels. Also, there is no limit to the amount of **foreign currency** you can bring into or out of Jamaica.

Finally, whenever you leave your hotel, take along some **small bills** and coins. They will come in handy, as tips are generally expected for even the smallest service.

ATMs ATMs are linked to an international network that most likely includes your bank at home. **Cirrus** (© **800/424-7787;** www.mastercard. com) and **PLUS** (© **800/843-7587;** www.visa.com) are the two most popular networks; check the back of your ATM card to see which network your bank belongs to. Use the toll-free numbers to locate ATMs in your destination.

Ask your bank for a list of ATMs in Jamaica. Be sure to check the daily withdrawal limit before you depart, and ask whether you need a new personal ID number.

CREDIT CARDS Plastic is invaluable when traveling in Jamaica. Credit cards are a safe way to carry money, and they provide a convenient record of all your expenses. You can also withdraw cash advances from your credit cards at any bank (though you'll start paying hefty interest on the advance the moment you receive the cash, and you won't receive frequent-flier miles on an airline credit card). At most Jamaican banks, you don't even need to go to a teller; you can get a cash advance at the ATM if you know your PIN. (If you've forgotten your PIN or didn't even know you had one, call the phone number on the back of your credit card and ask the bank to send it to you. It usually takes 5–7 business days, though some banks will provide the number over the phone if you tell them your mother's maiden name or pass some other security clearance.)

TRAVELER'S CHECKS Traveler's checks are something of an anachronism at many destinations. They are still widely used, however, in Jamaica because of inadequate ATM machines. If you also want the security of knowing you can get a refund if your wallet is stolen in Jamaica, you may want to purchase traveler's checks, which you can do at almost any bank. American Express offers denominations of $10, $20, $50, $100, $500, and $1,000. You'll pay a service charge ranging from 1% to 4%. You can also get American Express traveler's checks over the phone by calling ✆ **800/221-7282;** by using this number, Amex gold and platinum cardholders are exempt from the 1% fee.

Visa (✆ **800/732-1322**) offers traveler's checks at **Citibank** locations nationwide and several other participating banks. The service charge

ranges from 1.5% to 2%; checks come in denominations of $20, $50, $100, $500, and $1,000. AAA members can obtain Visa checks without a fee at most AAA offices or by calling ✆ **866/339-3378. MasterCard** also offers traveler's checks. Call ✆ **800/ 223-9920** for a location near you.

WHAT TO DO IF YOUR WALLET IS STOLEN Be sure to block charges against your account the minute you discover a credit card has been lost or stolen. Then be sure to file a report at the nearest Jamaican police station.

Every credit card company has an emergency 800-number to call if your card is stolen. They may be able to wire you a cash advance off your credit card immediately, and in many places they can deliver an emergency credit card in a day or two. The issuing bank's 800-number is usually on the back of your credit card—though of course, if your card has been stolen, that won't help you unless you recorded the number elsewhere.

Citicorp **Visa**'s U.S. emergency number is ✆ **800/336-8742. American Express** cardholders and traveler's-check holders should call ✆ **800/221-7282. MasterCard** holders should call ✆ **800/307-7309.** Otherwise, call the toll-free number directory at ✆ **800/ 555-1212.**

Odds are that if your wallet is gone, the Jamaican police won't be able to recover it for you. However, it's still worth informing them. Your credit card company or insurer may require a police report number or record of the theft. Likewise, if you carry traveler's checks, be sure to keep a record of their serial numbers separate from the checks. You'll get a refund faster if you do.

MONEYGRAMS Sponsored by American Express, Moneygram (✆ **800/926-9400**) is the fastest-growing money-wiring service in the world. Funds can be transferred from one individual to another in less than

10 minutes between thousands of locations throughout the world. An American Express phone representative will give you the names of four or five offices near you. (You don't have to go to an American Express office; some locations in Jamaica are pharmacies or convenience stores in small communities.) Acceptable forms of payment include cash, Visa, MasterCard, and Discover, and occasionally, a personal check. Service charges collected by American Express are $40

for the first $500 sent, with a sliding scale of commissions for larger sums. Included in the transfer is a 10-word telex-style message. The deal also includes a free 3-minute phone call to the recipient. Funds are transferred within 10 minutes, and they can then be retrieved by the beneficiary at the most convenient location when proper photo ID, and in some cases, a security code established by whomever provides the funds, is presented.

5 When to Go

HIGH SEASON VS. LOW SEASON: SOME PROS & CONS

With its fabled weather balmy all year, Jamaica is more and more a year-round destination. Nevertheless, it has a distinct **high season** running roughly from mid-December through mid-April. Hotels charge their highest prices during this peak winter period, when visitors fleeing cold north winds crowd the island. (We've quoted each hotel's rack rates throughout this guide, but you don't have to pay that much, even in high season, if you book a package instead of calling the hotel directly.)

Reservations should be made 2 to 3 months in advance for trips during the winter. At certain hotels, think about booking a year ahead for Christmas holidays or February.

The **off season** in Jamaica (roughly mid-Apr to mid-Dec) amounts to a summer sale. In most cases, hotel rates are slashed a startling 20% to 60%. Some package-tour charges are as much as 20% lower, and individual excursion airfares are reduced from 5% to 10%. In addition, airline seats and hotel rooms are much easier to come by. It's a bonanza for cost-conscious travelers, especially families.

ANNUAL TEMPERATURE & RAINFALL CHART

	Jan	Feb	Mar	Apr	May	June	July	Aug	Sept	Oct	Nov	Dec
Temp. (°F)	86	85	86	87	88	90	90	90	89	89	87	87
Temp. (°C)	30	29	30	31	31	32	32	32	32	32	31	31
Rainfall (in.)	1.2	0.9	0.9	1.5	4.1	3.8	1.8	4.2	5.0	6.8	3.8	1.6

OFF-SEASON ADVANTAGES

Although Jamaica may appear inviting in the winter to those who live in northern climates, there are many reasons why your trip may be much more enjoyable if you go in the off season:

- A less-hurried way of life prevails. You'll have a better chance to appreciate food, culture, and customs.
- Swimming pools and beaches are less crowded—perhaps not crowded at all.

- Year-round resort facilities are offered, often at reduced rates, which may include snorkeling, boating, and scuba diving.
- To survive, resort boutiques often feature summer sales, hoping to clear excess merchandise.
- You can often appear without a reservation at a top restaurant in, say, Montego Bay and get a table.

- The endless waiting game is over: no waiting for a rented car, tee time, or tennis court.
- Some package-tour fares are as much as 20% lower, and individual excursion fares are also reduced between 5% and 10%.
- Accommodations and flights are easier to book.
- Finally, the very best of Jamaica attractions remain undiminished in the off season—sea, sand, and surf, with lots of sunshine.

OFF-SEASON DISADVANTAGES

Let's not paint too rosy a picture, though. Although the advantages of off-season travel outweigh the disadvantages, there are drawbacks to summer travel:

- You might be staying at a construction site. Jamaican hoteliers save their serious repairs and their major renovations until the off season.
- Services are often reduced.
- Not all restaurants and bars will be fully operational at resorts.
- Hotels and resorts may be operating with reduced staffs.

CLIMATE

Jamaica has one of the most varied climates of any Caribbean island. Along the seashore, where most visitors congregate, the island is air-conditioned by northeasterly trade winds, and temperature variations are surprisingly slight. Coastal readings average between 71°F (22°C) and 88°F (31°C) year-round. The Jamaican winter is similar to May in the United States or northern Europe; there can be chilly times in the early morning or at night. Winter is generally the driest season, but can be wet in mountain areas; expect showers, especially in northeastern Jamaica.

Inland, temperatures decrease by approximately .55°C for every 91m (about 1°F for every 300-ft.) increase in elevation.

Rainfall is heaviest along the eastern edge of the island's North Coast, with Port Antonio receiving the most intense downpours. The island has two rainy seasons: May, and October through November.

THE HURRICANE SEASON The curse of Jamaican weather, the hurricane season, officially lasts from June 1 to November 30—but there's no need for panic. Satellite weather forecasts generally give adequate warning so that precautions can be taken. If you're heading to Jamaica during the hurricane season, you can call your local branch of the **National Weather Service** (listed in your phone directory under the U.S. Department of Commerce) for a weather forecast.

Another easy way to receive the weather forecast in the city you plan to visit is by contacting the information service associated with The Weather Channel. It works like this: Dial ℂ **800/WEATHER** and listen to the recorded announcement. When you're prompted, enter the account number of a valid Visa or MasterCard. After the card is approved, at a rate of 95¢ per query, punch in the name of your city. On the Internet you can also stop by www.weather.com to get the same forecasts for free.

HOLIDAYS

Jamaica observes the following public holidays: New Year's Day (Jan 1), Ash Wednesday, Good Friday, Easter Sunday and Monday, National Labour Day (late May), Independence Day (a Mon in early Aug), National Heroes Day (3rd Mon in Oct), Christmas Day (Dec 25), and Boxing Day (Dec 26).

JAMAICA CALENDAR OF EVENTS

January

Accompong Maroon Festival, St. Elizabeth. Annual celebration of Maroons of Western Jamaica, with traditional singing and dancing, feasts, ceremonies, blowing of the *abeng* (cow's horn), playing of Maroon drums. ℂ 876/952-4546. January 6.

Jamaica Sprint Triathlon, Negril. Hundreds participate in a three-part competition joining swimming, cycling, and running in one sweat-inducing endurance test. Contact the Jamaica Tourist Board (see "Visitor Information," p. 15). Late January.

February

Tribute to Bob Marley—Symposium in Music, Ocho Rios. Seminars for students of music. ℂ 876/926-5726. First week in February.

Bob Marley Birthday Bash, Montego Bay. An annual concert that celebrates a local star. ℂ 876/978-2991. February 6.

Reggae Summerfest, Ocho Rios. Annual reggae bash, featuring top reggae stars. Call ℂ 876/960-1904 for dates in 2005. See "Catch a Fire: Jamaica's Reggae Festivals," on p. 65.

March

Montego Bay Yacht Club's Easter Regatta. Annual sailing event of several races staged along the North Coast over a 6-day period around Easter. (ℂ 876/979-8038). March 23 to March 28, 2005.

April

Carnival in Jamaica, Kingston, Ocho Rios, and Montego Bay. Weeklong series of fetes, concerts, and street parades. Contact local tourist offices. First week of April.

June

Ocho Rios Jazz Festival, Ocho Rios and Montego Bay. International performers play alongside Jamaican jazz artists; other events include barbecues. ℂ 888/637-8111 or 876/927-3544 (www.ochoriosjazz.com). Second week in June.

National Dance Theatre Company's Season of Dance, Kingston. Traditional and modern dance, as well as notable singers. ℂ 876/926-6129. June through August.

August

Reggae Sunfest, Catherine Hall, Montego Bay. Annual 5-day music festival. ℂ 876/952-0889 (www.reggaesumfest.com). First week of August. See "Catch a Fire: Jamaica's Reggae Festivals," on p. 65.

September

Falmouth Blue Marlin Tournament, Montego Bay. A big deal locally. ℂ 876/954-5934. Late September.

October

Port Antonio International Fishing Tournament. One of the oldest and most prestigious sportfishing events in the Caribbean, with participants from Europe and North America. ℂ 876/927-0145. October 15 to 22, 2005.

November

Air Jamaica Jazz & Blues Festival, Montego Bay. Series of concerts at Rose Hall Great House. ℂ 876/952-4425. Third week of November.

December

Motor Sports Championship Series, Dover Raceway, St. Ann. Prestigious championship event. ℂ 876/960-3860. Early December.

6 Travel Insurance

It's wise to visit the troubled land of Jamaica with full insurance coverage, protecting you against loss of property, theft, or any medical problem that might arise. With medical insurance it's best to secure, if possible, a policy that offers immediate payment—not one where you must shell out in Jamaica, then wait for reimbursement.

If you're an adventure tourist who likes to indulge in scuba diving, hiking in the Blue Mountains, or motorcycling along Jamaica's potholed roads, try to get a policy that does not exclude what most insurers call "hazardous activities." Some motorized watersports also fall under hazardous activities.

Before going, check your existing policies before you buy additional coverage covering trip cancellation, lost luggage, medical expenses, or car-rental insurance. You're likely to have partial coverage, though it may be inadequate. U.S. medical insurance plans seldom cover health costs incurred outside the United States, unless supplemental coverage is purchased. Further, most U.S. Medicare and Medicaid programs do not provide payment for medical services outside the country.

For information, contact one of the following popular insurers:

- **Access America** (© 866/807-3982; www.accessamerica.com)
- **Travel Guard International** (© 800/826-4919; www.travel guard.com)
- **Travel Insured International** (© 800/243-3174; www.travel insured.com)
- **Travelex Insurance Services** (© 888/457-4602; www.travelex-insurance.com)

TRIP-CANCELLATION INSURANCE (TCI)

There are three major types of trip-cancellation insurance: one for when you prepay a Jamaican cruise or tour that gets canceled, and you can't get your money back; a second for when you or someone in your family gets sick or dies, and you can't travel (but beware that you may not be covered for a preexisting condition); and a third for when bad weather, such as a Jamaica hurricane, makes travel impossible. Some insurers provide coverage for events like jury duty; natural disasters close to home, like floods or fire; even the loss of a job. A few have added provisions for cancellations because of terrorist activities. Always check the fine print before signing on, and don't buy this insurance from a tour operator that may later be responsible for cancellation; buy only from a reputable travel insurance agency. Finally, don't overbuy: You won't be reimbursed more than the cost of your trip.

MEDICAL INSURANCE

With the exception of certain HMOs and Medicare/Medicaid, your medical insurance will seldom cover medical treatment—even hospital care—in Jamaica, so you may need to pay the bill upfront. Members of **Blue Cross/Blue Shield** can use their cards at select hospitals in most major cities worldwide (© 800/810-BLUE or www.bluecares.com for a list of hospitals).

Some credit cards (American Express and certain gold and platinum Visa and MasterCards, for example) offer automatic flight insurance against death or dismemberment in case of an airplane crash, if you charged the cost of your ticket.

If you require additional insurance, try one of the following companies:

- **MEDEX International,** 9515 Deereco Rd., Timonium, MD 21093-5375 (© 800/527-0218 or 410/453-6300; fax 410/453-6301; www.medexassist.com)

- **Travel Assistance International** (© **800/821-2828;** www.travel assistance.com), 9200 Keystone Crossing, Suite 300, Indianapolis, IN 46240 (For general information on services, call the company's Worldwide Assistance Services, Inc., at © **800/777-8710.**)
- **The Divers Alert Network (DAN)** (© **800/446-2671** or 919/684-8111; www.diversalert network.org)

CAR-RENTAL INSURANCE

If you hold a private auto insurance policy in the U.S., check to see if you are covered in Jamaica for loss or damage to the car, and liability in case a passenger is injured. The credit card you used to rent the car also may provide some coverage. Policies vary widely from holder to holder. Most American Express cardholders, for example, don't need a damage waiver option, as most Jamaican car-rental agencies recognize Amex's policy, especially if you're dealing with a U.S.-affiliated firm such as Hertz or Avis. However, many local car-rental companies in Jamaica don't recognize the policy; therefore, you may feel safer dealing with a U.S. affiliate rather than a domestic car-rental agency.

Car-rental insurance (about $20 a day) probably does not cover liability if you caused the accident. Check your own auto insurance policy, the rental company policy, and your credit card coverage for the extent of coverage: Is Jamaica covered? Are other drivers covered? How much liability is covered if a passenger is injured? (If you rely on your credit card for coverage, you may want to bring a second card with you, as damages may be charged to the card.)

7 Health & Safety

Traveling to Jamaica should not adversely affect your health. Finding a good doctor in Jamaica is no real problem, and all of them speak English, of course.

Keep the following suggestions in mind:

- It's best to drink bottled water in Jamaica.
- If you experience diarrhea, moderate your eating habits and drink only bottled water until you recover. If symptoms persist, consult a doctor.
- The Jamaican sun can be brutal. Wear sunglasses and a hat, and use sunscreen liberally. Limit your time on the beach the first day. If you do overexpose yourself, stay out of the sun until you recover. If your exposure is followed by fever or chills, a headache, or a feeling of nausea or dizziness, see a doctor.
- Some of the biggest annoyances in Jamaica are the insects called "no-see-ums," which appear mainly in the early evening. You can't see these gnats, but you sure can "feel-um." Screens can't keep these critters out, so carry your favorite bug repellent.

You don't need to get any particular shots or vaccinations to travel in Jamaica, and most common medicines are available over the counter. If you need special medication, however, try to arrive in Jamaica with an adequate supply for the duration of your trip.

If you're traveling in the countryside, it's wise to take a small medical kit with you containing antacid, antiseptics, calamine lotion, Band-Aids, sunscreen, lip balm, water purification tablets, and insect repellent.

WHAT TO DO IF YOU GET SICK AWAY FROM HOME

If you suffer from a chronic illness, consult your doctor before your departure for Jamaica. For conditions like epilepsy, diabetes, or heart problems, wear a **Medic Alert Identification Tag** (© 800/825-3785; www.medicalert.org), which will immediately alert doctors to your condition and give them access to your records through Medic Alert's 24-hour hot line.

Pack **prescription medications** in your carry-on luggage, and carry prescription medications in their original containers. Also bring along copies of your prescriptions in case you lose your pills or run out. Carry the generic name of prescription medicines, in case a local pharmacist is unfamiliar with the brand name.

And don't forget sunglasses and an extra pair of contact lenses or prescription glasses.

Contact the **International Association for Medical Assistance to Travellers (IAMAT)** (© 716/754-4883 or 416/652-0137; www.iamat.org) for tips on travel and health concerns in Jamaica and lists of local doctors, all of whom speak English. If you get sick, consider asking your hotel concierge to recommend a local doctor—even his or her own. You can also try the emergency room at a local hospital: Many have walk-in clinics for emergency cases that are not life-threatening. You may not get immediate attention, but you won't pay the same price as an emergency-room visit (usually at least $300).

STAYING SAFE

Except for Haiti, Jamaica is the most potentially dangerous destination in the Caribbean. You can get into a lot of trouble in Jamaica or you can have a carefree vacation. Much depends on you, where you go, and what you do. Women traveling alone or even in pairs are especially vulnerable, as rapes are alarmingly common.

Walking alone at night, or even with a loved one, on a moonlit Jamaican beach is a romantic idea—but not smart. You could be mugged. And hitchhiking for both women and men is never a good idea in Jamaica. There have been cases of "disappearances" in the remote hinterlands.

Petty crime also continues to be a major problem on the island, especially in the capital city of Kingston. Americans on many occasions have been robbed, the bandit turning violent if he faces resistance.

Bus travel in Jamaica is definitely not recommended. Buses are invariably overcrowded and the greatest venue for the pickpocket to practice his trade.

The good news? In major resort areas such as Montego Bay, the government is hiring more special foot police and bike patrols to enhance security. These megaresorts are virtually walled compounds with 24-hour guards. Smaller inns don't have such protection, however, so make sure that all your doors and windows are securely locked.

8 Specialized Travel Resources

TRAVELERS WITH DISABILITIES

Jamaican hotels rarely give much publicity to the facilities (if any) they offer persons with disabilities, so it's always wise to contact the hotel directly, in advance. Tourist offices probably won't be able to help you with such questions.

Get a free copy of *Air Transportation of Handicapped Persons* from the **U.S. Department of Transportation.** Write for Free Advisory Circular No.

AC12032, Distribution Unit, U.S. Department of Transportation, Publications Division, 3341Q 75 Ave., Landover, MD 20785 (© **301/322-4961;** fax 301/386-5394; http://isddc.dot.gov). Only written requests are accepted.

Flying Wheels Travel (© **507/451-5050;** fax 507/481-1685; www.flyingwheelstravel.com) offers escorted tours and cruises that emphasize sports and private tours in minivans with lifts. **Access Adventures** (℡ 716/889-9096) offers customized itineraries for a variety of travelers with disabilities. **Accessible Journeys** (℡ 800/846-4537 or 610/521-0339; www.disability travel.com) caters specifically to slow walkers and wheelchair travelers and their families and friends.

The **MossRehab Hospital** (℡ 215/456-5995; www.mossresourcenet.org) provides a helpful **Travel Information Service** by phone. **The Society for Accessible Travel and Hospitality** (℡ 212/447-7284; fax 212/725-8253; www.sath.org) offers a wealth of travel resources for all types of disabilities and informed recommendations on destinations, access guides, travel agents, tour operators, vehicle rentals, and companion services. Annual membership costs $45 for adults, $30 for seniors and students.

FOR BRITISH TRAVELERS The **Royal Association for Disability and Rehabilitation (RADAR),** Unit 12, City Forum, 250 City Rd., London, EC1V 8AF (℡ 020/7250-3222; fax 020/7250-0212; www.radar.org.uk), publishes holiday "Fact Packs" for £2 ($3.30) each or three for £5 ($8.25).

GAY & LESBIAN TRAVELERS

Jamaica is the most homophobic island in the Caribbean, with harsh anti-gay laws, even though there's a large local gay population.

Many all-inclusive resorts, notably the famous Sandals of Jamaica, maintain strict no-gay policies. However, Hedonism II in Negril does allow gay travelers. So does the Grand Hotel Lido in Negril. Still, avoid open displays of affection—such as handholding on the streets—in Jamaica: You could be assaulted for trying it.

The **International Gay & Lesbian Travel Association (IGLTA)** (℡ 800/448-8550 or 954/776-2626; fax 954/776-3303; www.iglta.com) links travelers up with gay-friendly hoteliers, tour operators, and airline and cruise-line

representatives. It offers monthly newsletters, marketing mailings, and a membership directory that's updated once a year. Membership is $200 yearly, plus a $100 administration fee for new members.

Above and Beyond Tours (℡ 800/397-2681; www.abovebeyondtours.com) offers gay and lesbian tours worldwide and is the exclusive gay and lesbian tour operator for United Airlines. **Now, Voyager** (℡ 800/255-6951; www.nowvoyager.com) is a San Francisco–based gay-owned and -operated travel service. **Olivia Cruises & Resorts** (℡ 800/631-6277 or 510/655-0364; www.olivia.com) charters entire resorts and ships for exclusive lesbian vacations all over the world.

Out and About (℡ 800/929-2268 or 415/644-8044; www.outandabout.com) offers guidebooks and a newsletter 10 times a year packed with information on the global gay and lesbian scene. *Spartacus International Gay Guide* and *Odysseus* are good, annual English-language guidebooks focused on gay men, with some information for lesbians. You can get them from most gay and lesbian bookstores, or order them from **Giovanni's Room** bookstore, 1145 Pine St., Philadelphia, PA 19107 (℡ 215/923-2960; www.giovannisroom.com). *Gay Travel A to Z: The World of Gay & Lesbian Travel Options at Your Fingertips,* by Marianne Ferrari (Ferrari Publications), is a good guidebook series.

SENIOR TRAVELERS

Except for a possible reduction on certain domestic airfares offered aboard **Air Jamaica Express,** the island itself is virtually devoid of discounts for senior citizens. Some car-rental companies may extend discounts to seniors, but arrange that before you land on the island. Once on the island, a senior is likely to pay the same prices that anybody else does.

FAMILY TRAVEL

Jamaica is one of the top family-vacation destinations in the Caribbean, and many of the island's resorts offer supervised children's activities, babysitters, family discounts, and special meals for kids.

Family Travel Times is published 10 times a year by Travel with Your Children (TWYCH), and includes a weekly call-in service for subscribers. Subscriptions cost $40 a year from TWYCH, 40 Fifth Ave., New York, NY 10011 (© 212/477-5524; www.familytraveltimes.com).

How to Take Great Trips with Your Kids (The Harvard Common Press) is also full of good general advice.

Family Travel Network (www.familytravelnetwork.com) offers travel tips and reviews of family-friendly destinations. **Travel with Your Children** (www.travelwithyourkids.com) is a comprehensive site offering sound advice for traveling with children.

MULTICULTURAL TRAVELERS

Agencies and organizations that provide resources for black travelers include: **Rodgers Travel** (© 215/473-1775; www.rodgerstravel.com), a Philadelphia-based travel agency with an extensive menu of tours in destinations worldwide, including heritage and private group tours; and the **African-American Association of Innkeepers International** (© 877/422-5777; www.africanamericaninns.com), which provides information on member B&Bs in the U.S., Canada, Bermuda, and the Caribbean.

The Internet offers a number of helpful travel sites for the black traveler. **Black Travel Online** (www.blacktravelonline.com) posts news on upcoming events and includes links to articles and travel-booking sites. **Soul of America** (www.soulofamerica.com) is a more comprehensive website, with travel tips, event and family reunion postings, and sections on historically black beach resorts and active vacations.

Tying the Knot in Jamaica

In high season some Jamaican resorts witness several weddings a day. Many of the larger resorts can arrange for an officiant, a photographer, and even the wedding cake and champagne. Some resorts will even throw in the wedding with the cost of your honeymoon at the hotel. Both the Jamaican Tourist Board and your hotel can assist with paperwork; participants must simply be in Jamaica for 24 hours before the ceremony. Bring birth certificates and affidavits saying you've never been married before. (If you've been divorced or widowed, bring copies of your divorce papers or a copy of the deceased spouse's death certificate.) The license and stamp duty costs J$4,000 (US$66), and the ceremony can cost from J$4,000 to J$7,000 (US$66–US$116), depending on how much legwork you do. Apply in person at the **Ministry of National Security and Justice,** 12 Ocean Blvd., Kingston, Jamaica (© 876/906-4908).

The single best hotel for arranging wedding packages is **Half Moon Golf, Tennis & Beach Club** (© 800/626-0592) in Montego Bay. **Sandals** properties in Montego Bay, Negril, and Ocho Rios (© 800/SANDALS) also have good packages.

For more information, check out the following collections and guides: *Go Girl: The Black Woman's Guide to Travel & Adventure* (Eighth Mountain Press), a compilation of travel essays by writers including Jill Nelson and Audre Lorde, with some practical information and trip-planning advice; *Travel and Enjoy Magazine* (© 866/266-6211; www.travelandenjoy.com; subscription $24/year), which focuses on discounts and destination reviews.

SINGLE TRAVEL

Many people prefer traveling alone. Unfortunately, the solo traveler is often forced to pay a punishing "single supplement" charged by many resorts, cruise lines, and tours for the privilege of sleeping alone.

Travel Companion Exchange (TCE) (© 631/454-0880; www.travelcompanions.com) is one of the original roommate finders for single travelers. **Travel Buddies Singles Travel Club**

(© 800/998-9099; www.travelbuddiesworldwide.com) runs small, intimate, single-friendly group trips and will match you with a roommate for no extra charge. **TravelChums** (© 212/787-2621; www.travelchums.com) is an Internet-only travel-companion matching service hosted by the respected New York–based Shaw Guides travel service.

The Single Gourmet Club (© 212/980-8788; fax 212/980-3138; www.singlegourmet.com), is an international social, dining, and travel club for singles of all ages, with 21 offices in the U.S. and Canada. Membership is $75 for the first year, $50 to renew.

Traveling Solo: Advice and Ideas for More than 250 Great Vacations, by Eleanor Berman (Globe Pequot), gives advice on traveling alone. *Outdoor Singles Network* (P.O. Box 781, Haines, AK 99827; http://kcd.com/ci/osn) is a quarterly newsletter for outdoor-loving singles. Subscriptions are $55; single issues are $15.

9 Planning Your Trip Online

SURFING FOR AIRFARES

The "big three" online travel agencies, **Expedia.com, Travelocity,** and **Orbitz,** sell most of the air tickets bought on the Internet. (Canadian travelers should try Expedia.ca and Travelocity.ca; U.K. residents can go to Expedia.co.uk and Opodo.co.uk.) Each has different business deals with the airlines and may offer different fares on the same flights, so it's wise to shop around. Expedia and Travelocity will also send you **e-mail notification** when a cheap fare becomes available to your favorite destination. Of the smaller travel agency websites, **SideStep** (www.sidestep.com) has gotten the best reviews from Frommer's authors. It's a browser add-on that purports to "search 140 sites at once," but in reality only beats competitors' fares as often as other sites do.

Also remember to check **airline websites,** especially those for low-fare carriers such as Southwest, JetBlue, AirTran, WestJet, and Ryanair, whose fares are often misreported or simply missing from travel agency websites. Even with major airlines, you can often shave a few bucks from a fare by booking directly through the airline and avoiding a travel agency's transaction fee. But you'll get these discounts only by **booking online:** Most airlines now offer online-only fares that even their phone agents know nothing about. For the websites of airlines that fly to and from your destination, go to "Flying to Jamaica," below.

Great **last-minute deals** are available through free weekly e-mail services provided directly by the airlines. Most of these are announced on Tuesday or Wednesday and must be purchased

Frommers.com: The Complete Travel Resource

For an excellent travel-planning resource, we highly recommend **Frommers.com** (www.frommers.com), voted Best Travel Site by *PC Magazine*. We're a little biased, of course, but we guarantee that you'll find the travel tips, reviews, monthly vacation giveaways, bookstore, and online-booking capabilities thoroughly indispensable. Among the special features are our popular **Destinations** section, where you'll get expert travel tips, hotel and dining recommendations, and advice on the sights to see for more than 3,500 destinations around the globe; the **Frommers.com Newsletter,** with the latest deals, travel trends, and money-saving secrets; our **Community** area featuring **Message Boards,** where Frommer's readers post queries and share advice (sometimes even our authors show up to answer questions); and our **Photo Center,** where you can post and share vacation tips. When your research is done, the **Online Reservations System** (www.frommers.com/book_a_trip) takes you to Frommer's preferred online partners for booking your vacation at affordable prices.

online. Most are only valid for travel that weekend, but some (such as Southwest's) can be booked weeks or months in advance. Sign up for weekly e-mail alerts at airline websites or check megasites that compile comprehensive lists of last-minute specials, such as **Smarter Living** (smarterliving.com). For last-minute trips, **site59.com** and **lastminutetravel.com** in the U.S. and **lastminute.com** in Europe often have better air-and-hotel package deals than the major-label sites. A website listing numerous bargain sites and airlines around the world is **www.itravelnet.com**.

If you're willing to give up some control over your flight details, use what is called an **"opaque" fare service** like **Priceline** (www.priceline.com; www.priceline.co.uk for Europeans) or its smaller competitor **Hotwire** (www.hotwire.com). Both offer rock-bottom prices in exchange for travel on a "mystery airline" at a mysterious time of day, often with a mysterious change of planes en route. The mystery airlines are all major, well-known carriers—and the possibility of being sent from

Philadelphia to Chicago via Tampa is remote; the airlines' routing computers have gotten a lot better than they used to be. But your chances of getting a 6am or 11pm flight are pretty high. Hotwire tells you flight prices before you buy; Priceline usually has better deals than Hotwire, but you have to play their "name our price" game. If you're new at this, the helpful folks at **BiddingForTravel** (www.biddingfortravel.com) do a good job of demystifying Priceline's prices and strategies. Priceline and Hotwire are great for flights within North America and between the U.S. and Europe. *Note:* In 2004 Priceline added non-opaque service to its roster. You now have the option to pick exact flights, times, and airlines from a list of offers—or opt to bid on opaque fares as before.

For much more about airfares and savvy air-travel tips and advice, pick up a copy of *Frommer's Fly Safe, Fly Smart* (Wiley Publishing, Inc.).

SURFING FOR HOTELS

Shopping online for hotels is much easier in the U.S., Canada, and Caribbean than it is in the rest of the world. Also, many smaller hotels and B&Bs—especially outside the U.S.—don't show up on websites at all. Of the "big three" sites, **Expedia** may be the best choice, thanks to its long list of special deals. **Travelocity** runs a close second. Hotel specialist sites **hotels.com** and **hotel discounts.com** are also reliable. An excellent free program, **TravelAxe** (www. travelaxe.net), can help you search multiple hotel sites at once, even ones you may never have heard of.

In the opaque website category, **Priceline** and **Hotwire** are even better for hotels than for airfares; with both, you're allowed to pick the neighborhood and quality level of your hotel before offering up your money.

Priceline's hotel product even covers Europe and Asia, though it's much better at getting five-star lodging for three-star prices than at finding anything at the bottom of the scale. On the down side, many hotels stick Priceline guests in their least desirable rooms. Be sure to go to the **Bidding-ForTravel** website (see above) before bidding on a hotel room on Priceline; it features a fairly up-to-date list of hotels that Priceline uses in major cities. For both Priceline and Hotwire, you pay up front, and the fee is nonrefundable. *Note:* Some hotels do not provide loyalty program credits or points or other frequent-stay amenities when you book a room through opaque online services.

10 The 21st-Century Traveler

INTERNET ACCESS AWAY FROM HOME

Travelers have any number of ways to check their e-mail and access the Internet on the road. Of course, using your own laptop—or even a PDA (personal digital assistant) or electronic organizer with a modem—gives you the most flexibility. But even if you don't have a computer, you can still access your e-mail and even your office computer from cybercafes.

WITHOUT YOUR OWN COMPUTER

It's hard nowadays to find a city that *doesn't* have a few cybercafes. Although there's no definitive directory for cybercafes—these are independent businesses, after all—three places to start looking are at **www.cybercaptive. com**, **www.netcafeguide.com**, and **www.cybercafe.com**.

Most major airports now have **Internet kiosks** scattered throughout their gates. These kiosks, which you'll also see in shopping malls, hotel lobbies, and tourist information offices around the world, give you basic Web access for a per-minute fee that's usually

higher than cybercafe prices. The kiosks' clunkiness and high prices means they should be avoided whenever possible.

To retrieve your e-mail, ask your **Internet service provider (ISP)** if it has a Web-based interface tied to your existing e-mail account. If your ISP doesn't have such an interface, you can use the free **mail2web** service (www. mail2web.com) to view (but not reply to) your home e-mail. For more flexibility, you may want to open a free, Web-based e-mail account with **Yahoo! Mail** (mail.yahoo.com). (Microsoft's Hotmail is another popular option, but Hotmail has severe spam problems.) Your home ISP may be able to forward your e-mail to the Web-based account automatically.

If you need to access files on your office computer, look into a service called **GoToMyPC** (www.gotomypc. com). The service provides a Web-based interface for you to access and manipulate a distant PC from anywhere—even a cybercafe—provided your "target" PC is on and has an always-on connection to the Internet (such as with Road Runner cable).

Flying with Film & Video

Never pack film—developed or undeveloped—in checked bags, as the new, more powerful scanners in U.S. airports can fog film. The film you carry with you can be damaged by scanners as well. **X-ray damage** is cumulative; the faster the film, and the more times you put it through a scanner, the more likely the damage. Film under 800 ASA is usually safe for up to five scans. If you're taking your film through additional scans, U.S. regulations permit you to demand hand inspections. In international airports, you're at the mercy of airport officials. On international flights, store your film in transparent baggies, so you can remove it easily before you go through scanners. Keep in mind that airports are not the only places where your camera may be scanned: Highly trafficked attractions are X-raying visitors' bags with increasing frequency.

Most photo supply stores sell **protective pouches** designed to block damaging X-rays. The pouches fit both film and loaded cameras. They should protect your film in checked baggage, but they also may raise alarms and result in a hand-inspection.

You'll have little to worry about if you are traveling with **digital cameras.** Unlike film, which is sensitive to light, the digital camera and storage cards are not affected by airport X-rays, according to Nikon. Still, if you plan to travel extensively, you may want to play it safe and hand-carry your digital equipment or ask that it be inspected by hand.

Scanners of carry-on items will not damage **videotape** in video cameras, but the magnetic fields emitted by the walk-through security gateways and handheld inspection wands will. Always place your loaded camcorder on the screening conveyor belt or have it hand-inspected. Be sure your batteries are charged, as you may be required to turn the device on to ensure that it's what it appears to be.

The service offers top-quality security, but if you're worried about hackers, use your own laptop rather than a cybercafe to access the GoToMyPC system.

WITH YOUR OWN COMPUTER

Major Internet service providers (ISPs) have **local access numbers** around the world, allowing you to go online by simply placing a local call. Check your ISP's website or call its toll-free number and ask how you can use your current account away from home, and how much it will cost.

Most business-class hotels throughout the world offer dataports for laptop modems, and a few thousand hotels now offer high-speed Internet access using an Ethernet network cable. You'll have to bring your own cables either way, so **call your hotel in advance** to find out what the options are.

USING A CELLPHONE IN JAMAICA

The three letters that define much of the world's **wireless capabilities** are GSM (Global System for Mobiles), a big, seamless network that makes for easy cross-border cellphone use throughout Europe and dozens of other countries worldwide. In the U.S., T-Mobile, AT&T Wireless, and Cingular use this quasi-universal system; in Canada, Microcell and some Rogers customers are GSM; and all Europeans and most Australians use GSM.

If your cellphone is on a GSM system, and you have a world-capable phone such as many (but not all) Sony Ericsson, Motorola, or Samsung models, you can make and receive calls across civilized areas on much of the globe, from Andorra to Uganda, and certainly Jamaica. Just call your wireless operator and ask for "international roaming" to be activated on your account. Unfortunately, per-minute charges can be high.

World-phone owners can bring down their per-minute charges with a bit of trickery. Call up your cellular operator and say you'll be going abroad for several months and want to "unlock" your phone to use it with a local provider. Usually, they'll oblige. Then, in Jamaica, pick up a cheap, prepaid phone chip at a mobile-phone store and slip it into your phone. (Show your phone to the salesperson,

as not all phones work on all networks.) You'll get a local phone number—and much, much lower calling rates.

Otherwise, **renting** a phone is a good idea. While you can rent a phone from any number of overseas sites, including kiosks at airports and at car-rental agencies, we suggest renting the phone before you leave home. That way you can give loved ones your new number, make sure the phone works, and take the phone wherever you go—especially helpful when you rent overseas, where phone-rental agencies bill in local currency and may not let you take the phone to another country.

Two good wireless rental companies are **InTouch USA** (✆ **800/872-7626;** www.intouchglobal.com) and **Roadpost** (✆ **888/290-1606** or 905/272-5665; www.roadpost.com). Give them your itinerary and they'll tell you what wireless products you need. InTouch will also, for free, advise you on whether your existing phone will work in Jamaica; simply call ✆ **703/222-7161** between 9am and 4pm EST, or go to http://intouchglobal.com/travel.htm.

11 Flying to Jamaica

THE MAJOR AIRLINES

There are two **international airports** on Jamaica: Donald Sangster in Montego Bay (✆ **876/952-3124**) and Norman Manley in Kingston (✆ **876/924-8452;** www.manley-airport.com. jm). The most popular flights are from New York and Miami. Remember to reconfirm all flights no later than 72 hours before departure. Flying time from Miami is 1¼ hours; from Los Angeles, 5½ hours; from Atlanta, 2½ hours; from Dallas, 3 hours; from Chicago and New York, 3½ hours; and from Toronto, 4 hours.

Some of the most convenient service to Jamaica is provided by **American Airlines** (✆ **800/433-7300** in the U.S.; www.aa.com) through hubs in New York and Miami. Throughout the year, one daily nonstop flight departs from New York's Kennedy Airport for Montego Bay. From Miami, at least two daily flights depart for Kingston and two daily flights depart for Montego Bay.

US Airways (✆ **800/428-4322;** www.usairways.com) offers one flight daily from Charlotte, North Carolina, Philadelphia, and Boston. **Northwest**

Travel in the Age of Bankruptcy

Airlines go bankrupt, so protect yourself by **buying your tickets with a credit card,** as the Fair Credit Billing Act guarantees that you can get your money back from the credit card company if a travel supplier goes under (and if you request the refund within 60 days of the bankruptcy). **Travel insurance** can also help, but make sure it covers against "carrier default" for your specific travel provider. And be aware that if a U.S. airline goes bust mid-trip, a 2001 federal law requires other carriers to take you to your destination (albeit on a space-available basis) for a fee of no more than $25, provided you rebook within 60 days of the cancellation.

Airlines (© 800/225-2525; www. nwa.com) flies directly to Montego Bay daily from Minneapolis.

Air Jamaica (© **800/523-5585** in the U.S.; www.airjamaica.com) operates one or more flights daily to Montego Bay and Kingston from such cities as Miami, Fort Lauderdale, Orlando, Atlanta, Baltimore/Washington, D.C., Philadelphia, Chicago, Newark, Boston, Houston, Los Angeles, and New York's JFK. The airline has connecting service within Jamaica through its reservations network to **Air Jamaica Express,** whose planes usually hold between 10 and 17 passengers. Air Jamaica Express flies from the island's international airports at Montego Bay and Kingston, and also to smaller airports around the island, including Boscobel (near Ocho Rios) and Tinson Pen (near Kingston).

Air Canada (© **888/247-2262** in Canada, or 800/268-7240 in the U.S.; www.aircanada.ca) flies from Toronto to Jamaica daily. The connection to Kingston is nonstop, but the flight to Montego Bay involves a change of planes in Miami. **British Airways** (© **0870/850-9850** in Britain; www. britishairways.com) has four nonstop flights weekly to Montego Bay and Kingston from London's Gatwick Airport.

NEW AIR TRAVEL SECURITY MEASURES

In the wake of the terrorist attacks of September 11, 2001, the airline industry began implementing sweeping security measures in airports. Expect a lengthy check-in process and extensive delays. Although regulations vary from airline to airline, you can expedite the process by taking the following steps:

- **Arrive early.** Arrive at the airport at least 2 hours before your scheduled flight.
- **Try not to drive your car to the airport.** Parking and curbside access to the terminal may be limited. Call ahead to check.
- **Don't count on curbside check-in.** Some airlines and airports have stopped curbside check-in altogether, while others offer it on a limited basis. Check with the individual airline.
- **Be sure to carry plenty of documentation.** A government-issued photo ID (federal, state, or local) is now required. You may need to show this at various checkpoints. With an E-ticket, you may be required to have with you printed confirmation of purchase, and perhaps even the credit card with which you bought your ticket. Be sure that your ID is **up-to-date.**
- **Prepare to be searched.** Expect spot-checks. Electronic items, such as a laptop or cellphone, should be readied for additional screening. Also, try to limit the number of metallic items you wear.

- **No ticket, no gate access.** Only ticketed passengers are allowed beyond screener checkpoints, except those with specific medical or parental needs.

FLYING FOR LESS: GETTING THE BEST AIRFARE

Airlines periodically lower prices on their most popular routes. Check the travel section of your Sunday newspaper for advertised discounts or call the airlines directly and ask if any **promotional rates** or special fares are available. You'll almost never see a sale during the peak winter season in Jamaica, or during the Thanksgiving or Christmas seasons. If your schedule is flexible, say so, and ask if you can get a cheaper fare by staying an extra day, flying midweek, or flying in less-trafficked hours.

Join a travel club such as **Moment's Notice** (© 718/234-6295; www. moments-notice.com) or **Sears Discount Travel Club** (© 800/433-9383 or 800/255-1487 to join; www. travelersadvantage.com), which supply unsold tickets at discounted prices. You pay an annual membership fee to get the club's hot line number. Of course, you're limited to what's available, so you have to be flexible. Or else join **frequent-flier clubs.** It's best to accrue miles on one program, so you can rack up free flights and achieve elite status faster. But it also makes sense to open as many accounts as possible: You'll get the best choice of seats, faster response to phone inquiries, and prompter service if luggage is stolen, a flight is canceled or delayed, or you need to change your seat.

Internet users today can tap into the same travel-planning databases that were once accessible only to travel agents—and do it at the same speed. Sites such as **Frommers.com**, **Travelocity.com**, **Expedia.com**, and **Orbitz.com** enable consumers to comparison-shop for airfares, access special bargains, book flights, and reserve hotel rooms and rental cars. But don't fire your travel agent just yet: A seasoned, reliable travel agent remains an invaluable resource, particularly for complex itineraries.

Some websites, such as Expedia. com, send you **e-mail notification** when a cheap fare becomes available.

TSA Carry-On Regulations

The **Transportation Security Administration (TSA)** has stabilized what you can carry on and what you can't. The general rule is that sharp things are out, nail clippers are okay, and food and beverages must be passed through the X-ray machine—but that security screeners can't make you sip your carry-on beverage (to prove it isn't toxic). Bring food in your carry-on rather than checking it, as explosive-detection machines used on checked luggage have been known to mistake food (especially chocolate, for some reason) for bombs. Travelers in the U.S. are allowed one carry-on bag, plus a "personal item" such as a purse, briefcase, or laptop bag. Carry-on hoarders can stuff all sorts of things into a laptop bag; as long as it has a laptop in it, it's still considered a personal item. For a list of restricted items, log on to **www.tsa.gov/public/index.jsp.**

12 Packages for the Independent Traveler

Unlike many places, Jamaica is not a big market for escorted tours where you're hauled around on a bus and looked after constantly by a guide. You can, of course, take locally guided tours once you land.

Package tours are not the same thing as escorted tours. With a package tour to Jamaica, you travel independently but pay a group rate. Packages usually include airfare, a choice of hotels, and car rentals, and packagers often offer several options at different prices. In many cases, a package that includes airfare, hotel, and transportation to and from the airport will cost you less than just the hotel alone would have cost. That's because Jamaican packages are sold in bulk to tour operators—who then resell them to the public at a cost that sharply undercuts regular rates.

The best place to find a package tour is the travel section of your local Sunday newspaper. Also check the ads in the back of national travel magazines like *Arthur Frommer's Budget Travel, Travel & Leisure, National Geographic Traveler,* and *Condé Nast Traveler.*

Liberty Travel (© **888/271-1584** to be connected with the agent closest to you; www.libertytravel.com) is one of the biggest packagers in the Northeast, and usually has a full-page ad in Sunday papers. Check out its **Last Minute Travel Bargains** site, offered in conjunction with Continental Airlines (www.lastminute.com), with deeply discounted vacation packages and reduced airfares. **Northwest Airlines** (www.nwa.com) offers a similar service: Posted on Northwest's website every Wednesday, its **Cyber Saver Bargain Alerts** offer special hotel rates, package deals, and discounted airline fares.

Among the airlines themselves, your package options include those from **American Airlines Vacations** (© **800/321-2121;** www.aavacations. com), **Delta Vacations** (© **800/221-6666;** www.deltavacations.com), and **US Airways Vacations** (© **800/455-0123;** www.usairwayvacations.com). Contact the airline that services your hometown most frequently. In addition, **Air Jamaica Vacations** (© **800/LOVEBIRDS;** www.air jamaicavacations.com) is affiliated with the national airline, and these folks know the country well.

The biggest hotel chains and resorts in Jamaica (such as **Sandals**) also offer package deals. If you know where you want to stay, call that resort about air-and-land packages.

To save time comparing the prices and values of all the package tours out there, consider calling **TourScan, Inc.,** P.O. Box 2367, Darien, CT 06820 (© **800/962-2080** or 203/655-8091; fax 203/655-6689; www. tourscan.com). Each season the company computerizes travel brochures containing some 10,000 vacations at 1,600 Caribbean hotels, including some in Jamaica. Write for a catalogue; the price ($4) can be credited toward any TourScan vacation.

FOR BRITISH TRAVELERS

Caribbean Connection, Concorde House, Forest Street, Chester CH1 1QR (© **01244/355-300**), offers all-inclusive packages (airfare and hotel) to Jamaica and customizes tours for independent travel. It publishes two catalogs.

Other Jamaican specialists operating out of the U.K. include big **Kuoni Travel,** Kuoni House, Dorking, Surrey RH5 4AZ (© **01306/747-002;** www.kuoni.co.uk), and **Caribtours,** Kiln House, 210 New Kings Rd., London SW6 4NZ (© **020/7751-0660;** www.caribtours.co.uk)—a small, very knowledgeable specialist.

What the Meal Plans Mean

AP (American Plan): This plan includes three meals a day (sometimes called "full board" or "full pension").

CP (Continental Plan): A continental breakfast (that is, bread, jam, and coffee) is included in the room rate.

EP (European Plan): This rate is always cheapest, as it offers only the room—no meals.

MAP (Modified American Plan): Sometimes called "half-board" or "half-pension," this rate includes breakfast plus dinner or lunch.

SPECIAL-INTEREST VACATIONS

BIKING

Some of the best bike tours in Jamaica are offered in Negril at **Rusty's X-cellent Adventures** (© 876/957-0155). See p. 112.

Note that bike repair shops are almost nonexistent. Take along a repair kit if you plan to do some solo cycling.

GOLF

Jamaica has the best golf courses in the West Indies, with Montego Bay alone sporting four championship links.

The course at **Wyndham Rose Hall Golf & Beach Resort** (© 876/953-2650) is ranked among the top five golf courses in the world by some; it's an unusual and challenging seaside and mountain course.

The excellent course at **Tryall Club Jamaica** (© 876/956-5660) is the site of the Jamaica Classic Annual. The **Half Moon** (© 876/953-2560) at Rose Hall features a championship course designed by Robert Trent Jones Jr. **Ironshore Golf & Country Club** (© 876/953-2800) is another good course in Montego Bay. See "Golf," in chapter 3.

On the North Shore there's **Super-Clubs' Runaway Golf Club** (© 876/973-2561) at Runaway Bay and

Sandals Golf & Country Club (© 876/975-0119) at Ocho Rios. See "Golf," in chapter 6.

In Mandeville, **Manchester Country Club,** Brumalia Road (© 876/962-2403), is Jamaica's oldest golf course, though it has only 9 holes. Beautiful vistas unfold 660m (2,200 ft.) above sea level. See p. 132.

HIKING

Because of possible dangers involved, it's often best to go on an organized tour, the best of which are offered by **Sun Venture Tours,** 30 Balmoral Ave., Kingston, Jamaica W.I. (© 876/960-6685; www.sunventuretours.com). See p. 212.

Besides the high Blue Mountains, where Sunventure goes, another great place for hiking is from Port Antonio (p. 176). You can hike various trails through the **Rio Grande Valley;** highlights include the 7-hour White River Falls jaunt along the banks of the White River and an easier walk to Scatter Wall Falls, floating on a bamboo raft across the Rio Grande. The 11km (7-mile) Guava River Trail goes along the Guava River into the heart of the Blue Mountains.

The **Maroon Country,** near Montego Bay, is also a place of challenging hikes—though it's best to hire a guide here.

HORSEBACK RIDING

The best riding is on the North Shore. Jamaica's most complete equestrian center is **Chukka Cove Polo Club** (© 876/972-2506; www.chukkacove.com), at Richmond Llandovery, less than 6km (4 miles) east of Runaway Bay. See p. 158.

Another good program is offered at **Rocky Point Riding Stables** (© 876/953-2212), Half Moon Club, Rose Hall, Montego Bay, housed in the most beautiful barn and stables in Jamaica. See p. 75.

SCUBA DIVING

Diving is sometimes offered as part of all-inclusive packages by the island's major hotels. There are also well-maintained facilities independent of the hotels.

Near Montego Bay, **Seaworld Resorts** (© 876/953-2180), at the Cariblue Hotel on Rose Hall Main Road, offers scuba-diving excursions to offshore coral reefs that are among the most spectacular in the Caribbean. There are also PAIC-certified dive guides, one dive boat, and all necessary equipment for either inexperienced or certified divers. See p. 73.

Negril is a hotbed of diving. **Negril Scuba Centre** (© 800/818-2963 or 876/957-9641), in the Negril Beach Club Hotel, Norman Manley Boulevard, is the area's most modern, best-equipped scuba facility (p. 113). Equally good is **Marine Life Divers,** a PADI-approved, five-star dive shop

located at the Samsara Hotel (© 876/957-3245; www.mldiversnegril.com).

SNORKELING

The offshore reefs bordering the coast at Negril are excellent for snorkeling, many shallow enough to lure the beginner. The shoreline east of Ocho Rios to Galina Point is fringed by a coral reef of rainbow-hued marine life. Most resorts provide snorkeling equipment, but the activity isn't very well organized.

TENNIS

All-Jamaica Hardcourt Championships are played in August at the **Manchester Country Club,** Brumalia Road, P.O. Box 17, Mandeville (© 876/962-2403). The courts are open for general play during the rest of the year. See p. 132.

Grand Sport Villa Golf Resort & Spa, Main Street, Ocho Rios (© 876/974-1027), focuses more on tennis than does any other resort in the area. It offers three clay-surface and three hard-surface courts, all lit for nighttime play. Nonresidents must call and make advance arrangements with the manager. See p. 141.

In Montego Bay you'll find excellent tennis facilities at **Wyndham Rose Hall Golf & Beach Resort,** at Rose Hall (© 876/953-2650); at **Half Moon Golf, Tennis & Beach Club** (© 876/953-2211); and at **Tryall Club Jamaica,** St. James (© 876/956-5660). See p. 75.

13 For the Cruise-Ship Traveler

Most cruise ships heading for Jamaica travel at night, arriving the next morning at the day's port of call, perhaps Montego Bay or Ocho Rios. In port, passengers can go ashore for sightseeing, shopping, and a local meal. Prices vary widely; consult a travel agent for the latest.

Agencies and tour companies offering cruise packages to Jamaica include:

Ambassador Tours, 120 Montgomery St., Suite 400, San Francisco, CA 94104 (© 800/989-9000 or 415/357-9876); **Cruises, Inc.,** 1415 NW 62 St., Suite 205, Fort Lauderdale, FL 33309 (© 800/854-0500 or 954/958-3681); **Cruises of Distinction,** 2750 S. Woodward Ave., Bloomfield Hills, MI 48304 (© 800/634-3445);

Cruise Masters, Century Plaza Towers, 2029 Century Park E., Suite 950, Los Angeles, CA 90067 (℃ **800/ 242-9000** or 310/556-2925); **Kelly Cruises,** 1315 W. 22nd St., Suite 105, Oak Brook, IL 60521 (℃ **800/837- 7447** or 630/990-1111); and **Hartford Holidays Travel,** 129 Hillside Ave., Williston Park, NY 11596 (℃ **800/828-4813** or 516/746-6670).

Also stay tuned to last-minute price wars brewing among such mega-carriers as Carnival, Princess, Royal Caribbean, and Holland America (see below), as well as such low-budget contenders as Premier.

THE CRUISE LINES

Here's a brief rundown of some of the cruise lines serving Jamaica and the Caribbean. For detailed information, pick up a copy of one of our companion guides in this series, *Frommer's Caribbean Cruises & Ports of Call, Frommer's Caribbean Ports of Call,* or *The Unofficial Guide to Cruises.*

- **Carnival Cruise Lines** (℃ **800/ 327-9501;** www.carnival.com): Offering affordable vacations on some of the biggest and most brightly decorated ships afloat, Carnival is the boldest, brashest, most successful mass-market cruise line in the world. Its vessels depart for Ocho Rios from Miami and New Orleans. The cruises offer good value and feature non-stop activities. Food and party-colored drinks are plentiful, and the overall atmosphere is comparable to a floating theme park. Lots of single passengers opt for this line, as do families attracted by the line's well-run children's program.
- **Celebrity Cruises** (℃ **800/722- 5941** or 305/539-6000; www. celebritycruises.com): Celebrity maintains eight stylish, medium to large ships with cruises that last between 7 and 10 nights to Ocho Rios, among other destinations. It's classy but not stuffy, several notches above mass-market lines. Accommodations are roomy and well equipped, cuisine is refined, and service is impeccable. Unlike many competitors, Celebrity has a very young fleet.
- **Costa Cruise Lines** (℃ **800/462- 6782** or 954/266-5600; www. costacruises.com): Costa, the U.S.-based branch of a cruise line that has thrived in Italy for about a century, maintains hefty to megasize vessels. Two of Costa's vessels offer similar jaunts through the eastern Caribbean on alternate weeks, departing from Fort Lauderdale and calling at Ocho Rios. There's an Italian flavor and lots of Italian design onboard here, and an atmosphere of relaxed indulgence.
- **Holland America Line– Westours** (℃ **800/426-0327** or 206/281-3535; www.holland america.com): Holland America is the most high-toned of the mass-market cruise lines. They offer solid value, with very few jolts or surprises, and attract a solid, well-grounded clientele of primarily older travelers (late-night revelers and serious partygoers might want to book cruises on other lines, such as Carnival). Cruises stop at deep-water mainstream ports such as Ocho Rios or Montego Bay, and last an average of 7 days, but in some cases 10 days, visiting such ports as Key West, Grand Cayman, St. Maarten, St. Lucia, Curaçao, Barbados, and St. Thomas.
- **Royal Caribbean International (RCI)** (℃ **800/398-9819** or 305/ 539-6000; www.royalcaribbean. com): RCI leads the industry in the development of megaships. Though accommodations are more than adequate, they are not

upscale and tend to be a bit more cramped than the industry norm. Using either Miami, Fort Lauderdale, or San Juan as their home port, Royal Caribbean ships call regularly at Ocho Rios. Most of the company's cruises last 7 days.

14 Getting Around

BY RENTAL CAR

Jamaica is big enough—and public transportation is unreliable enough—that a car is a necessity if you plan to do much independent sightseeing. Unfortunately, prices of car rentals in Jamaica have skyrocketed; it's now one of the most expensive rental scenes in the Caribbean. And fraud is a very real concern; stick with our choices below.

Most rental cars in Jamaica are picked up at the airport, not delivered to your hotel. Some hotels have car-rental desks, but in all cases we've found those desks' prices higher than if arrangements were made in advance. Most car-rental firms in Jamaica grant unlimited mileage; if the firm you're calling doesn't, switch to one that does.

You can usually book a rental car as part of a package tour, but if you're going on your own, here are some tips:

WHERE TO RENT Try **Budget** (© **800/472-3325** in the U.S., 876/952-3838 at the Montego Bay Airport, or 876/924-8762 in Kingston; www.budget.com); with Budget, a daily collision-damage waiver is mandatory and costs $15. **Hertz** (© **800/654-3131** in the U.S.; www.hertz.com) operates branches at the airports in Montego Bay (© 876/979-0438) and Kingston (© 876/924-8028).

If you'd like to shop for a better deal with one of the local companies in Montego Bay, try **Jamaica Car Rental,** 23 Gloucester Ave. (© **876/952-5586**), with a branch at the Sangster International Airport at Montego Bay (© **876/952-9496**). You can also try **United Car Rentals,** 49 Gloucester Ave. (© **876/952-3077**), which rents Mazdas, Toyotas, Hondas, and Suzuki jeeps, costing from $48 per day for a standard, $62 for automatic.

In Kingston try **Island Car Rentals,** with a branch at Montego Bay's Sangster International Airport (© **876/952-7225**). It rents Hondas and Samurais with rates beginning at $90 daily in winter and $68 in the off season.

Expedia.com (www.expedia.com) and **Travelocity** (www.travelocity.com) can help you compare prices for rentals—and locate bargains—in Jamaica.

DRIVING IN JAMAICA   *Drive on the left side of the road.* You should exercise more than usual caution, and be especially cautious at night: Male drivers here are too reckless for comfort. Speed limits in towns are 48kmph (30 mph), and 80kmph (50 mph) outside towns. Gas is measured by the imperial gallon (a British unit of measurement that's about 25% more than a U.S. gal.); most stations don't accept credit cards. Your valid driver's license from home is acceptable for short-term visits to Jamaica.

ROAD MAPS   A coastal route designated by an "A" plus a number encircles Jamaica. It's well marked and easy to follow. More complicated are secondary roads, urban streets, and feeder roads, whose markings sometimes are infuriatingly unclear. Recognizing this problem, the Jamaica Tourist Board has issued one of the best maps of the island, the *Discover Jamaica* road map. It contains a detailed overview of the entire island, as well as blowups of Kingston, Montego Bay, Negril, Mandeville, Spanish Town, Port Antonio, and Ocho Rios; there's also a very useful street index to Kingston. Get it from any Jamaica Tourist Board office or car-rental agency.

MILEAGE INFORMATION   Subject to road conditions, driving time from Montego Bay to Negril (about 84km/52 miles) is 1½ hours; between Montego Bay and Ocho Rios (108km/67 miles), 1½ hours; between Ocho Rios and Port Antonio (106km/ 66 miles), 2½ hours; between Ocho Rios and Kingston (87km/54 miles), 2 hours; between Kingston and Mandeville (98km/61 miles), 1½ hours; and between Kingston and Port Antonio (98km/61 miles), 1½ to 2 hours.

AUTO BREAKDOWNS   In case of a breakdown, telephone your car-rental agency for assistance.

BY TAXI & BUS
Most cabs in Jamaica are older vehicles. Taxis in Kingston don't have meters, so agree on a price before you get in the car. In Kingston and the rest of the island, special taxis and buses for visitors are operated by JUTA (Jamaica Union of Travellers Association) and have the union's emblem on the side of the vehicle. Look for a red Public Passenger Vehicle (PPV) plate.

Taxis can be flagged down on the street or summoned by phone. Rates are per car—not per passenger—and 25% is added to the metered rate between midnight and 5am.

Technically, JUTA cabs are supposed to have meters, but most of them are not in working order. Therefore, again, *agree on the price of the trip before booking*. Cab fares should be posted inside the taxi; if you don't see

them, you have the right to request a copy from the driver. A 10% to 12% tip is usually added.

Avoid pirate or unlicensed taxis. Not only are they not metered—they are illegal and rarely carry insurance.

BY MOPED & MOTORCYCLE
The front desk of your hotel can usually arrange the rental of a moped or motorcycle. Expect a daily rate of about $45 for a moped or $70 for a Honda 550. Depending on the vehicle rented, a deposit of $100 to $300 is generally required.

BY PLANE
Most travelers enter the country via Montego Bay (although American Airlines also flies to Kingston). If you want to fly elsewhere on the island, you'll need to use the island's domestic air service, which is provided by **Air Jamaica Express.** Reservations are handled by **Air Jamaica** (© **800/523-5585;** www.airjamaica.com in the U.S., or 876/952-4300). You can also reserve from home through a travel agent or American Airlines.

Air Jamaica Express offers scheduled flights daily between the resort areas. There are seven flights a day from Kingston to Montego Bay, two flights a day between Kingston and Ocho Rios, and two flights between Montego Bay and Ocho Rios—each about $70 per leg. Car-rental facilities are not available at Jamaica's smaller airports.

International Air Link (© **876/ 940-6660;** www.intlairlink.com) also provides shuttle service between Montego Bay and Negril for $66 one-way.

15 Tips on Accommodations
Because of the island's size and diversity, Jamaica offers the widest array of accommodations in the Caribbean.

One increasingly popular option is the **all-inclusive resort.** Well-publicized, solidly financed, and

boasting a wealth of facilities, these tend to be large resorts where all your drinking, dining, and sporting diversions are offered within the hotel compound as part of one all-inclusive price. Although they tend to limit your exposure to local life, they are convenient. (See "The All-Inclusive: Safe Haven, or Not for You?" box below.)

Another option is the **small hotel.** Jamaica offers many of these, a few of which are the finest in the Caribbean. There, on any given day, you'll be given an option of dining either within the hotel or at any of the independent restaurants that flourish nearby.

Other options include renting a **self-catering villa** or **apartment,** where you can save money by making your own meals in your own kitchen. Also noteworthy are Jamaica's simple but decent **guesthouses,** where low costs combine with maximum exposure to local life. Unfortunately,

these sometimes lie far from beaches and offer few diversions or activities.

BOOKING A HOTEL ROOM

Reservation services usually work as consolidators, buying or reserving rooms in bulk, then dealing them out to customers at a profit. They do offer special deals that range from 10% to 50% off; but remember, these discounts apply to the inflated rack rates that guests rarely end up paying. You're better off dealing directly with a hotel.

Here are a few of the best reservations services for Jamaican travel: **Accommodations Express** (© 800/ 950-4685; www.hotels.com); **Hotel Discount Reservations** (© 800/ 715-7666; www.hoteldiscount.com);

The All-Inclusive: Safe Haven, or Not For You?

Of all the resorts of Jamaica, the all-inclusive has virtually taken over Ocho Rios, although Mo Bay and Negril have their fair share. The concept was pioneered by Jamaica's Butch Stewart with his Sandals properties (© 888/SANDALS) and has since swept the Caribbean, including such islands as St. Lucia. Sandals caters only to couples (male/female), although most other resorts welcome all known couplings.

All-inclusives are not for the independent traveler. At the all-inclusive, you get all your meals and most activities paid for as part of a package. Some dine-around plans help you break the monotony of eating at the same resort every night. With their 24-hour security force, these all-inclusives give you more protection than the smaller, independent inns without such expensive patrolling.

If you're an adventure traveler, you may not want such womblike security. You may prefer to stay at a small inn or little hotel where you're free to roam throughout the day, returning to your bed after a night of rum and reggae on the town.

Like a mother hen, the all-inclusive will pamper you during your entire stay, even pick you up at the airport and haul you back there for your return flight. At the little independent inn or small hotel, you're more or less on your own. The choice is yours.

If you don't want to stick to the all-inclusives, one of the best travel agencies specializing in hotel deals is **Changes in L'Attitudes** (© 800/ 330-8272; www.changes.com). Its website is fast-loading and informative. For villas in Mo Bay, Ocho Rios, and Port Antonio, contact **Elegant Resorts International** (P.O. Box 80, Montego Bay, Jamaica; © 800/237 3237; fax 876/953-9563).

Quikbook (© **800/789-9887,** includes fax-on-demand service; www.quikbook.com); and **Room Exchange** (© **800/846-7000** in the U.S.).

Online, try booking with **Frommers.com** and save up to 50%. **Microsoft Expedia** (www.expedia. com) features a "Travel Agent" that directs you to affordable lodgings.

LANDING THE BEST ROOM Somebody has to get the best room in the house, and it might as well be you. In Jamaica the first question for most visitors is, "How far is my room from the beach?" Find this out before you go. Find out also what's included in the price—beach chairs, towels? It could make a big difference in your final bill.

Corner rooms are usually more spacious, more tranquil, and closer to the elevator. They often have more windows and light than standard rooms, and don't always cost more.

If you like to retire early, book a room away from the entertainment and the kitchen. Also ask if your windows can open, and if there are ceiling fans and/or air-conditioning.

Finally, when reserving ask if the hotel is under renovation. This is more likely to occur off season.

GUESTHOUSES

An entirely different type of accommodation is the guesthouse, where most Jamaicans themselves stay when they travel. Prices average anywhere from $50 to $100 for a double per night, although this can vary widely.

The term "guesthouse" can mean anything, however. Some resemble simple motels built around swimming pools; others are made up of small individual cottages with kitchenettes, constructed around a main building containing a bar and restaurant serving local food. Some are surprisingly comfortable, often with private baths and a swimming pool. (You may or may not have air-conditioning; rooms are often cooled by ceiling fans or breezes through open windows—a security concern.)

Guesthouses can't be topped for value, however. Though bereft of frills, the guesthouses we've recommended are clean and safe for families or single women.

CONDOS, COTTAGES & VILLAS

If you're going as a family or group of friends, a housekeeping holiday can be one of the least-expensive ways to vacation in Jamaica. Self-catering accommodations are now available in many locations.

The more upscale **villas** have a staff, or at least a maid who comes in a few days a week, and they also provide the essentials for home life, including bed linens and cooking paraphernalia. **Condos** usually come with a reception desk and are often comparable to life in a suite in a big resort hotel. Nearly all condo complexes provide swimming pools (some have more than one pool).

Some **private apartments** in Jamaica are rented, either with or without maid service. This is more of a no-frills option than are the villas and condos. The apartments may not be in buildings with swimming pools, and they may not maintain a front desk to help you. Jamaican **cottages** often contain no more than a simple bedroom, small kitchen, and bath. During the winter, you'll need to reserve at least 5 or 6 months in advance.

Villas of Distinction, P.O. Box 55, Armonk, NY 10504 (© **800/289-0900** in the U.S., or 914/273-3331; fax 914/273-3387; www.villasof distinction.com), offers private villas with one to six bedrooms and a pool. Domestic help is often included. Descriptions, rates, and photos of the villas are available online.

At Home Abroad, 405 E. 56th St., Suite 6H, New York, NY 10022-2466 (© 212/421-9165; fax 212/752-1591; www.athomeabroadinc.com), has a roster of private upscale homes for rent in Jamaica, most with maid service.

VHR, Worldwide, 235 Kensington Ave., Norwood, NJ 07648 (© 800/633-3284 in the U.S. and Canada, or 201/767-9393; fax 201/767-5510), offers the most comprehensive portfolio of luxury villas, condominiums, resort suites, and apartments for rent in the Caribbean, including Jamaica. The company can also arrange for airfare and car rental.

Hideaways International, 767 Islington St., Portsmouth, NH 03801 (© 800/843-4433 in the U.S., or 603/430-4433; fax 603/430-4444; www.hideaways.com), publishes *Hideaways Guide,* a pictorial directory of home rentals worldwide, including Jamaica. It includes full descriptions so you know what you're renting. For most rentals, you'll deal directly with the owners. Other services include yacht charters, cruises, airline ticketing, car rentals, and hotel reservations. Annual membership is $145; membership information, listings, and photos are available online.

16 Tips on Dining Out

The bad news is that dining in Jamaica is generally more expensive than in either the United States or Canada. Restaurant prices are more in tune with Europe, as virtually everything must be imported except the fish and Caribbean lobster. Service charges are automatically added to most restaurant tabs, usually 10% to 15%. Even so, if service has been good, it's customary to tip extra.

To save money, many visitors prefer the Modified American Plan (MAP), which includes room, breakfast, and one main meal per day, almost always dinner. You can then have lunch somewhere else, or if your hotel has a beach, order a light a la carte lunch at the hotel, the cost of which is added to your bill. On some MAP plans, you can arrange in advance to exchange lunches for dinners, so you can go out a few times. This is true for affiliated resorts such as Sandals, which has more than one hotel in the same resort, as it does in Mo Bay and Ocho Rios.

Warning A Word on Marijuana

You will almost certainly be approached by someone selling *ganja* (marijuana)—in fact, that's why many travelers come here. However, drugs, including marijuana, are illegal, and imprisonment is the penalty for possession. You don't want to experience the Jamaican penal system first-hand. Don't smoke pot openly in public. Of course, hundreds of visitors do and get away with it, but you may be the one who gets caught, and the person selling to you might even be a police informant. Above all, don't try to bring marijuana back into the United States. There are drug-sniffing dogs stationed at the Jamaican airports, and they will check your luggage. U.S. Customs agents, well aware of the drug situation on Jamaica, have arrested many tourists who have tried to bring some home.

The American Plan (AP), on the other hand, includes all three meals each day. Drinks, including wine, are usually extra. On this plan, it's cheaper and you don't need to rent a car or taxi at night, but you'll miss out on different dining experiences around your resort.

Before booking a hotel, it's wise to have a clear understanding of what is included in the various meal plans offered.

If you plan to eat out, here are some tips:

- In summer, only the most elegant establishments require men to wear jackets. Most top-rated places today ask only that a man wear a shirt with a collar.
- Check to see if reservations are required. In the winter you may find all the tables gone at some of the more famous places. Savvy guests often ask the concierge of a hotel to make reservations. At all places, wear a cover-up if you're lunching; don't enter a restaurant attired in a bikini.
- To save money, stick to regional food whenever possible. For a main dish, that usually means Caribbean lobster or fish (see "Jamaican Food & Drink," p. 232).
- Getting to a restaurant at night is difficult if you drive a rented car. The roads are badly marked, driving is on the left, and road conditions are poor. It's better to go by taxi. Some popular upscale restaurants will send a minivan to your hotel.

17 Tips on Shopping

Crafts are a popular take-home item while in Jamaica. **Woodcarvings** run the gamut from the horrible to the delightful; **baskets** are woven from palm fronds or the straw of an island plant known as the *jipijapa*. The

The Java of Kings

One of the world's most sought-after coffees, Blue Mountain Coffee, is the drink of connoisseurs, favored from Tokyo to New York. The coffee is known for its good acidity, refined taste, particular sweetness, exquisite flavor, and an intense aroma.

The Blue Mountains north of Kingston reach a peak of 2,220m (7,400 ft.), making the coffee bean here one of the highest-elevation-grown coffees in the world. Introduced to Jamaica in 1728, the coffee is handpicked, and every stage of its production from hulling to sorting and grading is carefully supervised.

In Jamaica a ground 57-gram (2-oz.) gift pack usually retails for about $8, but it's probably far more expensive in your hometown if it's available at all. (Blue Mountain coffee beans in Japan, for example, sell for more than $60 per lb.)

The coffee is sold in most upscale gift shops in Jamaica, and makes an aromatic souvenir of your visit. We prefer to buy our supply while trekking through the Blue Mountains themselves. To locate where to buy the brew on-site (or nearly so), see "Exploring the Blue Mountains," on p. 211.

island's inventory of woodcarvings and weavings is supplemented by establishments selling **leather goods** (sandals and shoes are often a good buy); locally made **jewelry** fashioned from gold, silver, onyx, and bone; and **clothing** (especially casual wear and sportswear) whose light textures nicely complement the heat of the tropics. Also noteworthy are the many **handbags** woven from straw or palm fronds, which are sometimes rendered more ornate through colorful embroidery applied by any of the island's "straw ladies."

Also noteworthy is the handful of **art galleries** that stock the paintings

of local artists. Some art critics say the island's most valuable export, after aluminum, is its art. These paintings range from the banal and uninspired to evocative portrayals of universal themes.

Premium coffee is one of Jamaica's major exports, and you can buy it here much cheaper than at home.

Bargaining is welcome with handicrafts, especially in informal markets, but not in more formal stores. Expect a discount of around 15% to 20% off the original price.

18 Recommended Books

BOOKS
GENERAL
Catch a Fire: The Life of Bob Marley, by Timothy White (Guernsey Press, 1983), chronicles the reggae musician's life and career, from poverty to international fame.

Jamaican Folk Tales and Oral Histories, by Laura Tanna (Institute of Jamaica Publications, 1984), is a collection culled from the best Jamaican storytelling and told with humor and style.

The Cimaroons, by Robert Leeson (William Collins, 1978), is the story of an enslaved people who fought stubbornly for their freedom. Their story does not appear in many history books, yet is true and exciting.

X/Self, by Edward Kamau Brathwaite (Oxford University Press, 1987), one of the finest of the Caribbean poets, traces his African/Caribbean ancestry in an extraordinarily rich, imaginative sequence of poems.

HISTORY
The Gleaner Geography & History of Jamaica (Gleaner Company, 22nd edition, 1991) is a textbook through

which Jamaican schoolchildren learn about their country. The latest edition is available in major bookstores around Jamaica.

TRAVEL
Tour Jamaica, by Margaret Morris (Gleaner Company, 1988), describes an island of infinite variety with interesting and warmhearted people. Covering six regions, the book provides data on places of interest, local personalities, and historic and topical anecdotes. Featured are 19 recommended tours.

The Adventure Guide to Jamaica, by Steve Cohen (Hunter Publishing, 1988), leads you on a tour of unforgettable parts of the island few visitors know how to reach.

CUISINE
The Jamaican Chef, by Byron Murray and Patrick Lewin (Life Long Publishers, 1990), provides recipes for an array of island dishes.

Traditional Jamaican Cookery, by Norma Benghiat (Penguin, 1985), includes local recipes never before written down, having been passed down by word of mouth.

FAST FACTS: Jamaica

Business Hours Banks are open Monday through Friday from 9am to 5pm. Store hours vary, but as a rule most business establishments open at 8:30am and close at 4:30 or 5pm Monday through Friday. Some shops open Saturday until noon.

Currency Exchange There are Bank of Jamaica exchange bureaus at both international airports (near Montego Bay and Kingston), at cruise-ship piers, and in most hotels.

Doctors Many major resorts have doctors on call. If you need any particular medicine or treatment, bring evidence such as a letter from your home doctor.

Electricity Most places use the standard electrical voltage of 110, as in the U.S. However, some establishments still operate on 220 volts, 50 cycles. If your hotel is on a different current than your U.S.-made appliance, ask for a transformer and adapter.

Embassies, Consulates & High Commissions Calling embassies or consulates in Jamaica is a challenge. Phones will ring and ring before being picked up, if they are answered at all. Extreme patience is needed to reach a live voice on the other end. The embassy of the **United States** is located at the Jamaica Mutual Life Building, 2 Oxford Rd., Kingston 5 (© **876/929-4850**). The High Commission of **Canada** is situated at 3 Wet Kings House Rd., Kingston 10 (© **876/926-1500**), and there's a consulate at 29 Gloucester Ave., Montego Bay (© **876/952-6198**). The High Commission of the **United Kingdom** is found at 28 Trafalgar Rd., Kingston 10 (© **876/510-0700**).

Emergencies For police and air rescue, dial © **119**; to report a fire or call an ambulance, dial © **110**.

Hospitals See "Fast Facts," in each regional chapter for the most convenient medical services to each destination.

Mail Instead of going to a post office, you can, in most cases, give mail to the hotel reception. Most hotels also sell stamps. Allow about 1 week for an airmail postcard or letter to reach North America. Increases in postal charges may be implemented at any time, so ask about the current rate before depositing mail. For mail to any business listed in this book, remember to include "Jamaica, W. I." in the address. The island has no zip codes. Call © **876/922-9430** in Kingston with questions. For important items, consider a courier service such as DHL (© **876/922-7333**) or Federal Express (© **876/952-0411** or 876/960-9192).

Newspapers & Magazines Jamaica supports three daily newspapers (*Daily Gleaner, The Jamaica Record,* and *Daily Star*), several weekly periodicals, and a handful of other publications. U.S. newsmagazines, such as *Time* and *Newsweek,* as well as occasional copies of the *Miami Herald,* are available at most newsstands.

Nudity Nude sunbathing and swimming are allowed at a number of hotels, clubs, and beaches (especially in Negril), but only where signs state that swimsuits are optional. Elsewhere, law enforcement officials won't even allow topless sunbathing.

Passports Passport requirements vary according to your country of origin.

For residents of the United States: Whether you're applying in person or by mail, you can download passport applications from the U.S. State Department website at **http://travel.state.gov.** For general information, call the **National Passport Agency** (ⓒ 202/647-0518). To find your regional passport office, either check the U.S. State Department website or call the **National Passport Information Center** (ⓒ 900/225-5674); the fee is 55¢ per minute for automated information and $1.50 per minute for operator-assisted calls.

For Residents of Canada: Passport applications are available at travel agencies throughout Canada or from the central **Passport Office,** Department of Foreign Affairs and International Trade, Ottawa, ON K1A 0G3 (ⓒ 800/567-6868; www.ppt.gc.ca).

For residents of the United Kingdom: To pick up an application for a standard 10-year passport (5-year passport for children under 16), visit your nearest passport office, major post office, or travel agency, or contact the **United Kingdom Passport Service** at ⓒ 0870/521-0410 or search its website at www.ukpa.gov.uk.

For residents of Ireland: You can apply for a 10-year passport at the **Passport Office,** Setanta Centre, Molesworth Street, Dublin 2 (ⓒ 01/671-1633; www.irlgov.ie/iveagh). Those under age 18 and over 65 must apply for a 12€, 3-year passport. You can also apply at 1A South Mall, Cork (ⓒ 021/272-525) or at most main post offices.

For residents of Australia: You can pick up an application from your local post office or any branch of Passports Australia, but you must schedule an interview at the passport office to present your application materials. Call the **Australian Passport Information Service** at ⓒ 131-232, or visit the government website at www.passports.gov.au.

For residents of New Zealand: You can pick up a passport application at any New Zealand Passports Office or download it from their website. Contact the **Passports Office** at ⓒ 0800/225-050 in New Zealand or 04/474-8100, or log on to www.passports.govt.nz.

Pharmacies Prescriptions are only accepted by local pharmacies if they were issued by a Jamaican doctor. Luckily, hotels have doctors on call. If you need any particular medicine or treatment, bring evidence, such as a letter from your own physician. For the most convenient local pharmacies, refer to "Fast Facts" in each regional chapter.

Police Dial ⓒ 119.

Radio & TV Jamaica is served by two major radio broadcasters. Radio Jamaica (RJR) is the more popular of the two, partly because of its musical mix of reggae, rock 'n' roll, and talk-show material. RJR's two island-wide services are known as Supreme Sound and FAME FM. The second broadcaster is Jamaica Broadcasting Corporation (JBC), which also operates the island's only television station (JBC-TV, established in 1963). Many of the better hotels offer Cable News Network (CNN) and other satellite channels.

Taxes The government imposes between 10% to 15% room tax, depending on your category of hotel. You'll be charged a J$1,000 (US$28) departure tax at the airport, payable in either Jamaican or U.S. dollars. There's also a 20% government tax on rental cars and a 20% tax on all overseas phone calls.

Telephone, Telex & Fax Even the island's smallest hotels maintain their own fax machines. For telexes, contact the local branch of **Cleveland Walace Jamaica,** the country's telecommunications operators. In Kingston its address is 47 Halfway Tree Rd. (℃ **876/926-9700**).

Time During the winter, Jamaica is on Eastern Standard Time, the same as New York and Montréal. When the United States is on daylight savings time, however, it's 6am in Miami and 5am in Kingston; Jamaica does not switch to DST.

Tipping Tipping is customary in Jamaica. Typically 10% or 15% is expected in hotels and restaurants on occasions when you would normally tip. Most places add a service charge to the bill, but a little extra (3%–5%) is often expected for good service. Tipping is not "officially" allowed at all-inclusive resorts.

Useful Telephone Numbers Ambulance, ℃ **110**; fire, ℃ **110**; police, ℃ **119**; time, ℃ **117**; toll operator and telephone assistance on local and intraisland calls, ℃ **112**; overseas calls operator, ℃ **113**; **Post and Telephone Department,** ℃ **876/922-9430.** You reach **MCI** at ℃ **800/888-8000; AT&T** at ℃ **800/CALLATT;** and **Sprint** at ℃ **800/877-8000.**

Water It's usually safe to drink tap water island-wide; however, it's prudent to drink bottled water, if available. We do.

3

Montego Bay & the Northwest Coast

Despite a large influx of visitors, **Montego Bay** retains its own identity. A thriving business-and-commercial center, it functions as the main market town for most of western Jamaica, supporting both cruise-ship tourism and a growing industrial center. Mo Bay, as it's known, is even served by its own airport, **Donald Sangster International.**

This is the most cosmopolitan of Jamaican resorts, not as hedonistic as Negril but also not as crowded as Ocho Rios. As such, Montego remains the grande dame of island resorts. The draw of Mo Bay is its deluxe hotels, such as the Ritz-Carlton, Half Moon, Round Hill, and Tryall.

As in much of Jamaica, your choice of resort here often matters more than your choice of area. If you're determined to honeymoon with your sweetie, go for one of the Sandals properties; if you want to hang with the jet-set, take a villa at Round Hill.

If you're seeking authentic or traditional Jamaica, however, this area is probably not for you.

1 Orientation

ARRIVING BY PLANE   Most arrivals in Jamaica are at **Donald Sangster International Airport** (*C* 876/952-3124), 3km (1¾ miles) east of the center of Montego Bay. Those booked into resorts at Ocho Rios and its satellite, Runaway Bay, or Negril also use the Mo Bay airport as a point of entry into Jamaica.

In winter, the busy season for tourism in Jamaica, lines move smoothly. Things move more slowly during the summer months, despite dwindling numbers of tourists—partly because many Jamaicans from Canada and the United States arrive during those months to visit family. They often bring suitcases packed with gifts and supplies; inspection of these items can cause endless delays. (Jamaica's Customs and Immigration officers are zealous.)

After clearing Customs, there is a **currency exchange office.** You can change money here into Jamaican dollars. Nearly all places on the island eagerly accept the Yankee dollar—in fact, most vendors will specifically request it—but if you plan to go to local dives, they might deal only in Jamaican dollars. Our advice? Pick up a little Jamaican cash here at the airport, where you'll get a far better exchange rate than at your hotel. Plus, it's safer here than at a late-night city ATM.

Although it's true that there are **ATMs** at the airport, some Frommer's readers have complained bitterly when they discovered some of these machines to be chronically out of cash.

Warning: Once you retrieve your luggage at the airport, hang on to it. Luggage theft is fairly commonplace here, and in Kingston it becomes much more so.

GETTING FROM THE AIRPORT INTO THE CITY   Some of the major resorts, such as the Sandals properties, keep vans waiting at the airport to carry guests right to the hotel for free. Other properties do not, however, especially the less expensive ones. If you're staying at one of these, you must take a taxi (unless you're picking up a rental car at the airport); there is no public bus service from the airport into Montego Bay.

Use only special taxis or vans operated by **JUTA,** the **Jamaica Union of Travelers Association** (© 876/952-0813). Do *not* get into a "pirate taxi," even though drivers will promise to cut the going rate in half; cheating tourists is disturbingly common. JUTA tariffs are controlled, and you'll recognize its vehicles by the union emblems. A list of official tariffs is posted at the airport—but it's still important to agree on the price before setting out, to avoid potential disagreements later.

VISITOR INFORMATION   The main office of the **Jamaica Tourist Board** is at Gloucester Avenue (© 876/952-4425), opposite the entrance to Cornwall Beach. It is open Monday to Friday 8:30am to 4:30pm and on Saturday from 9am to 1pm. There is a small branch office (information booth) at the Craft Market at the corner of Market and Harbour streets and another in the arrivals hall of Donald Sangster Airport. When visiting, ask for a free map of Montego Bay.

GETTING AROUND   Taxis are generally the way to get around, as there is no practical bus service in Montego Bay and no public tourist shuttles except those maintained by hotels—which are strictly for the use of guests. (A taxi shuttle service did operate briefly during the 1990s, but the taxi lobby managed to kill it off.)

You can walk to most places within the center of Mo Bay itself, especially along Gloucester Avenue. In other cases, summon a licensed taxi. These have red license plates and meters, with fares posted inside each vehicle. If you want to hail a taxi to go somewhere outside of town, most of the cabs can be found along Gloucester Avenue.

For the more adventurous, getting around by bike or motorcycle is another possibility—though cyclists in Mo Bay must deal with loco drivers who seem to feel they own the highway. If you still want to risk life and limb, your hotel might either lend you a bike or rent you one.

If not, check with **Sun Cruise Bike Rental** at 32 Gloucester Ave. (© 876/979-0614), next to the Wexford Court Hotel. Bikes here rent for $20 a day, with a $200 credit card deposit taken at the time of the rental. You can also rent scooters at the same location for $40 to $45 a day, though a $1,000 deposit is taken on your credit card. Sun Cruise is open daily 8am to 6pm.

FAST FACTS: Montego Bay

Banks   For money exchanges and/or other banking needs, the two best choices are **Scotiabank** (© 876/952-4440) and **National Commercial Bank** (© 876/952-3640), both on Sam Sharpe Square in the center of Mo Bay. Each maintains a 24-hour ATM and opens Monday to Thursday 8:30am to 3pm, Friday 8:30am to 4:30pm, and Saturday 10am to 1pm. Both are part of the Cirrus system, so participating cards work in their machines.

Montego Bay

ACCOMMODATIONS ■
Blue Harbour Hotel **16**
Breezes Montego Bay **13**
Casa Blanca Beach Club **19**
Coral Cliff Gaming Lounge
& Resort **17**
Coyaba **10**
Doctor's Cave Beach Hotel **9**
El Greco Resort **11**
FDR Pebbles **1**
Half Moon Golf, Tennis
& Beach Club **4**
Holiday Inn Sunspree **2**
Montego Beach Resort **8**
Richmond Hill Inn **26**
Ridgeway Guest House **12**
Ritz Carlton Rose Hall Jamaica **2**
Round Hill Hotel & Villas **30**
The Sandals Inn **6**
Sandals Montego Bay **5**
Sandals Royal Caribbean **4**
Sea Castles Resort **4**
Starfish Trelawny Beach **1**
Sunset Beach Resort & Spa **28**
Toby's **7**
Tryall Club Jamaica **2**
Verney House Resort **15**
Wexford Court Hotel **16**
Wyndham Rose Hall
& Country Club **14**

DINING ◆

The Brewery **23**
The Castles **3**
Chef Oliver Magnus **21**
Day-O Plantation Restaurant **33**
Guangzhou **24**
The Houseboat Grill **29**
Julia's **32**
Margueritaville Sports Bar
  & Grill **20**
Marguerite's Seafood
  by the Sea **20**
The Native Restaurant **25**
The Pelican **22**
Pork Pit **25**
Reading Reef Club Restaurant **34**
Richmond Hill Inn **26**
Round Hill Dining Room **31**
Sugar Mill Restaurant **3**
Three Palms **3**
Town House **27**

Remember that ATMs dispense Jamaican dollars, and US$1 equals about 43 Jamaican dollars, so you'll have to request larger amounts.

Bookstores If you'd like to do some light reading on the beach, you can go to **Sangster's Bookshop,** 2 St. James St. (© 876/952-0319), the largest book outlet in Montego Bay. It's open Monday to Saturday 8:30am to 6pm. Another retailer is **Henderson's Book Store,** 27 St. James St. (© 876/ 952-2551), open Monday to Saturday 8:30am to 6pm.

Business Hours Stores' policies vary, but in general they open Monday to Friday 8:30am to 4:30 or 5pm. Some smaller shops also open on Saturday until noon. Sunday gets sleepy in Montego Bay, except at the hotels.

Doctors & Dentists All major hotels have a doctor or dentist on call. For emergency treatment, go to the hospital (see "Hospital," below). If you will need medicine or any particular treatment while in Montego Bay, bring a letter from your home physician before arriving on the island.

Drugstores One of the best pharmacies in Montego Bay is **Clinicare Pharmacy,** 14A Market St. (© 876/952-8510), open Monday to Saturday from 9am to 8pm and Sunday 10am to 6pm. Note that local pharmacies will only accept a prescription if it has been issued by a Jamaican doctor.

Emergencies Dial © **110** to report a fire or call an ambulance. Dial © **119** for the police.

Hospital Patients in emergency situations are often flown to Puerto Rico or Miami, where medical facilities are far superior. The major hospital in Montego Bay is **Cornwall Regional Hospital** at Mount Salem (© 876/ 952-5100).

Internet Access Your best bet if your hotel isn't equipped is **Internet West,** 17 Harbour St. (© 876/971-6057; irietech2@cwjamaica.com). It's open Monday to Saturday 9am to 7pm.

Laundry & Dry Cleaning If your hotel doesn't offer guest laundry facilities, you can drop off laundry at **Fabricare Centre,** 4 Corner Lane (© 876/952-6897), which also features 1-hour dry cleaning. Hours are Monday to Saturday 7:30am to 5pm. Offering much the same service, including 1-hour dry cleaning, is **Ucon Laundry & Dry Cleaners,** 11 Perry St. (© 876/952-6105), open Monday to Saturday 7:30am to 5:30pm.

Mail Include "Jamaica, W.I." in all island addresses. The island has no zip codes.

Maps Go to the tourist office (see above) for a good map of Montego Bay.

Photo Supplies Film can be purchased at **Salmon's,** 32 St. James St. (© 876/952-4527), open Monday to Saturday 9am to 6pm; and **Ventura,** 22 Market St. (© 876/952-2937), open Monday to Friday 9am to 5pm and Saturday 9am to 6pm. Each of these stores also processes photos.

Post Office Many visitors buy Jamaican stamps as collector's items, as they are often flamboyant. The chief post office in Montego Bay is in the center of town at 122 Barnett St. (© 876/952-7389). It is open Monday to Friday 8am to 5pm.

Safety Montego Bay is far safer as a destination than Kingston. All the major resorts, especially the all-inclusives, have private security guards patrolling the grounds; on-site you'll probably run into few problems. However, trouble often rises when you leave your hotel. One annoyance is the string of hustlers—peddling flesh, drugs, or whatever—who will attach themselves to you. Most of them are harmless; a few, though, are muggers or pickpockets, so be careful around them. As for wandering around Montego Bay's narrow, dark streets at night—suffice to say that it's a very bad idea.

Telephone Hotels sometimes add outrageous surcharges to long-distance calls. For that reason, some frugal travelers purchase a **Cable & Wireless Phone Card**—available at most hotel desks—for J$200 (US$3.30), allowing you to talk to places in the U.S. and Canada for about 11 minutes. For more information, call ℂ **888/225-5295**.

Travel Agencies There is no local representative for American Express in Montego Bay. However, with an American Express card you can get a personal check cashed at **Great Vacations,** 2 Market St. (ℂ **876/971-6750**), open Monday to Friday 8:30am to 4:30pm, Saturday 9am to 1pm. This office can also make travel arrangements for you. Another leading travel agent is **International Travel Services,** 14B Market St. (ℂ **876/952-2485**), open Monday to Friday 8:30am to 5pm, Saturday 10am to 1pm.

2 Where to Stay

The Montego Bay region boasts a superb selection of hotels, ranging from very expensive world-class resorts to notable bargains. There's also a broad scale and diverse selection of all-inclusive resorts, which are all reviewed together for easy comparison at the very end of this section. Most of the big full-service resorts are frequently included in package tours. Booking a package will make the rates much more reasonable. See "Packages for the Independent Traveler," p. 36, and "Tips on Accommodations," p. 41.

Each type of property attracts a different crowd. The deluxe properties such as Round Hill, Tryall, and Half Moon are for veterans of Caribbean travel. Many guests at these resorts are repeat visitors, and in some cases have visited them 20 or more times; if you're not a member of this club, however, you might feel a bit out of place.

The all-inclusive resorts tend to attract young, starry-eyed couples and honeymooners on their first trips to Jamaica. These places tend to be a little noisy, decadent, and no-holds-barred as a result.

Finally, the smaller resort properties listed here as moderately or inexpensively priced tend to attract middle-age couples (as opposed to the young crowd at Sandals-type places). Guests at these smaller properties tend to be more experienced travelers, often Europeans, and are independent-minded enough to view the hotel mostly as a place to bunk down at night.

MAKING RESERVATIONS

If you arrive without a reservation (not recommended in Jamaica), begin your search for a room as early in the day as possible. If you arrive late at night without a reservation, you may have to take what you can get—often in a price range much higher than you'd like to pay.

Montego Bay has become a year-round destination, and summers aren't as tranquil as they once were. Nonetheless, hotels still have lower occupancy from mid-April to mid-December. Off-season discounts, which can be substantial, are granted at resorts during slow times.

VERY EXPENSIVE

Half Moon Golf, Tennis & Beach Club ✦✦✦   Opening onto 16 hectares (400 acres) that take in .8km (½ mile) of white-sand beach, this is one of the Caribbean's grand hotels, without the snobbery of Round Hill or Tryall (see below). It also has far more activities, excitement, amenities, restaurants, and a better beach. About 13km (8 miles) east of Montego Bay's city center and 10km (6¼ miles) from the international airport, this is a classic, and one of the 300 best hotels in the world according to *Condé Nast Traveler.* It's a grand and appealing place, a true luxury hideaway with taste and style.

Accommodations include conventional hotel rooms, suites, and a collection of superbly accessorized private villas (most villas have private pools and a full-time staff). Each unit is comfortably furnished with an English colonial/Caribbean motif, with a private balcony or patio, plus a state-of-the-art bathroom with a shower/tub combo. Queen Anne–inspired furniture is set off by vibrant Jamaican paintings, and many units contain mahogany four-poster beds.

The Sugar Mill Restaurant, our favorite in Montego Bay, is beside a working water wheel from a bygone sugar estate (see "Where to Dine," below). The Seagrape Terrace offers delightful meals alfresco. Il Giardino, set within a convincing replica of a Renaissance palazzo, serves savory Italian cuisine. The resort also has a pan-Asian restaurant, a steakhouse, and an English pub.

Half Moon Post Office, Rose Hall, St. James, Montego Bay. ⓒ **800/626-0592** in the U.S., or 876/953-2211. Fax 876/953-2731. www.halfmoonclub.com. 419 units. Winter $390–$490 double, $590–$1,190 suite; $1,170–$2,940 villa; off season $240–$290 double, $350–$790 suite, $720–$1,740 villa. MAP (breakfast and dinner) $70 per person extra. Ask about golf and spa packages. AE, DC, DISC, MC, V. **Amenities:** 7 restaurants; 6 bars; 3 outdoor pools; 18-hole golf course; 13 tennis courts (7 lighted); spa; Jacuzzi; 2 saunas; deep-sea fishing; dive shop; bike rental; car-rental desk; limited room service; babysitting; laundry service; horseback riding; croquet. *In room:* A/C, TV, dataport, kitchenette (in some units), minibar, hair dryer, iron/board, safe, beverage maker.

Ritz-Carlton Rose Hall Jamaica ✦✦✦ *(Kids*   The most up-to-date and spectacular of the grande dames of Mo Bay (that includes Half Moon and Round Hill), this complex sprawls across a dazzling stretch of white-sand beach. The major draw is the White Witch golf course, a 10-minute shuttle ride away. This resort offers the ambience of a traditional Jamaican great house with all modern comforts, including a full-service spa. In the old plantation country of Jamaica, just a 10-minute ride from the airport (every half-hour), the hotel is secluded, standing in carefully landscaped grounds. First-rate guest rooms, in tropical motifs, feature stoned-columned balconies and deluxe bathrooms with shower/tub combos. Some accommodations are suitable for those with disabilities. Those who can afford it live in even greater luxury in the executive suites. Among the top resorts of Jamaica, only Half Moon equals its cuisine. This resort has a good range of activities for kids, both indoor and outdoor, including arts and crafts, making sandcastles, and hearing stories of old Jamaica, the latter usually reserved for a rainy day.

Rose Hall, Montego Bay. ⓒ **800/241-3333** in the U.S. or Canada, or 876/953-2800. Fax 876/953-8980. www.ritzcarlton.com. 427 units. Winter $365–$395 double, $495–$1,500 suite; off season $195–$225 double, $325–$1,500 suite. Children under age 12 stay free in parent's room. AE, DC, DISC, MC, V. **Amenities:**

6 restaurants; 2 bars; outdoor pool; 18-hole golf course; 2 tennis courts; health club and spa; Jacuzzi; water-sports; children's activities; business center; 24-hr. room service; babysitting; laundry service; dry cleaning; nonsmoking rooms; rooms for those with limited mobility. *In room:* A/C, TV, minibar, hair dryer, iron/board, safe, beverage maker.

Round Hill Hotel and Villas ★★★ Opened in 1953 on a small, private white-sand beach, Round Hill is a legend and the most prestigious address in Jamaica, although it hasn't kept up with the times like Half Moon. Still, that doesn't stop the likes of Steven Spielberg and Harrison Ford from checking into villas on the 39-hectare (98-acre) estate. The guest rooms are in a richly appointed seaside building known as the Pineapple House, and each opens onto views of the water and beach. Each spacious, breezy unit has plantation-style decor with refinished antique furniture and a king-size or two twin beds, plus spacious bathrooms with shower/tub combinations. Privately owned villas dot the hillside, and each is individually decorated, sometimes lavishly. Rates for the villas include the services of a maid, a cook, and a gardener; 21 have their own private pools.

Breakfast is brought to your room or served on the dining terrace. Informal luncheons are held in an intimate straw hut with an open terrace in a little sandy bay. Standard Jamaican and Continental dishes are served on a candlelit terrace or in the Georgian colonial room overlooking the sea. Ralph Lauren, a some-times visitor, decorated the cocktail area.

Rte. A1 (P.O. Box 64), Montego Bay. © **800/972-2159** in the U.S., or 876/956-7050. Fax 876/956-7505. www.roundhilljamaica.com. 74 units. Winter $420–$510 double, $600–$850 villa; off season $260–$310 double, $370–$550 villa. Extra person $70. MAP (breakfast and dinner) $80 per person extra. AE, DC, DISC, MC, V. **Amenities:** Restaurant; 3 bars; outdoor pool; 5 tennis courts; health club and spa; dive shop; limited room service; babysitting; laundry service; nonsmoking rooms. *In room:* A/C, dataport, kitchen, fridge, coffeemaker, hair dryer, safe, beverage maker.

The Tryall Club ★★★ *Kids* This is a top choice for vacationers who are seri-ous about golf. With more spacious grounds than almost any other Jamaican hotel, this stylish and upscale resort sits 19km (12 miles) west of town on the site of a 880-hectare (2,200-acre) former sugar plantation. It has neither the fine beach of Half Moon, nor the elegant house-party atmosphere of Round Hill, but it's one of Jamaica's grandest resorts. The property lies along a 2km (1¼-mile) beachfront and is presided over by a 165-year-old Georgian-style great house.

The accommodations in luxurious villas are decorated in cool pastels with English colonial touches. All contain ceiling fans and some have air-condition-ing, along with picture windows framing sea and mountain views. Bedrooms are exceedingly spacious, with luxurious beds, private patios or terraces, and tile floors. Bathrooms are roomy, with plenty of counter space and a shower/tub combination. The resort's villas are set amid lush foliage and are designed for pri-vacy, each with a private pool. The most formal of the resort's dining areas is in the great house, but it's not the equal of the options available at Half Moon and the Ritz-Carlton. There's also a casual beach cafe, more for convenience than good food.

Many clients here are CEOs, so the hotel has opened an Internet room. On other fronts, Tryall is winning recognition as one of the most eco-sensitive resorts in the Caribbean, winning acclaim as a "Green Globe Hotel."

St. James (P.O. Box 1206), Montego Bay. © **800/238-5290** in the U.S., or 876/956-5660. Fax 876/956-5673. www.tryallclub.com. 69 villas. Winter $400–$1,700 villa; off season $250–$1,000 villa. MAP (breakfast and dinner) $77 per person extra. AE, DC, DISC, MC, V. **Amenities:** 2 restaurants; 4 bars; cafe; outdoor pool with swim-up bar; championship 18-hole par-71 golf course; 9 Laykold tennis courts; health club; deep-sea fishing; snorkeling; windsurfing; children's programs; salon; limited room service; massage; babysitting; laundry service; nonsmoking rooms; rooms for those with limited mobility. *In room:* A/C (in some units), TV, kitchen, fridge, coffeemaker, hair dryer, safe.

EXPENSIVE

Coyaba 😾😾   On a lovely strip of private beachfront, this small all-inclusive resort evokes a British colonial atmosphere. It was established in 1994 by American/Jamaican-Chinese entrepreneurs, the Robertson family, and built from scratch at a cost of $4 million. Set a 15-minute drive east of the center of Montego Bay, it's centered on an adaptation of an 18th-century great house.

Accommodations in the main building overlook the garden; those in the pair of three-story outbuildings lie closer to the beach and are somewhat more expensive. The decor is plantation-style, with traditional prints, expensive chintz fabrics, French doors leading onto private patios or verandas, and mahogany furniture. Hand-carved bedsteads, often four-posters, are fitted with luxury coverings. The roomy bathrooms have combination shower/tubs. Its bedrooms are modern and well maintained, and some units have been upgraded to junior suites with small refrigerators and such special amenities as irons and ironing boards. The hotel's main and most formal restaurant, the Vineyard, serves first-rate Jamaican and Continental dinners. Less upscale is Docks Caribbean Bar & Grill.

Little River, Montego Bay. © 877/232-3224 or 876/953-9150. Fax 876/953-2244. www.coyabaresort jamaica.com. 50 units. Winter $300–$400 double; off season $200–$350 double. All meals $105 per person extra. Children age 11 and under get a 50% discount on meals. AE, MC, V. **Amenities:** 3 restaurants; 3 bars; outdoor pool; lighted tennis court with free tennis clinic; health club and spa; Jacuzzi; watersports; car-rental desk; limited room service; massage; laundry service; nonsmoking rooms; rooms for those wIth limited mobility; nanny service. *In room:* A/C, TV/VCR, coffeemaker, hair dryer, iron/board, safe.

Wyndham Rose Hall & Country Club 😾 *Kids*   If you have to be directly on a great beach, this place isn't for you, but if you want to escape the more impersonal all-inclusives like the Sandals clones in favor of a more authentic Jamaican experience, then check in here. On a thin strip of white-sand beach, this 12-hectare (30-acre) resort stands along the north-coast highway 14km (9 miles) east of the airport. On a former sugar plantation, the hotel abuts the 200-year-old home of the legendary "White Witch of Rose Hall," (see the box on p. 78) now a historic site (p. 79). The seven-story H-shaped structure features a large, attractive lobby on the ground floor; upstairs, guest rooms all have sea views and come with a small private balcony. The tiled bathrooms with tubs and showers are well maintained.

Facing massive competition from the newly opened Ritz-Carlton (which is far superior), Wyndham has spent millions on renovations, improving and upgrading its accommodations with new designer furniture. Bathrooms have received a makeover with granite countertops, new plumbing fixtures, and Bath & Body Works amenities. The hotel's six restaurants are good but not sublime.

Rose Hall (P.O. Box 999), Montego Bay. © 800/996-3426 in the U.S., or 876/953-2650. Fax 876/518-0203. www.wyndham.com. 493 units. Winter $410–$440 double, from $600 suite; off season $355–$415 double, from $590 suite. Rates are all-inclusive. AE, DC, DISC, MC, V. **Amenities:** 6 restaurants; 4 bars; 3 pools (2 with swim-up bar); 18-hole golf course; 6 lighted all-weather Laykold tennis courts; health club; sailboats; children's programs; limited room service; massage; babysitting; laundry service; nonsmoking rooms; rooms for those with limited mobility. *In room:* A/C, TV, dataport, hair dryer, iron/board, safe, beverage maker.

MODERATE

Coral Cliff Gaming Lounge & Resort 😾 *Value*   For good value, the Coral Cliff may be your best bet in Montego Bay, lying only a 2-minute walk from

Doctor's Cave Beach. The hotel grew from a colonial-style building that was once the private home of Harry M. Doubleday (of the famous publishing family). It's located about 2km (1¼ mile) west of the center of town. Many of the light, airy, and spacious bedrooms open onto sea-view balconies. The rooms, as befits a former private house, come in a wide variety of shapes and sizes, most of them containing old colonial furniture, wicker, and rattan. Most units have twin beds. The bathrooms are small in the older bedrooms, but more spacious in the newer wing out back. Each is tidily maintained and has a combination shower/tub.

Decent Jamaican and international dishes are served at Ma Loos restaurant.

165 Gloucester Ave. (P.O. Box 253), Montego Bay. ℭ 876/952-4130. Fax 876/952-6532. www.coralcliff jamaica.com. 19 units. Winter $100–$180 double, $120–$160 triple, from $180 suite; off season $80–$90 double, $92–$105 triple, from $140 suite. MC, V. **Amenities:** 2 restaurants; bar; casino; health club; spa; babysitting; laundry service; library. *In room:* A/C, TV, dataport, safe.

Doctors Cave Beach Hotel ⭐ *Value*   This three-story hotel offers great value and lies in the bustle of the town's commercial zone. It's across from Doctor's Cave Beach, the busiest and most crowded, but with the best sands, in the Montego Bay area. It has its own gardens on 2 hectares (4 acres) of tropical gardens. The well-maintained rooms are simply but comfortably furnished, and suites have kitchenettes. Rooms are rated standard or superior; the latter are more spacious and have balconies with a view. All units have tile floors, queen-size or twin beds (suites have king-size beds), and small but efficiently organized tiled bathrooms with combination shower/tubs. The food is more authentic than at the resorts recommended above.

Gloucester Ave. (P.O. Box 94), Montego Bay. ℭ 800/44-UTELL in the U.S., or 876/952-4355. Fax 876/952-5204. www.doctorscave.com. 90 units. Winter $130–$150 double, $125 suite for 2; off season $95–$100 double, $120 suite for 2. Extra person $25. MAP (breakfast and dinner) $29 per person extra. AE, DC, MC, V. **Amenities:** 3 restaurants; bar; outdoor pool; health club; Jacuzzi; limited room service; babysitting; nonsmoking rooms; rooms for those with limited mobility. *In room:* A/C, TV, kitchenette, safe, beverage maker.

Montego Beach Resort   This old Jack Tar has changed its stripes and blossomed anew as the Montego Beach Resort. It offers an affordable worry-free beach vacation for those seeking moderately priced lodgings. The 1.3-hectare (3¼-acre) beachfront resort encompasses a pair of buildings 3km (1¾ miles) north of the commercial core of Montego Bay. Lying only a 5-minute ride from the Montego Bay airport, this renovated property caters to couples, singles, children (ages 12–17), golfers, and honeymooners. Four championship golf courses lie only a short drive from the resort. The resort underwent a $4-million renovation in which each of the bedrooms was upgraded. The guest units are modern if bland, and they do sit a few steps from the beach with views of the water. Private balconies open directly onto Montego Bay, and guests practically live in their bathing suits. All units are furnished with rather bland motel-standard bathrooms with tub/shower combinations.

Lunch is served beachside or in the main dining room, and there's nightly entertainment. The international food isn't wildly creative or refined, but it's at least plentiful.

2 Gloucester Ave. (P.O. Box 144), Montego Bay. ℭ 800/858-2258 or 876/952-4340. Fax 876/971-3275. www.montegobeachresort.com. 131 units. Winter $160–$200 double; off season $125–$160 double. AE, MC, V. No children accepted. **Amenities:** Restaurant; bar; freshwater pool; putting green; tennis clinic and courts; Jacuzzi; sauna; windsurfing; water-skiing; snorkeling; sailing; business center; massage; nonsmoking rooms; rooms for those with limited mobility; reggae dance lessons. *In room:* A/C, TV, iron/board, safe.

Richmond Hill Inn ★ *Finds*   If you're an avid beach lover, you should know in advance that the nearest beach is a 15-minute drive away from this hotel. It was built as the homestead of the Dewar family (the scions of scotch). Very little of the original villa remains, but what you'll find is a hilltop aerie ringed with urn-shaped concrete balustrades, a pool terrace suitable for sundowner cocktails, and comfortable, slightly fussy bedrooms done up in lace-trimmed curtains, homey bric-a-brac, and pastel colors. Each accommodation comes with a midsize bathroom with tub/shower combination. Maid service is included in the rates, and there are both a bar and a restaurant looking out over Montego Bay.

Union St. (P.O. Box 362), Montego Bay. © 876/952-3859. Fax 876/952-6106. www.richmond-hill-inn.com. 20 units. Winter $115 double, $189 1-bedroom suite, $300 3-bedroom suite; off season $90 double, $168 1-bedroom suite, $250 3-bedroom suite, MC, V. **Amenities:** Restaurant; bar; pool; limited room service; babysitting; maid service. *In room:* A/C, TV, fridge, coffeemaker, iron/board, safe.

SeaCastles Beach Resort   If you seek isolation from the bustle of the over-crowded resorts in the center of Mo Bay, this might be the place for you. An airy, widely separated compound of postmodern buildings vaguely influenced by British colonial models, the resort contains only suites—each with a kitchen or kitchenette. Because all units are suites, accommodations are larger and more spacious than in the average resort, with roomy bathrooms, each with a tub-and-shower combination. Lawns slope down to the beach, past arbors, gazebos, bars, and watersports kiosks. The Castles restaurant (p. 69) overlooks the graceful swimming pool; less formal meals and drinks are offered in the Clifftop Bar.

Rte. A1, Rose Hall (P.O. Box 55), Montego Bay. © 876/953-4671. Fax 876/953-0891. 198 units. Winter $215 suite; off season $184 suite. Rates are all-inclusive. AE, MC, V. **Amenities:** Restaurant; bar; outdoor pool; watersports facilities; tour desk; babysitting; laundry service. *In room:* A/C, TV, kitchen, iron/board, safe.

INEXPENSIVE

Blue Harbour Hotel   On a hillside overlooking the harbor, midway between the airport and town off Route A1, this small hotel offers basic service in a friendly atmosphere. Rooms here are simple, while the suites offer kitchenettes to help you save even more money. For dinner, the hotel offers the option of a dine-around plan that includes 10 of Montego Bay's restaurants. (Transportation to and from the restaurants is provided.) Facilities include a swimming pool, air-conditioned lounge, and coffee shop serving breakfast and light lunch. Tennis courts are nearby; arrangements can also be made for golf, deep-sea fishing, scuba diving, and island tours. The hotel operates a shuttle once a day to Doctor's Cave Beach, leaving at 10am.

6 Sewell Ave. (P.O. Box 212), Montego Bay. © 876/952-5445. Fax 876/952-8930. http://fly.to/jamaica. 25 units. Winter $58–$68 double, $70–$86 triple; off season $54 double, $70 triple. Each additional person $15. Children 11 and under stay free in parent's room. Rates include continental breakfast. AE, MC, V. **Amenities:** Coffee shop; lounge; outdoor pool; nearby sports, such as golf and tennis; tour desk; limited room service; nonsmoking rooms; rooms for those with limited mobility. *In room:* A/C, TV, kitchenette, hair dryer, iron/board, safe.

Casa Blanca Beach Hotel *Value*   After a long decline, this landmark property opening onto a large white-sand beach is back in business. It's the reincarnation of the 19th-century Hotel Casa Blanca that first put Montego Bay on the tourist map. The new Casa Blanca attracts a middle-class tourist interested in getting good value at a low-rise near popular Doctor's Cave Beach.

Facing the sea, bedrooms are for the most part midsize and open onto balconies or patios. Several of the beds are of the old-fashioned four-poster variety, and all units come with neatly tiled bathrooms with showers.

The hotel offers free watersports such as snorkeling, surfing, and sailing virtually at its doorstep. The location places guests right in the center of the action along "Hip Strip," a plus or a minus depending on your outlook. Activities planned for guests include weekly calypso and reggae music, and native shows with limbo dancing. Boat excursions are also arranged.

Gloucester Ave., Montego Bay. © 876/952-0720. Fax 876/952-1424. 80 units. Year-round $85 double. MC, V. **Amenities:** Outdoor pool; beach; watersports; game room; nonsmoking rooms. *In room:* A/C, TV, hair dryer, iron/board, safe.

El Greco Resort   This three-story, cream-colored hotel sits at the top of a rocky bluff, high above the surf, sand, and well-oiled bodies of Doctor's Cave Beach. A private elevator links the hotel's cliff-top site to a point near the beachfront. Surrounded by a landscaped garden into which are nestled both a swimming pool and a pair of tennis courts (lit for night play), the resort is well maintained and well priced. It's smack in the middle of Montego Bay's densest concentration of honky-tonk commercialism—yet the location enables guests to rise above the congestion a bit. This hotel catches the trade winds, and most (but not all) of the rooms offer a sweeping view over the sea. Apartments contain full kitchenettes and have pure white ceramic floor tiles. The bedrooms are air-conditioned, though not the living rooms, which have ceiling fans instead; 32 larger two-bedroom units occupy the building's uppermost floor. Each unit comes with a midsize private bathroom with a shower. There's both a bar and a restaurant on the premises, although many of the guests opt to cook.

11 Queens Dr. (P.O. Box 1624), Montego Bay. © 888/354-7326 in the U.S., 800/597-7326 in Canada, or 876/940-6116. Fax 876/940-6115. www.elgrecojamaica.com. 96 apts. Year-round $115–$120 1-bedroom apt; $172 2-bedroom apt. Rates include breakfast. AE, MC, V. **Amenities:** Restaurant; bar; outdoor pool; tennis court; limited room service; rooms for those with limited mobility. *In room:* A/C, TV, dataport, kitchen, fridge, iron, safe.

Ocean View Guest House *(Value)*   Stay here for a great deal; you won't get state-of-the-art maintenance or service, but the price is adjusted accordingly. The simple and uncomplicated bedrooms are supplemented with a small shared library and TV room (satellite reception is available). Most open onto a veranda or the spacious front porch. It's quietest at the back.

26 Sunset Blvd. (.8km/½ mile west of Sangster airport; P.O. Box 210), Montego Bay. © 876/952-2662. 5 units. Winter $45 double, $65 triple; off season $35 double, $45 triple. No credit cards. **Amenities:** TV lounge; library. *In room:* A/C, no phone.

Ridgeway Guest House *(Finds)*   This warm B&B, far removed from the impersonal megaresorts (and their megaprices), is a great find. The helpful owners offer free pickup from the airport and transport to Doctor's Cave Beach, a 15-minute walk or 5 minutes by car. They are constantly improving their property—a two-story white-painted building set among flowers and fruit trees from which guests may help themselves, perhaps having an orange-and-grapefruit salad. The large rooms are decorated in a tropical motif with two or three queen-size beds. The marble bathrooms have modern fixtures, including a combo tub and shower, and TV is available in a public area. Some rooms feature air-conditioning, TVs, and phones; others are equipped with ceiling fans only, and lack televisions or phones. The hotel next door opens its restaurant to Ridgeway guests.

34 Queens Dr. (P.O. Box 1237), Montego Bay. © 876/952-2709. www.ridgewayguesthouse.com. 4 units. Year-round $69 double. Children 11 and under stay free in parent's room. MC, V. **Amenities:** Nearby restaurant; rooftop garden; TV lounge; car-rental desk; laundry service. *In room:* A/C, TV, fridge, hair dryer, no phone (in some units).

Honeymooning at Half Moon

Although the couples-only Sandals properties offer honeymoon packages, our advice is to skip those and opt for either a wedding or a honeymoon (perhaps both) at **Half Moon Golf, Tennis & Beach Club** (p. 56). We consider its romance packages the best in the Caribbean.

The resort offers three different wedding packages and one honeymoon package. Couples planning to celebrate both even get a special bonus if they book at least 25 rooms for attending family and friends: Half Moon gives the bride and groom a complimentary ceremony and 7 nights' free accommodations, a savings of up to $7,500.

You can also order services a la carte. The Standard Wedding Plan includes a marriage officer, a bottle of champagne, a bouquet of flowers for the bride and a boutonniere for the groom, a wedding cake, a professional video, a roll of 36 pictures and negatives, and—if needed—a best man and maid of honor to act as witnesses, all at a total cost of $850. The Royal Wedding Plan includes all of the above, plus a $50 gift voucher redeemable at selected shops in the Half Moon Shopping Village, a bottle of Half Moon rum, two Half Moon watches, and the services of a calypso band for 15 minutes. That package costs $1,150. For more information, call © **876/953-2211** (© 800/626-0592 in the U.S.), or log on to **www.halfmoonclub.com**.

Toby's Resort   This resort is a 5-minute walk from Doctor's Cave Beach. Despite the traffic and crowds around it, the almond, mango, and grapefruit trees that surround the two-story main building, cottages, and swimming pools create a sense of rural isolation. You'll also find a restaurant serving Jamaican cuisine, a flower shop, a minigym, a bandstand for occasional concerts, and a bar. Bedrooms all have either a terrace or a balcony, and each unit's small, tiled bathroom has a shower. This hotel is also a showcase for Jamaican and foreign art.

1 Kent Ave. (P.O. Box 467), Montego Bay. © **876/952-4370.** Fax 876/952-6591. www.tobyresorts.com. 65 units. Winter $80 double; off season $70 double. AE, DISC, MC, V. **Amenities:** Restaurant; 2 bars; 2 outdoor pools; small gym; game room; limited room service; rooms for those with limited mobility. *In room:* A/C, TV, iron/board, no phone.

Verney House Resort   In a verdant setting that's a 10-minute walk from the urban congestion of Montego Bay, this hotel offers a feeling of remote calm. You can still get to where the action is by making a short trek downhill, or kick back on the sand by heading to one of several beaches (such as Cornwall Beach) that lie about 5 minutes away by foot. The inn also provides free van transportation to and from the beach. Each unit sports white walls and simple furnishings, creating the sense that you're in a private home. The restaurant (the Kit-Kat) and bar both overlook the swimming pool.

3 Leader Ave. (P.O. Box 18), Montego Bay. © **876/952-2875.** Fax 876/979-2944. www.afst.com/ vhouse/vh.htm. 25 units. Winter $65 double, $70 triple, $80 quad; off season $45 double, $55 triple, $70 quad. AE, MC, V. **Amenities:** Restaurant; bar; outdoor pool; babysitting. *In room:* A/C, TV, iron, safe.

Wexford Court Hotel *(Kids)*   Especially good for families on a budget, this hotel lies within a 5-minute walk of Doctor's Cave Beach. This hotel has a small pool and a patio (where calypso is enjoyed in season). The apartments have living/dining areas and kitchenettes, so you can cook for yourself. All the rooms have patios shaded by gables and Swiss chalet–style roofs, and each has a tiled, shower-only bathroom. The restaurant serves some zesty Jamaican dishes in a setting that evokes a 1950s Howard Johnson's.

39 Gloucester Ave. (P.O. Box 108), Montego Bay. © **876/952-2854.** Fax 876/952-3637. 61 units. Winter $105–$110 double, $120 apt; off season $95–$100 double, $110 apt. MAP (breakfast and dinner) $34 per person extra. AE, DISC, MC, V. **Amenities:** Restaurant; bar; outdoor pool; limited room service; babysitting; laundry service; rooms for those with limited mobility. *In room:* A/C, TV, kitchenette (in some units), safe.

ALL-INCLUSIVE RESORTS

All-inclusive resorts charge one price for a lengthy stay (usually a week), folding accommodations and dining into one package. Once you've paid up, you can forget about watching the dinner bill or getting dinged for every little tour, hike, or boat ride you take on the property.

Note that when you book into one of the following all-inclusives, you either take your meals on-site or buy a dine-around plan that enables you to patronize the eateries at other, similar resorts. Either way, though, you're likely to find most of the food rather mediocre. In no case will it compare to the fare served at sophisticated restaurants in such major U.S. cities such as New York or Boston.

Of course, those big-city restaurants don't open onto a beach—and the weather here's much better in wintertime. So there are advantages to these Mo Bay resorts, but just remember: Creative cuisine is not one of them.

Breezes Montego Bay 𝄇𝄇 A five-story complex, this SuperClub—called "a sandbox for your inner child"—is the only major hotel directly on the sands of Montego Bay's most popular public beach, Doctor's Cave. It's adult and indulgent, but without the raucous partying of Hedonism II (a member of the same chain). Bedrooms are tastefully furnished and breezy, overlooking either the beach or the garden that separates the hotel from the traffic of Montego Bay's main commercial boulevard, Gloucester Avenue. Rooms range from intimate cabins to lavish suites. The cabin rooms, 31 in all, are similar to a ship's cabin, with a queen-size bed. Slightly larger are the deluxe rooms, with twins or a king-size bed. The best are the deluxe oceanfront rooms, with king-size beds, and the oceanfront suites. All units have bathrooms with shower/tub combinations.

Informal but good meals are served at Jimmy's Buffet, a terrace overlooking the pool and the beach. More formal meals, with a more refined cuisine, are dished out at the candlelit Martino's, an Italian rooftop restaurant.

Gloucester Ave., Montego Bay. © **800/417-5288** in the U.S., or 876/940-1150. Fax 876/940-1160. www.s uperclubs.com. 124 units. All-inclusive rates for 3 nights: Winter $1,112 double; off season $680 double. Rates include all meals, drinks, and most activities. AE, DC, DISC, MC, V. No children under 14 accepted. **Amenities:** 2 restaurants; 4 bars; outdoor pool; 2 tennis courts; health club; rooftop Jacuzzi; dive shop; kayaking; sailing; snorkeling; windsurfing. *In room:* A/C, TV, hair dryer, iron/board, safe, beverage maker.

FDR Pebbles 𝄇 *Kids* No, it's not named after the U.S. president. This resort, which pioneered at Runaway Bay, has invaded Montego Bay and almost overnight become the most family-friendly place in the area. It's even better than its parent outside Ocho Rios. FDR lies a 35-minute drive east of the airport, opening onto the waterfront and a beach. The resort is an all-inclusive property of cedar-wood accommodations designed with real Jamaican flair, offering spacious living and bedroom areas, shower/tub combination bathrooms, plus generous balconies opening onto a view. It's most suited for families with two children, although a larger family can be very comfortable in adjoining units. Everything is geared towards family fun, with an array of activities including fishing and swimming in a nearby river and hiking along nature trails. Each family is assigned a "vacation nanny" who helps with housekeeping and babysitting.

First-rate ingredients are fashioned into a rather standard repertoire of both Jamaican and American dishes. Portions are exceedingly generous.

Main St., Trelawny (P.O. Box 1933). (C) **888/FDR-KIDS** in the U.S. or 876/617-2500. Fax 876/617-2512. www. fdrholidays.com. 96 units. Winter $275–$350 double; off season $252–$330 double. Children under age 6 stay free. Rates are per person per night and all-inclusive. AE, DISC, MC, V. **Amenities:** 2 restaurants; 3 bars; outdoor pool; lighted tennis court; watersports; kids club; teen center; babysitting; nonsmoking rooms; rooms for those with limited mobility; dance club; cybercafe; hikes. *In room:* A/C, TV, kitchenette, hair dryer, iron/board, beverage maker.

Holiday Inn SunSpree (Kids)

This is the only Holiday Inn resort in Jamaica that can be booked on all-inclusive terms. It opened in 1995 following a $13-million renovation of another property and continues a tradition of catering to singles, couples, and honeymooners—but the resort also has a new emphasis on programs for families with children. The 5-hectare (12-acre) property fronts nearly a .8km (½ mile) of white-sand beach on Jamaica's north shore. Well-furnished, modern rooms and suites are for the most part spacious and are housed in eight free-standing buildings; all have such amenities as a private balcony or patio. Of these, 76 are oceanfront units, and 27 suites come complete with indoor Jacuzzis. Each unit contains a midsize private bathroom with tub-and-shower combination, too. (*A tip:* If you turn in early, seek a room away from the dining, entertainment, and pool areas.) A wide range of dining options is available even though the resort is all-inclusive. Two nights each week are devoted to buffet theme nights, when guests dine on the beach and listen to Jamaican music. The Sports Bar with its big TV is a macho hangout; the Witches Disco attracts a younger crowd.

8km (5 miles) east of Montego Bay International Airport (P.O. Box 480), Rose Hall. (C) **800/HOLIDAY** or 876/953-2485. Fax 876/953-3274. www.sixcontinenthotels.com. 524 units. Winter $290–$390 double, from $550 suite; off season $249–$290 double, from $350 suite. Rates are all-inclusive. AE, MC, V. **Amenities:** 4 restaurants; 4 bars; 2 snack bars; 3 pools; 4 tennis courts; health club; dive shop; snorkeling; windsurfing; basketball court; volleyball court; disco; Kids Spree Vacation Club staffed by trained counselors; room service (breakfast only); babysitting. *In room:* A/C, TV.

The Sandals Inn

The Sandals Inn is a couples-only (male-female) hotel built around a large pool and patio, with a beach a short walk across a busy highway. This is the least expensive, least glamorous, least spacious, and least attractive of Sandals's all-inclusive resorts scattered across Jamaica. But it's a trade-off: Though you don't get luxury, you do get proximity to downtown Montego Bay, reasonable rates, and free day passes (including free transportation) to both of the other Sandals resorts at Mo Bay. Thirty-eight rooms open onto the pool; all units contain private midsize bathrooms with tub-and-shower combos. There is also now a so-called environmentally friendly linen service, whereby sheets and towels are not changed unless you request that they be changed.

Food is served in bountiful portions in the resort's only dining room, and there's nightly entertainment. A restaurant called Carlyle, specializing in flambé dishes, breaks the routine of the main dining room.

Kent Ave. (P.O. Box 412), Montego Bay. (C) **800/SANDALS** in the U.S. and Canada, or 876/952-4140. Fax 876/ 952-6913. www.sandals.com. 52 units. All-inclusive rates for 4 days/3 nights: winter $1,240–$2,320 double; off season $1,520–$2,000 double. All-inclusive 7-day rates: winter $3,220–$4,060 double; off season $2,660–$3,500 double. AE, MC, V. Free airport shuttle. No children accepted. **Amenities:** 2 restaurants; 2 bars; outdoor pool; tennis court; exercise room; Jacuzzi; outdoor hot tub; saunas; salon; Internet center; nonsmoking rooms; rooms for those with limited mobility; sports program; nighttime entertainment. *In room:* A/C, TV, coffeemaker, hair dryer, iron, safe.

Fun Fact Catch a Fire: Jamaica's Reggae Festivals

Every August, during what might otherwise have been a slow tourist season, Montego Bay comes alive with the pulsating sounds of reggae when two well-known reggae festivals are presented almost back-to-back. Beginning in early August and running for at least a week, the first of the two events is **Reggae Summerfest** (it was, until very recently, known as Reggae Sunsplash). Its events are usually presented at different sites within Montego Bay, usually at beach-fronting soundstages ringed with bars and food stands. Sometime during the second week in August, a different set of entrepreneurs produce **Reggae Sunfest** at Catharine Hall, a government-funded housing development beside the Roseway Bypass in Montego Freeport.

Performers at either of these festivals have included Ziggy Marley, Cocoa Tea, the Melody Makers, Barefoot Hammond, the Mystic Revelers, and some of the biggest names in reggae, both from Jamaica and abroad. Many local hotels are fully booked for the festival, so advance reservations are necessary.

The Jamaican Tourist Board's U.S. and Canadian offices can give you information about packages and group rates for the festivals and fill you in on other events held throughout the year on Jamaica.

Sandals Montego Bay ✿ This honeymoon haven lies next to Whitehouse Village on the largest private beach in Mo Bay, even better than the one at Sandals Royal Caribbean. Located on a 7.6-hectare (19-acre) site, this all-inclusive also has a big party atmosphere (whereas Sandals Royal Caribbean is more refined and subdued). Everything is covered in the price: meals, snacks, nightly entertainment (including the notorious toga parties), and unlimited drinks night or day at one of four bars. Lots of entertainment and sports facilities are available on the property, and many guests never leave its walls. There's one big drawback, though: The resort lies literally at the edge of the airport, and planes fly overhead all day long, rattling the rum glasses. Also, the building's a bit dated.

Accommodations are either in villas spread along 510m (1,700 ft.) of the white-sand beach or in the main house, where most bedrooms face the sea and include private balconies. Try to avoid booking a room over the dining area; these don't have balconies and may be noisy. The best units are the grand luxe ocean- or beachfront units, with private balconies or patios. Each unit here is equipped with a first-rate bathroom with a tub/shower combo. The cuisine is in the typical Sandals chain-style format—plenty of it, but nothing too imaginative. The best option is Tokyo Joe's, serving six-course Asian dinners. Oleander Deck, with its "white-glove service," features Jamaican and Caribbean cuisine.

Kent Ave. (P.O. Box 100), Montego Bay. © **800/SANDALS** in the U.S. and Canada, or 876/952-5510. Fax 876/952-0816. www.sandals.com. 245 units. 4 days/3 nights: winter $2,060–$3,080 double, $3,520–$5,920 suite; off season $2,000–$3,080 double, $3,280–$5,920 suite. 7-day rates: winter $3,990–$5,809 double, $6,160–$10,360 suite; off season $3,500–$5,390 double, $4,480–$10,360 suite. Rates include all meals, drinks, and activities. AE, MC, V. **Amenities:** 5 restaurants; 4 bars; 4 pools; 8 tennis courts; health club; 4 Jacuzzis; sauna; watersports; dive shop; Internet center; salon; massage; laundry service; nonsmoking rooms; rooms for those with limited mobility. *In room:* A/C, TV, dataport, coffeemaker, hair dryer, iron/board, safe.

Sandals Royal Caribbean ✿✿ This all-inclusive, couples-only (male-female) resort with a tranquil atmosphere lies on its own private beach. Some of the British colonial atmosphere remains (the formal tea in the afternoon), but there are modern touches as well, including a private, clothing-optional island reached by boat.

The spacious rooms range from standard to superior to deluxe. Best are the grand luxe beachfront rooms, with private patios or balconies. Each unit has a small but well-equipped private bathroom with a shower/tub combination. The cuisine is more varied here than at other Mo Bay Sandals, with, for example, Royal Thai, an Indonesian restaurant on an offshore island. The Regency and The Pavilion serve a rather good Jamaican-inspired cuisine, among other options. Children are not allowed at this resort.

Mahoe Bay (P.O. Box 167), Montego Bay. © **800/SANDALS** in the U.S. and Canada, or 876/953-2232. Fax 876/953-2788. www.sandals.com. 208 units. All-inclusive rates for 4 days/3 nights: winter $1,845–$2,070 per couple, from $1,760 suite for 2; off season $1,125–$1,733 per couple, from $1,845 suite for 2. Rates include all meals, drinks, and activities. AE, DISC, MC, V. Children not accepted. **Amenities:** 5 restaurants; 5 bars; 4 outdoor pools; 3 tennis courts; health club; 5 Jacuzzis; sauna; watersports; limited room service; massage; coin-operated laundry; nonsmoking rooms; rooms for those with limited mobility. *In room:* A/C, TV, hair dryer, iron/board, safe, beverage maker.

Sunset Beach Resort & Spa *(Kids* This all-inclusive hotel opened in 1998 and aims for a marketing niche less glamorous (and less expensive) than that occupied by the Beaches and Sandals groups. The complex consists of three separate beaches; two pale-pink, 11-story towers containing a total of 300 units; and a 120-room annex, the Beach Inn, whose low-rise design allows guests closer and more immediate access to the sand. Accommodations are outfitted in a subdued motif that includes vague references to tropical design, but tends to be more soothing (and blander) than the decor of many of its competitors. Rooms are fairly spacious, with comfortable beds, plus medium-size bathrooms with tubs and showers.

Meals, featuring a varied cuisine, are served at each of the property's four restaurants and are in the all-inclusive rates. Silk Road offers Pacific Rim cuisine, Botticelli serves Italian cuisine, and the Sunset Grill is an indoor/outdoor pool-and-beach restaurant. The Banana Walk is the resort's all-purpose dining room, with ongoing buffets. There's also nightly entertainment.

Montego Freeport Peninsula, P.O. Box 1168, Montego Bay. © **800/261-5013** or 876/979-8800. Fax 876/953-6744. www.sunsetbeachresort.com. 420 units. Winter $750–$930 double, from $1,350 suite for 2; off season $690–$870 double; from $1,200 suite for 2. Rates are all-inclusive for 3 nights. AE, MC, V. **Amenities:** 4 restaurants; 6 bars; 3 pools; minigolf; 4 lighted tennis courts; health club; spa; Jacuzzi; children's programs; game rooms; Internet cafe; coin-operated laundry; rooms for those with limited mobility; shuffleboard courts; giant chess and checkerboards; beachfront volleyball; disco; nighttime entertainment. *In room:* A/C, TV, mini-bar (in some units), hair dryer, safe, sauna.

Starfish Trelawny Beach & Fun Resort *(Kids* Following a $5-million much-needed renovation, this all-inclusive is one of the best value vacations on the island. Opening onto a stretch of powder-white, soft, sandy beach, it offers activities for both children and adults. The location is 37km (23 miles) east of the Mo Bay airport. The most spacious rooms are the cottages at the rear of the hotel, which each house three adults and two children. For those who must have an ocean view, the resort rents some "superior" rooms, suitable for three adults and one child, with a balcony overlooking the beach. The least expensive units have a mountain or garden view, with a balcony, each housing three adults and one child. The wide range of sports and amenities make this an alluring choice. The food is fairly standard but there's a sushi bar with teppanyaki tables and a pasta-and-pizza restaurant. Four-course gourmet dinners are served in the Casablanca Restaurant.

North Coast Hwy., Falmouth. ⓒ **800/659-5436** or 876/954-2451. Fax 876/954-2173. www.starfish resorts.com. 350 units. Winter $416–$480 double, $540 cottage; off season $364–$416 double, $510 cottage. Rates are all-inclusive. AE, DC, MC, V. **Amenities:** 5 restaurants; 4 bars; disco bar; 4 pools; 4 tennis courts; health club; sauna; dive shop; children's center; Internet cafe; babysitting; laundry service; nonsmoking rooms; badminton court. *In room:* A/C, TV, minibar, hair dryer, iron/board, safe, beverage maker.

3 Where to Dine

The Montego Bay area offers some of the finest—and most expensive—dining in Jamaica. But if you're watching your wallet and don't have a delicate stomach, some intriguing food is sold right on the street. For example, on Kent Avenue you might try spicy jerk pork. Seasoned spareribs are also grilled over charcoal fires and sold with extra-hot sauce. Naturally, either dish goes down better with a Red Stripe beer. Cooked shrimp are sold on the streets of Mo Bay; they don't look it, but they're very hotly spiced, so be forewarned. If you're cooking your own meals, you might want to buy a fresh lobster or the catch of the day from a Montego Bay fisherman on the harbor.

EXPENSIVE

Day-O Plantation Restaurant 🔾 *Finds* INTERNATIONAL/JAMAICAN Here's your chance to wander back to Jamaica's plantation heyday. This place was originally built in the 1920s as the home of the overseer of one of the region's largest sugar producers, the Barnett Plantation. The restaurant occupies a long, indoor/outdoor dining room that's divided into two halves by a dance floor and a small stage. Here, owner Paul Hurlock performs as a one-man band, singing and entertaining the crowd while his wife, Jennifer, and their three children manage the dining room and kitchen.

Every dish is permeated with Jamaican spices. Try the chicken plantation-style, with red-wine sauce and herbs; filet of red snapper in Day-O style, with olives, white wine, tomatoes, and peppers; or, even better, one of the best versions of jerked snapper in Jamaica. We also like the grilled rock lobster with garlic butter.

Day-O Plantation, Lot 1, Fairfield, Montego Bay. ⓒ **876/952-1825**. Reservations suggested. Main courses $15–$33. AE, MC, V. Tues–Sun 6–11pm. It's an 8-min. drive west of town off the A-1 highway toward Negril; minivan service will pick up diners at any of the Montego Bay hotels and return them after their meals.

Finds Mo Bay Street Meat

The densest concentration of street food in Montego Bay is available at the junction of Gloucester Avenue and Kent Road. (The .8km/½-mile strip of beach-fronting boulevard stretching along both sides of that junction is also known as Bottom Rd. or, less formally, as the "Hip Strip," the edges of which are lined with bars, food stands, and shops catering to the beach trade.) At any of these stands, you might try authentic jerk pork or seasoned spareribs, grilled over charcoal fires and sold with extra-hot sauce; order a Red Stripe beer to go with it. Cooked shrimp are also sold on the streets of downtown Mo Bay, especially along Saint James Street; they don't look it, but they're very spicy, so be warned. And if you have an efficiency unit with a kitchenette, you can buy fresh lobster or the catch of the day and make your own dinner.

Julia's ⚓ CONTINENTAL   Julia's food, although competently prepared and using fresh ingredients whenever possible, can hardly compete with the view. The winding jungle road you take to get here is part of the before-dinner entertainment. After a jolting ride to a setting high above the city and its bay, you pass through a walled-in park that was the site of a private home built in 1840 for the Duke of Sutherland. The long, low-slung modern house boasts sweeping, open-sided views over the rolling hills and faraway coastline. Wills Green, the man running the place, draws on the styles of both the Caribbean and central Europe to prepare filet of fresh fish with lime juice and butter, lobster, shrimp, and many different kinds of pasta. Also look for such dishes as the mixed grilled seafood, cheesecake of the day, and their delicious raspberry tart.

Julia's Estate, Bogue Hill. ℂ 876/952-1772. Reservations required. Main courses $18–$36. AE, DISC, MC, V. Daily 5:30–11pm. Private van transportation provided; ask when you reserve.

Richmond Hill Inn ⚓ INTERNATIONAL/CONTINENTAL   This plantation-style house dates from 1806, when it was built by owners of the Dewars whiskey distillery. Today it's run by a family who prepare well-flavored food for an appreciative clientele. Dinners include a sautéed shrimp, an excellent house salad, stuffed breast of chicken, filet of red snapper, and a choice of dessert cakes. Many of the dishes are of a relatively standard international style, but others, especially the lobster, are worth the trek up the hill.

Top of Union St. ℂ 876/952-3859. Reservations recommended. Main courses $17–$42. DISC, MC, V. Daily 7am–10pm. Take a taxi (a 4-min. ride uphill, east of the town's main square) or ask the restaurant to have you picked up at your hotel.

Round Hill Dining Room ⚓ INTERNATIONAL   One of the top dining rooms in Montego Bay, this place has attracted a smattering of celebrities with its sophisticated surroundings. To reach the dining room, you'll have to pass through the resort's open-air reception area and proceed through a garden. Many visitors opt for a drink in the large and high-ceilinged bar area, designed by Ralph Lauren, before moving on to dinner served either on a terrace perched above the surf or (during inclement weather) under an open-sided breezeway. The menu changes nightly, offering an array of well-prepared dishes, from Mediterranean to Jamaican, from American to Italian pastas. For example, shrimp and pasta Caribe is sautéed with chopped herbs, cream, and wine; and Rasta pasta is tossed with vegetables and basil. Caribbean veal is stuffed with spicy crabmeat and seared, and the catch of the day is served jerked, broiled, or steamed with butter, herbs, and ginger. Of course, you can also order more classic dishes, including rack of lamb, pan-seared scallops, or a medallion of lobster sautéed with cream and served over fettuccine. Afternoon tea and sandwiches are served daily at 4pm.

In the Round Hill Hotel and Villas, along Rte. A1, 13km (8 miles) west of the center of Montego Bay. ℂ 876/956-7050. Reservations required for 10 or more. Main courses $30–$48. AE, DC, MC, V. Daily 12:30–2:30pm and 7:30–9:30pm.

Sugar Mill Restaurant ⚓⚓ INTERNATIONAL/CARIBBEAN   This restaurant, near the ruin of what used to be a water wheel for a sugar plantation, is reached after a drive through rolling landscape. The lovely setting and exquisite cuisine make this place a perennial favorite. Guests dine by candlelight either indoors or on an open terrace with a view of a pond, the water wheel, and plenty of greenery. Lunch can be a relatively simple affair, a daily a la carte offering, preceded by Mama's pumpkin soup and followed with homemade rum-and-raisin ice cream. For dinner, try one of the chef's zesty versions of jerk pork, fish, or chicken. He also prepares the day's catch with considerable flair. Smoked North Coast marlin is a specialty. On any given day, you can ask the waiter what's cooking in the curry pot. Chances are it will be a Jamaican specialty such as goat, full of flavor and served with island chutney.

At the Half Moon Golf, Tennis & Beach Club, Rose Hall, along Rte. A1. ⓒ **876/953-2314.** Reservations required. Main courses $27–$42. AE, MC, V. Daily 7–9pm. A minivan can be sent to most hotels to pick you up.

Three Palms ✿ JAMAICAN/INTERNATIONAL   This restaurant sits across from one of the largest hotels in Montego Bay. With its cedar-shingled design and trio of steeply pointed roofs, it has the air of a country club. Not everything is ambrosial on the menu, but the cooks turn out a predictable array of good pasta and seafood dishes. Many of the flavors are Mediterranean, especially the lobster tails and other seafood dishes. Two intriguing chef's specialties are "grouper round down" (grouper served with shrimp, squid, and mussels) and pan-seared snapper with beans, rice, and fresh vegetables.

Across from the Wyndham Rose Hall Resort, Rose Hall. ⓒ **876/953-2650.** Reservations recommended. Main courses $20–$25. AE, MC, V. Thurs–Tues 6–9:30pm.

Town House ✿ JAMAICAN/INTERNATIONAL   Housed in a redbrick building dating from 1765, the Town House is a tranquil dining choice. It offers sandwiches and salads, or more elaborate fare if your appetite demands it. At night it's floodlit, with outdoor dining on a veranda overlooking an 18th-century parish church. You can also dine in what used to be the cellars, where old ship lanterns provide a warm atmosphere. Pepper-pot or pumpkin soup is a delectable start to a meal. The chef offers a wide selection of main courses, including the local favorite, red snapper *en papillote* (baked in parchment). We're fond of the large rack of barbecued spareribs with the owners' special Tennessee sauce. The pasta and steak dishes are also good, especially the homemade fettuccine with whole shrimp and the perfectly aged New York strip steak.

16 Church St. ⓒ **876/952-2660.** Reservations recommended. Main courses $14–$36. AE, DISC, MC, V. Mon–Fri noon–3pm; daily 6–10pm. Free limousine service to and from many area hotels if you eat dinner here.

MODERATE

The Castles INTERNATIONAL   The Castles is one of the most elegant restaurants between Montego Bay and Falmouth. The chefs scour the globe in their search for dishes such as gazpacho, spicy spaghetti in meat sauce, or a beef consommé julienne appetizer. In a formal setting that's open to the breezes, guests peruse a menu that is usually divided among seafood selections—such as a delicious lobster thermidor—and main dishes and roasts, perhaps tenderloin of pork with honey and thyme or a savory roast prime rib of beef. There's also a selection of Italian dishes ranging from veal parmigiana to chicken with peppers, though these tend to vary in quality. Carrot cake is the pastry chef's prized dessert. Although the restaurant serves its regular guests nightly, it is open to the general public only on Tuesday, Wednesday, and Sunday.

In the SeaCastles Beach Resort, Rose Hall (along A1 east of Montego Bay, toward Falmouth). ⓒ **876/953-4671.** Reservations required. Main courses $16–$26. AE, DC, MC, V. Daily 7am–10pm.

Chef Oliver Magnus INTERNATIONAL   Set on a hill overlooking faraway cruise ships, this restaurant is housed in a villa with a tile roof. Chef Oliver Magnus dazzles with an array of appetizers ranging from gazpacho to smoked marlin; salads are also interesting, especially the marinated papaya with the

---

Fun Fact **If Only Columbus Had Prevailed**

When Christopher Columbus and his men sailed into what is now Montego Bay, the explorer named it *El Golfo de Buen Tiempo* or "The Gulf of Good Weather." The name didn't stick. The Spanish conquistadores preferred the name *Bahía de Manteca*. Literally translated, that means "Lard Bay." The Spanish fleets used to anchor in the bay and send men ashore to hunt down wild hogs. From the fatty flesh of these animals, they made "hog butter" to cook with on the long journey back to Europe. Eventually Manteca evolved into Montego.

---

tangy balsamic green-onion vinaigrette. Main dishes include a snapper Camembert with a ranch sauce topped with cheese and toasted almonds. We're also fond of the *misto di mare,* a medley of shrimp, crab, and other fish stewed in a tomato pesto ragout. The grilled lamb from New Zealand is given added Jamaican flair with the use of a mild jerk spice.

Corniche Rd. ℭ **876/952-2988.** Main courses J$465–J$1,200 (US$7.70–US$20). MC, V. Daily 6:30–10:30pm.

The Houseboat Grill INTERNATIONAL   The setting for this unusual and very laid-back restaurant is a houseboat built around 1960 that floats at permanent anchor from a pier beside Freeport Road. You can enjoy a pre-dinner drink and watch the sunset from a chair on the main deck before descending into the boat's innards for a meal that's composed of culinary ideas from virtually everywhere. Specialties include New Zealand mussels in a Thai-style red curry; pan-seared pork medallions with apple-pecan stuffing and a brandy-flavored cream sauce; and filet of red snapper with Thai-style tamarind sauce and garlic-flavored green beans. Although the kitchen closes around 10pm, the bar opens every day at 4pm and remains open until whenever the owners feel like shutting it down.

Freeport Rd. ℭ **876/979-8845.** Reservations recommended. Main courses $16–$20. MC, V. Tues–Sun 6–10pm. Closed 2 weeks in Aug.

Marguerite's Seafood by the Sea and Margueritaville Sports Bar & Grill INTERNATIONAL/SEAFOOD   This two-in-one restaurant across from the Coral Cliff Hotel specializes in seafood served on a breeze-swept terrace overlooking the sea. There's also an air-conditioned lounge with an adjoining "Secret Garden." The chef specializes in exhibition cookery at a flambé grill. The menu is mainly devoted to seafood and fresh fish, but there are also numerous innovative pastas and rather standard meat dishes. The changing dessert options are homemade, and a reasonable selection of wines is served. The sports bar and grill features a 34m (110-ft.) water slide, live music, satellite TV, watersports, a sun deck, and a straightforward menu of seafood, sandwiches, pasta, pizza, salads, and snacks—nothing fussy. Naturally, the bartenders specialize in margaritas.

Gloucester Ave. ℭ **876/952-4777.** Reservations recommended for Marguerite's Seafood by the Sea. Main courses $12–$42; snacks and platters from $9. AE, MC, V. Restaurant daily 6–10:30pm; sports bar daily 10am–3am.

INEXPENSIVE

The Brewery AMERICAN/JAMAICAN   This is more a bar than a full-scale restaurant, but lunch and dinner are served. Basic hamburgers, salads, and sandwiches are available, and there's also a daytime special buffet featured on Monday, Wednesday, and Friday, costing J$300 (US$5). You can enjoy drinks and a meal on the outside patio overlooking the ocean. The best time to come for drinks is during happy hour, from 4 to 6pm daily. On Friday and Saturday nights, they have disco nights, and the bar has karaoke on Thursday.

In Miranda Ridge Plaza, Gloucester Ave. (C) **876/940-2433**. Main courses J$450–J$660 (US$7.45–US$11). AE, MC, V. Daily 11am–2am.

China House *Value* CHINESE   Forget the tacky commercial surroundings, which evoke a fast-food outlet in the States. The cooks here dish up an array of lip-smackingly good dishes, platter after platter of fresh, tasty Chinese food. In the densest concentration of stores and souvenir shops on Montego Bay's tourist strip, this high-ceilinged restaurant lies across Gloucester Avenue from the sea. The well-prepared food is served in copious portions. Lobster in black-bean sauce is a specialty, and the cooks also prepare several Cantonese dishes exceedingly well.

32 Gloucester Ave. (C) **876/952-5240**. Main courses J$300–J$900 (US$5–US$15). AE, MC, V. Daily 10am–10pm.

Guangzhou CHINESE   This is about your only choice for Chinese food along the "Hip Strip." If you live in such places as New York or San Francisco, don't get too excited about dining here. Nonetheless, what you're served isn't bad. The food is also very familiar: a selection of lobster, shrimp, chicken, and pork from lo mein to Singapore noodles. The same menu is served at both lunch and dinner. We've found lunch here a bit gloomy, but dinner is better. The chefs, incidentally, are actually from China.

Gloucester Ave. (C) **876/952-6200**. Main courses J$260–J$695 (US$4.30–US$12). DC, MC, V. Mon–Sat noon–9:45pm; Sun 5–9:45pm.

The Native Restaurant ⌖ JAMAICAN/INTERNATIONAL   Open to the breezes, this casual restaurant with panoramic views serves some of the finest Jamaican dishes in the area. Appetizers include ackee and salt fish and jerk reggae chicken, or smoked marlin, which you can follow with steamed fish or jerk chicken. A more exotic specialty is Boonoonoonoos; billed as "A Taste of Jamaica," it's a big platter with a little bit of everything—meats, fish, and vegetables.

29 Gloucester Ave. (C) **876/979-2769**. Reservations recommended. Main courses $12–$32. AE, DISC, MC, V. Daily 7–10:30pm.

The Pelican JAMAICAN   A Montego Bay landmark, the family-friendly Pelican has been serving good food at reasonable prices for more than a quarter century. Most of the dishes are at the lower end of the price scale, unless you order shellfish. Many diners come here at lunch for one of the well-stuffed sandwiches, juicy burgers, or barbecued chicken. You can also choose from a wide array of Jamaican dishes, including stewed peas and rice, curried goat, Caribbean fish, fried chicken, and curried lobster. A "meatless menu" is also featured, and includes such dishes as a vegetable plate. The soda fountain serves old-fashioned sundaes with real whipped cream.

Gloucester Ave. (C) **876/952-3171**. Reservations recommended. Main courses $12–$23. AE, MC, V. Daily 7am–11pm.

Pork Pit ⌖ JAMAICAN   This joint is the best place to go for the famous Jamaican jerk pork and jerk chicken, and the location is right in the heart of

---

Moments **A True Taste of Jamaica**

Wherever you go in Jamaica, you'll see ramshackle stands selling **jerk pork**. There is no more authentic local experience than stopping at one of these stands and ordering a lunch of jerk pork, preferably washed down with a Red Stripe beer. Jerk is a way of barbecuing spicy meats on slats of pimento wood, over a wood fire set in the ground. You can never be quite sure what goes into the seasoning, but the taste is definitely of peppers, pimento (allspice), and ginger. You can also order jerk chicken, sausage, fish, and even lobster. The cook will haul out a machete and chop the meat into bite-size pieces for you, then throw them into a paper bag.

Montego Bay, near Walter Fletcher Beach. Many beachgoers desert their towels at noontime and head over here for a big, reasonably priced lunch. Picnic tables encircle the building, and everything is open-air and informal. A half-pound of jerk meat, served with a baked yam or baked potato and a bottle of Red Stripe, is usually enough for a meal. The menu also includes steamed roast fish.

27 Gloucester Ave. © 876/952-3663. 1 lb. of jerk pork $9.50. MC, V. Daily 11am–11pm.

4 Beaches, Golf & Other Outdoor Pursuits

BEACHES

Cornwall Beach (© 876/952-3463) is a long stretch of white sand with dressing rooms, a bar, and a cafeteria. The grainy sand and good swimming have made it a longtime favorite. Unlike some of Jamaica's remote, hard-to-get-to beaches, this one is near all the major hotels, especially the moderately priced ones. Unfortunately, it can be crowded in winter (mostly with tourists, not locals). This is a good beach for kids, with gentle waters and a gently sloping ocean bottom. The beach is open daily from 9am to 5pm. Admission is $2.50 for adults, $1.50 for children.

Doctor's Cave Beach, on Gloucester Avenue (© **876/952-2566** for the beach club), is arguably the loveliest stretch of sand bordering Montego Bay. Its gentle surf, golden sands, and fresh turquoise water make it an inviting place to swim, and there's always a beach-party atmosphere. Placid and popular with families, it's the best all-around beach in Montego Bay. Sometimes schools of tropical fish weave in and out of the waters, but usually the crowds of frolicking people scare them away. Since it's almost always packed, especially in winter, you have to get there early to stake out a beach-blanket-size spot. Admission is $5 for adults, $2.50 for children age 12 and under. Open daily 8:30am to sunset. The beach club here has well-kept changing rooms, showers, restrooms, a food court, a bar, a cybercafe, and a sundries shop. Beach chairs and umbrellas can be rented daily.

Walter Fletcher Beach (© 876/979-9447), in the heart of Mo Bay, is noted for its tranquil waters, which makes it a favorite of families with children. It's one of the most beautiful beaches along Jamaica's southern coast. Easy to reach, it's generally crowded in winter and enjoyed by visitors and locals alike. If you bring a picnic, be careful not to litter, as patrols might fine you. From December to March there seems to be a long-running beach party here. Visitors show up in almost anything (or lack of anything), although actual nudity is prohibited. There are changing rooms, a restaurant, and lifeguards. Hours are daily from 10am to 10pm. Admission is J$200 (US$3.30) for adults, J$100 (US$1.65) for children.

Frankly, you may want to skip all these public beaches entirely and head instead for the **Rose Hall Beach Club** (© **876/680-0969** for the beach club), on the main road 18km (11 miles) east of Montego Bay. The club offers .8km (½ mile) of secluded white-sand beach with crystal-clear water, plus a restaurant, a bar, a covered pavilion, an open-air dance area, showers, restrooms, hammocks, changing rooms, beach volleyball courts, beach games, and a full watersports program. Admission is $6 for adults, $3 for children. Hours are daily from 9am to 5pm.

SPORTS & OUTDOOR PURSUITS

DEEP-SEA FISHING   **Seaworld Resorts,** whose main office is at the Cariblue Hotel, Rose Hall Main Road (© **876/953-2180**), operates flying-bridge cruisers, with deck lines and outriggers, for fishing expeditions. A half-day fishing trip costs $380 for up to four participants.

DIVING, SNORKELING & OTHER WATERSPORTS   Some of the best dive sites in the area include **Rose Hall Reef,** a shallow reef teeming with marine life and underwater visibility of 7 to 14m (20–40 ft.). A large pillar of coral rising to the surface is called "Fairy Castle" by local divers. Nurse sharks often swim at this reef, and you can invariably see grunts, soldier fish, and red snapper. Named after the James Jones novel, *Go to the Widowmaker,* the ominously named **Widowmakers Cave** starts at 12m (40 ft.) with its entrance cave stretching for 24m (80 ft.). As you swim into its cavernous depth, you're greeted with barracuda, reef fish, and other denizens of the deep, along with such natural wonders as gorgonians, black coral, and sponges. At the aptly named **Chub Reef,** the site is teeming with Bermuda Chubs and other rainbow-hued marine life in 8m (24 ft.) of water. The coral caverns here are particularly stunning. Finally, **The Point,** whose wall drops to 60m (200 ft.), is for very experienced divers only. Expect strong currents and exotic black coral, deep-water gorgonians, sponges, and other marine life. **Seaworld Resorts** (see above) also operates scuba-diving excursions, plus sailing, windsurfing, and more. Its dives plunge to offshore coral reefs, among the most spectacular in the Caribbean. There are three certified dive guides, one dive boat, and all the necessary equipment for

---

Kids A Waterworld for Families

The $20-million **Aguasol Theme Park** (© **876/940-1344**), Walter Fletcher Beach, lures with its array of watersports activities including a giant water slide, plus a go-kart track, a large sandy beach, and planned amusements that cover everything from fashion shows to presentations of reggae. There's also an outdoor restaurant and a sports bar featuring 42 big-screen televisions, and at press time there was a health club under construction, and some "go-buggy" electric carts. An upper deck is ideal for sunbathing, and there's also a picnic area. At night a dance club dominates the action. Open daily from 10am to 10pm, the attraction charges J$200 (US$3.30) adults, J$100 (US$1.65) for children age 12 and under. Rentals of beach chairs or umbrellas go for J$600 (US$9.95) each.

both inexperienced and already-certified divers. One-tank dives cost $45; night dives are $65.

Dive Jamaica (© 876/953-2021), run by PADI-certified instructor Rodney Davis, originally from New Orleans, offers everything from resort courses to specialty certification, with outings to a variety of sites, including Rose Hall Beach, where you'll see basket sponges, sea fans, nurse sharks, parrotfish, and perhaps even a turtle or dolphin if you're lucky. The best deal here is a two-tank dive at $70 per person.

Cool Aqua Sun Sport (© 876/953-2021), run by PADI-certified instructor Percival Plummer, offers everything from resort courses to specialty certification, with outings to a variety of sites, including the Basket Reef, where you'll see basket sponges, sea fans, parrotfish, and perhaps even a turtle or dolphin.

North Coast Marine Sports (© 876/953-2211), located at the Half Moon Golf, Tennis & Beach Club, offers everything from scuba diving to Sunfish, snorkel gear, kayaks, and more. They can arrange for deep-sea fishing trips and snorkel cruises, too.

Doctor's Cave Beach is part of the **Montego Bay Marine Park,** which was established to protect the wide variety of marine life among the coral reefs right offshore from the popular beaches. You can rent snorkel gear from the beach club at Doctor's Cave, or from the beach clubs at any of the local beaches.

You might also like to head across the channel to check out **Coyaba Reef, Seaworld Reef,** and **Royal Reef,** which are full of barjacks, blue and brown chromis, yellow-headed wrasses, and spotlight parrotfish. You must have a guide here, as the currents are strong and the wind picks up in the afternoon. If you're not staying at a resort offering snorkeling expeditions, then Seaworld is your best bet. For about $30 per hour, a guide swims with you and points out various fish.

GOLF   The **White Witch of Rose Hall Golf Course,** part of the Ritz-Carlton Rose Hall (© 876/953-2204), is one of the most spectacular courses in the Caribbean, situated on 80 hectares (200 acres) of lush greenery in Jamaica's old plantation country. The course is named after Annie Palmer, the notorious "White Witch" (see the box on p. 78) and mistress of Rose Hall nearby (p. 79). Ten minutes from the deluxe resort by wheels, the course was created by Robert von Hagge, who designed the course to wind up and down the mountains, with panoramic vistas of the sea visible from 16 of the 18 holes. Greens fees are $159 for hotel guests, $179 for nonguests.

Wyndham Rose Hall Golf & Beach Resort ☆☆, Rose Hall (© 876/953-2650), has a noted course with an unusual and challenging seaside-and-mountain layout, built on the shores of the Caribbean. Its eighth hole skirts the water, then doglegs onto a promontory and a green thrusting 182m (600 ft.) into the sea. The back nine are the most scenic and interesting, rising up steep slopes and falling into deep ravines on Mount Zion. The 10th fairway abuts the family burial grounds of the Barretts of Wimpole Street. The 90m-high (300-ft.) 13th tee offers a rare panoramic view of the sea and the roof of the hotel, and the 15th green is next to a 12m (40-ft.) waterfall, once featured in a James Bond movie. Amenities include a fully stocked pro shop, a clubhouse, and a professional staff. Guests pay $125 for 18 holes, or $75 for 9 holes; nonguests pay $150 for 18 holes and $105 for 9 holes. Cart rental and the use of a caddy are included in the greens fees.

The excellent course at the **Tryall Club Jamaica** ☆☆☆ (© 876/956-5660), 19km (12 miles) from Montego Bay, is so regal that it's often the site of major tournaments. For 18 holes, guests of Tryall are charged $80 in winter, $40 the

Moments **Swimming with the Dolphins**

Montego Bay's **Half Moon Resort** (p. *56*) features daily sessions of swimming with the dolphins at its **Dolphin Lagoon** in a natural cove in the vicinity of Sunrise Beach. For $155 per person, you get into the water with some of Flipper's cousins for a bottlenose kiss and a dorsal-fin ride. A trimmed-down close encounter with the dolphins—called "Beach Encounter"—costs $89 per person. Before joining the program, a trainer gives a briefing about the "politically correct" ways to mingle with these friendly sea animals. For more information or to make reservations in advance, call ✆ **800/626-0592.**

rest of the year. In winter the course is usually closed to nonguests; the rest of the year, they pay a steep $115.

Half Moon, at Rose Hall (✆ **876/953-2560**), features a championship course designed by Robert Trent Jones Sr. with manicured and diversely shaped greens. Half Moon hotel guests pay $125 for 18 holes including caddy and cart; nonguests pay $130. Carts cost $35 for 18 holes, and caddies (which are mandatory) are hired for $17.

The **Ironshore Golf & Country Club,** Ironshore, St. James, Montego Bay (✆ **876/953-3681**), is another well-known 18-hole, par-72 course. Privately owned, it's open to all golfers. Greens fees for 18 holes are $50, plus $35 for a cart and $16 for a caddy.

HORSEBACK RIDING   A good program is offered at the **Rocky Point Riding Stables** at the Half Moon Club, Rose Hall, Montego Bay (✆ **876/953-2286**). Housed in the most beautiful barn and stables in Jamaica, it offers around 30 horses and a helpful staff. A 90-minute beach or mountain ride costs $60.

RAFTING   **Mountain Valley Rafting,** P.O. Box 23, Montego Bay (✆ **876/956-4920**), offers somewhat tame and touristy excursions on the Great River, which depart from the Lethe Plantation, about 16km (10 miles) south of Montego Bay. Skip that, and head over to Falmouth, 45km (28 miles) to the east, where rafting on the **Martha Brae** is an adventure. To reach the starting point from Falmouth, drive approximately 5km (3 miles) inland to **Martha Brae's Rafters Village** (✆ **876/952-0889**). The rafts are similar to those on the Rio Grande, near Port Antonio; you sit on a raised dais on bamboo logs. The cost is $45, with two riders allowed on a raft, plus a small child if accompanied by an adult (but use caution). The trips last 1¼ hours and operate daily from 9am to 4pm. It's not necessary to wear swimsuits. Along the way, you can stop and order cool drinks or beer along the banks of the river. There's a bar, a restaurant, and two souvenir shops in the village.

TENNIS   **Half Moon Golf, Tennis & Beach Club** ✿✿✿, outside Montego Bay (✆ **876/953-2211**), has the finest courts in the area. Its 13 state-of-the-art courts, seven of which are lit for night games, attract tennis players from around the world. Lessons cost $30 to $35 per half-hour, $50 to $65 per hour. Residents play free, day or night. The pro shop, which accepts reservations for court times, is open daily from 7am to 9pm. If you want to play after those hours, you switch on the lights yourself. If you're not a hotel guest, you must purchase a day pass ($40 per person) at the front desk; it allows access to the resort's courts, gym, sauna, Jacuzzi, pools, and beach facilities.

Tryall Club Jamaica, St. James (© **876/956-5660**), offers nine hard-surface courts, three lit for night play. Day games are free for guests; nonguests pay $30 per hour. There's a $20 per hour charge to light the courts after dark. At least four on-site pros provide lessons for $25 to $35 per half-hour, or $45 to $60 per hour.

Wyndham Rose Hall Golf & Beach Resort, Rose Hall (© **876/953-2650**), outside Montego Bay, is an outstanding tennis resort, though not the equal of Half Moon or Tryall. Wyndham offers six hard-surface courts, each lit for night play. The resident pro charges $40 per hour for lessons, $35 for 45 minutes, or $30 for 30 minutes.

5 Seeing the Sights

Most of the Montego Bay area's first-rate sights, such as the great houses, lie outside the city.

But the downtown area does at least merit a morning of your time for a look around. Everyone at some point seems to stroll **Gloucester Avenue,** home to hotels, restaurants, shops, street vendors, taxi drivers, and hair braiders. From there, it's possible to make a brief tour of the town.

WALKING TOUR   A STROLL THROUGH MONTEGO BAY

If you don't mind fending off hustlers, you can stroll through the center of Montego Bay. Allow about 1½ hours to see the major landmarks.

We like to begin our walk north of Walter Fletcher Beach at:

❶ Fort Montego
Above Gloucester Avenue and up Miranda Hill on Queen's Drive, the fort is long gone. Originally it had 17 cannons, of which only a trio remain. The fort never saw much action, and what it did see was of the comic variety—a Jamaican slapstick film.

Immediately south of the fort and reached by going southeast along Gloucester Avenue is a roundabout at the beginning of Howard Cooke Drive. This is the site of the:

❷ Old Fort Craft Park
See "Shopping," below for more details. You'll be awash in T-shirts, woodcarvings, shell jewelry, baskets to fit cobras of any size, and vendors peddling fruits and vegetables.

Afterward, you can walk 1 block to the east along Union Street until you reach the landmark:

❸ Georgian House
This 18th-century residence—really two buildings—was built by a rich tradesman who wanted one house for his wife and the other for his mistress.

Return to Fort Street, going only 1 block to the south to reach:

❹ Sam Sharpe Square
Sam Sharpe was the local hero who spearheaded the Christmas Rebellion of 1831 that eventually led to the freeing of Jamaica's slaves. The cobblestone square bearing his name is still a rallying point for protests and political speeches.

At the northwest corner of the square is a bronze statue commemorating Sharpe, who was hanged in this very square.

In the northwest corner you can also see another grim monument called:

❺ "The Cage"
This foreboding brick structure dates from 1806. Its name is apt: It was used as a lockup for both escaped slaves and drunks arrested on the street, most often British sailors on shore leave.

Leaving Sam Sharpe Square, head east along Market Street for 2 blocks until you come to:

6 Burcell Memorial Baptist Church

Dating from 1824, this church is named for its founder, the preacher Thomas Burcell; Sam Sharpe himself once served as a deacon here. The present church is a reconstruction, as slave owners burned the original church to protest Burcell's support of the emancipation movement. Sharpe's remains lie in the church's vault.

Continue to walk east along Market Street for another block until you approach the intersection with East Street. Take East Street south to Church Street. Once here, head west again in the direction of Sam Sharpe Square. On your left you'll come to:

7 St. James Parish Church

Shaped like a Greek cross, this is one of the best examples of mid-18th-century architecture on the island. The present church is a reconstruction; the original church was destroyed in the devastating earthquake that rocked Mo Bay in 1957.

Facing the church is the:

8 Town House Restaurant

If you're here at lunchtime, this is the best dining choice in the center of town. A wealthy merchant constructed this home of red brick in 1765. A bullet hole in the mahogany staircase can still be seen.

THE BEST ATTRACTIONS IN & AROUND MONTEGO BAY

If you can tear yourself away from the beach to take some excursions, here's the pick of the litter.

TOURS & CRUISES

Croydon Plantation, P.O. Box 1348, Catadupa, St. James (© **876/979-8267**), is a 38km (24-mile) ride from Montego Bay. It can be visited on a half-day tour from Montego Bay (or Negril) on Tuesday and Friday. Cruise-ship passengers can visit on Wednesday. Included in the $50 price are round-trip transportation from your hotel, a tour of the plantation, a taste of tropical fruits in season, and a barbecued-chicken lunch. Most hotel desks can arrange this tour, which is rather touristy and not worth a half-day for most visitors.

SEEING THE SIGHTS
TOURS & CRUISES

A **Hilton High Day Tour,** booked through Beach View Plaza (© **876/952-3343**), includes round-trip transportation on a scenic drive through historic plantation areas. Your day starts with continental breakfast at an old plantation house. You can roam the 40 hectares (100 acres) of the plantation and visit the German village of Seaford Town or St. Leonards village nearby. Calypso music is played throughout the day, and a Jamaican lunch is served at 1pm. The

---

⌒Moments Meeting Some Feathered Friends

At the **Rocklands Wildlife Station,** about 2km (1¼ mile) outside Anchovy on the road from Montego Bay, St. James (© **876/952-2009**), you can have a Jamaican doctor bird perch on your finger to drink syrup, feed small doves and finches millet from your hand, and watch dozens of other birds flying in for their evening meal. Don't take children age 5 and under to this sanctuary, as they tend to bother the birds. Admission is $10; open daily from 9am to 5:30pm.

cost is $55 per person for the plantation tour, breakfast, lunch, and transportation. Tour days are Tuesday, Wednesday, Friday, and Sunday.

Day and evening cruises are offered aboard the *Calico,* a 17m (55-ft.) gaff-rigged wooden ketch that sails from Margaritaville on the Montego Bay waterfront. An additional vessel, *Calico B,* also carries another 40 passengers. You can be transported to and from your hotel for either cruise. The daily voyage departs at 10am and returns at 1pm offering sailing, sunning, and snorkeling (with equipment). The cruise costs $35. On the *Calico's* evening voyage, which goes for $25 and is offered daily from 5 to 7pm, cocktails and wine are served as you sail through the sunset. For information and reservations, call **North Coast Cruises** (✆ **876/952-5860**) a few days in advance.

THE GREAT HOUSES

Occupied by plantation owners, each great house of Jamaica was built on high ground so that it overlooked the plantation itself and was in sight of the next house in the distance. It was the custom for the owners to offer hospitality to travelers crossing the island by road. While these homes are intriguing and beautiful, it's important to remember that they represent the sad legacy of slavery—they were built by slaves, and the lavish lifestyle of the original owners was supported by the profits of slave labor. The two great houses below can be toured in the same day.

Greenwood Great House ⓡ   Some people find the 15-room Greenwood even more interesting than Rose Hall (see below) because it's undergone less

---

The White Witch of Rose Hall

Annie Mary Paterson, a beautiful bride of only 17, arrived at the **Rose Hall Great House** near Montego Bay on March 28, 1820, to take up residence with her new husband, John Palmer. The house was said to affect her badly from the moment she entered it.

When John Palmer found out she was having an affair with a young slave, he is said to have beaten her with a riding whip. John Palmer died that night, and before long rumors were swirling that his young wife had poisoned his wine.

With her husband buried, Annie Palmer began a reign of terror at Rose Hall. Fearing her slave lover might blackmail her, she watched from the back of a black horse while he was securely tied, gagged, and flogged to death. Legend says that she then began to drift into liaison after liaison with one slave after another. But she was fickle: When her lovers bored her, she had them killed.

Her servants called her the "*Obeah* (voodoo) woman," the daughter of the devil, and "the White Witch of Rose Hall."

Although some scholars claim that they can produce no evidence of this legendary figure's cruelty or even of her debauchery, her story has been the subject of countless paperback Gothic novels.

When Ms. Palmer was found strangled in her bed in 1833, few speculated who her murderer might have been. Her household servants just wanted her buried as soon as possible in the deepest hole they could dig.

> **Tips Getting Past the Security Guard**
>
> Jamaica, especially the area about Montego Bay, is filled with great houses left over from the plantation era fueled by a slave economy. With few exceptions, these great houses—often decaying—are closed to the public. Over the years, we've found that exchanging some money with the local groundskeeper or security guard will gain us entry into the private grounds and gardens. Of course, you shouldn't actually go inside a great house and invade people's living quarters, but it's a great way to see a *Gone with the Wind* side of Jamaica rarely viewed by the casual visitor.

restoration and has more literary associations. Erected between 1780 and 1800, the Georgian-style building was the residence of Richard Barrett (cousin of poet Elizabeth Barrett Browning). Elizabeth Barrett Browning herself never visited Jamaica, but her family was one of the largest landholders here. An absentee planter who lived in England, her father once owned 33,600 hectares (84,000 acres) and some 3,000 slaves. On display is the original library of the Barrett family, with rare books dating from 1697, along with oil paintings of the family, Wedgwood china, rare musical instruments, and a collection of antique furniture.

On Rte. A1, 23km (14 miles) east of Montego Bay. © 876/953-1077. Admission $12 adults, $6 children under age 12. Daily 9am–6pm.

Rose Hall Great House The legendary Rose Hall is the most famous great house on Jamaica. The subject of at least a dozen Gothic novels, it was immortalized in the H. G. deLisser book, *White Witch of Rose Hall.* The house was built from 1778 to 1790 by John Palmer, a wealthy British planter. At its peak, this was a 2,640-hectare (6,600-acre) plantation, with more than 2,000 slaves. However, it was Annie Palmer, wife of the builder's grandnephew, who became the focal point of fiction and fact (see "The White Witch of Rose Hall" box below). Annie was said to have murdered several of her husbands while they slept and eventually suffered the same fate herself. Long in ruins, the house has now been restored. Annie's Pub is on the ground floor.

Rose Hall Hwy., 15km (9¼ miles) east of Montego Bay. © 876/953-2323. Admission $15 adults, $10 children. Daily 9am–6pm. Last tour at 5:15pm.

6 Shopping

Be prepared to be pursued by aggressive vendors. Selling a craft item may mean the difference between having a meal or going hungry, and that situation often leads to a feverish attempt to peddle goods to potential customers, all of whom are viewed as rich. *Warning:* Occasionally this harassment turns ugly or even violent, so watch your back if you decide to turn it on an angry vendor.

The main shopping areas are at **Montego Freeport,** within easy walking distance of the pier; **City Centre,** where most of the duty-free shops are, aside from those at the large hotels; and the **Holiday Village Shopping Centre,** located across from the Holiday Inn, on Rose Hall Road, heading from Montego Bay toward Ocho Rios.

If you have time for only one shopping complex, make it **Old Fort Craft Park,** as its handicrafts are more varied. It's grazing country for both souvenirs

---

Tips   When "Duty-Free" Isn't

Some so-called "duty-free" prices are actually lower than stateside prices, but then the government hits you with a 10% "general consumption tax" on all items purchased. Even so, you can still find good duty-free items here, including Swiss watches, Irish crystal, Italian handbags, Indian silks, and liquors and liqueurs. Appleton's rums are an excellent value. Tía María (coffee-flavored) and Rumona (rum-flavored) are the best liqueurs. Khus Khus is the local perfume. Jamaican arts and crafts are available throughout the resorts and at the Crafts Market (see below).

---

and more serious purchases. This shopping complex with 180 vendors (all licensed by the Jamaica Tourist Board), fronts Howard Cooke Boulevard (up from Gloucester Ave. in the heart of Montego Bay, on the site of Fort Montego). You'll see wall hangings, hand-woven straw items, and wood sculpture. You can even get your hair braided. Be aware that vendors can be very aggressive. If you want something, be prepared to bargain.

At the **Crafts Market,** near Harbour Street in downtown Montego Bay, you can find a good selection of handmade souvenirs of Jamaica, including straw hats and bags, wooden platters, straw baskets, musical instruments, beads, carved objects, and toys. That jipijapa straw hat is important if you're out in the island sun.

Tips   Avoiding the Mo Bay Hustle

With some two million tourists arriving each year, often with fat wallets, the Mo Bay hustle developed. Although the government has improved the situation considerably, time was in the 1990s that you couldn't walk more than a few steps before a hustler approached or cornered you.

Rivaled by Ocho Rios, the Mo Bay hustler is still an annoying presence and works hard to keep you from walking around the resort and enjoying it on your own terms.

Sometimes even a simple "no" is not enough to free yourself from the bondage of your uninvited guest. If a hustler will not leave, you can threaten to call a resort patrol, a group of police officers hired by the government to prevent harassment of visitors. The patrol (both men and women) wear dark-blue quasi-military uniforms with black berets and are easy to spot.

Some vendors try to peddle themselves as guides. Some try to sell junky souvenirs such as carvings. Many are peddling drugs, especially ganja (marijuana).

Be careful of pickpockets when shopping the markets, and don't let a carver etch your name on a piece of wood. He will later claim you ordered him to do so. Resist having jewelry put on your body; similarly, if someone places a straw hat on your head, you'll be billed whether you want it or not.

Grooving on Marley's Reggae Beat

The Bob Marley Experience at the Half Moon Shopping Village, North Coast Highway (© 876/953-3946; www.bobmarleyexperience.com/legend.htm), provides a keen insight into the reggae star's life. On-site you can visit a shop stuffed with Marley memorabilia, everything from CDs to T-shirts, from postcards to incense. Marley's exclusive clothing line, the "Tuff Gong Collection" of denim wear, is also sold here—and there's a free 15-minute documentary on Marley's life and music showing continuously in a wide-screen theater seating about 70.

One of the most intriguing places for shopping is an upscale minimall, **Half Moon Plaza,** on the coastal road about 13km (8 miles) east of the commercial center of Montego Bay. It caters to the guests of the Half Moon Club, and the carefully selected merchandise is upscale and expensive. On the premises are a bank, about 25 relatively upscale boutiques, and a private and well-respected prep school named in honor of the longtime manager of Half Moon, Heinz Simonowitz.

Klass Kraft Leather Sandals, 44 Fort St. (© 876/952-5782), offers sandals, caps, and leather accessories made on location by a team of Jamaican craftspeople.

Golden Nugget, 8 St. James Shopping Centre, Gloucester Avenue (© 876/952-7707), is a duty-free shop with an impressive collection of watches and a fine assortment of jewelry, plus cameras and a wide assortment of French perfumes.

Copasetic, Half Moon Shopping Village (© 876/953-3838), is a good outlet for Jamaican crafts, including pottery, jewelry, and straw products.

The best selection of native art is found at the **Gallery of West Indian Art,** 11 Fairfield Rd. (© 876/952-4547), with a wide selection of paintings not only from Haiti and Jamaica, but Cuba as well, along with Jamaican hand-carved wooden animals—even some painted hand-turned pottery.

Mezzaluna, Half Moon Shopping Village, Half Moon Plaza (© 876/953-9683), is an upscale women's boutique selling lingerie, La Perla perfumes, and various garments, along with chic accessories such as belts.

7 Montego Bay After Dark

Nightlife is not guaranteed at Montego Bay's top hotels. In winter the restaurants and bars of the Ritz-Carlton or Half Moon have the most diverse amusements. After dark it's sleepy at Round Hill and Tryall.

The following clubs attract mainly a crowd of 20- to 40-somethings.

The number-one nightspot in Mo Bay is a two-in-one restaurant, **Marguerite's Seafood by the Sea** and **Margueritaville Sports Bar & Grill,** Gloucester Avenue (© 876/952-4777), across from the Coral Cliff Hotel. It specializes in moderately priced seafood and margaritas served on a breezy terrace overlooking the sea. The sports bar and grill features a 33m (110-ft.) Hydroslide, live music, satellite TV, a sun deck, a CD jukebox, and a straightforward menu of seafood, sandwiches, pasta, pizza, salads, and snacks—nothing fussy.

Moments **Hunting the Green Flash**

In Jamaica, people gather for what's known as a "sundowner" to watch the day's last flickering rays.

The place we head for our sundowner is **Richmond Hill Inn** (p. 60). This 1806 plantation-style house was once owned by the Dewars, of Scotch whiskey fame. Perhaps out of memory of the long-ago occupants, a Scotch will do. But those fruit punches seem to win out instead. In a building constructed of limestone and molasses, you can wander among antiques and take your drink out onto the terrace for a grand sweep of the resort and the bay.

Count yourself lucky if you see a sudden "green flash" the moment the sun sets. This rare refraction of sunlight, which sometimes occurs in the West Indies on cloudless evenings, is said to guarantee true love to couples who witness it.

Cricket Club, at Wyndham Rose Hall (© 876/953-2650), is more than just a sports bar; it's where people go to meet and mingle with an international crowd. Televised sports, karaoke singalongs, tournament darts, and backgammon are all part of the fun. It's open daily from 8pm to 2am; there's no cover.

We've enjoyed the atmosphere at **Sun Daze,** 39 Gloucester Ave. (© 876/952-9391), which has an authentic Jamaican laid-back feel—complete with a constant flow of calypso and reggae music from as early as 10am daily (for the diehards) until 2am. This restaurant/club draws an equal mixture of locals and visitors, nearly all under age 40.

If you want to stick to the more familiar, try **Witches Nightclub,** Holiday Inn SunSpree Resort (© 876/953-2485). Nonguests of the hotel can pick up a pass at the front desk for $85, which allows them all-inclusive privileges at the nightclub. The pass includes a buffet and all the drinks and dancing you can handle. The house/disco/jazz music is as imaginative as what you'll find at a club in the United States. It's open daily from 6pm to 2am.

The Brewery, Gloucester Avenue (© 876/940-2433), is one of the city's most popular nightlife hangouts. It's a cross between an English pub and a Jamaican jerk-pork pit. There's a woodsy-looking bar where everyone is into Red

Moments **Rum & Reggae—and an Escape**

When you want to escape, head for **Time 'n' Place,** just east of Falmouth (© 876/954-4371). From Montego Bay, you'll spot the sign by the side of the road before you reach Falmouth: "If you got the time, then we got the place." On an almost deserted 3km (1¾-mile) beach sits this funky beach bar built of driftwood. Sit back in this relaxed, friendly place and listen to the reggae from the local stations. You can order the island's best daiquiris, made from fresh local fruit, or stick around for peppery jerk chicken or lobster. Time 'n' Place isn't completely undiscovered—somehow the fashion editors of *Vogue* have swooped down on the place, using it as a backdrop for beach fashion shots.

Stripe and reggae, lots of neo-medieval memorabilia, and a covered veranda in back overlooking busy Gloucester Avenue.

When it comes to gambling parlors, Mo Bay is no San Juan, much less Las Vegas. If you must, there's the **Coral Cliff Gaming Room** at Gloucester Avenue (© 876/952-4130), open 24 hours for slot machines. Don't expect large jackpots. There are some 100 video slot machines, as well as a macho big-screen TV and bar, drawing a Bud-swilling sports crowd.

8 Falmouth: Decaying Georgian Charm

The port town of **Falmouth** lies on the north coast of Jamaica, 37km (23 miles) east of Montego Bay. It makes for an interesting morning or afternoon tour. Laid out in 1790, Falmouth is the best-preserved Georgian town on the island, although it is ramshackle. Talks of restoration are just hot air at this point, and it's hard to imagine that such a sleepy town was once the busiest port in Jamaica (most of its port business shifted east to the larger harbor at Kingston long ago). Don't be surprised to share the streets today with wandering donkeys and goats.

Leave your car at Water Square; you can explore the town on foot in about an hour.

WALKING TOUR   STROLLING THROUGH FALMOUTH

The best place to begin your walk is:
❶ Water Square
The town's center, this is a large, spacious plaza at the east end of Falmouth. It was named for a large old circular stone-built reservoir erected in 1798 to store water from the Martha Brae River.

Facing Water Square is:
❷ Albert George Shopping & Historical Centre
This is still a market, rather claptrap but thriving, with little handicrafts stores. It was constructed in 1895.

From here, walk 1 block east toward the water to see:
❸ Phoenix Foundry & Central Wharf
At the corner of Lower Harbour Street and Thorpe Street, the foundry dates from 1810. In its heyday it manufactured iron bedsteads for the British army. In back is a sad reminder of Falmouth's past, the Central Wharf, where slaves were brought ashore to be auctioned off to plantation owners.

To the immediate west of the foundry stands:
❹ Tharp House
Near the junction of Thorpe Street and Seaboard Street, this was the in-town residence of John Tharp, notorious as the largest slave owner on the island. Today it's still disliked by locals, but for a different reason: It shelters the Falmouth tax office.

After viewing the property, continue northwest along Seaboard Street to:
❺ Falmouth Courthouse
This is the grandest building in town, a Georgian courthouse constructed in the Palladian style with Doric columns. The courthouse is guarded by cannons on each side. Originally the courthouse dated from 1815, but a fire swept through it in 1926. The present building is a reconstruction.

From the courthouse, head northwest along Seaboard Street until you come to Market Street, cutting right at this point and heading in the direction of the sea. You'll come to:
❻ Barrett House
This was the Falmouth town house of Edward Barrett, a rich planter, and

one of many houses owned by the Barrett family (of which Elizabeth Barrett Browning was a member).

From Barrett House, walk south again as if returning to Water Square. At the intersection of Market and Cornwall streets, you come to the:

❼ Baptist Manse

This was once the abode of the island's most passionate abolitionist, William Knibb, a Baptist preacher who angered sugar planters with his fiery speeches attacking slavery.

After seeing the manse, continue down Market Street until you come to Duke Street, at which point you head west. After 1 block, turn left on King Street to see:

❽ William Knibb Memorial Church

At the corner of George and Duke streets, this chapel was rebuilt following its burning by the British during the Christmas Rebellion of 1831.

Return to Duke Street and continue 4 blocks west to:

❾ St. Peter's Anglican Church

Built in 1795 and enlarged in 1842, this is the oldest extant building in Falmouth and the second oldest church on the island. Visit its interior to see its stained-glass windows.

WHERE TO STAY

Fisherman's Inn Dive Resort (Rose's by the Sea)   Set on the coastal road just outside the commercial center of Falmouth, immediately adjacent to also-recommended Glistening Waters, this is a well-designed roadside inn that might remind you of a pub-hotel in Britain. Much attention is devoted to the woodsy-looking restaurant, where main courses at lunch cost from $5 to $20 and dinners range from $13 to $40; menu items include filet mignon, stir-fried beef with soy and oriental herbs, and chicken breast stuffed with cheese and chopped callaloo. Despite its appeal as a restaurant, there's an interesting hotel configuration here as well: It includes a swimming pool set in a concrete wharf jutting into the waters of the phosphorescent bay, a gazebo-style pool bar, and a walkway and wooden pier accessing the bedrooms—which are built on pilings above the sea. Each of these has a private veranda or patio, white tile floors, white-painted furniture, and a sense of low-key coziness that only a small, intimately organized hotel can convey. All the units come with small private bathrooms with shower.

Rock Falmouth, Trelawny. ℂ 876/954-4078. 10 units. Year-round $120–$135 double. AE, MC, V. **Amenities:** Restaurant; bar; outdoor pool; 24-hr. room service; babysitting; nonsmoking rooms; rooms for those with limited mobility. *In room:* A/C, TV, iron, safe.

WHERE TO DINE

Glistening Waters Restaurant and Marina *(finds* SEAFOOD   Residents of Montego Bay often make the 45km (28-mile) drive out here along Route A1 just to sample the ambience of old Jamaica. This well-recommended restaurant and sports bar, with a veranda overlooking the lagoon, is housed in what was originally a private clubhouse for the aristocrats of nearby Trelawny. (The furniture here may

---

⌒Moments Market Day

On Wednesday morning from 8am to noon, Falmouth hosts the biggest flea market in the country, with hundreds of booths linking the marketplace and overflowing into the streets. Take time out to buy a loaf of bammy (cassava bread) and pick up the makings of a picnic.

Walking Tour: Strolling Through Falmouth

1 Water Square
2 Albert George Shopping
  & Historical Centre
3 Phoenix Foundry
  & Central Wharf
4 Tharp House
5 Falmouth Courthouse
6 Barrett House
7 Baptist Manse
8 William Knibb Memorial
  Church
9 St. Peter's Anglican
  Church

remind you of a stage set for *Night of the Iguana*.) Menu items usually include local fish dishes, such as snapper or kingfish. Other specialties include three different lobster dishes, three different preparations of shrimp, three different conch viands, fried rice, and pork chops. The food is just what your mama would make—if she came from Jamaica. And the waters of the lagoon contain a rare form of phosphorescent microbe which, when the waters are agitated, glows in the dark. Ask about evening booze cruises, which cost $15 per person, including one drink, where you can observe this phenomenon. Departures are nightly at about 7pm.

Rock Falmouth, Trelawny (between Falmouth and the Trelawny Beach Hotel). © **888/991-9901** toll-free in Jamaica, or 876/954-3229. Main courses $8–$31. AE, MC, V. Daily 10am–9:30pm.

9 Interior St. James Parish

Most visitors, including many who have visited Montego Bay multiple times, never leave the coastline. Yet you can take an interesting self-guided driving tour deep into the lush interior of St. James Parish. This tour touches only on destinations nearer to Montego Bay.

At the village of **Reading,** west of Montego Bay, take Route B8 (it's signposted) into the tropical interior. The elevation rises as you drive along the aptly named **Long Hill,** which runs parallel to the Great River Valley. From below you can see tropical palms and ferns.

Six kilometers (3¾ miles) south of Reading, you come to village of:

LETHE   This is a base for rafting the Great River. Before driving down from Montego Bay, rafting trips should be arranged in advance. **Mountain Valley Rafting,** Lethe Hanover (© **876/956-4920**), offers excursions on the Great River, which depart from the Lethe Estate, 16km (10 miles) south of Montego Bay. Rafts are available for $38 for up to two people. Trips last 45 minutes and operate daily from 8am to 5pm. The rafts are composed of bamboo trunks with a raised dais to sit on. In some cases, a small child can accompany two adults on the same raft, although due caution should be exercised if you choose to do this. Ask about pickup by taxi at the end of the rafting run. For $55 per person, a half-day experience includes transportation to and from your hotel, an hour's rafting, lunch, a garden tour of the Lethe property, and a taste of Jamaican liqueur.

Also at Lethe you'll find one of the most graceful **stone bridges** ✿ in Jamaica, spanning the Great River and dating from 1828. Who built this bridge of heavy stones? Slave labor, of course. The decaying ruins of a former sugar mill standing forlornly on the riverbank will make you reach for your camera. It's one of the most evocative sights in St. James of a long-gone plantation era.

Nearby lies another attraction:

ROCKLANDS WILDLIFE STATION   For more information, including times of visit, refer to the box, "Meeting Some Feathered Friends," above. To reach this site, you must turn off the B8 some 183m (600 ft.) south of the signposted turnoff to Lethe. A steep dirt road leads up to Rocklands, which is one of the most favored spots in all the West Indies for birders, who have been flocking here since a feeding station opened in 1958. The area abounds in bird life, including the hummingbird, orange quit, ground dove, and saffron finch. You also might see the national bird of Jamaica, the streamer-tailed doctor bird.

10 The Maroon Country

A strange, eerie part of Jamaica lies in the hills southeast of Montego Bay. Few visitors from abroad venture here. The landscape begins 2km (1¼ miles) south of Montego Bay along Fairfield Road (which is not in the best of shape).

BACK-ROADING SOUTHEAST OF MONTEGO BAY

If you follow bumpy Fairfield Road, you will eventually reach Maroon Town, lying on the periphery of the rugged and bleak **Cockpit Country** (see below).

The first hamlet of historical interest is:

KENSINGTON   A tiny town some 21km (13 miles) south of Mo Bay. Kensington doesn't offer much to see today. But history buffs will be interested to know that in this remote outpost the famous slave uprising of 1831 was launched, bringing on the Christmas Rebellion that eventually led to the emancipation of slaves in the British colonies. A ridge-top plantation was set afire, and the rebellion broke out of control before the slaves were eventually subdued.

The only sign of this rebellion today is a plaque along the road, placed here by the Jamaican National Heritage Trust to commemorate the moment.

Continue 5km (3 miles) southeast to:

MAROON TOWN   This town was settled by the remnants of the Trelawny Town Maroons. A Jamaican colonel, John Guthrie, signed a peace treaty here with the Maroons in 1745, though it only lasted until 1795.

11 The Cockpit Country

The foreboding landscape of the Cockpit Country is one of the most desolate and eerie territories in all the West Indies. For those who'd like to combine some adventure into that holiday by the beach, a tour through this rugged terrain is recommended—if you're in good shape, that is.

The forest-clad limestone hills of the Cockpit Country are shaped like witches' hats. This is wild "karst" terrain, of the type also found in Puerto Rico. The land is filled with weathered limestone covering some 1,295 sq. km (500 sq. miles). Much of the Cockpit Country remains uninhabited and, even today, still hasn't been explored in depth.

Conical hillocks were dissolved by an elaborate drainage system of caves and sinkholes. No other region of the Caribbean has such intriguingly named settlements: Wait-a-Bit, Rest and Be Thankful, and Me No Sen You No Come.

Jamaica at present classifies the Cockpit Country as a **National Reserve,** although there is a movement afoot to have it declared a national park. Because the Maroons function almost independently of the Jamaican government, they are fiercely opposed to national park status, fearing it would intrude upon their independence.

Warning: Trails here are overgrown, so guides (see below) are imperative. No foreigner should attempt this exploration without skilled guidance. Sinkholes appear suddenly and without warning, and hikers who fall into them can be seriously injured or killed. The land is also a mosquito breeding factory. These pests are hungry for blood—*yours*—so be prepared. You should also take plenty of water and adequate provisions.

The company we recommend most for guided tours is **Cockpit Country Adventure Tours** (© **876/610-0818;** www.stea.net). Guides are experienced and were trained by the U.S. Peace Corps. The easiest tour is called "Burnt Hill Natural History Tour," costing $54 per person. The second tour, "Rock Spring Cave," is a medium adventure including some visits to caves. The cost here is $65 per person. The most difficult jaunt is the "Quashie River Sink and Cave," costing $71 per person, and going into the difficult territory of the Quashie River, as well as exploring the 4km (2½-mile) Quashie Cave, known for its "cathedral room" and its underground waterfall.

In all cases, it is necessary to hire two guides for each trip, even if only one person goes along. So it's recommended that you go with other people.

4

Negril

On the arid western tip of Jamaica, Negril has had a reputation for bacchanalia, hedonism, marijuana smoking, and nude bathing since hippies discovered its sunny shores during the 1960s. The resort became more mainstream during the early 1990s as big-money capitalists built megaresorts, most of them managed by SuperClubs or Sandals. Yet some resorts still reserve stretches of beach for nude bathers, and illegal ganja is still peddled openly.

Clothed or unclothed, visitors are drawn to white Seven Mile Beach and some of the best snorkeling and scuba diving in Jamaica. Opening onto a tranquil lagoon protected by a coral reef, the beach here is set against a backdrop of sea grapes and coconut palms. The low-rise resorts blend gracefully into the flat, sandy landscape.

There are really two Negrils. The West End is the site of modest cottages and character-filled local restaurants. The other Negril is on the East End, along the road from Montego Bay; the best hotels line this panoramic beachfront. The town center itself offers little of interest.

WHICH ONE'S FOR YOU: NEGRIL OR MO BAY?

Negril, especially during the past 2 decades, has become the most serious touristic competitor to Montego Bay. These two resorts are markedly different in what they offer: Despite some new first-class hotels opening up, Negril is not anywhere near the same league as Montego when it comes to posh hostelries.

For the serious golfer, Mo Bay wins again; it offers some of the finest courses in the Caribbean. And for those who view sightseeing as part of their holiday, Montego Bay offers the most diversified attractions in Jamaica; Negril, other than its beaches, is not blessed with great sights.

What does Negril offer, then? There is no more laid-back place in all the Caribbean for sunning by day and "sinning" when darkness comes. For those who want to *literally* hang out, Negril also offers the only officially sanctioned nude beach in all Jamaica. Negril is a sensual, fun-loving Eden where you can find shelter in everything from a Rastafarian hut to an overcrowded Jacuzzi where fellow guests might all be naked. If you like hallucinogenic brownies and 11km-long (6¾-mile) beaches but hate fancy French brasseries, Negril is the place for you.

For some reason, Negril is also becoming increasingly attractive as a family destination.

One caution: Though the temptation to take a moonlit walk on Negril's beach is powerful, resist. It's possible you could be mugged at night, or worse.

1 Orientation

ARRIVING BY PLANE

If you're coming from abroad, leaving such cities as Miami or New York, try to fly into the **Donald Sangster International Airport** in Montego Bay. See p. 50 for more details.

From the airport at Montego Bay, it is an 81km (50-mile) drive southwest to Negril, a trip that usually takes 2 hours but could take more or less, depending on traffic conditions. The road winds scenically past ruins of sugar estates and great houses.

It is unwise to fly into Kingston if you plan to go on to Negril. Kingston is 242km (150 miles) to the east and at least a 4-hour drive, maybe more.

GETTING FROM THE AIRPORT TO NEGRIL

If you've booked into one of the all-inclusives such as Sandals, a hotel van will carry you from the airport at Mo Bay into Negril. Arrangements for your arrival and pickup are made in advance, at the time of booking.

If you don't have a Sandals pickup arranged, we do not recommend the public bus between Montego Bay and Negril, even though it's a cheap, one-way ride costing about $4 per passenger. The crowded minibus is uncomfortable, there isn't room for much luggage, and pickpockets are known to prey upon the tourists.

It's better to take a private minivan. We've found the most reliable to be **Tour Wise** (© 876/952-4943), charging $21 one-way. This van will drop you right at your final destination in Negril. If you don't see a Tour Wise minivan waiting at the Mo Bay airport, call © **876/974-2323.**

Another option is to go from Sangster Airport to Negril by taxi, though this is a pricey choice. The one-way fare ranges from $60 to $80; always negotiate it *before* getting into the car with your things.

Still another option is renting a car. Information on car rentals is given on p. 40. From the airport in Montego Bay, you drive west along Route A1 for about 90 minutes to reach Negril.

En route, the only town of any size you'll pass through is **Lucea,** built around a harbor at a point 40km (25 miles) east of Negril. If you're driving, it hardly merits a stopover, although in British colonial days it was more important than Mo Bay.

Locals call it "Lucy." If you visit at all, the best time to stop is on Saturday morning when the market around the harbor is both active and colorful, from about 7am to noon. Otherwise, we'd suggest you drive on, heading straight for the more glamorous retreats of Negril.

Fun Fact How Not to Arrive in Negril

When Jimmy Buffett flew into Negril on his private seaplane to stay at Chris Blackwell's posh island outpost The Caves, the singer got quite a welcome—and no margaritas. The Negril police opened fire on his plane from their "fortress" at the Negril Lighthouse, mistakenly believing the singer's plane was carrying drugs from a neighboring island. Buffett escaped alive, and the bullet-dodging incident led to a new song, *Jamaica Mistaka.*

Fun Fact Ill-Gotten Gains from Pirate Gold

Lucea was one of the ports favored by the notorious pirate Henry Morgan. He used to anchor his pirate vessels here, and it is said that he once owned about 2,023 hectares (5,000 acres) of land in the hinterlands around Lucea.

Finally, if you're really in a hurry, Negril has a small airport for short-hop domestic flights. **International Air Link** (© **866/952-5807** or 876/940-6660; www.intlairlink.com) flies the Kingston-to-Negril run as a direct charter for $580 per planeload.

These shuttle flights land at the **Negril Aerodrome** at Bloody Bay, 11km (6¾ miles) north of Negril's central hotel belt. There's no scheduled bus service from the airstrip to Negril Village, but taxis are plentiful: Though the fare is to be negotiated with a driver, count on spending at least $8 for the short ride.

VISITOR INFORMATION

The local office of the **Jamaica Tourist Board** (© **876/957-4243**) is on the second floor of the Coral Seas Plaza, opposite a traffic circle. It dispenses local maps, events schedules, and other useful material. Hours are Monday to Friday 8:30am to 4:30pm, and Saturday 9am to 1pm.

ORIENTING YOURSELF IN NEGRIL

Of all the resorts of Jamaica, Negril offers the simplest geography. Many visitors view Negril as one long street.

The South Negril River divides the resort in two, with Long Bay and its beaches lying north of the river and West End lying to the south of it.

Set inland from the beach about 91 to 137m (300–450 ft.), **Norman Manley Boulevard** begins near the Norman Manley Sea Park, close to the point where the South Negril River empties into Long Bay. This two-lane highway, flanked by hotels and restaurants, continues north to Long Bay Beach Park and eventually the airport.

Negril Village (the heart of Negril) consists mainly of two unimpressive shopping plazas, a bank or two, some tacky stores, and some housing developments in the distance in a section known as "Red Ground." (Most of Negril's local population lives here.)

The two main squares, **Negril Plaza** and **Coral Seas Plaza,** lie south of the traffic circle fronting **Negril Square.** At the parking lot here, you can hail a taxi to take you where you want to go. This sector marks the beginning of **Sheffield Road,** the main highway leading out of town to the city of Savanna-la-Mar. Here you'll find the most convenient gas station in Negril, along with a health clinic and the police station.

South of the South Negril River is a rock-studded limestone plateau. When American hippies arrived back in the 1960s, they settled here, calling the place **"the Rock."** Hotels here are of the intimate variety, attracting an independent backpacker clientele.

Eventually, West End Road leads to the **West End** and becomes Lighthouse Road as it winds its way to **Negril Lighthouse** 🕭, some 5km (3 miles) south of

Sunshine Village at Negril Village. The lighthouse stands 30m (100 ft.) above the sea at the westernmost tip of Jamaica. The West End is the only sector that evokes the Negril of old, though it becomes increasingly congested and developed with each passing year. As you travel beyond the lighthouse, you'll find a few places to escape the madding beach crowds.

GETTING AROUND NEGRIL

Negril is very spread out, stretching for miles. Some visitors walk where they want to go, but it's a long hike if you're heading to the northern edge of Long Bay or to the West End—some of these places may be 11 to 16km (6¾–10 miles) from your hotel. Also, walking the roads of Negril at night isn't recommended because of potential muggers.

So you'll need transit. The upscale resorts, including the all-inclusives, operate shuttles from the northern tip of Long Bay into Negril Village. Because the West End's hotels aren't on the beach, the more prosperous ones also operate shuttles to the beach; small inns don't.

Otherwise, you can do as the locals do and take the minibus that runs all day long up and down Norman Manley Boulevard and even into the West End. Most rides cost $2; the bus runs until early evening, sometimes later.

In lieu of the uncomfortable minivan, you might hail a taxi. Cabbies operate all over Negril, the licensed ones displaying a red medallion. In theory, fees are regulated by the government, but in years of going to Negril, we've never encountered a meter that wasn't broken.

So negotiate your fare before getting into the cab. Most trips should cost from $4 to $5, depending on where you're going. If a cabbie demands $20, look for another taxi. Taxis are most plentiful at Coral Seas Plaza and the Negril Crafts Market. Your hotel will often call a cab for you; if they won't, phone the JUTA (© **876/957-9197**) cab association for one.

You can also get around Negril by bike. Bicycles are available at most resort properties.

Instead of peddling up and down Seven Mile Beach or across the rocky cliffs of the West End, many visitors prefer to rent a motor scooter. The best supplier of those is the aptly named **Dependable Bike Rental,** at Vernon's Car Rental, Plaza de Negril (© **876/957-4354** or 876/957-3585). This outfitter doesn't rent bicycles, only motor scooters costing from $25 to $30 per day plus a $250 deposit taken on your credit card. Jeeps can be rented here, as well: A Suzuki convertible jeep begins at $50 a day.

Unlike in the States, helmets are not mandatory in Jamaica, but you should wear one for your own safety: Roads are potholed and often dangerous, with patches of sand and gravel making it easy to skid out of control. Helmets are included in the rental fee.

If you'd like to escape the traffic and the crowds along Norman Manley Boulevard, the best place to go biking, in our view, is into the **Negril Hills,** which lie beyond the Negril Lighthouse along West End Road (see above). A bike tour here can be in relative isolation as you pass along the most often deserted beaches of greater Negril and even past some landing strips where private planes depart with illegal cargoes of marijuana for the mainland United States.

FAST FACTS: Negril

Airport For information about domestic short-hop flights, call the Negril Aerodrome at ℂ **876/957-5016.**

Banks The best, most central bank is **Scotiabank,** Plaza de Negril (ℂ **876/957-4236**), open Monday, Thursday, and Friday 8:15am to 4pm, and Tuesday and Wednesday 8:15am to 3pm. Its ATMs are open 24 hours.

Emergencies For emergencies, dial ℂ **119.** The Negril Police Headquarters (ℂ **876/957-4268**) lie some 183m (600 ft.) east of the Shell gas station on Sheffield Road. For an ambulance or to report a fire, dial ℂ **110.**

Internet Access The best place to go, outside your hotel, is **The Coral Seas Beach Hotel,** Norman Manley Boulevard (ℂ **876/957-3997**), open daily 9am to 5pm. Nonguests are permitted to use the facilities.

Library The small **Negril Library,** West End Road (ℂ **876/957-4917**), is open Monday to Friday 10am to 6pm, Saturday 9am to 1pm.

Mail Include "Jamaica, W.I." in all island addresses. The island has no zip codes.

Medical Services For a non-life-threatening emergency, there are several choices. The **Negril Beach Medical Centre,** Norman Manley Boulevard (ℂ **876/957-4888**), is open daily from 9am to 5pm. And the **Negril Health Center** sits on Sheffield Road (ℂ **876/957-4926**) between the police station and the Shell gas station. Each charges about J$100 (US$1.65) to see a doctor.

Newspapers & Magazines American magazines and newspapers, including the *Miami Herald* and the *New York Times,* are sold at newsstands and the first-class resorts in Negril.

Post Office & Mail The **Negril Post Office** (ℂ **876/957-9654**) is located on West End Road next to the Craft Market. It is open Monday to Friday 8am to 5pm. Expect long lines. Instead of the overcrowded post office, we use the **Airpak Express** (ℂ **876/957-5051**) at the Negril Aerodrome, 11km (6¾ miles) outside town. UPS packages arrive here, and letters can be mailed internationally.

Pharmacy The best outlet is the **Negril Pharmacy,** shop no. 14 in the Coral Seas Plaza (ℂ **876/957-4076**), open Monday to Saturday 9am to 7pm.

Safety The all-inclusives and the first-class resorts have 24-hour security guards. The lower-rent properties rarely do, and theft—including night burglary—is distressingly commonplace in these places. Try to secure your room at night, and don't leave windows open no matter how tempting cooling trade winds are.

Tourists are rarely robbed at gunpoint, but muggings and pickpocketing occur daily. Guard your valuables, and take all the usual precautions while traveling in Negril. Be extremely careful, especially at night, about opening your door to strangers—even those who claim to be members of the hotel staff.

Also be careful of the drivers who race around Negril in battered cars. Once they get behind the wheel, these Jamaican males think they are "king of the road," and it is a fool who doesn't get out of their way. Regrettably, the same machismo also afflicts most cabbies in Negril. You may need to warn your driver that you prefer to take a few minutes longer on your ride.

Telephone Resort hotels often add ridiculous surcharges to overseas calls. To beat this game, head for **Negril Calling Service,** shop no. 19, Plaza de Negril (© **876/957-3212**), open 8:30am to 7:30pm daily.

Tourist Information See "Visitor Information," above.

Travel Agents If you need to make travel arrangements once you've landed here, the most reliable agency is **Caribic Vacations,** Norman Manley Boulevard (© **876/957-3309**).

2 Where to Stay

The choice and variety of lodgings in Negril are a bit bewildering, from funky and rustic to first-class and opulent; no place in the West Indies offers more bizarre accommodations than Negril. You can stay in a deluxe four-poster bed that was recently warmed before you by a departing Jimmy Buffett; a guesthouse where Bob Marley and a girlfriend used to hang out; or the B&B of an eccentric lady from England who will serve you a proper "cuppa" on her Wedgwood tea set. It's all up to you.

Most visitors want a hotel or resort along **Seven Mile Beach** opening onto Long Bay. Here are all the famous (or infamous) all-inclusive resorts that have secured the best beachfront property, leaving the lesser resorts to fight for their own places in the sun. Many had to build across the main street as a result—something to consider.

For the escapist, the **West End**'s inns and small B&B-type places are the places to go, although these properties open onto rocky cliffs instead of a beach. Nevertheless, they are much preferred by independent types and are certainly more adventurous. (Note that some of these cliff-side resorts will not allow families with children under 8 to check in, for fear they might fall from the cliffs; most of the paths don't have protective rails.) West End cottages and huts are far cheaper than the resorts on Long Bay. Regrettably, they are also easy for night burglars to penetrate. (See "Safety" in "Fast Facts: Negril," above.)

If you're seeking really rock-bottom bargains in simple rustic huts that are almost camplike, try to book one of the dozen units offered by **Da Gino's,** an Italian restaurant (see "Where to Dine," p. 107). Other dining spots that rent cheap rooms include **LTU Pub** (p. 109) and **Kuyaba on the Beach** (p. 110).

Note: Negril's all-inclusive resorts, most of which would fall into the "Very Expensive" or "Expensive" categories, are treated separately beginning on p. 102.

EXPENSIVE

Negril Cabins Resort *Value Kids* This place appeals to travelers who want to get away from it all without spending a fortune; it's an especially good choice for families with kids. These wooden cabins (which have been featured in *Architectural Digest*) are in a forest, across the road from a beach called Bloody Bay. The 4 hectares (9 acres) of gardens are planted with royal palms, bull thatch, and a rare variety of mango tree.

The simple but stylish cabins are small timber cottages, none more than two stories high, rising on stilts. Each offers two spacious and comfortable bedrooms, plus a balcony and shower-only bathroom. Many units have been recently upgraded and improved, and all are brightened with vibrant Jamaican fabrics. The best are rented as "executive suites," with a sunken living and dining area, plus a pull-out queen-size sofa bed for small families. The executive units also come with air-conditioning and an iron and ironing board. Simple but tasty Jamaican and international dishes are served.

Norman Manley Blvd. (P.O. Box 118), Negril. ℂ 800/382-3444 in the U.S., or 876/957-5350. Fax 876/957-5381. www.negril-cabins.com. 82 units. Winter $240 cabin for 2; off season $220 cabin for 2. Rates are all-inclusive. Children cost an additional $25 each. AE, MC, V. **Amenities:** 2 restaurants; bar; pool; tennis court; fitness center; Jacuzzi; scuba diving; snorkeling; bike rental; car rental; room service (7am–10pm); babysitting; laundry service; nonsmoking rooms; rooms for those with limited mobility. *In room:* A/C, TV (in some units), hair dryer, iron/board, safe.

Sea Splash Resort ⍟   Partly because of its small size, this beachfront resort has a friendly, personable feeling and none of the snobbishness exhibited by the staff of The Caves (p. 103). Much more intimate than the megaresorts nearby, it lies on a small but carefully landscaped sliver of beachfront land planted with tropical vegetation. Suites are spacious and stylishly decorated. All are the same size and contain the same amenities—a kitchenette, a balcony or patio, large closets, and either a king-size bed or twin beds—although the suites on the upper floor have higher ceilings and feel more spacious than the others. Living areas contain sofa beds, ideal for small families. The small bathrooms come with showers.

Norman Manley Blvd. (P.O. Box 3123), Negril. ℂ 800/254-2786 in the U.S., or 876/957-4041. Fax 876/957-4049. www.seasplash.com. 22 units. Winter $199–$219 suite for 2; off season $135–$155 suite for 2. Extra person $24. Full board $65 per person extra. AE, DC, DISC, MC, V. **Amenities:** Restaurant; bar; pool; Jacuzzi; limited room service; babysitting; laundry service; rooms for those with limited mobility. *In room:* A/C, TV, kitchenette, coffeemaker, hair dryer, safe.

MODERATE

Charela Inn ⍟   Simplicity, quiet elegance, and good value for the money are the hallmarks of this seafront inn reminiscent of a Spanish hacienda. This place sits on the main beach strip on 1 hectare (3 acres) of landscaped grounds. The building's inner courtyard, with a tropical garden and a round, freshwater pool, opens onto one of the widest (75m/250 ft.) sandy beaches in Negril. Try for 1 of the 20 or so rooms with a view of the sea. Accommodations are generally spacious, often with a bit of Jamaican character to their wicker furnishings and ceiling fans. All have private patios or balconies. Most of the good-size bathrooms have shower/tub combinations, but some have showers only.

Le Vendôme (p. 107), facing the sea and the garden, offers both an a la carte menu and a five-course fixed-price meal that changes daily. Thursday and Saturday nights there's live entertainment.

Norman Manley Blvd. (P.O. Box 3033), Negril. ℂ 876/957-4648. Fax 876/957-4414. www.charela.com. 49 units. Winter $158–$210 double; off season $108–$148 double. MAP (breakfast and dinner) $40 per person extra. 5-night minimum stay in winter. AE, MC, V. **Amenities:** Restaurant; bar; pool; kayaking; Sunfish sailing; windsurfing; limited room service; laundry service; nonsmoking rooms; rooms for those with limited mobility. *In room:* A/C, TV, dataport, hair dryer, safe, beverage maker (in some units).

CocoLaPalm Resort   This is a well-conceived hotel on Seven Mile Beach with very little plastic or glitter and lots of opportunity for relaxation and rest. The complex consists of a pair of long and narrow two-story buildings whose slender ends face the beach, and whose long sides form the edges of a carefully landscaped garden containing a Jacuzzi and a kidney-shaped swimming pool. Rooms are shaped like octagons, and each has a patio or balcony and white-painted furniture. On the premises are a bar and restaurant.

Negril

ACCOMMODATIONS ■
Banana Shout Resort **41**
Beaches Negril **7**
Beaches Sandy Bay **3**
Blue Cave Castle **32**
The Caves **44**
Charela Inn **20**
CocoLaPalm Resort **19**
Country Country **15**
Couples Negril **2**
Couples Swept Away Negril **11**
Crystal Waters **16**
Devine Destiny **40**
Drumville Cove Resort **39**
Firefly Beach Cottages **18**
Foote Prints on the Sand **12**
Fun Holiday Beach Resort **13**
Grand Lido **4**
Hedonism II **9**
Home Sweet Home **31**
Idle Awhile Resort **22**
Jackie's on the Reef **46**
Kuyaba **26**
Negril Cabins Resort **1**
Negril Inn **25**
Negril Yoga Centre **27**
Our Past Time Villas **6**
Point Village Resort **8**
Rock Cliff Hotel **37**
Rockhouse **36**
Sandals Negril Resort & Spa **10**
Sea Splash Resort **14**
Tensing Pen **43**
Thrills Resort **35**
White Sands **21**
Xtabi **34**

DINING ◆
Chicken Lavish **30**
Choices **33**
Cosmo's Seafood
  Restaurant & Bar **5**
Da Gino's **24**
Hungry Lion **38**
Juicy J's **29**
Kuyaba on the Beach **26**
Le Vendrôme **23**
LTU Pub **45**
Margueritaville **17**
Norma's **14**
Rick's Café **42**
Rockhouse Restaurant **36**
Sweet Spice **28**

ⓘ Information
✉ Post Office

To Montego Bay

Bloody Bay

Negril Airport

THE GREAT MORASS

Booby Cay

Caribbean Sea

SEVEN MILE BEACH

Long Bay

A 1

Norman Manley Blvd.

PARISH OF HANNOVER
PARISH OF WESTMORELAND

ROYAL PALM RESERVE

South Negril River

Norman Manley Sea Park
Crafts Market

Negril Yacht Club

Police Station

Jamaica Tourist Board

Plaza de Negril

Sheffield Rd.

Whitehall Rd.

WHITE HALL

Westland Mountain Rd.

West End Rd.

WEST END

Negril

JAMAICA

Kingston

Norman Manley Blvd., Negril. ℂ **800/320-8821** or 876/957-4227. Fax 876/957-3460. www.cocolapalm. com. 80 units. Winter $135–$220 double, $210–$250 suite; off season $105–$165 double, $165–$185 suite. MC, V. **Amenities:** 3 restaurants; bar; 2 pools; Jacuzzi; babysitting; laundry service; rooms for those with limited mobility. *In room:* A/C, TV, fridge, coffeemaker, hair dryer, safe.

Crystal Waters *(Kids* This is an excellent choice for families with young children. Unlike other resorts, the housekeeper assigned to you here is like a personal maid who takes over all the cooking and babysitting. The place is a long-established old-timer and much respected locally for simple accommodations at reasonable prices. The accommodations are tropically decorated, furnished with a mixture of hardwoods and wicker, plus a small bathroom with shower. The villas include ceiling fans (plus air-conditioning) and full kitchens, and each is staffed with a housekeeper who will cook breakfast, lunch, and dinner for you. There's also a freshwater pool.

Norman Manley Blvd. (P.O. Box 3018), Negril Beach, Negril. ℂ **876/957-4284.** Fax 876/957-4889. www. crystalwaters.net. 10 villas. Winter $145–$160 1-bedroom villa, $250–$290 2-bedroom villa, $410 3-bedroom villa; off season $110–$120 1-bedroom villa, $170–$210 2-bedroom villa, $295 3-bedroom villa. Maximum of 2 people per bedroom. MC, V. Closed in Sept. **Amenities:** 2 pools; Jacuzzi; watersports; children's pool and playground equipment; activities desk; 24-hr. room service; in-room massage; babysitting; laundry service. *In room:* A/C, TV, dataport, kitchen, fridge, coffeemaker, hair dryer, iron/board, safe, cellphone, microwave.

Firefly Beach Cottages With a lot of Jamaican flair, this laid-back hodgepodge of white concrete and wooden buildings opens directly onto a "skinny-dipping" beach. There's even a so-called penthouse in the garden with sleeping lofts, plus studios and cottages—including one large two-bedroom unit that can sleep up to eight (in cramped conditions). All units are cooled by air-conditioning and ceiling fans, and many beds are canopied. Each unit comes with a small bathroom containing a shower, while all rooms have verandas and kitchens, but there's no restaurant. However, there is a breakfast bar. Local eateries and the beach (you don't even need a suit) are close at hand.

Norman Manley Blvd. (P.O. Box 54), Negril. ℂ **876/957-4358.** Fax 876/957-3447. www.jamaicalink.com. 18 units. Winter $134–$210 double (up to 4 people);off season $96–$158 double (up to 4 people). AE, MC, V. **Amenities:** Breakfast bar; small exercise room; Jacuzzi; massage (not in room); babysitting; laundry service; rooms for those with limited mobility; cellphone rental. *In room:* A/C, kitchenette, fridge, no phone (except for penthouse).

Idle Awhile Resort ⋆ *(Finds* One of Negril's newest resorts is also among its most intimate and personal. Right on a choice spot on Seven Mile Beach, the inn offers deluxe bedrooms with king-size beds and large verandas, and eight junior suites, each with a kitchenette and enclosed patio. There are also larger suites available with more living area and a more spacious veranda. Catering to families, singles, or couples, the resort offers guest privileges at the large sports complex at Swept Away nearby. Bedrooms are nestled in tropical gardens. On a luxury-living note, if you book a one-bedroom suite, you can hire a cook for another $15 per day, plus groceries. The chef will go grocery shopping for you and prepare you regional Jamaican dishes.

Norman Manley Blvd., Negril. ℂ **877/243-5352.** Fax 876/957-9567. www.idleawhile.com. 13 units. Winter $170–$210 double, $210 junior suite, $275 1-bedroom suite; off season $110–$125 double, $160 junior suite, $170–$190 1-bedroom suite. AE, MC, V. **Amenities:** Restaurant; bar; room service (7am–7pm); babysitting; laundry service/dry cleaning. *In room:* A/C, TV, dataport, kitchenette (in some rooms), minibar, safe.

Jackie's on the Reef *(Finds* The setting is a soaring concrete building that looks as though it was never quite completed; the result evokes a postmodern cathedral, thanks to long corridors that spill into sunlit communal areas. In

Jackie Lewis's own words, "This is a healing joint," welcoming a revolving series of practitioners imported for temporary sojourns from Manhattan. Treatments might include facials, body massages, reflexology, and more. Most bedrooms are generous in size with mosquito netting draped over beds in old plantation style; however, there are no TVs, phones, air-conditioning, or even fans, and furnishings are rather simple, with usually just twin beds and small tables in the rooms. Each comes with a shower-only bathroom. The hotel lies 11km (6¾ miles) from the nearest beach, but there's a small seawater pool and a ladder down to the reef for swimming.

West End Rd., Negril. ⓒ 876/957-4997, or 718/469-2785 (New York State). www.jackiesonthereef.com. 3 units, 1 cottage. Year-round $150 per person. Rates include breakfast, dinner, and yoga class. No credit cards. Drive 4km (2½ miles) past the oldest lighthouse in Negril; just keep heading out the West End until you come to the sign. Children not accepted. **Amenities:** Dining room; small seawater pool; spa; snorkeling; outdoor massage; laundry service; yoga; meditation. *In room:* No phone.

Tensing Pen 𝍐𝍐   Our favorite nest in Negril lies on the western tip and has grown and evolved since its hippie era in the early 1970s. On a cliff a 10-minute stroll from the landmark lighthouse, it is 6km (3¾ miles) south of the center of Negril. Hidden away from the world, the place is a little gem. Those aggressive beach vendors will never find you here, tucked behind a high wall. On ¾ of a hectare (2 acres) of grounds, you're surrounded by tropical planting. Laze in the hammocks or sunbathe on the terraces hewn out of rock. Sleep in a rustic stone cottage covered in thatch in a four-poster draped in mosquito netting, plantation house–style. Some of the huts are elevated, evoking treehouse living. Local tiles, tropical woods, bamboo rockers, ceiling fans, and louvered windows set the tone. Bathrooms with shower/tub combinations are a bit cramped. There's a communal kitchen where guests sometimes cook for each other. The nearest beach is a 10- to 15-minute drive or a 30-minute walk away.

Lighthouse Rd. (P.O. Box 13), Negril. ⓒ 876/957-0387. Fax 876/957-0161. www.tensingpen.com. 15 units. Winter $128–$279 double; off season $87–$180 double. AE, MC, V. **Amenities:** Restaurant; bar; communal kitchen; babysitting; laundry service; rooms for those with limited mobility. *In room:* Fridge, no phone, ceiling fan.

INEXPENSIVE

Banana Shout Resort   Set on 1 hectare (2½ acres) of landscaped grounds with waterfalls, lily ponds, tropical flowers, and fruit trees, this property comprises four cottages, three of which are poised on a cliff overlooking the sea. A series of tiered decks with concrete steps leads down the rocks to water. Each secluded unit contains a kitchenette and ceiling fan. The rooms are furnished with locally crafted pieces of artwork from Jamaica, Haiti, and Asia, and each is equipped with a small bathroom with shower. There's a cafe across the street.

4 West End Rd. (P.O. Box 4), Negril. ⓒ 941/927-6996 in the U.S., or tel/fax 876/957-0384. www.banana shout.com. 4 cottages. Winter $80–$100 cottage for 1 or 2, $120 cottage for 4; off season $40–$60 cottage for 1 or 2, $70 cottage for 4. MC, V. **Amenities:** In-room massage; laundry service. *In room:* Kitchenette, fridge, coffeemaker, no phone, ceiling fans, hammocks.

Blue Cave Castle   Filled with a sense of whimsy and fun, this little mock castle is a terrific deal. Battlements and turrets re-create medieval days, and the resort is built over a cave; it duplicates a Czechoslovakian castle. There are steps down to the cave from the garden, where local wedding receptions are regularly held. Guest rooms are decorated with handmade mahogany furniture and antique Turkish carpets covering the walls. Three rooms are air-conditioned, although there are no room phones or TVs. (There's no pool, either, but you can swim off the cliffs in lieu of a beach.) All rooms have sea views, refrigerators, ceiling fans, and balconies. A good restaurant in front is open to the public; the oceanside dining area is reserved for guests only.

Lighthouse Rd., Negril. ℂ and fax **876/957-4845.** www.bluecavecastle.com. 10 units. Winter $60–$100 double; off season $40–$55 double. Extra person $10. DISC, MC, V. **Amenities:** Restaurant (next door, under different management); laundry service; safe in office. *In room:* A/C (7 units), TV (7 units).

Country Country ℛ   The owners of this intimate hotel were determined to outclass their competitors, so they turned to celebrity decorator Ann Hodges, the creative force behind the gorgeous decor in many of the much more expensive Island Outpost properties. A narrow meandering path stretches from the coastal boulevard to the white-sand beach, where watersports await. Along the way is a collection of neo-Creole, clapboard-sided buildings that drip with elaborate gingerbread and cove moldings, each inspired by an idealized vision of vernacular Jamaican colonial architecture. The buildings are a rainbow of peacock hues highlighting the separate architectural features of each building. Inside, concrete floors keep the spacious interiors cool. Each unit has a vaguely Victorian feel, with comfortable furnishings, plus a shower-only bathroom. There's a beachfront bar and grill, plus the only Chinese restaurant in Negril, the Hunan Garden, offering good-tasting, moderately priced dishes in a setting that evokes Shanghai during the British colonial era.

Norman Manley Blvd. (P.O. Box 39), Negril. ℂ **876/957-4273.** Fax 876/957-4342. www.countrynegril.com. 14 units. Dec 15–Apr 14 $145–$165 double; off season $115–$135 per night double. AE, MC, V. **Amenities:** Restaurant; bar; limited room service; nonsmoking rooms. *In room:* A/C, TV, fridge, hair dryer, safe, beverage maker.

Devine Destiny ℛ *Finds*   This is one of the best and best-designed resorts in the West End, utterly devoid of the funky-hippie motif that characterizes most of its competitors. Set in an isolated neighborhood 366m (1,200 ft.) from the sea and cliffs, it's a relatively large complex plunked down in the middle of a counterculture neighborhood that until quite recently shunned resorts.

   The architecture might remind you of an upscale hacienda in Argentina, with sprawling wings, terra cotta, tile work, mahogany furniture, and such decorative touches as a stone column in the lobby where water drips from a fountain. More than any of its competitors, this place gives the feeling of a coherently planned resort. There's a shuttle bus to Seven Mile Beach, which beats the 2-hour walk, and an on-site restaurant serves simple fare. Many clients here come on European group tours.

Summerset Rd., West End (P.O. Box 117), Negril. ℂ **876/957-9184.** Fax 876/957-3846. www.devinedestiny. com. 43 units. Winter $69–$119 double, $169 suite; off season $49–$74 double, $119 suite. Children 11 and under stay free in parent's room. AE, MC, V. **Amenities:** Restaurant; bar; outdoor pool; Jacuzzi; pool table; shuttle bus to beach; laundry service . *In room:* A/C, TV (in some units), kitchenette, safe (available to rent).

Drumville Cove Resort   Rooms at this rustic retreat are housed in cream-colored structures trimmed in brown (some are in pink), overlooking the sea near the lighthouse, while cottages are scattered throughout the property. All units have ceiling fans, though only seven rooms (and none of the cottages) are air-conditioned; five rooms offer TVs. Each unit is equipped with a small bathroom with shower and tub. Included on the property is a restaurant serving Jamaican specialties with a few American dishes. The nearest good beach is a 5-minute drive away (the hotel provides transportation), and there's a freshwater swimming pool for guest use.

West End Rd. (P.O. Box 72), Negril. (C) **876/957-4369.** Fax 876/957-0198. www.drumvillecove.com. 18 units. Winter $67–$112 double, $92–$112 cabana for up to 4; off season $45–$65 double, $60–$70 cabana for up to 4. AE, MC, V. **Amenities:** Restaurant; bar; outdoor pool; shuttle bus to beach; laundry service. *In room:* A/C (in some units), TV, kitchenette, iron/board, safe, no phone, ceiling fan.

Foote Prints in the Sand Dane and Audrey Foote started this enterprise in the mid-1980s; it has since expanded and occupies some of the choicest beach-front along Seven Mile's sandy stretch. The rooms, four of which contain kitchenettes, are tropically outfitted with hardwood furnishings, air-conditioning, and private bathrooms with shower and tub. The hotel restaurant serves three meals daily, specializing in Jamaican and American food. Barbecues and music liven up the place on Friday nights.

Norman Manley Blvd. (P.O. Box 100), Negril. (C) **888/790-5264** or 876/957-4300. Fax 876/957-4301. 30 units. Winter $135–$145 double, $165 double with kitchenette; off season $85–$95 double, $115 double with kitchenette. Extra person $30 in winter, $20 off season. MC, V. **Amenities:** Restaurant; bar; limited room service; babysitting; laundry service. *In room:* A/C, TV, kitchenette (some units), coffeemaker, hair dryer, iron/board.

Fun Holiday Beach Resort *(Kids)* In the center of Negril's Seven Mile Beach, this new resort was designed for fun in the sun. All its comfortably furnished bedrooms are spacious, each with two double beds and a first-class bathroom. Some of the accommodations have connecting doors, which can be unlocked if a family checks in and needs more space. The most desirable bedrooms open onto the ocean, the rest fronting the gardens. The rooms also have private patios or porches. There's a lot more to this place than a bed for the night. Its beach-front restaurant serves fresh and well-prepared seafood, with fish cooked as you like it, and 3 nights a week live reggae music is provided. The beach bar is also known for serving the best daiquiris along Seven Mile Beach. There is also an array of other activities which you can hook into, including jet-ski and banana-boat rides. There's a car-rental agency on-site.

Norman Manley Blvd., Negril. (C) **876/957-9688.** Fax 876/957-4693. www.funholidaybeachresort.com. 35 units. Winter $90–$140 double; off season $60–$120 double. Extra person $15. AE, MC, V. **Amenities:** Restaurant; bar; outdoor pool; watersports; car rental; limited room service; airport transfers arranged; live entertainment. *In room:* A/C, TV, kitchenette (in some units).

Home Sweet Home *(Finds)* This is a cozy, down-home place that almost re-creates Negril's hippie heyday. You might find your groove here just as writer Terry McMillan did; she visited while doing research for her novel *How Stella Got Her Groove Back.* "Home" is a concrete building with a garden with lots of greenery and flowering plants. When you see the bedrooms, you'll realize many visitors have slept here before you. All accommodations have ceiling fans, a radio and a cassette player, plus a balcony or veranda, but no TV or phone (only suites have a phone). Every unit is equipped with a small bathroom with shower. There's a sun deck on the cliffs, and you can swim, dive, or snorkel. A simple restaurant serves three inexpensive Jamaican meals a day.

West End Rd., Negril. (C) and fax **800/925-7418** in the U.S., or 876/957-4478. www.homesweethome resort.net. 14 units. Winter $100–$250 double, $200 penthouse; off season $74–$180 double, $150 penthouse. Extra person $15. Children 11 and under stay free in parent's room. AE, DC, MC, V. **Amenities:** Restaurant; bar; outdoor pool; Jacuzzi; bike rentals; 24-hr. room service; massage in room or on the cliff; babysitting; laundry service; rooms for those with limited mobility. *In room:* A/C, kitchenette, coffeemaker, safe, no phone.

Kuyaba *(Value)* This is one of the more appealing hotels along Negril's beach, with an artfully designed collection of bedrooms and a clientele that has included the ambassadors from both Mexico and Chile. It occupies a long and narrow strip of sandy soil stretched between the coastal road and the beach. Accommodations are within buff-colored, Iberian-inspired, two-story buildings that contain terra-cotta floors, mahogany four-poster beds, tub/shower bathrooms, lots of mahogany louvers and trim, and rates that—considering the quality of the rooms—are a relative bargain. The suites are an especially good value. Part of the appeal of this place derives from the in-house, beachfront restaurant, the Kuyaba. Permeated with a Polynesian whimsy, it has the most elaborately engineered setting of any restaurant on Negril's beach (see "Where to Dine," p. 107).

Norman Manley Blvd., Negril. ℂ 876/957-4318. Fax 876/957-9765. www.kuyaba.com. 18 units. Winter $62–$97 double, $106 suite; off season $48–$77 double, $85 suite. Extra person $12 per night. AE, MC, V. **Amenities:** Restaurant; bar. *In room:* A/C, TV (in some units), kitchenette (in some units), safe, no phone.

Negril Yoga Centre *Finds*   Set on 1.4 flat and verdant hectares (3½ acres) of thriving vegetation across the road from the beach, this place offers a collection of artfully mismatched accommodations that have evolved over time. It began as the original yoga school in Negril.

Three of the units lie within La Casa Blanca, a cement-sided building whose angularity evokes a work by Le Corbusier. The remaining units all lie within funky-looking wood-and-concrete cottages, each with a ceiling fan but no air-conditioning. Overall, the aura is artfully spartan and carefully synchronized with nature, permeated with a Zen-like calm. The social center is an open-aired pavilion where the owner teaches Hatha yoga for $10 per class. Meals cost from $6 to $15 and are served at 3 and 7pm, depending on which seating is available.

Norman Manley Blvd. (P.O. Box 48), Negril. ℂ and fax 876/957-4397. www.negrilyoga.com. 12 units. Winter $44–$70 double; off season $29–$58 double. MC, V. **Amenities:** Dining room; massage; nonsmoking rooms; rooms for those with limited mobility; yoga. *In room:* Kitchenette, fridge, no phone.

Our Past Time Villas *Value*   Picture this as a good value B&B on attractively landscaped grounds. In a town full of all-inclusive resorts, this is an oasis of independence for the self-sufficient type of visitor who likes renting a unit with a kitchenette and preparing some meals in house, although there's also a good alfresco restaurant on-site serving tasty Jamaican specialties. The location is choice as well, at the beginning of Seven Mile Beach. Accommodations here are fairly simple but tastefully decorated in a vaguely Caribbean motif, and each comes with a private balcony or a patio. The better units open onto views of the sea. Each rental contains a small bathroom with shower, and accommodations fall into three categories: a regular double room, a studio and kitchenette, and a two-bedroom apartment with kitchenette.

Norman Manley Blvd. (P.O. Box 45), Negril. ℂ 876/957-5422. Fax 876/957-5503. 17 units. Winter $100–$120 double, $110–$130 studio, $210–$240 2-bedroom apt; off season $50–$90 double, $70–$120 studio, $130–$200 2-bedroom apt. Additional person $20. MC, V. **Amenities:** Restaurant; bar; limited room service; babysitting; laundry service. *In room:* A/C (in most units), TV, kitchenette (in some units), safe.

Rock Cliff Hotel   This hotel is one of the better of the dozens of raffish guesthouses that lie among the palms and sea grapes west of Negril's center. Set atop a low cliff overlooking the sea, and popular with divers, it features two restaurants, two bars, and a Sunday-night all-you-can-eat lobster buffet. There's a pool on the premises, and you can inch your way down the cliff for sea dips offshore from the rocks, though most people trek 3km (1¾ miles) to the nearest beach. The suites (but not the conventional bedrooms) contain kitchenettes. The bedrooms have mahogany furniture, pastel-colored draperies, and off-white walls, plus small bathrooms with shower/tub combinations.

West End Rd. (P.O. Box 3065), Negril. © **876/957-4331.** Fax 876/957-4108. www.rockcliffhotel.com.jm.
33 units. Winter $132 double, $333 suite for 2; off season $70–$125 double, $240 suite for 2. AE, MC, V.
Amenities: 2 restaurants; 2 bars; pool; Jacuzzi; dive shop; babysitting; laundry service; volleyball; basketball.
In room: A/C, kitchenette (in some units), no phone.

Rockhouse ⨀   This funky boutique inn stands in stark contrast to hedonistic
all-inclusive resorts like Sandals, and it offers very affordable rates. It's a cross
between a South Seas island retreat and an African village, with thatched roofs
capping stone-and-pine huts. A team of enterprising young Aussies restored and
expanded this place, which was one of Negril's first hotels (the Rolling Stones
hung out here in the 1970s). The rooms have ceiling fans, four-poster beds
draped in mosquito netting, and open-air showers. All units contain queen-size
beds; and four cottages have sleeping lofts with extra queen-size beds. Less than
half a kilometer (¼ mile) from the beach, Rockhouse has a ladder down to a cove
where you can swim and snorkel. After a refreshing dip in the cliff-side pool, you
can dine in the open-sided restaurant pavilion, which serves excellent, spicy local
fare three times a day.

West End Rd. (P.O. Box 24), Negril. © **876/957-4373.** Fax 876/957-0557. www.rockhousehotel.com. 26
units. Winter $130 studio, $250 villa; off season $100 studio, $175 villa. Children age 11 and under stay free
in parent's room. AE, MC, V. **Amenities:** Restaurant; 2 bars; outdoor pool; snorkeling; nonsmoking rooms;
rooms for those with limited mobility. *In room:* A/C, minibar, hair dryer, iron/board, safe.

Thrills Resort   Southwest of the center of Negril, on sloping, palm-dotted land
that descends toward a rocky beach, this is a simple but well-managed resort. It's
set about .8km (½ mile) inland from the far-western end of West End Road, incon-
veniently uphill from the West End dining and drinking. It's small and receives lots
of English package tours. The centerpiece is a hexagonal tower set adjacent to a
low-slung motel-like complex containing the rooms, each simply decorated with
white walls, island-made mahogany furniture and louvered doors, shower-only
bathrooms, and tiled floors. An in-house restaurant serves international cuisine.

Beach lovers negotiate a 10-minute drive (or a 20-min. walk) eastward to the
famous sands of Negril's legendary beach, and Thrills also provides shuttle service. Snorkelers, however, find ample opportunities off the low cliffs and caves
along the coast. The resort has its own tennis courts and swimming pool, too,
and a wide range of dive shops and watersports are nearby.

West End (P.O. Box 99, Negril Post Office), Westmoreland. © **876/957-4390.** www.thrillsresort.com. 30
units. Winter $55 double; off season $45 double. MC, V. **Amenities:** Restaurant; bar; pool; tennis courts;
limited room service; shuttle bus to beach. *In room:* A/C, TV, iron/board, safe, no phone.

White Sands ⨀ *Kids*   This low-key property is informal and family-run, offering good value. Most of its bedrooms open onto the beach, although some less
desirable units are across the street. Accommodations range widely from a basic
double to a four-bedroom, four-bathroom villa with a pool. The smallest units
on the property, with either double beds or twins, attract the frugal traveler.
Deluxe rooms have vaulted ceilings and overlook the beach. Families prefer the
one-bedroom apartments, with a bedroom, living room, dining room, and
kitchen. Most units come with full bathroom with shower only. The four-
bedroom villa, across the road from the beach, is ideal for families or groups.
Families also appreciate that children 11 and under stay free.

Norman Manley Blvd. (P.O. Box 60), Negril. © **876/957-4291.** Fax 876/957-4674. www.whitesandsjamaica.
com. 40 units, 1 villa. Winter $89 double, $123 1-bedroom apt, $340 villa; off season $75 double, $92
1-bedroom apt, $240 villa. AE, DISC, MC, V. **Amenities:** Beach bar and grill; outdoor pool; game room; rooms
for those with limited mobility. *In room:* A/C, kitchen, fridge, coffeemaker, iron, no phone.

Xtabi   The land that's owned by this resort is bisected by West End Road in a way that places the simpler, less-expensive units on the landward side, and the larger, more-glamorous units (in this case, cottages) on a cliff above the sea. Units on the landward side have air-conditioning and efficient, unpretentious layouts and furnishings. Those near the sea don't have air-conditioning but are larger and benefit from more-direct access to sea breezes. All the units contain a neatly kept private bathroom with shower. If you stay here, don't expect direct access to a sandy beach. Ladders climb, somewhat precariously, down to a set of rock-sided inlets where the surf roils around during heavy seas. Safer and easier is a dip in the hotel's pool. The resort's social center is an octagonal bar area with a large ocean-fronting patio. Drinks are served at almost any hour of the day or night; lunches are simpler affairs of conch or salad; dinners are more elaborate, with grilled pork chops and filet mignon, lobster thermidor, and conch steaks.

Light House Rd., Negril. © **876/957-4336.** Fax 876/957-0827. www.xtabi-negril.com. 24 units. Winter $55–$65 double, $160 seafront cottage for 2; off season $45–$50 double, $110 seafront cottage for 2. Extra person $8–$12 each. AE, MC, V. **Amenities:** Restaurant; bar; pool; babysitting; laundry service. *In room:* A/C (in some units), kitchenette, iron, safe, no phone.

ALL-INCLUSIVE RESORTS

All-inclusive resorts fold the cost of lodging, meals, and often extras like drinks or sports into one price. The advantage of staying at one of these places is that you can more or less chart the cost of your vacation in advance, providing you don't spend a lot of extra money on entertainment, shopping, excursions, or transportation. Another element all-inclusives offer that most other properties, especially smaller ones, don't is security: Most of these resorts can afford to hire guards to protect the grounds 24 hours a day.

However, because you're paying for food in advance, you'll feel obligated to dine on-site every night—and the food tends to be unremarkable at best. If you view food as an integral part of your holiday, it might be better to check into a property where you are not a part of a meal plan.

Beaches Negril ⊛ *Kids*   One of the biggest resorts in Negril was established in 1997 as the family-oriented wing of the Sandals chain—an all-inclusive outfit that remains stoically opposed to allowing children in its other resorts. The resort occupies a highly desirable 8-hectare (20-acre) lot studded with palms and sea grapes adjacent to a sandy beach. At Beaches Negril you can either spend time with your kids or relax on the beach in the knowledge that they're entertained and supervised elsewhere, thanks to a roster of child and teen activities in segregated areas (where adults can enter only at their children's invitation, believe it or not). Accommodations are clustered in three individual villages, each of which is subdivided into a cluster of cement and wood buildings accented with cedar shingles. All units come equipped with midsize private bathrooms with tub or shower.

The resort's five restaurants include the unpretentious Blazing Paradise Beach Grill, and the formal Seville Room, where the standard Jamaican and international cuisine and the decor evoke Andalusia. There's live entertainment nightly, usually music from a local reggae band.

Norman Manley Blvd., Negril. © **800/BEACHES** or 876/957-9270. Fax 876/957-9269. 215 units. Winter $2,040–$2,760 double, $2,940–$6,391 suite for 2; off season $1,770–$2,580 double, $2,520–$5,880 suite for 2. Rates are all-inclusive for 3 nights. AE, MC, V. **Amenities:** 5 restaurants; 7 bars; 2 pools; 2 tennis courts; exercise room; Jacuzzi; 3 whirlpools; sauna; watersports; tour desk; massage; babysitting; laundry service; dry cleaning. *In room:* A/C, TV, coffeemaker, hair dryer, iron/ board, safe.

Beaches Sandy Bay ⟨R⟩ *(Kids)*   In the wake of 3.5 million dollars in renovation, this ocean-bordering resort reopened its doors in late 2003. Spread across 2.4 hectares (6 acres) of lush landscaping, it fronts 305m (1,000 ft.) of white-sand beach. Unlike many Negril resorts, which cater only to male/female couples or adults-only, this sprawling property caters to singles, couples, and families alike. The place never looked so good, especially in its retiled pool decks, jazzed up decorations, landscaping, and redecorated guest bedrooms. A nursery and a kids' camp has made Beaches more family-friendly than ever. Guests receive exchange privileges at Beaches Negril, a sibling resort, where scuba diving is included. Part of the Sandals family, the resort is laidback and casual. Since meals are included, it comes as good news that the hotel has hired an array of talented chefs to feed you well at various venues that feature both Italian and Caribbean fare—there's even a beachfront grill.

Norman Manley Blvd., Negril. ⟨C⟩ **800/BEACHES** or 876/957-5100. Fax 876/957-5229. www.beaches.com. 128 units. Winter $550–$610 double, $670–$970 suite; off season $490–$550 double, $610–$910 suite. 2-night minimum stay. Rates all-inclusive. **Amenities:** 3 restaurants; bar; 2 outdoor pools; 2 tennis courts; fitness center; watersports; kids activities; salon; laundry service/dry cleaning; entertainment; rooms for those with limited mobility. *In room:* A/C, TV, kitchenette (in some units), hair dryer, safe, beverage maker.

The Caves ⟨R⟩   Although the nearest beach is a 12-minute ride away, Negril's most atmospheric and elegant small inn still attracts international celebrities. In spite of its fame, however, there are drawbacks. There's a sense of snobbishness at this member of Chris Blackwell's Outpost hotels, generally the finest in the Caribbean, and the prices are very high compared to the competition. The hotel is on ¾ of a hectare (2 acres) of land that's perched above a honeycombed network of cliffs, 10m (32 ft.) above the surf on a point near Negril's lighthouse, close to Jamaica's westernmost tip. The setting, though lavishly publicized, is difficult to negotiate with its stairwells and catwalks.

Accommodations, well suited for groups of friends traveling together, are in breezy units within five cement and wood-sided cottages, each with a thatched roof and sturdy furniture. Matisse could have designed them. None has air-conditioning, and the windows are without screens. A TV and VCR can be brought in if you request them. Many of the units contain alfresco showers.

Sumptuous meals are prepared only for guests and are included, along with domestic Jamaican drinks from the bar, as part of the all-inclusive price.

P.O. Box 313, Lighthouse Station, Negril. ⟨C⟩ **800/OUT-POST** in the U.S. and Canada, or 876/957-0270. Fax 876/957-4930. www.islandoutpost.com. 10 units. Year-round $445–$575 double. Rates include all meals and self-service bar. AE, MC, V. No one under 18 allowed. **Amenities:** 2 restaurants; bar; saltwater pool; spa; Jacuzzi; sauna; snorkeling equipment; bikes; airport transfers; laundry service; nonsmoking rooms. *In room:* Dataport, minibar, hair dryer, iron/board, safe, beverage maker, ceiling fan.

Couples Negril ⟨R⟩   If you're a man and a woman in love (others stay away!), you're welcomed at this romantic resort, lying on 300m (1,000 ft.) of white-sand beach, 8km (5 miles) from the center of Negril. The formula worked in Ocho Rios (p. 140), so it was repeated here. A rival of Sandals properties, this love nest is the site of many weddings and honeymoons. On 7 hectares (18 acres) facing crescent-shaped Negril Harbour, this resort caters to those who want back-to-back scheduled activities, ranging from tennis tournaments to fashion shows. Each good-size unit has a king-size bed and a CD player (bring your own tunes), plus a balcony or patio with a view of the bay or of the lush gardens. Furnishings, though standard, are comfortable, and everything is new, including the shower/tub combination bathrooms. The best doubles are the deluxe beachfront suites, which have Jacuzzis and hammocks. No building in the complex is higher than the tallest coconut tree. On the east side of the property, nude sunbathing is permitted.

The food is good, and you have a choice of three restaurants, including Otaheite, serving a Caribbean fusion cuisine. Mediterranean and Continental menus are also served. A resident band plays nightly and there's special entertainment planned throughout the week, including Caribbean dinner buffets with music.

Bloody Bay, Negril. © **800/COUPLES** in the U.S., or 876/957-5960. Fax 876/957-5858. www.couples.com. 234 units. All-inclusive rates for 3 nights: winter $1,590–$2,780 double, from $2,070 suite for 2; off season $1,470–$1,750 double, from $1,590 suite for 2. Rates include all meals, drinks, and activities. AE, DC, MC, V. No one under 18 allowed. **Amenities:** 3 restaurants; 5 bars; 2 outdoor pools; golf; 14 tennis courts; fitness room with aerobics classes; watersports; dive shop; glass-bottom-boat trips; Sunfish sailing; game room; tour desk; limited room service; laundry service; basketball court. *In room:* A/C, TV, minibar (in some units), coffeemaker, hair dryer, iron/board, safe.

Couples Swept Away Negril ★★ This is one of the best beachside hotels in Negril—it's certainly the one most conscious of both sports and relaxation. All-inclusive, it caters to singles and couples eager for an ambience of all possible diversions available but absolutely no organized schedule and no pressure to participate if you just want to relax. As a staff member told us (privately, of course), "We get the health-and-fitness nuts, and Sandals or Hedonism get the sex crazed." The resort occupies 8 flat and sandy hectares (20 acres), which straddle both sides of the highway leading in from Montego Bay.

The accommodations (the hotel calls them "veranda suites" because of their large balconies) are in 26 two-story villas clustered together and accented with flowering shrubs and vines, a few steps from the 11km (6¾-mile) beachfront. Each lovely, airy, and spacious unit has a ceiling fan, a king-size bed, and (unless the vegetation obscures it) sea views. Wooden shutters let sunlight and breezes in. Units contain showers only.

The cuisine here is more health conscious and of better quality than that served at Sandals and Hedonism II. The resort's social center is its international restaurant, Feathers, which lies inland, across the road from the sea. There's also an informal beachfront restaurant and bar, plus a veggie bar serving fresh fruit, juices, pita sandwiches, salads, and vegetarian dishes.

Norman Manley Blvd. (P.O. Box 3077), Negril. © **800/COUPLES** in the U.S. and Canada, or 876/957-4061. Fax 876/957-4040. www.sweptaway.com. 134 units. Winter $530–$665 double; off season $485–$620 double. Rates are all-inclusive. Ask about spa packages. AE, MC, V. Children under 18 not accepted. **Amenities:** 3 restaurants; 5 bars; 2 outdoor pools; 10 tennis courts; racquetball; squash; health club and spa; 2 Jacuzzis; sauna; glass-bottom-boat trips; sailing; scuba diving; sea kayaking; snorkeling; water-skiing; windsurfing; bikes; tour desk; airport transfers; room service (continental breakfast only); laundry service. *In room:* A/C, TV, coffeemaker; hair dryer, iron/board, safe.

Grand Lido *(Overrated* The Grand Lido sits on a landscaped 8.9-hectare (22-acre) stretch of beachfront adjacent to the more raucous Hedonism II. Although it is touted as the most upscale of Jamaica's SuperClubs resorts, it falls far below expectations. The impersonal lobby evokes an airplane hangar and sets the tone for a largely impersonal place lacking good service or quality cuisine.

Rooms aren't bad, though. Each spacious suite contains either a patio or a balcony that (except for a few) overlooks the beach. Most units are split-level, with CD players, king or twin beds, and large bathrooms with tubs and showers. The elegant hardwood furniture in the rooms was handmade in Jamaica. In addition to a cavernous main dining room, a trio of restaurants serves pedestrian cuisine. Guests can also sample an all-night disco, piano bar, pool tables, and nine bars.

The best restaurant here is the Piacere, but it's hard to get a table when the house is full. Even after the six restaurants close, there are three different dining enclaves that remain open throughout the night. Note that the smaller of the resort's two beaches is reserved for nudists; if you don't like looking at nude bathers out your window, ask for a "swimwear-side" unit. Also, children are not allowed here; only couples and singles over 15 years old.

Bloody Bay (P.O. Box 88), Negril. © 877/GO-SUPER in the U.S., 800/701-5923 in Canada, or 876/957-5010. Fax 876/518-5148. www.grandlido.com. 210 units. Winter $1,793–$2,920 suite for 2; off season $1,634–$2,570 suite for 2. Rates are all-inclusive for 4 days/3 nights. Minimum stay of 4 days/3 nights. AE, MC, V. Children not accepted. **Amenities:** 6 restaurants; 3 all-night eateries; 9 bars; disco; 2 outdoor pools; 4 tennis courts; gym; health club; spa facility; 4 Jacuzzis; sauna; pool tables; business center; salon; 24-hr. room service; laundry service; nonsmoking rooms; rooms for those with limited mobility. *In room:* A/C, TV, minibar (in some units), hair dryer, safe.

Hedonism II ⚜   Devoted to the pursuit of sophomoric pleasure, and with less class than Couples Negril, Hedonism II packs the works into a one-package deal, including all the drinks and partying anyone could want. The complex lies at the northern end of Negril Beach. Of all the members of the SuperClubs chain, this is the most raucous. It's a meat market, deliberately inviting its mainly single guests to go wild for a week. One manager boasted that the resort holds the record for the most people in a Jacuzzi at once.

The rooms are stacked in dull two-story clusters dotted around a sloping 9-hectare (22-acre) site about 3km (1¾ miles) east of the town center. This is not a couples-only resort—singles are both accepted and encouraged. The hotel will find you a roommate if you'd like to book on the double-occupancy rate. Accommodations don't have balconies but are very spacious. Each has a king-size or twin beds fitted with fine linen and with mirrors hanging over the beds. Each bathroom has a shower/tub combination.

On one section of this resort's beach, clothing is optional. It's called the "Nude" section; the other is known as "the Prude." The resort also has a secluded beach on nearby Booby Cay, where guests are taken twice a week for picnics.

There's nightly entertainment, along with a live band, a high-energy disco, and a piano bar. International cuisine, a bit bland, is served in daily buffets. There's also a clothing-optional bar, a prude bar, and a grill.

Negril Beach Rd. (P.O. Box 25), Negril. © 800/859-7873 in the U.S., or 876/957-5070. Fax 876/957-5214. www.superclubs.com. 280 units. All-inclusive rates: winter $234–$581 double; off season $374–$445 double. Rates include all meals, drinks, and activities. AE, DC, DISC, MC, V. Children not accepted. **Amenities:** 4 restaurants; 6 bars; 2 grills; 2 outdoor pools; dance club; 6 tennis courts; 2 badminton courts; 2 indoor squash courts; exercise rooms; sauna; dive shop; glass-bottom-boat rides; sailing; scuba diving; snorkeling; water-skiing; windsurfing; free airport transfers; Internet cafe; massage; nonsmoking rooms; 1 room for those with limited mobility; basketball court; volleyball court; aerobics. *In room:* A/C, coffeemaker, hair dryer, safe.

Negril Inn ⚜   About 5km (3 miles) east of the town center in the heart of the 11km (6¾-mile) beach stretch, this is one of the smallest and most reasonably priced all-inclusive resorts in Negril. Because of its size, it's very low-key. The resort, not confined to couples only, offers very simple but comfortably furnished

---

(*Fun Fact* **The Naked Truth**

Nude bathing is allowed at a number of hotels, clubs, and beaches (especially in Negril), but only where there are SWIMSUITS OPTIONAL signs. Elsewhere, the law will not even allow topless sunbathing.

guest rooms with private balconies, in a series of two-story structures in a garden setting. Each unit has a small tiled bathroom with a shower/tub combination.

Included in the package are all meals, all alcoholic drinks (except champagne), and nightly entertainment. The restaurant is rather good.

Norman Manley Blvd. (P.O. Box 59), Negril. © 876/957-4209. Fax 876/957-4365. www.negril.com. 46 units. Winter $240 double, $300 triple; off season $180 double, $210 triple. Rates are all-inclusive, including airport transfers. AE, MC, V. Children not accepted in winter. **Amenities:** Restaurant; bar; outdoor pool; 2 tennis courts; fitness center; Jacuzzi; airport transfers; room service (breakfast only); laundry service; nonsmoking rooms piano room. *In room:* A/C, hair dryer, iron/board, no phone.

Point Village Resort *Kids*
This condo complex is especially family-friendly, so couples with children make up a large part of the clientele. The inn lies between the larger resorts of Grand Lido and Hedonism II. Of the two beaches fronting the hotel, one is clothing-optional. This is just fine with the many German families who check in here; however, other families who object to nudity might want to seek different accommodations. The resort is a cluster of three-story, tile-roofed buildings nestled within the edges of a 5.6-hectare (14-acre) sandy peninsula dotted with sea grapes and salt-resistant shrubs. (The strip is narrow, though, and separated from the broader sands of Seven Mile Beach by a barrier.) You can opt for all-inclusive rates or, if you want to cook some of your meals yourself—all units contain a kitchenette—you can skip the meal plan. Babysitting services and child care are provided without charge each day from 8:30am to 5:30pm, after which "childminders" can be arranged for $5 per child per hour.

Rutland Point (P.O. Box 105), Negril. © **877/POINTJA** or 876/957-5170. Fax 876/957-5351. www.point village.com. 256 units, 143 of which are available for rentals. Winter $300 double, $370 suite for 2; off season $248 double, $268 suite for 2. Rates are all-inclusive. AE, MC, V. **Amenities:** 3 restaurants; 3 bars; 3 pools; Jacuzzi; Internet cafe; babysitting; coin-operated laundry. *In room:* A/C, TV, kitchenette, fridge, safe.

Sandals Negril Beach Resort & Spa *R*
On 5 hectares (13 acres) of prime beachfront land a short drive east of the center of Negril, Sandals Negril is an all-inclusive, couples-only (male-female) resort that attracts a basically young, convivial, and unsophisticated audience. It's far more active and freewheeling than the more formal Sandals properties in Ocho Rios and Montego Bay. The casual, well-furnished rooms have a tropical motif. Recently renovated, they come in a wide range of styles, but are generally spacious, each with a marble bathroom with a shower/tub combination. The best units open directly onto the beach. Honeymooners usually end up in a Jamaican-built four-poster mahogany bed. For a balcony and sea view, you have to pay the top rates.

Rates include all meals; snacks; unlimited drinks, day and night, at one of four bars (including two swim-up pool bars); and nightly entertainment, including theme parties. Coconut Cove is the main dining room, but guests can also eat at one of the specialty rooms. The Sundowner offers white-glove service and Jamaican cuisine, and low-calorie health food is served beside the beach. Kimono features Japanese cuisine. In the typical Sandals style, the food is rather standard, but there is great variety and no one goes hungry.

Norman Manley Blvd., Negril. © **800/SANDALS** in the U.S. and Canada, or 876/957-5216. Fax 876/957-5338. www.sandals.com. 223 units. All-inclusive rates: winter $335–$415 double, $430–$650 suite; off season $325–$400 double, $430–$650 suite. Rates include all meals, drinks, and activities. AE, DISC, MC, V. Children under 16 not accepted. **Amenities:** 5 restaurants; 4 bars; 2 outdoor pools; 4 tennis courts; fitness center with saunas, canoeing; scuba diving; snorkeling; Sunfish sailing; windsurfing; airport transfers; limited room service; massage; coin-operated laundry; nonsmoking rooms; aerobics classes. *In room:* A/C, TV, minibar (in some units), hair dryer, iron/board, safe, beverage maker.

3 Where to Dine

Negril has more raffish, fun dining spots than anywhere else in Jamaica; this town makes some of the dining spots in Mo Bay look duller than a British teahouse.

The best item on almost any menu is fresh fish (it's often fried, but you can usually get it grilled). Jerk chicken is another popular local dish. Pasta is found on almost every menu. Finally, you'll find more vegetarian options here than anywhere else in the country. Don't be surprised to even occasionally encounter ganja cakes on some menus in the West End. (Yes, they *are* hallucinogenic—and technically illegal to consume.)

EXPENSIVE

Le Vendôme 🀄 JAMAICAN/FRENCH   This place some 6km (3¾ miles) from the town center enjoys a good reputation. You don't have to be a hotel guest to sample the cuisine, which owners Daniel and Sylvia Grizzle describe as a "dash of Jamaican spices" with a "pinch of French flair." Dine out on the terracotta terrace, with its view of the swaying palms on the beach. Start off with a homemade pâté, or perhaps a fresh-vegetable salad, and then follow with baked snapper, duckling à l'orange, or a seafood platter. Wines and champagnes are imported from France.

In the Charela Inn, Negril Beach. ℂ **876/957-4648.** Reservations recommended for Sat dinner. Continental breakfast $5; English breakfast $10; main courses $25–$39; fixed-price meal $26–$39. AE, MC, V. Daily 7:30am–9:30pm.

Norma's 🀄🀄 INTERNATIONAL/JAMAICAN   Norma Shirley is hailed as the finest chef in Jamaica (also see "Norma's on the Terrace," on p. 198). Having closed down in Montego Bay, she now operates this eatery in Negril. Although Norma is not likely to be on the premises when you arrive, the chefs use her recipes for their inspiration—a cookery characterized by such regional products as callaloo (a spinachlike vegetable), papaya, and corn-fed free-range chicken. The menu is seasonally adjusted; offerings might include lobster tails, jerk chicken, grilled Atlantic salmon, perfectly cooked rack of lamb, savory Cornish game hen, or delicately poached salmon.

In the Sea Splash Resort, Norman Manley Blvd. ℂ **876/957-4041.** Reservations recommended. Breakfast $4.95–$8.95; lunch main courses $5.95–$21; dinner main courses $13–$25. AE, DC, MC, V. Daily 7:30–10:30pm.

Rick's Café 🀄 SEAFOOD/STEAKS   At sundown, everybody in Negril heads toward the lighthouse along the West End strip to Rick's Café, whether they want a meal or not. Of course, the name was inspired by the old watering hole of Bogie's *Casablanca.* There was a real Rick (Richard Hershman), who first opened this bar back in 1974, but he's long gone. This laid-back cafe was made famous in the 1970s as a hippie hangout, and ever since it's attracted the bronzed and the beautiful (and some who want to be). Management claims the sunset here is the most glorious in Negril, and after a few fresh-fruit daiquiris, you'll agree with them. (Actually, the sunset is just as spectacular at any of the waterfront hangouts in Negril, if nothing is blocking the view.) Casual dress is the order of the day, and reggae and rock comprise the background music. If you want dinner, you can order imported steaks along with a complete menu of blackened dishes, Cajun style. The fish (red snapper, fresh lobster, or grouper) is always fresh. The food is rather standard, and expensive for what you get, but that doesn't keep the touristy crowds away from the sunset party. You can also buy plastic bar tokens at the door, which you can use instead of money, a la Club Med. A bit tacky, we'd say. Bogie would never have tolerated this.

West End Rd. (C) 876/957-0380. Reservations accepted for parties of 6 or more. Main courses $19–$28. AE, MC, V. Daily noon–10pm.

Rockhouse Restaurant ⚜ INTERNATIONAL   This is a gorgeous setting for enjoying some of the best food in Negril. Set on the premises of the previously recommended Rockhouse, it was developed by a team of Australian and Italian entrepreneurs who designed a bridgelike span, equivalent to a railway trestle, high above the surging tides of a rocky inlet on Negril's West End. You may get a touch of vertigo if you lean over the railing. This place attracts a hip international crowd. Enjoy a drink or two at the bar, which is built with glossy tropical hardwoods and coral stone, before your meal. Menu items, which are always supplemented with daily specials, might include a seasonal platter of smoked marlin or an upscale version of Jamaican peppered pork with yams.

In the Rockhouse, West End Rd. (C) 876/957-4373. Reservations required for dinner in high season, otherwise not necessary. Main courses $9.50–$27. AE, MC, V. Daily 7am–10:30pm.

MODERATE

Da Gino's ITALIAN   Four octagonal, open-sided dining pavilions, separated from Negril's beachfront by a strip of trees, evolved as the escapist dream of Gino Travaini, the Italy-born owner. Pastas and bread are made fresh daily. The best chef's specialties feature linguine with lobster, filet of beef with peppercorns, various forms of scaloppine, and huge platters of grilled seafood.

On the premises are a dozen very simple huts, each octagonal, rustic, and camplike, that rent for between $60 and $120 each, double occupancy, depending on the season. Each has a TV, a very basic kitchenette, and a ceiling fan but no air-conditioning.

In the Hotel Mariposa Hideaway, Norman Manley Blvd. (C) 876/957-4918. Reservations recommended. Main courses $13–$26. MC, V. Daily 8am–10pm.

Gambino's ⚜ ITALIAN   Adjacent to the more visible and better-known Margaritaville, with an outdoor deck that opens directly onto the sands of the beach, this restaurant mixes Jamaican and Italian food better than almost any other eatery in Negril. You might begin with a psychedelic house special drink (they include Beachcomber's rum punch, a Miami Vice, and a strawberry daiquiri); then head for a chair at one of the wrought-iron tables for a meal. Menus here run to fresh salads, grilled fish, spaghetti Alfredo, veal or chicken parmigiana, and a very good version of fettuccine with lobster.

In the Beachcomber Club Hotel, Norman Manley Blvd. (C) 876/957-4170. Reservations recommended for dinner, not necessary at lunch. Lunch burgers, salads, and platters $6–$12; dinner main courses $8–$25. AE, MC, V. Daily 7:30–11am, noon–3pm, and 7–10:30pm.

Hungry Lion ⚜ *Finds* RASTAFARIAN/INTERNATIONAL   Some of the best seafood and vegetarian dishes are found at this laid-back alfresco hangout on the cliffs. Instead of the usual Red Stripe beer, you can visit the juice bar and sample the tropical punches with or without rum. Menus change daily, depending on what's available in the local markets. About seven main courses are offered nightly—mostly seafood and vegetarian platters, featuring grilled kingfish steak and pan-fried snapper. Lobster is prepared in many different ways, and everything is accompanied by rice and peas along with steamed vegetables. The homemade desserts are luscious, especially the pineapple-carrot cake, our favorite.

West End Rd. ⓒ 876/957-4486. Main courses $9–$20. AE, MC, V. Daily 5:30–11pm.

LTU Pub INTERNATIONAL   Built from concrete, with an outside that's painted red and white, the place doubles as a simple 10-room hotel. But it's best known for the restaurant, atop a cliff 11m (35 ft.) above the sea. Meals might consist of grilled fish, especially snapper filets, several different preparations of shrimp, grilled steaks, burgers, or salads, including an especially flavorful version made with lobster. You'll find this place around the corner from Rick's Café.

The 10 rooms at this hotel occupy five concrete "villas" set within the garden; all have air-conditioning and ceiling fans; none has TV or phone.

West End Rd. ⓒ 876/957-0382. Sandwiches and salads $4–$15; main courses $10–$22. AE, MC, V. Daily 7:30am–11pm.

INEXPENSIVE

Chicken Lavish ⭐ *Finds* JAMAICAN   We've found that Chicken Lavish, whose name we love, is the best of the low-budget eateries in Negril. Just show up on the doorstep of this place along the West End beach strip and see what's cooking. Curried goat is a specialty, as is fresh fried fish. The red snapper is caught in local waters. But the big draw is the restaurant's namesake, the chef's special Jamaican chicken. It's amazingly consistent, fried or served with curry or sweet-and-sour sauce. He'll tell you, and you may agree, that it's the best on the island. Ironically, this utterly unpretentious restaurant has achieved something like cult status among counterculture travelers who have eaten here since the 1970s. You can dine on the roofed veranda, or ask for takeout.

West End Rd. ⓒ 876/957-4410. Main courses $4.50–$10. MC, V. Daily 10am–10pm.

Choices JAMAICAN   This no-frills, open-air restaurant offers local food in a bustling atmosphere. This is a clapboard-sided roadside hut painted in bright reggae colors of blue, green, and yellow. Customer seating is on plastic tables and chairs beneath an open-air parapet. The food is simple and portions are hearty. Breakfast includes ackee and salt cod prepared with Jamaican spices, onions, green peppers, and tomatoes. Daily soup specials might include conch, pumpkin, or red pea. For a real island experience, try spicy jerk chicken, fish, or pork. Other dishes might include stewed beef, curried goat, or a dish of oxtail. Most dishes come with salad and a vegetable.

West End Rd. ⓒ 876/957-4841. Lunch main courses J$100–J$230 (US$1.65–US$3.80); dinner main courses J$250–J$800 (US$4.15–US$13). No credit cards. Daily 7am–11pm.

Cosmo's Seafood Restaurant & Bar ⭐ *Finds* SEAFOOD/JAMAICAN   One of the best places to go for local seafood enters on a Polynesian thatched *bohío* (beach hut) open to the sea and bordering the main beachfront. In this rustic setting, Cosmo Brown entertains locals and visitors. You can order his famous conch soup, or conch in a number of other ways, including steamed or curried. He's also known for his savory kettle of curried goat, or you might prefer freshly caught seafood or fish, depending on what the catch turned up. Unless you order shellfish, most dishes are rather inexpensive.

Norman Manley Blvd. ⓒ 876/957-4784. Main courses $5–$15. AE, MC, V. Daily 9am–10pm.

Juicy J's JAMAICAN   The more you look at this place, the more you'll probably like it. At breakfast, try ackee and salt fish or fish stewed in brown sauce and served with plantain—a fine, thoughtfully prepared example of what most Jamaicans consider standard morning fare. To acclimate yourself, head past the mismatched chairs and tables of the front rooms to the pinewood bar in back, meet the staff, and have a glass of fruit punch, coffee, beer, or rum. Then select from a list of good-tasting food that includes grilled, steamed, or (our favorite) *escoveitch* of fish; four different preparations of chicken, including a version with curry; lasagna; or lobster.

Negril Sq. (behind Scotia Bank). ℭ 876/957-4213. Breakfast platters J$180–J$301 (US$3–US$5); lunch and dinner main courses J$250–J$900 (US$4.15–US$15). MC, V. Daily 7am–11pm.

Kuyaba on the Beach ⭐ *Value* INTERNATIONAL   The setting is about as rustic, laid-back, and funky as you'll find—the perfect venue for slugging back two or three of the house special cocktails, which include "screaming bananas" and a party-colored, rum-based concoction known as a "kuyaba rainbow." Tables are set on a wooden deck, built on poles buried deep in the sands of the beach. The menu has been considerably improved—better market-fresh ingredients and more flavor. Starters that are specialties include jerk sausage served with shrimp wrapped in bacon, or a bowl of "real Jamaica"—a choice of red peas (actually beans), cream of pumpkin, or pepper pot. Pasta dishes are winning, especially conch-laced spaghetti with a garlic, wine, and tomato sauce or angel-hair pasta studded with cream. Caribbean lobster is a standard feature. Some of our favorite dishes include crab and pumpkin cakes with a papaya mustard, or coconut curried conch with a mango-and-papaya chutney. For dessert, there's nothing finer than the Jamaican rum cake or the mango cheese cake. The name is Arawak for "feasting, drinking, and dancing," something that happens whenever a musician drops by to play some live reggae or soca.

In the Hotel Kuyaba, Norman Manley Blvd. ℭ 876/957-4318. Main courses $10–$23; sandwiches and salads $6–$9. AE, MC, V. Daily 8am–11pm.

Margaritaville AMERICAN/INTERNATIONAL   It's practically Disney gone Jamaican at this rowdy bar, restaurant, and entertainment complex. Thanks to the loaded buses that pull in for a field trip from some of Negril's all-inclusive hotels, it's a destination in its own right. People party here all day and night. There's an on-site art gallery where most of the works are by the very talented U.S.-born artist Geraldine Robbins, and at the gift shops you might actually be tempted to buy something. Every evening beginning around 9pm, there's live music or perhaps karaoke. Permanently moored a few feet offshore is a pair of Jamaica's largest trampolines, whale-size floaters that feature high-jumping contests by any participant whose cocktails haven't affected them yet. Rock climbing is also available. Drinks are deceptively potent. In all this party atmosphere, you don't expect the food to be that good, but it might happily surprise, even though it consists of such fare as shrimp-and-tuna kebobs. You'll find Southern fried chicken, along with the standard club steaks and burgers.

Norman Manley Blvd. ℭ 876/957-4467. Burgers and sandwiches $8.75–$9.75. Main courses $12–$25. AE, MC, V. Daily 8am–11pm.

Sweet Spice ⭐ *Kids* JAMAICAN   This is everybody's favorite mom-and-pop eatery, a real local hangout. It's set beside the road leading south out of Negril, within a clapboard-sided house that seems to grow bigger each year, and which is painted an electric shade of blue. Food is simple, cheap, and bountiful, served amid a decor of plastic tablecloths, tile floors, and windows covered with louvers and screens (but without glass). The Whytes welcome guests warmly and serve portions that are large, satisfying, and home-style. Bring Grandma, Mom, Dad, the kids—many Jamaican families do. You get what's on the stove or in the kettle that night, perhaps the fresh catch of the day or a conch steak. The grilled chicken is done to perfection, and shrimp is steamed and served with garlic butter or cooked in coconut cream. A number of curry dishes tempt, including concoctions made with goat, lobster, and chicken. Meals come with freshly cooked, Jamaica-grown vegetables. The fruit juices served here in lieu of alcoholic beverages are truly refreshing, and the menu is the same at lunch and dinner.

1 White Hall Rd. ℂ 876/957-4621. Reservations not accepted. Main courses J$200–J$1,000 (US$3.30–US$17). MC, V. Daily 9am–11pm.

4 Hitting the Beach & Other Outdoor Pursuits

BEACHES
HITTING THE BEACH
Beloved by the hippies of the 1960s, **Seven Mile Beach** 🏝🏝 is still as beautiful as ever, but it's no longer the idyllic retreat it once was. Resorts now line this beach, attracting an international crowd. Nudity, however, is just as prevalent: This beach promotes a laid-back lifestyle and carefree ambience more than any other in Jamaica or, perhaps, in the Caribbean. Clean aquamarine waters, coral reefs, and a backdrop of palm trees add to the appeal. When you tire of the beach, you'll find all sorts of resorts, clubs, beach bars, open-air restaurants, and the like. Vendors hawk everything from Red Stripe beer to ganja.

Except for the crowds and harassment, this is one of the prettiest beaches in Jamaica—though the harassment can be a big turnoff. One Frommer's reader found the constant hassle "high-octane—never ending. I was offered everything almost on an hourly basis from the hustler himself to drugs. A simple 'no' often wouldn't do."

In the spirit of the place, topless bathing is common along the entire stretch of the beach, although a small section near Cosmo's Restaurant officially condones total nudity. Many of the big resorts also have nude beaches. The hottest and most exotic is found at **Hedonism II,** although **Grand Lido** next door draws its fair share. When these hotels rent "rooms with a view," theirs is no idle promise: Nude beaches at each of these resorts are in separate and "private" areas of the resort property. Security guards keep Peeping Toms at bay; photography is not permitted. Most of the resorts also have a nude bar, a nude hot tub, and a nude swimming pool.

If you want to escape the hair-braiders, hustlers, aloe masseurs, nude bodies, reggae music, and the rest, escape to **Long Bay Beach Park** at the far northern end of Negril Beach. Out beyond the hotel belt, this stretch of beach is set against a backdrop of picnic tables and changing rooms. We've found it the least crowded of all Negril's beaches, even during the busy winter months. On our latest visit, we didn't even detect a whiff of ganja here.

If you have kids in tow, take them to **Anancy Fun Park** on Norman Manley Boulevard, close to the Poinciana Beach Resort. It offers an array of activities ranging from miniature golf to a merry-go-round, train ride, pedal boating, fishing, and other attractions. The park is open daily from sunup to sundown, charging no admission—you are charged, however, for rides or activities. The park is corny but recommended for children.

A favorite retreat for us—and we're letting you in on a secret—is the half-moon-shaped **Bloody Bay Beach** 🏝 lying beyond Long Bay Beach Park. Nude bathers do frequent the place, and because of its relative emptiness there is some danger of a possible mugging or theft, even during the day. That's the only downside; otherwise, it's wonderful. Use the center of the beach, near an open-air barbecue where the smell of jerk pork permeates the air.

BIKE TOURS

Rusty's X-cellent Adventures, Hilton Avenue, P.O. Box 104 (© 876/957-0155), choreographs some of Jamaica's most hair-raising and best-conceived bike tours. The outfit was founded by Ohio-born Rusty Jones. Tours begin and end at his house, on a side road (Hilton Ave.) just west of Negril's lighthouse. He's the region's expert on the dozens of relatively dry—that is, not muddy—single-track goat and cow paths that provide aerobic exercise and drama for all levels of bike riders. Customized tours last between 2 and 4 hours, cost $35 per person, and never include more than four riders at a time. Tours are primarily geared to "hard-core mountain bikers," even though there are ample opportunities for newcomers to the sport, as well. There's a running commentary on cultural and horticultural diversions en route. Bikes, helmets, water canteens, and accessories are included in the price as part of the experience; advance reservations are essential.

You can also rent a bike and explore at will, although you're not likely to find as dramatic scenery as you will on a guided tour. See "Getting Around Negril," on p. 91 for more details on renting bicycles.

BOATING

Boating is a major sport in Negril, but you don't see a lot of large craft, especially fishing vessels, prevalent on the North Coast. In Negril, visitors mainly take to the waters in canoes, runabouts, and dugouts. The major hotels rent Sailfish, Sunfish, and windsurfers.

The best outfitter is **Aqua Nova Water Sports** at the Negril Beach Club (© 876/957-4754). Its program features an array of activities, including a morning snorkel and lunch cruise, an island picnic, a sunset snorkel cruise, and a clothing-optional cruise. It also offers the best array of watersports, including fishing trips, jet skiing, WaveRunners, water-skiing, parasailing, and glass-bottom reef trips.

Depending on what you want to do, prices are wide-ranging, with fishing trips being the most expensive. You can, for example, take the morning snorkel lunch cruise for $55, the sunset snorkel cruise for $65, or a glass-bottom reef trip for $25. Parasailing costs $35, and a 4-hour fishing trip costs about $400.

GOLF

Negril Hills Golf Course, Sheffield Road (© 876/957-4638), is Negril's only golf course. Although it doesn't have the cachet of such Montego Bay courses as Tryall, it's your only choice in western Jamaica. The 91-hectare (225-acre) course lies in the foothills of Negril at Sheffield, 5km (3 miles) east of the resort. The course is known for its water hazards and undulating fairways. This is one place where if your ball goes into the water, you shouldn't try to retrieve it—unless you want to fight a crocodile for it. On-site are a restaurant (the food is mediocre) and pro shop.

HORSEBACK RIDING

Check out **Country Western Horse Rental** (© 876/955-7910), Bay Road, Little London. Here you can go for a 2-hour ride for $50. Rides follow the coastline before venturing into the Negril Hills. See **Rhodes Hall Plantation** under "Exploring the Area," below, for yet another option.

SCUBA DIVING & SNORKELING

Negril offers some of the best and most challenging underwater life for scuba divers of any resort in Jamaica. There are no really deep walls prevalent along the North Coast, but the offshore reefs here teem with marine life. Many of them are shallow, making them ideal for neophytes who want to break into the sport. Even in front of Seven Mile Beach are undercuts and caverns, attracting the diver or snorkeler.

The most famous dive site is **"The Throne Room"** ⚘, with a depth ranging from 12 to 21m (40–70 ft.). The site enables divers to enter at one end and ascend into the open air at the other. The orange elephant ear sponges that flourish here are the largest we've ever seen in Jamaica.

The Sands Reef Club, named after a nearby hotel, has a depth range of 12 to 24m (40–80 ft.). This shallow reef drops off to a sandy shelf, and is noted for its purplish sea fans and its gorgonians and coral heads. There is much to see here, from black durgeons to tube sponges, from squirrelfish to goatfish.

With a depth of 12 to 21m (40–70 ft.), **"The Caves"** indeed consists of sea caverns—one large, the other small. There is a linking tunnel between the two. Black coral and sponges grow in profusion along with gorgonians. There is a sea kingdom of other residents, too, including sea cucumbers and stingrays.

Long a favorite with divers, **Kingfish Point** ⚘, with depths of around 27m (90 ft.), lures the most experienced divers because of its depths. The marine life here is the most varied of the dive sites, including both the elephant ear and the yellow tube sponge, the hogfish and the damselfish, along with both brain and star coral and marigold-colored crinoids. The huge boulders of star coral are among the most dramatic along the coast, along with deepwater sea fans and sea plumes.

Negril Scuba Centre, in the Negril Beach Club Hotel, Norman Manley Boulevard (© **800/818-2963** or 876/957-9641), is the most modern, best-equipped scuba facility in Negril. Beginners dive lessons are offered daily, as well as multiple-dive packages for certified divers; full scuba certifications and specialty courses are also available. A resort course, designed for first-time divers with basic swimming abilities, costs $75 and includes all instruction, equipment, a lecture on water and diving safety, and one open-water dive. A one-tank dive costs $30 per dive plus $20 for equipment rental (not necessary if divers bring their own gear). More economical ($55) is a two-tank dive, which must be completed in 1 day.

Watersports equipment is readily available at any of at the kiosks along Negril's beaches. Each of these outlets is operated by **Seatec Water Sports** (© **876/957-4401**), charging roughly the same rates as Negril Scuba Centre (see above). Jet skis cost $40 to $50 for a 30-minute ride; snorkeling is $15 to $20 per person for a 60-minute excursion by boat to an offshore reef with equipment; 20-minute banana-boat rides are $10; parasailing is $30 for a 12-minute ride; and water-skiing is $30 for a 15-minute tow-around.

SPORTFISHING

Stanley's (© **876/957-0667**) does deep-sea fishing trips in the waters off Negril. Catches turn up such game fish as wahoo, tuna, blue marlin, and sailfish. Bait, tackle, and beverages are included in the price. Six people can rent a fishing boat for $400 for a trip lasting 4 hours. An 8- to 9-hour trip, including lunch, will cost six fishermen about $750.

5 Exploring the Area

The chief attraction of Negril is **Seven Mile Beach** (see "Beaches," above). Many beach buffs visit Negril and don't care to see much else. There are actually a few sights, though Negril has none of the multifaceted or historical attractions found in a place like, say, Montego Bay.

ROYAL PALM RESERVE

The 122-hectare (300-acre) **Royal Palm Reserve** 🔆 recreation site carved into the Great Morass is the easiest part of the massive local wetlands to explore. To reach it, take the road to Savanna-la-Mar at the southern end of Negril, turning left at the signpost and going along a dirt road to reach the beginning of the reserve. Here you'll find much wildlife, including sea hawks, ospreys, and the Jamaican woodpecker. The swamp is also home to egrets, butterflies, doctor birds, herons, and the endangered Jamaican black parakeet. Wooden boardwalks enable you to walk 2km (1¼ miles) or so into the wetlands for a close encounter with it all. Take along plenty of mosquito repellent.

The showpiece of the reserve is Cotton Tree Lake, home to numerous waterfowl, including wild ducks and the Jamaican pond turtle. A nature museum informs about the plant and animal life of the reserve. There is also a riverside bar and another lakeside restaurant and bar specializing in natural juices and Jamaican dishes.

The visitor center (© **876/957-3736**) is open daily from 9am to 6pm, and tours cost $10 for adults and $5 for children 12 and under.

IN THE ENVIRONS

Should you wish to escape and discover that Jamaica is not just a beach, you can take a day off and head for **Rhodes Hall Plantation,** especially if you like to ride horses. Both neophyte and champion riders are catered to here. A 2-hour ride takes you through banana and coconut groves and high into the hills. A crocodile watch is one of the highlights of the tours. You can also tour the 202-hectare (500-acre) plantation and go scuba diving or fishing.

Horseback riding is available Sunday through Friday from 7am to 5pm, averaging $60 per ride. For more information, call © **876/957-6333.** The location of the plantation is 5km (3 miles) north of Negril at Green Island.

GREEN ISLAND

You can explore the area north of Negril on your scooter or in a rented car. Follow the main highway, the A1, as it passes through the wetlands of The Great Morass. A good stop along the way is at the shady **Hurricane Park** (you'll see a sign) with a bar. You can order a rum punch here, a cold soft drink, or perhaps the grilled catch of the day.

Another recreational site is reached by traveling 914m (3,000 ft.) or so to the west of Hurricane Park. Here you'll come to **Half Moon Beach,** which takes its name from sands likened to "crushed diamonds." Expect to find a thatched dive serving some Jamaican dishes, most often seafood the local fishermen brought in.

Continue 3km (1¾ miles) west of Green Island Harbour to **Rhodes Mineral Springs and Beach,** with several thatched bars aggressively seeking to slake your thirst. The beach is small but inviting. It's the site of a spontaneous beach party most Sunday nights.

MAYFIELD FALLS & MINERAL SPRINGS 𝒜𝒜

Another intriguing excursion takes you to Miskito Cove, 6km (3¾ miles) east of
Lucea on Bamboo Bay—an idyllic spot discovered by yachters who often anchor
there. If you're there at noon, you're greeted with the smell of jerk chicken cooking in various shacks.

Rising south of the cove is a series of green hills called the Dolphin Head
Mountains. Reach them via the A1 road to **Mayfield Falls & Mineral Springs**
(𝒞 **876/953-3034**), at Mayfield. This is a working farm near the village of Pen-
nycooke, 16km (10 miles) south of Miskito Cove. Take in the waterscapes as you
walk through a bamboo village. There are more than a dozen waterfalls, and you
can swim into an underwater cave. The full-day tour is $65 including transfers.

The easiest way to enjoy the experience without the hassle is booking a half-
day excursion through **Caribic Vacation** (𝒞 **876/957-3309** in Negril). You're
transported to the site and fed lunch for a total cost of $48 per person; this daily
tour lasts from 8am to 1pm.

BLENHEIM

Those with a sense of Jamaican history, especially Jamaican Americans, might
want to journey to the tiny hamlet of Blenheim, 6km (3¾ miles) inland from
Green Island. Administered by the Jamaican National Trust, this is the site of the
free **Sir Alexander Bustamante Museum** 𝒜 (𝒞 **876/922-1287**). Bustamante
was a national hero, the nation's first prime minister; he is kind of the George
Washington of Jamaica. Born in modest surroundings (as this rustic three-room
shack reveals), he eventually rose to the position of prime minister and helped
break British colonial rule. Queen Elizabeth II later knighted him. The hilltop
museum displays mostly photos and memorabilia.

6 Shopping

At long last, Negril has a shopping mall to equal the ones found in Mo Bay or
Ocho Rios. It's the **Time Square Mall** (𝒞 **876/957-9263**), lying on Norman
Manley Boulevard across from the much-frequented nightclub Bourbon Each.
More than five duty-free shops and souvenir stores await you, including a court-
yard cafe.

This mall offers Negril's best selection of watches (from Chaumet to Patek
Philippe), jewelry (including some from the collections of Chopard and Miki-
moto), and gifts and accessories such as a wide assortment of pens and writing
instruments. Crafts are sold here, along with perfumes, books, cigarettes, cigars,
film, liquor, dresses, and Blue Mountain coffee. The first and only cigar store
(Cigar World) in Negril is also here, with a walk-in humidor, selling genuine
Habanos or Cuban cigars. Jamaican cigars are also sold.

If you're staying in a housekeeping or self-catering apartment, you can pick
up groceries at the **Hi-Lo Grocery Store** in the Hi-Lo Shopping Centre on West
End Road. Here's your chance to enjoy Blue Mountain coffee, Jamaican spices,
and locally grown fruits and vegetables.

Just off Norman Manley Boulevard, as you head south into Negril Village,
you come upon the **Negril Crafts Market.** A collection of shacks, this is the
largest center for crafts in the area, though they're sold virtually everywhere,
including along the beach. Woodcarvings, beds, jewelry, and other items fill the
market. Haggling is expected; begin by offering half the price you're quoted.

The worst shopping is at the overpriced boutiques found at first-class hotels, especially the all-inclusives. But they come in handy when you're seeking postcards, souvenirs, suntan lotion, or swimwear in a pinch.

Other vendors can be found at **Fi Wi Plaza** on West End Road, between a traffic circle and "Sunshine Village." The most expensive (but not always best) crafts are sold at **Rutland Point Market** in the north of Negril.

7 Negril After Dark

Some of the best reggae bands in Jamaica, often from Kingston and often Bob Marley wannabes, show up in Negril. Alfred's and Risky Business are both major venues for reggae performances. All establishments listed below are located on Norman Manley Boulevard unless otherwise noted.

Alfred's (© 876/957-4735), is a Jamaican experience where travelers will still feel welcome. Though catering more to locals, there's much intermingling, no cover, and a mix of ages here. You can also order a bite to eat until 11pm. Particularly interesting is the beach-party area, with a stage for live reggae and jazz acts. You can also boogie on the dance floor inside, shaking to hits you'll hear at clubs stateside. Alfred's puts on a show 3 nights a week (Sun, Tues, Fri) and there is a $3 cover charge.

Bourbon Beach (© 876/957-4405), is the most popular and versatile hangout on Negril Beach. The club features live reggae 3 nights a week. The rum and Red Stripe flow freely through the day and night—at least from 9am to 11pm (and often much later). The club also serves food, including jerk chicken or fresh fish and lobster.

The hotspot during spring break, **Margaritaville** (© 876/957-4467), is a popular venue at night. It attracts the Bud and Marlboro crowd to its four openair bars with large-screen TVs playing both music and sports videos. Karaoke is a Sunday regular, and various events are staged here, including bikini and wet T-shirt competitions.

Cosmo's Seaford Restaurant & Bar (© 876/957-4784), is also popular after dark. Located on the beach, it offers recorded music, everything from old hits to soca. You can play pool, drink, and mingle.

Risky Business (© 876/957-3008), sits a few feet from the waves. It can be sleepy or manic, depending on what music is playing. In season you can order burgers and sandwiches, and the Red Stripe is cheap year-round. Basically, it's a young hangout whose traditional party nights are Monday, Thursday, and Saturday, beginning at 9pm. Friday night (crazy Fridays) features karaoke. There's no cover, even when the place is rocking.

Action is also lively at the **Sea Splash Resort** (© 876/957-4041), whose bar is located amid allamander vines, midway between a swimming pool and the edge of the sea. This place attracts a slightly older crowd than the two previously described spots. Sheltered from the sun by a teepee-shaped roof of palm leaves and thatch, it offers a tempting array of tropical drinks, such as Calico Jack's rum punch and a white sands. The bar is open daily from 7am to 11pm.

For the hottest night in Negril, don a toga and head for **Hedonism II** (© 876/957-5200), the most notorious all-inclusive in Jamaica. It's known for wild and raunchy parties. Nonguests are allowed entrance if they purchase a $75 night pass. At first this might seem steep, but it's really not when you consider that for this fee you are allowed all the food and drink you can consume—plus the entertainment. Fellow guests in thong bikinis and bondage suits are just part of the scenery. On-site is the resort's hottest disco, where action begins at 11pm and often goes on until 3am.

MXIII, on West End Road (no phone), more than any other nightclub in Negril, can either blow you away with its high-energy pulsations or simply present a ripped-up bandstand without energy and lights, depending on whether or not there's a musical act scheduled. There's no permanent bar—only temporary vendors selling colorful drinks from coolers. Expect a spontaneous, difficult-to-pin-down schedule heavy on soca and reggae.

The Jungle, in Mariner's Negril Beach Club (© **876/957-4005**), is the most crowded, horny, exuberant, and famous disco and nightclub in Negril, with a penchant for attracting sports and music-industry celebrities. (Even trash-TV king Jerry Springer did a turn here.) The scene gets so mobbed during spring break that movie crews have actually flown in from the United States to film it. Most of the perspiration here is spilled on the ground level, where four bars and dance floors rock and roll with music that varies according to the night's individual theme. Head for the upper level for the much-needed "cool-downs" that, at least here, have developed into a laid-back art form all their own. Red Stripe and rum punches are the drinks of choice for a crowd that really seems to enjoy their estrogen and testosterone highs. The cover charge is $9 for men and $7 for women. The Jungle Arcade is a gaming room with around 100 slot machines. The club is open Wednesday to Sunday from 10pm until the last patron staggers back to his or her hotel.

5

The South Coast & Mandeville

While Negril (see chapter 4) gets the crowds, the **South Coast** of Jamaica has only recently begun to attract visitors. The Arawak once lived in sylvan simplicity along these shores before their civilization was destroyed. Early Spanish settlers came here searching for gold; today's traveler comes looking for the untrammeled sands of its secluded beaches. Fishermen still sell their catch at colorful local markets, and the prices, as they say here, are "the way they used to be" in Jamaica.

Most visitors here come east from Negril through Savanna-la-Mar to the high-country, British-style town of **Mandeville,** then on to a boat tour up the Black River, home of freshwater crocodiles. (Those with more time hit Treasure Beach first before going on to Mandeville.)

The area attracts an adventure-oriented visitor who doesn't want to be picked up in a minivan and hauled to an all-inclusive hotel behind a guarded compound with canned entertainment. It's a sleepy place devoid of duty-free stores, musicians in yellow shirts singing "Yellow Bird," and toga parties. Instead of air-conditioning, you get mosquito nets and ceiling fans.

Yet the beaches here are the equal of those of Mo Bay or Ocho Rios. Restaurants, for the most part, are of the sort you'd have found along the roadside in Jamaica in the 1950s—and some of them are still charging 1950s prices. Local lifestyles, too, remain mostly unchanged by time.

This last frontier of Jamaica will no doubt be invaded by tourism within the next decade or so. But for now it appears, at least in its more remote parts, a sleepy dream from long ago.

1 The South Coast (★

Think of this as the undiscovered Jamaica, though the region is beginning to attract more visitors every year; they're drawn by Jamaica's sunniest climate.

Local adventures are plentiful on the South Coast. Among the most popular is a boat tour up the Black River, once a major logging conduit. Another favorite is the trip to the Y. S. Falls, where seven spectacular cascades tumble over rocks in the foothills of the Santa Cruz Mountains, just north of the town of Middle Quarters.

BLUEFIELDS & BELMONT
These twin fishing villages are approached via the A1 highway, 19km (12 miles) to the southeast of Savanna-la-Mar. Bluefields Beach (actually a series of small beaches) is one of the finest in the area, drawing visitors every weekend from as far away as Kingston.

EXPLORING THE AREA
To reach the South Coast, head east from Negril, following the signposts to Savanna-la-Mar along Sheffield Road; the highway isn't particularly good until

it broadens into the A2 at Savanna. After passing through the village of **Blue-fields,** continue southeast to the small town of **Black River,** which opens onto Black River Bay.

From Black River you can take the A2 north and northeast to the city of **Mandeville.** Or you can continue along the coast to **Treasure Beach,** though the road narrows at this point. If you'd like to continue to the very end of the road, head east to attractions at quaintly named Lover's Leap, Alligator Pond, and Milk River Bath.

WHERE TO STAY

Shafston Great House (value)   For the uncomplaining frugal traveler who does not require state-of-the-art maintenance, this historic house is the domain of the best-known fellow in town, Frank Lohmann. The place is very popular with young people from Germany. On the grounds is the most-photographed tree in the area, a mammoth silk cotton tree framed against a backdrop of pimento fields. The view from this hilltop is panoramic, as well. Bedrooms are large, comfortably furnished, and quite plain; only two have private (shower-only) bathrooms, however. Ten more old-fashioned rooms are located in the great house, the rest in a newer extension, most sharing bathrooms; campsites are also available for rent, at $35 per night. There's a rustic Jamaican restaurant here, too, serving regional specialties.

Bluefields. ② 876/997-5076. www.shafston.com. 20 units (3 with private bathroom). Year-round $80 double without bathroom; $140 double with bathroom. Rates include meals. MC, V. **Amenities:** Restaurant; bar; pool; Jacuzzi; guided tours; laundry service; rooms for those with limited mobility. *In room:* No phone.

The Villas at Bluefields Bay ★★★ (finds)   These exclusive private waterfront villas—built by American architect Debbie Moncure—are an ideal retreat. Right on their own white-sand beach, with private pools, they are the ultimate in South Coast luxury. *Caribbean Travel & Life* even goes so far as to say they're Jamaica's best, though that's a bit of hyperbole. One local said that guests are "just married, just remarried, just ourselves, just ourselves and the kids, or just escaping the kids."

Set among lush foliage, these villas feel remote and secluded, yet lie only a 40-minute drive from Negril. Each villa is perfect for a honeymoon or romantic week; all are beautifully furnished with tub and shower combinations. Antique armoires and Irish linens provide additional grace notes. Two of the villas, Hermitage and San Michele, can even sleep up to eight guests. You dine on elegant crystal and fine china, and each villa has its own staff, including a chef, a waiter, a gardener, laundry worker, maid, and night attendant. Guests of the various villas meet at The Treehouse—a beach pavilion—for drinks, waterfront lunches, to change bathing suits, or to mingle.

Bluefields Bay, Bluefields. ② 202/232-4010 (Alexandria, Virginia). Fax 703/549-6517. www.bluefieldsvillas. com. 5 villas. Winter $4,400–$7,000 double; off season $3,400–$4,900 double. Rates are weekly and all-inclusive. No credit cards. **Amenities:** Villa kitchen with chef; beach pavilion for lunch and drinks; private pool; tennis court; spa treatments; deep-sea fishing; airport transfers; babysitting; laundry service; horseback riding nearby. *In room:* A/C, bar.

BEACHES & OUTDOOR PURSUITS

Bluefields Bay stretches for 10km (6¼ miles) along the coast and is broken up by a number of little coves. Here you'll find a string of sandy beaches separated from one another by mangroves. Walk along and select your favorite spot on the sands.

Along the western fringe of the bay stands **Paradise Park** ⟨ (☎ **876/955-2675**), a 404-hectare (1,000-acre) cattle-and-dairy farm that has been in the same family for more than a century. It is centered around an 18th-century property on a tropical savanna with luxuriant growth. Horseback riding can be arranged, and afterward explore the grounds of the estate on trails cut through a tropical forest full of bird life. In May and June, you can pick mangoes right off the trees. The waters here are ideal for swimming, and you can picnic in the park: Picnic tables and open barbecue grills are provided. You can also swim in the Sweet River. The park lies 2km (1¼ miles) west of Ferris Cross, along the main A2 highway between Negril and Black River. Admission costs $5, riding tours cost $30; the whole experience takes about 4 hours.

At a section called **Bluefields Beach Park,** you'll find most of the local vendors, terrible toilets, and jerk stalls. Because the fish is likely to be fresher than the pork or chicken, this is a good place to order jerk fish, along with a Red Stripe beer. Locals make highly prized hammocks, which are sold along the road in this area.

WHITEHOUSE ⟨

From Bluefields, the A2 road winds south to Whitehouse for 8km (5 miles) along the coast. Local life is expected to change permanently with the opening of a Beaches resort in the future, the first to go up along this coast. If you come before the change eventually occurs, you'll still find a fishing village of small shops and vegetable stalls (busiest on Wed and Sat mornings).

EXPLORING THE AREA

Just off the A2 at Belmont, you can visit the **Peter Tosh Mausoleum,** in a small green-and-gold building, open daily from 9am to 5pm. Technically, no admission is charged but you'll be asked for a donation. The Bob Marley mausoleum at Nine Mile, reached from Ocho Rios (p. 159), is more interesting, unless you liked reggae star Tosh's music better.

Bluefields was also the home of Philip Gosse (1810–88), an English naturalist who lived here for 18 months beginning in 1844 and wrote two books. His former abode is now privately owned and in poor condition, but you can walk by it, as it lies adjacent to the police station in Bluefields. In the gardens of the house grows a breadfruit tree said to have been planted as a seedling by Captain Bligh of *Mutiny on the Bounty* fame.

Snorkeling is good right off the shoreline. You can often get the owner of a local boat to take you over to nearby **Moor Reef** for $35 per hour. Some of the boats hold as many as six snorkelers.

WHERE TO DINE

Culloden Café ⟨ INTERNATIONAL   Set beside the coastal road stretching between Bluefields and Whitehouse, this restaurant is housed within an aristocratic-looking pink-sided villa that originally functioned as the childhood home of its owners and chef. The cozy and artfully minimalist interior opens to reveal a view of a formal garden and putting-green lawns that sweep down to the edge of the sea in vistas that evoke a tropical view of the English countryside. The owners include Ann Lyons, a former editor at a New York City publishing house, and her British-born husband, John Belcher. Together, they direct a polite, well-rehearsed staff who prepare flavorful food that's considerably broader in scope—and more sophisticated—than anything else in the area. Menu items include locally caught fish that might be blackened, New Orleans–style; *escoveitch* of fish (a whole fish served in a peppery vinegar sauce);

quesadillas stuffed with guacamole; or curried banana soup. Dessert might include Key lime cake or a frothy version of Pavlova—fruit and whipped cream in a meringue shell.

Culloden District, Whitehouse. © 876/963-5344. Reservations recommended. Main courses J$300–J$500 (US$5–US$8.30). MC, V. Wed–Mon noon–9pm.

BEACHES & OUTDOOR PURSUITS

The best beach is reached by going along a small trail past the Alexander Seaview Shopping Square. It's sleepy here during the day, but comes alive when fishermen return in the early evening, bringing the day's catch.

BLACK RIVER

The A2 continues to the southeast until you come to the waterfront settlement at Black River, the main town of **St. Elizabeth Parish.** There are more attractions to be visited from here than anywhere else along the South Coast. Allow 2 days for exploring the entire region if you have the time, including, if you so care, a day trip to Mandeville (p. 129).

EXPLORING THE AREA

Reached along A2 directly south of Whitehouse, going via South Sea Park, is **Scott's Cove,** a deep inlet that forms the frontier between the parishes of Westmoreland and St. Elizabeth. Here you'll find several fish and bammy stalls with vendors hawking their wares; bammy, for the uninitiated, is a fried cassava pancake.

Immediately to the southeast stands the 1,274-hectare (3,150-acre) **Font Hill Wildlife Sanctuary** , strung along 3km (1¾ miles) of seafront. Birders from all over the world flock here to see herons, egrets, and much rarer species such as blue-winged teals. Listen for the sound of the whistling duck. This is also a habitat for the ground dove, the smallest bird of that species. Give wide berth to the dozens of crocodiles that still inhabit the district.

You can follow a dirt trail here down to **Font Hill Beach,** a small strip of white sands set against a backdrop of sea grapes. The swimming is good here, as the waters are clear, which invites snorkelers to the offshore reefs. This is one of the ideal places for a picnic with supplies you picked up at Scott's Cove.

VISITOR INFORMATION

The local office of the **Jamaica Tourist Board** is in the Hendricks Building, 2 High St., Black River (© 876/965-2074), open Monday to Friday 8:30am to 4:30pm.

FAST FACTS: BLACK RIVER

Banks   A local branch of **Scotiabank,** 6 High St. (© 876/965-2251), can handle your banking needs. It opens Monday, Thursday, and Friday from 9am to 4pm, Tuesday and Wednesday from 9am to 3pm.

Mail   The **Black River Post Office,** North Street (© 876/634-3769), lies close to the local police station. It is open Monday to Friday 8am to 5pm.

Hospital   Medical services are available at **Black River Hospital,** 45 High St., Black River (© 876/965-2212), which has 24-hour service. It lies in a former barracks .8km (½ mile) west of Black River's center.

WHERE TO STAY

Invercauld Great House & Hotel   In 1889, when Black River's port was one of the most important in Jamaica, a Scottish merchant imported most of the

materials for the construction of this white-sided manor house. Today the renovated and much-enlarged house functions as a hotel. Rooms are clean, stripped
down, and simple, usually with mahogany furniture made by local craftspeople.
The hotel has gradually added five small houses filled with suites; these come
with either a king-size bed or twin beds, and the units each also have a fold-out
couch, are air-conditioned, have cable TVs and phones, and either patios or
verandas. Most rooms come with a tub and shower; the rest only have showers.

High St., Black River. ℂ 876/965-2750. Fax 876/965-2751. www.invercauldgreathouse.com. 52 units. Year-
round $68–$123 double; $85–$140 suite. MC, V. On the harborfront, a few blocks west of Black River's commercial center. **Amenities:** Restaurant; bar; pool; tennis court; limited room service; babysitting; laundry
service; rooms for those with limited mobility. *In room:* A/C, TV, iron/board.

Waterloo Guest House   We wouldn't want to recommend anything more
rickety, old-fashioned, and worn than this place—which drips character, at least,
from its wooden verandas and gingerbread trim. Accommodations are found in
the main house and also in a more modern, far less attractive motel-like unit
out back. The main-house accommodations feature air-conditioning and private bathrooms with showers; those in the duller unit don't always have air-
conditioning but do come with shower-only bathrooms. Furnishings are
extremely modest, and the place is quite worn, even battered. Locals do flock
here to the on-site restaurant and bar.

44 High St., Black River. ℂ 876/965-2278. Fax 876/965-2095. 20 units. Year-round J$1,500–J$2,500
(US$25–US$42) double. MC, V. **Amenities:** Restaurant; bar; outdoor pool; car-rental desk; limited room service; laundry service; rooms for those with limited mobility. *In room:* A/C (in some units), TV (in some units),
coffeemaker, iron/board.

WHERE TO DINE
Bridge House Inn JAMAICAN   This is a simple and very Jamaican restaurant. The cement-sided structure was built in the early 1980s; it's done with a
beachfront motif and set within a grove of coconut palms and sea grapes.
Patrons include mostly a cross section of Jamaicans, including the occasional
conference of librarians or nurses. Menu items—everything is home style—
include complete dinners (fish, chicken, curried goat, oxtail, stewed beef, or
lobster) with soup and vegetables, served politely and efficiently by a staff of
hardworking waiters. A separate bar area off to the side dispenses drinks.

14 Crane Rd., Black River. ℂ 876/965-2361. Full meals $15–$30. MC, V. Daily 7am–10pm. On the eastern
outskirts of Black River, on the opposite side of the town's only bridge from the commercial center.

EXPLORING THE TOWN
Come here for a glimpse of old Jamaica before it disappears completely. Because
the town appears to be in decay during the day, we prefer it under the kind, rosy
glow of sunset while walking along its waterfront. You might also walk along
High Street (the main street), taking in old colonial buildings, some in the West
Indian gingerbread style and others mere rip-offs of Georgian architecture.

At the east end of High Street sits the **Hendricks Building,** site of the tourist
office (see above). This battered old structure dates from 1813. Also on "The
High," you can see the old **courthouse** with its porticoes and the **town hall** with
its pillared facade opening onto a mammoth banyan tree. Nearby you'll spot the
Parish Church of St. John the Evangelist, dating from 1837.

BLACK RIVER 𝒜 & THE GREAT MORASS 𝒜𝒜
The second longest river in Jamaica and a vast marshland called the Great
Morass are the Jamaican equivalent of the Florida Everglades. This sprawling

(Finds) Plenty Water Deh 'Bout

Jamaica's most bizarre bar, the **Pelican Bar** at Parottee Point (© 876/354-4218), lies on a shoal off this point and stands in shallow water on stilts made from acacia trees. Surely there is no more ramshackle bar in the Caribbean than the little hut of Floyd (real name Denever Delroy Forbes). Under a half-thatched half-tarp roof, he serves yachties and boaters seeking a pit stop as they head up the Black River. This rickety structure looks as if it's going to fall into the sea at any minute, but is usually packed with patrons. Many drinkers enjoy their rum punches or their Red Stripe beer while standing in the shallow waters around the patchwork bar of wood and other materials called "tings." Amazingly, if you notify him in advance, Floyd will even cook your dinner—fresh fish, fried or steamed, or maybe freshly caught Caribbean lobster for that special treat. His stove? Two car wheel rims fired by wood. His house cocktail is Pelican Perfection, a concoction made with lime juice, sugar, white rum, and ginger beer.

---

mass of animals, bird life, and lush vegetation is the most evocative section in Jamaica—a Tarzan-like jungle setting.

Five Jamaican rivers meet in the 32,374-hectare (80,000-acre) Morass, a soggy mass of crocodile-filled swamps, mangroves, and marshland with plenty of bird life, such as egrets, herons, ducks (both the whistling and ringed-neck species), and the blue-winged teal, among others.

The savanna is also filled with rare plant life such as butterfly ginger, bull thatch, saw grass, water hyacinths, pancake lilies, guaco bushes, potato slips, and wild cane, to name just a few. The red mangrove seen here is especially stunning: It sends its roots as deep as 12m (40 ft.) into the murky swamplands. You can also see royal palms and the remains of the logwood trees that once brought prosperity to Black River.

For a look at the Black River, its mangrove swamps, and crocodiles, the best tours are offered by **South Coast Safaris.** The 1½-hour tour covers 19km (12 miles) upstream and back and costs $15 for adults, $7.50 for children; tours leave daily at 9 and 11am and 12:30, 2, and 3:30pm. Children under 3 go free but probably shouldn't be taken at all, unless they are held onto firmly. South Coast Safaris is at 1 Crane Rd., Black River (© **876/965-2513**). In addition, biologist Lloyd Linton operates **Irie Safari,** 12 High St. (© **876/965-2211**), featuring 90-minute "safaris" on pontoon boats costing $20 per person. He takes cruises through the wetlands to sneak up on these American saltwater crocodiles—but at a safe distance, of course.

EXPLORING THE AREA

Most visitors come here for a so-called "safari" adventure along the Black River and into the Great Morass. However, it's also possible to see many land-based sights, especially if you take the A2 north and east to Mandeville.

YS FALLS ⭐⭐⭐ *(Kids* Among the most spectacular falls in the West Indies, rivaled only by the tourist-trodden Dunn's River Falls at Ocho Rios (see chapter 6), these eight falls drop a panoramic 36m (120 ft.) in majestic tiers separated by beautiful pools ideal for swimming. The lush setting is framed by limestone cliffs and junglelike growth. The falls lie on the privately owned YS Estate, 6km (3¾ miles) to the north of the A2 highway; the turnoff is signposted 2km (1¼ miles) east after you leave the village of Middle Quarters, about 13km (8 miles) north of Middle Quarters.

Kids love this estate, which is open Tuesday to Sunday from 9:30am to 3:30pm, charging an admission of $12. There's a little thatched dining hut on-site serving chicken and burgers, if you didn't pack a lunch.

In the hamlet of **Middle Quarters,** women stand along the roadside hawking peppery shellfish. Fiery hot, these crayfish (locally called "swimps") are caught in the river and then cooked at little open-air roadside grills.

BAMBOO AVENUE 𝒜𝒜𝒜 Middle Quarters, along the A2 north from Black River, marks the beginning of Bamboo Avenue—the most beautiful drive in the West Indies. Lying between Middle Quarters and Lacovia, this 4km (2½-mile) stretch of bamboo trees is a grand scenic treat. Planted in the early 20th century to provide a respite from the hot sun for sugarcane workers, the bamboo trees stretch across the road, linking to form a canopy over the road, which narrows to a kind of tunnel that flutters in the trade winds. It's a dramatic sight, and along the road hawkers of coconuts and peanuts ply their trades. Stop anywhere along the way for a snack and a refreshing drink of coconut water.

CASHOO OSTRICH PARK *Kids* Ostriches are not associated with Jamaica, but they thrive on this 40-hectare (100-acre) estate lying 6km (3¾ miles) south of East Lacovia (at the eastern end of Bamboo Ave.). Some of these birds weigh more than 159 kilograms (350 lb.); their eggs alone can weigh 2 kilograms (4½ lb.) or more. The owner has also installed a little petting zoo and playground with rabbits, ducks, and donkeys, among other tame animals. For adults, there's a bar along the riverside where you can rest in hammocks, enjoying a respite from touring. (Crocodiles inhabit the river, so don't be tempted to take a dip.) The park is open Tuesday to Sunday from 10am to 5pm, costing J$250 (US$4.15) for admission or J$150 (US$2.50) for ages 12 and under. For more information, call © **876/966-2222.**

SANTA CRUZ The last town of any importance you'll pass after Bamboo Avenue en route to Mandeville is Santa Cruz, a thriving market town supported in part by a large factory. The best stopover is at **Hind's Restaurant & Bakery,** Santa Cruz Plaza (© **876/966-2234**), serving Jamaican cuisine daily from 6:30am to 8pm (closes at 2pm on Sun). Main courses cost J$140 to J$300 (US$2.30–US$5). Many locals come here for breakfast, the favorite dish being ackee and salt fish. Main meals include such hair-on-your-chest dishes as stewed oxtail, tripe and beans, and curried goat. The faint-of-heart can order baked goods such as a rum cake. No credit cards are accepted.

APPLETON RUM ESTATE This estate is the oldest rum producer in the English-speaking West Indies. The estate has been producing award-winning rums since 1749. At the end of a tour, in which you're shown how cane is turned into rum, you're treated to complimentary samples of cane juice, called "high wine," and all the flavorful rums they can produce. The tour takes 45 minutes and is available Monday to Saturday from 9am to 4pm, costing $12 per person. Call © **876/963-9215.**

TREASURE BEACH Departing from the main A2 at Black River, a secondary road dips to the southeast taking you to Treasure Beach. This section is very different from the rest of Jamaica, evoking at times the more arid parts of

Arizona. Sheltered by the Santa Cruz mountains to the north, it doesn't get the heavy rainfall that showers over the lusher parts of the island. You are more likely to encounter towering cacti instead of junglelike growth.

Since the opening of Jake's (see below), which *Vogue* dubbed the "chicest shack in the Caribbean," more and more international tourists are drawn to this remote part of Jamaica.

FAST FACTS: TREASURE BEACH

Banks   Scotiabank (© 876/965-8257), in the village center, is open Monday, Thursday, and Friday from 8:15am to 4pm, Tuesday and Wednesday 8:15am to 3pm.

Information   The nearest branch office of the Jamaica Tourist Board is at Black River (see above).

Telephone   To make a call or send a fax, you can go to the **Cable and Wireless Centre** (© 876/965-9930), directly east of Jake's (see below). The office is open Monday to Friday 8am to 5pm.

WHERE TO STAY

Golden Sands Guest House *Value*   Popular with backpackers and others, this is the best bargain along the coast, although it's not for everyone. Four buildings that make up this compound lie at the edge of a long beach of good sands. A garden separates the property from the beach. The bedrooms are very spartan but well kept, each cooled by an overhead fan. All the units contain twin beds and a small bathroom where the water is never hot but kind of tepid. Management provides bed linens and towels. Guests cut down on meal costs by purchasing supplies at one of the local markets and cooking their own meals. The outdoor bar is a popular gathering place at night, attracting an international crowd of visitors that range from Germany to Manitoba. The most luxurious and private way to stay here is to rent the one-bedroom cottage. Sometimes guests wait until the fishing boats come in, to unload their rainbow-hued catch of the day. Then they purchase their dinner right on the spot, with a guarantee that it's very fresh.

Calabash Bay. © 876/965-0167. 24 units. Year-round $35 double; $70 cottage. Rates include breakfast. No credit cards. **Amenities:** Breakfast room. *In room:* A/C (in cottage only), TV, kitchenette, no phone, ceiling fans.

Jake's *Finds*   This is one of the most eccentric hotels in Jamaica. Perched on a cliff side overlooking the ocean and set within a labyrinth of badly marked roads, adjacent to a rocky beach that benefits from the occasional dumping of truckloads of sand, Jake's is a special haven. It occupies a series of earth-colored Casbah-style buildings, each individually decorated and exploding with colors—everything from funky purple to Pompeian terra cotta. Each contains mosquito netting, flickering candles, and a CD player with a very hip collection. All units come with a well-maintained bathroom with tub-and-shower combination. Likewise, as a means of avoiding infestations of flying insects, lighting is kept deliberately dim. Our favorite accommodations here are the trio of Octopussy villas, each with a large amount of living space and a spacious bedroom with an open-air deck on the rooftop jutting out over the water. For an extra sense of romance, the villas offer alfresco showers.

Jake's is owned by Chris Blackwell, the man who brought the world Bob Marley and U2. It is run by Jason Henzell, son of Perry Henzell, who produced *The Harder They Come,* the hippest Caribbean film of all time.

There's also a raffish-looking bar attracting guests and well-meaning locals, an amoeba-shaped pool, and a barrage of fishers and drivers who'll familiarize you with local activities and tours. The hotel restaurant is recommended separately in "Where to Dine" below.

Calabash Bay, Treasure Beach. ℭ 800/OUTPOST or 876/965-0635. Fax 876/965-0552. www.islandoutpost. com. 15 cottages, 4 villas. Year-round $75–$225 double; $295–$325 villa, plus 20% service and taxes. AE, MC, V. **Amenities:** 2 restaurants; bar; pool; game room/media room; kayaks; bicycles; Internet room; limited room service; babysitting; laundry service. *In room:* A/C (in some units), full kitchen (in some units), minibar, fridge (in some units), coffeemaker, hair dryer, safe, no phone.

Mar Blue Domicil ⟨ℛ⟩ ⟨*Finds*⟩

A stylish little guesthouse with only three bedrooms has opened along this yet-to-be-discovered coast. Each of the comfortably furnished, though rather simple, bedrooms opens onto the sea. These oceanfront rooms contain private balconies where guests sit out to watch the sunset at night. During the day, guests can be seen wandering Treasure Beach. The staff will inform you of all the activities available in the area in addition to swimming; these include snorkeling and taking excursions into the Santa Cruz mountains. The furnishings are rather stylish and designed by the owners and handmade out of cedar wood. Beds are queen-size and covered in Egyptian cotton. Guests consistently praise the food served here, with a daily changing menu that includes such delights as shrimp and lobster with a garlic-laced aioli sauce.

Treasure Beach. ℭ 876/840-5772. www.marblue.com. 4 units. Winter $149 double; off season $129 double. Rates include breakfast. 2-night minimum stay. MC, V. **Amenities:** Restaurant; bar; outdoor pool; massages; laundry service; nonsmoking rooms. *In room:* A/C (in 3 units), TV, minibar, hair dryer, iron/board, beverage maker.

Sunset Resort Villas

On a masonry terrace above the seacoast, a short walk from the moored fishing boats of Calabash Bay, this hotel doesn't have the international cachet or the sense of fun of nearby Jake's. But for an older and more conservative clientele, it's a solid alternative. Built in stages beginning in the late 1970s, on a 2.2-hectare (5½-acre) site, Sunset Resort might remind you of an enlarged version of a 19th-century sea captain's house, thanks to a two-story central core and horseshoe-shape pair of symmetrical wings that enclose a pool. The bedrooms, however, are larger than those at Jake's, though with none of their decorative flair. Each has noncontroversial, low-slung furnishings, some made with New England–style knotty pine. Most rooms come with tub-and-shower combinations. There's a restaurant (The Red Lobster) and bar on-site.

Calabash Bay, Treasure Beach. ℭ 876/965-0143. For reservations, contact South Enterprises, 2875 S. Main St., Suite 203, Salt Lake City, Utah 84115. ℭ 800/786-8452 or fax 800/487-2749. www.sunsetresort.com. 12 units. Year-round $80–$140 double; $165 1-bedroom suite for 2; $200–$280 2- or 3-bedroom suite, with kitchen, for 2–6 occupants. AE, MC, V. **Amenities:** Restaurant; lounge; outdoor pool; free snorkeling gear; fishing; bike rentals; limited room service; babysitting; rooms for those with limited mobility; outdoor barbecue. *In room:* A/C, TV, coffeemaker, iron/board, safe, no phone.

Treasure Beach Hotel

Set on a steep, lushly landscaped hillside above a sand beach with active surf, this white-sided hotel was built in the mid-1970s about 2km (1¼ miles) west of Pedro Cross. Although its staff is young and inexperienced, this is the largest hotel in the area, and is often the hotel of choice for Jamaican honeymooners. The origins of this property actually date from the 1930s when it was a retreat for asthmatics. Its centerpiece is a long and airy rattan-furnished bar whose windows look down the hillside to the beach and the hotel's 4.4 hectares (11 acres). Bedrooms lie within a series of outlying cottages. Each unit has a ceiling fan and a veranda or patio, plus a small bathroom with tub-and-shower combination.

Treasure Beach, P.O. Box 5, Black River, St. Elizabeth. © **800/526-2422** or 876/965-0110. Fax 876/965-2544. www.jamaica-southcoast.com/treasurebeach. 32 units. Winter $110–$143 double; off season $90–$114 double. AE, MC, V. **Amenities:** Restaurant; bar; 2 outdoor pools; Jacuzzi; limited room service; babysitting; laundry service; rooms for those with limited mobility. *In room:* A/C, TV, fridge (in some units), hair dryer, iron, safe (in some units).

WHERE TO DINE

Jake's 𝒜𝒜 JAMAICAN/INTERNATIONAL   Even if the sheer eccentricity of Jake's prevents you from an overnight here, you should absolutely dine here. Part of its allure stems from its raffish charm and unpredictability—you never know who might show up to divert and entertain you during a meal. (Likely candidates include everyone from Kingston's most prominent doctors to loquacious local philosophers who will predict your future through a rum-induced haze.) Jake's offers two distinctly different dining experiences: a romantic and secluded covered veranda out back, and a much more sociable front porch where tables are hand-painted in psychedelic patterns inspired by the 1960s. Menu items are announced on a chalkboard and might include pumpkin, red bean, or pepper-pot soups; fish tea (a clear broth checkered with herbs); and conch, callaloo, or cod fritters. More substantial fare includes plantain chips or carrot strips served with smoked marlin dip; a marvelous steamed fish in coconut-flavored cream sauce; tender pepper steak; and a revolving array of spicy jerk chicken, beef, pork, and fish.

Calabash Bay, Treasure Beach. © **876/965-0635.** Reservations recommended for dinner only Dec–Apr. Main courses J$350–J$900 (US$5.80–US$15). AE, DISC, MC, V. Daily 7:30am–9:30pm.

Tiffany's 𝒜 *Finds* JAMAICAN/AMERICAN   Carmen Sutherland is the hard-working founder of this pleasant, unpretentious restaurant beside the main street of Treasure Beach. Established in 1993, it occupies a colonial-inspired concrete building whose simple interior is painted in pale tones of blue and pink. Named after one of the owner's favorite books and films *(Breakfast at Tiffany's)*, it features such items as soups, roast beef, T-bone steaks, and peppered steak, three different preparations of chicken (including a version inspired by Waikiki Beach, with pineapple slices), burgers, sandwiches, and salads.

Calabash Bay, Treasure Beach. © **876/965-0300.** Reservations recommended. Main courses J$250–J$600 (US$4.15–US$9.95). AE, MC, V. Daily noon–10pm.

Finds Reggae, Jerk Barbecue & Callaloo Fritters

At Treasure Beach there are ramshackle thatched-roof huts where you can order a Red Stripe beer and escape from the fierce sun under a cooling palm tree. Our favorite is **Winsome's on the Beach** at Frenchman's Beach (no phone), where you can order a freshly made fish chowder, callaloo fritters, and the house specialty: chicken adobe, which is cooked in a coconut milk and ginger-laced tomato sauce. Grilled kingfish in *escoveitch* (pickled carrots, onions, and specialties) is another specialty. Along Treasure Beach Road you come upon **Diners Delite** (no phone), serving such classic Jamaican dishes are okra and salt fish, chicken stew, and braised oxtail. Those seeking the best barbecue pile into **Chef Kit at Wild Onion** (off Treasure Beach Rd.; no phone). On weekends you can hear live reggae here.

> ### *Finds* Bammy with Your Fish Fry
>
> Escaping dining rooms, you can relax on the beach if you drive an hour east from Treasure Beach to the little fishing village of Alligator Pond. Once here, you'll see a thatched hut, **Little Ochi** (© **876/965-4405**), which serves the best and freshest fish in the area. Your choice, of course, is based on the day's catch, brought in fresh by the fishermen that morning. Select your own fish and tell the chef how you want it cooked. A fish dinner costs around $12, and it comes with bammy (the local name for cassava bread) and a "festival" (translated as cornmeal cake). To carb out, rice and peas accompany all fish platters.

BEACHES & OUTDOOR PURSUITS

Treasure Beach 🗡🗡 is a catchall name for four beaches: Frenchman's Bay, Great Pedro Bay, Billy's Bay, and Calabash Bay. Beaches here are either coral colored or of black sand. At times you can virtually have a beach to yourself. The sea is at its calmest in the morning, so this is the best time for snorkeling. Be cautious when swimming in the rough currents, however. The waves along here are moderate but good enough for bodysurfing. About 92m (300 ft.) offshore are beautiful coral reefs ideal for snorkeling.

The coastline between Treasure Beach and Lover's Leap (see below) is riddled with footpaths that make for ideal hiking. You can often secure a mountain bike at your hotel and can ride along this flat or hilly terrain, stopping perhaps at a small rum bar for a refreshment.

LOVER'S LEAP

Eleven kilometers (6¾ miles) east of Treasure Beach is **Lovers' Leap** 🗡🗡, Southfield, Yardley Chase (© **876/965-6634**), the most dramatic and widely publicized attraction along Jamaica's South Coast. It commemorates the Romeo and Juliet story of two runaway slaves who leaped to their deaths hand in hand rather than be separated and returned to captivity. During the 1990s the Jamaican government erected an observation deck, meeting space, restaurant, bar, and gift shop at the site of the famous double suicide—the top of a 533m (1,750-ft.) cliff, one of the steepest on the South Coast. If you're adventurous, you can follow a rocky and meandering footpath down to the sea, though most visitors opt just to enjoy the view that sweeps out over the coastline from the open-air platform. It's open daily 10am to 6pm, charging J$170 (US$2.80) adults, J$80 (US$1.35) children for a view of the site, lighthouse, and amazing panoramas.

If you have time, you can continue east along the coast, following the signs to Milk River. You'll first pass a small nature reserve called **Alligator Hole,** which charges no admission and is open daily from 9am to 4pm. This is the Jamaican home of the endangered manatee, called a "sea cow." The best time to see these marvelous but shy creatures is in the late afternoon.

The road continues from Alligator Hole east for 3 more kilometers (1¾ miles) to the end of our coastal journey at **Milk River,** the site of a hot mineral spring. **Milk River Mineral Bath** 🗡, Milk River, Clarendon (© **876/902-4657;** fax 876/986-4974), boasts some of the world's most radioactive mineral waters, recommended by some doctors for the treatment of arthritis, rheumatism, lumbago, neuralgia, sciatica, and liver disorders. The cost of a bath is J$100 (US$1.65) for adults and J$50 (US85¢) for children. Baths usually last about

15 minutes (it isn't good to remain too long in the waters). Use of the baths is free if you're staying at the Milk River Mineral Spa & Hotel—20 rooms (most with bathrooms, many with air-conditioning, TV, and phone) from $110 to $117 double—and the waters are changed after use by each bather. A restaurant offers fine Jamaican cuisine and health drinks in a relaxed old-world atmosphere.

2 Mandeville ⌐★

Called the "English Town" because of its lingering British influence, Mandeville lies on a plateau more than 600m (2,000 ft.) above the sea in the tropical high-lands of Don Figuerero Mountains. Much cooler than the coastal resorts, it's a possible base from which to explore the South Coast.

VISITOR INFORMATION

There is no Jamaica Tourist Board office here. Information is available from the **Central & South Tourism Committee** at the Astra Country Inn, on the west-ern outskirts (© **876/962-9758,** 876/376-6176, or 876/450-3443), open daily 9am to 5pm.

FAST FACTS: Mandeville

Banks A branch of **National Commercial Bank** (© **876/962-2083**) can be found at 9 Manchester Rd.; open Monday to Friday 8:30am to 3pm, Friday 8:30am to 4:30pm.

Hospital The town's major hospital, **Mandeville Hospital,** Hargreaves Avenue (© **876/962-2067**), is the best medical center in the Central High-lands of Jamaica.

Internet Access The **Internet Café** at Manchester Shopping Centre (© **876/961-1829**) is the largest in Jamaica, boasting 20 computers and charging J$200 (US$3.30) per half-hour. It is open Monday to Friday from 8:30am to 5pm.

Mail The **Mandeville Post Office,** South Racecourse (© **876/962-3229**), is open Monday to Friday 8am to 5pm. To mail packages, it's more effi-cient to use **Airpak Express,** 11 Caledonia Rd. (© **876/962-5101**). Include "Jamaica, W.I." in all island addresses. The island has no zip codes.

Pharmacy The most convenient drugstore is the **Caledonia Mall Phar-macy,** Shop G5, Caledonia Road (© **876/962-0038**), open Monday to Friday 8am to 5:30pm, Saturday 8am to 4pm.

Safety The police station, 8 Parkerson Rd. (© **876/962-2250**), is on the north side of the central village green. Of all Jamaica's cities, Mandeville is the safest; still, take all the usual precautions.

Travel Agencies The best one is **Sterling Travel,** Caledonia Plaza (© **876/ 962-2203**), open Monday to Friday 8:30am to 4:30pm.

WHERE TO STAY

Golf View Hotel   This hotel won't win any prizes for architectural finesse— it looks like a hospital. But despite its shortcomings, it's one of the best-maintained and most efficiently managed hotels in the area. It's a motel-like

---

Impressions
When you have troubles, don't cry—remember rum is standing by.
                                                           —Old Jamaican saying

---

property with a small pool that's found in an unattractive courtyard. We'd give the Mandeville Hotel (see below) higher marks, though it too is a bit spartan. About half of the rooms here overlook the verdant fairways of the local golf course (Manchester Country Club); others front a swimming pool and a banal courtyard. Rooms are outfitted motel-style with relatively comfortable furnishings. About a third of them have air-conditioning, and each is equipped with a shower-tub combination bathroom.

5½ Caledonia Rd, Mandeville. © **876/962-4477.** Fax 876/962-5640. www.thegolfviewhotel.com. 51 units. Year-round $52–$71 double; $75 1-bedroom suite; $85 2-bedroom suite. AE, DISC, MC, V. **Amenities:** Restaurant; bar; outdoor pool; airport transfers; business center; laundry service; rooms for those with limited mobility. *In room:* A/C (in some units), TV, iron, ceiling fan.

Mandeville Hotel   This ornate hotel dates from 1875, once housing part of the British military garrison. In the 1970s the original hotel was replaced with a modern structure. There's a spacious lounge and good food and service. Bedrooms range in size from small to spacious, furnished with Jamaican styling, often including a four-poster bed and mahogany furniture. Bathrooms are old-fashioned but tidily maintained, each with a shower and tub. There are attractive gardens, plus golf and tennis at the nearby Manchester Country Club.

There is no pretension to the food at all; it's simple, homemade fare. From the dining room, you'll have a view of the pool and the green hills of central Jamaica.

4 Hotel St. (P.O. Box 78), Mandeville. © **876/962-2460.** Fax 876/962-0700. www.mandevillehotel.com. 29 units. Year-round $88–$125 double. AE, MC, V. **Amenities:** Restaurant; bar; pool; limited room service; laundry service; rooms for those with limited mobility. *In room:* TV, kitchenette (in 1 unit), fridge, coffeemaker.

WHERE TO DINE

Bloomfield Great House INTERNATIONAL   This is the only restaurant in town that's viewed as a destination in its own right. Serving excellent food in an intricately restored setting of historic interest, it's a hangout for the town's expatriate Australians, Brits, Americans, and Scandinavians. Surrounded by 2 hectares (5 acres) of landscaping, it's perched on a hilltop about a .4km (¼ mile) south of the town's commercial core, in a verdant residential neighborhood of upscale private homes. Start off with a drink in the cozy mahogany-trimmed pub before dining on the rambling veranda (with views that sweep out over the town), or a high-ceilinged dining room with colonial-style trim and moldings. Superb menu items include lobster ravioli, charbroiled filet mignon with sherry sauce and crispy onions, plantain-crusted chicken served with passion-fruit vinaigrette, and a delicious version of jumbo shrimp stuffed with jalapeño pepper, wrapped in bacon, and served with barbecue sauce. The pastas are house-made.

8 Perth Rd. © **876/962-7130.** Reservations recommended for dinner. Lunch main courses J$250–J$1,050 (US$4.15–US$17); dinner main courses J$615–J$1,895 (US$10–$31). AE, MC, V. Mon–Sat noon–9pm.

The Den JAMAICAN   One of Mandeville's more venerated old favorites, this restaurant is installed in a century-old setting that was once a family home. You dine in what were the occupants' former bedrooms in a setting of wood and wicker furnishings, with an old rustic feeling. You can eat inside or outdoors,

Mandeville & Environs

ACCOMMODATIONS ■
Golf View Hotel **1**
Mandevile Hotel **3**

DINING ◆
Bloomfield
Great House **5**
The Den **2**
International Chinese
Restaurant **4**

JACKASS HILL

Eden St.

New Green Rd.

Clarks Town Rd.

Kendall Rd.

JAMAICA
Mandeville • ⊛ Kingston

BATTERSEA

Battersea Rd.

Jones Hwy.

Knowles Cres.

CLARKS TOWN

Knowles Rd.

Winston

Patrick Rd.

New Green Rd.

Bonito Cresent

Hanbury Rd.

BRUMALIA

Brumilia Rd.

Gordon Rd.

GREY ABBEY

Manchester Shopping Centre

North Racecourse Rd.

CALEDONIA

West Rd.

Wint Rd.

Caledonia

Hargreaves Ave.

Main St.

TUCKER'S TURN

Police Station

Levy Ln.

Villa Rd.

De Carteret Rd.

Ward Ave. ⓘ

Manchester Country Club

South Racecourse

1

2

THE VILLA

NEW-LEIGH

GREEN VALE

Brooks Park

Ward Ave.

Tudor Theatre

✉

Odeon Theatre

3

MANDEVILLE

Park Crescent

Greenvale Rd.

A 2

PUT TOGETHER

Court House

Parish Church

BALVENIE HEIGHTS

Manchester School

Market

Wesley Rd.

BLOOMFIELD

5

Perth St.

Manchester Rd.

4

✝ Church
⛳ Golf Course
ⓘ Information
✉ Post Office

0 ———— 0.5 mi
0 ———— 0.5 km

and sometimes—mostly on Friday night—there is live music in the garden, even jazz. The chefs know their pots and pans, and turn out a savory cuisine including well-prepared grilled curry chicken, a steak kabob (with onions, pineapple, and peppers), and both jerk chicken and pork. Fish 'n chips appears often, as does a mix of grilled steak, chicken, and pork.

35 Caledonia Rd. ⓒ 876/962-3603. Reservations recommended. Main courses J$300–J$500 (US$5–US$8.30). AE, MC, V. Mon–Sat noon–9pm.

International Chinese Restaurant ASIAN   This is a good place if you're seeking some change-of-pace dining; you can eat well and inexpensively here. Some of the Chinese dishes have been given a Jamaican dash of flavor: a baked seafood medley comes with shredded coconut. Other dishes could be served at your favorite hometown Chinese eatery, such as chicken with cashew nuts. Try the special fried rice served with a combination of meats that include lobster, chicken, beef, and shrimp, all laced together with flavorful, extra-black soy sauce.

117 Manchester Rd. ⓒ 876/962-1252. Main courses J$300–J$1,668 (US$5–US$28). MC, V. Mon–Fri noon–9pm; Sat noon–9:30pm; Sun noon–8pm.

DISCOVERING THE TOWN

Mandeville sprawls across hills, but its historic core is easy to walk. The town centers around **Cecil Charlton Park** ♉, named for a former mayor. The Mandeville Courthouse stands on the northern tier of this plaza. Built of cut limestone in 1816 in Georgian style, it has an unusual double staircase and is graced with Doric columns.

Adjoining the courthouse is the **Rectory**—the oldest structure in town, completed in 1820. Throughout its long history, it was both a tavern and a hotel before reverting to its current status as a private residence. On the south side of the square rises **St. Mark's Church,** also established in 1820. It's worth a look inside for its timbered clerestory. The graveyard is filled with tombs of British soldiers who died in a yellow-fever epidemic.

Shopping in the town is a pleasure, whether in the old center or in a modern complex such as **Grove Court.** The market in the center of town teems with life, particularly on weekends when country folk ride into town on their weekly visits. It's open Monday to Saturday 9am to 4pm.

A private garden in the area worth visiting is **Mrs. Stephenson's Garden** ✸, 25 New Green Rd. (© **876/962-2328**), one of the most beautiful and well maintained in the area. An artist, Carmen Stephenson, still supervises this flamboyant "secret garden" herself. Call ahead for an appointment. The cost is a well-spent $2.

EXPLORING THE AREA

The **Manchester Country Club,** Brumalia Road (© **876/962-2403**), is Jamaica's oldest golf course, though it only has 9 holes. Beautiful vistas unfold from 661m (2,201 ft.) above sea level. Greens fees are J$1,000 (US$17), with caddy fees running J$600 (US$9.95). The course has a clubhouse, and this is also one of the best places in central Jamaica to play tennis.

If you like coffee, visit the **Jamaican Standard Products Company** ✸ (© **876/963-4211**), 3km (1¾ miles) north of Mandeville in Williamsfield. Call Monday through Friday about free tours. The factory, which has a wonderful aroma, exports mainly to Japan; it packages Blue Mountain coffee beans and its own "High Mountain" coffee. The factory also turns out spices and sauces. Call from 8am to 5pm; tours begin at 9:30am.

6

Ocho Rios & Runaway Bay

Situated on Jamaica's northeast coast, the resort areas of **Port Antonio** (see chapter 7), and **Runaway Bay** and **Ocho Rios** helped to launch large-scale tourism in Jamaica. Known for its abundant rainfall, verdant landscapes, rolling hills, and jagged estuaries, this region was once the preferred hangout for Noël Coward, Errol Flynn, and a host of British and American literati. Ian Fleming, creator of the James Bond spy thrillers, lived at Goldeneye near Ocho Rios.

Some 31km (19 miles) west lies its chief rival, the resort of **Runaway Bay**—more secluded than Ocho Rios, and without the vendors or cruise-ship arrivals. There's no real town here; it's mainly just a beachfront strip of hotels.

Just 8km (5 miles) to the west of Runaway Beach is **Discovery Bay,** whose name refers to the belief that Columbus first landed here in 1494.

A 2-hour drive east from **Montego Bay** (see chapter 3), **Ocho Rios** was once a small banana and fishing port, but tourism long ago became its leading industry. Now Jamaica's cruise-ship capital, the bay is dominated by an ore terminal and hotels with sandy beaches fringed by palm trees. The place is fine for a lazy beach vacation, but it's definitely not for anyone seeking a remote hideaway.

Ocho Rios is far lusher than Montego Bay, and many of its resort hotels boast private sandy beaches. On the other hand, golfing and nightlife are better in Mo Bay; if you want hedonism, head for Negril. Ocho Rios? It's more tranquil (some say blander) than either of them.

1 Ocho Rios

ORIENTATION

ARRIVING BY PLANE Ocho Rios is served by the tiny **Boscobel Aerodrome** (© **876/975-3101**), but no international flights wing in here. It is mainly for domestic air services. To avoid the land route to Ocho Rios, you can fly into Montego Bay and then take one of the smaller domestic lines flying from Montego Bay to Boscobel. Offering up to two scheduled flights is **Air Jamaica** (© **876/922-4661,** or toll-free in Jamaica 888/FLYAIRJ). If you're going to Ocho Rios, you will fly into the **Donald Sangster Airport** in Montego Bay (p. 50). Some hotels, particularly the larger resorts, will arrange for airport transfers from that point. Be sure to ask when you book.

To avoid crowded buses and minivans, many visitors taxi from Montego Bay to Ocho Rios for $120 per car (up to four passengers).

It is cheaper to go by van, however. The best shuttles are operated by **Tour Wise** (© **876/979-1027** in Montego Bay, or **876/974-2323** in Ocho Rios). You're dropped off at your inn about 2 hours after leaving the airport at Montego Bay.

VISITOR INFORMATION   The local office of the **Jamaica Tourist Board** is at Shop 7 in Ocean Villa Plaza on Main Street (© **876/974-2582**). It is open Monday to Friday 8:30am to 4:30pm and Saturday 9am to 1pm.

SPECIAL EVENTS

The Caribbean's most important jazz festival is the weeklong **Ocho Rios Jazz Festival,** held at various venues during the second week in June. Big names like the Jimmy Smith Trio appear here. Although Jamaica is primarily associated with reggae music, it has also contributed great jazz artists to the world, including Bertie King on saxophone and Jiver Hutchinson on trumpet. For more details and information, contact the Ocho Rios Jazz Festival (© **888/637-8111** or 323/857-5358; fax 323/692-0460; www.ochoriosjazz.com).

THE TOWN LAYOUT

Ocho Rios is hardly a place you can explore on foot, except for its inner core. Most of its uncontrolled development lies to the east of the center. The actual town stretches some 6km (3¾ miles) between Dunn's River Falls to the west and White River to the east. Connecting these far corners is A3, often called "Main Street." Mercifully, this traffic-clogged road bypasses the congested heart of town; curved like a snake, Main Street borders Turtle Bay with its beach. In the very center of town stands a handy-as-a-landmark clock tower. Main Street and Da Costa Drive meet at this point.

If you'd like to explore this northern part of Jamaica in more depth, especially by car, purchase the big fold-out map called *Ocho Rios and Beyond,* sold at all news kiosks in the center of town.

GETTING AROUND   It is not really necessary to rent a car in Ocho Rios. Taxis will make pickups when called to hotels. Taxis are governed by **JUTA** (© **876/974-2292**). In the center of town, they are plentiful in the parking lot adjacent to Ocean Village Plaza. You can also try **Maxi Taxi Associates** at Pineapple Place (© **876/974-2971**).

There is no bus service within Ocho Rios.

FAST FACTS: Ocho Rios

Banks The most convenient bank is **Bank of Nova Scotia,** Main Street (© **876/974-2311**), open Monday, Thursday, and Friday 8:15am to 4pm, and Tuesday and Wednesday 8:15am to 3pm. It has foreign exchange facilities and an ATM.

Bookstores The best is **Everybody's Bookshop,** Shop 44 in Ocean Village Plaza (© **876/974-2932**), open Monday to Saturday 9am to 5:30pm.

Emergencies Call police or report a fire by dialing © **119**. The police station (© **876/974-2533** for routine calls) is off Da Costa Drive, east of the clock tower.

Internet Access Currently there are no Internet access points in Ocho Rios, outside of hotel phone lines.

Laundry If your hotel doesn't have facilities, use **The Laundry Market** (© **876/974-5519**), east of the center at the turnoff for Shaw Park. Hours are Monday to Saturday 9am to 6pm. An alternative is **Carib Laundromat** on Main Street (© **876/974-7631**), open Monday to Saturday 7am to 7pm.

Library The **Ocho Rios Public Library** is at Milford Road (☎ **876/974-2588**), open Monday to Friday 9am to 5pm and Saturday 9am to 1pm.

Mail The main **Ocho Rios Post Office** is on Main Street (☎ **876/974-2526**), and it's open Monday to Friday 8am to 5pm. You can send faxes or telegrams from here, too. The post office is crowded and not as efficient as it should be; many visitors send important mail via UPS. The local office is at **Airpak Express,** Shop 9, Ocean Village Shopping Centre (☎ **876/974-0910**). Hours are Monday to Friday 8am to 5pm. Include "Jamaica, W.I." in all island addresses. The island has no zip codes.

Medical Services There is no hospital in Ocho Rios; the nearest is **St. Ann's Bay Hospital** (☎ **876/972-0150**), 11km (6¾ miles) west. The **Central Medical Laboratory** (☎ **876/974-2614**), in the center of town, offers basic services Monday to Friday 8am to 4:30pm, Saturday 9am to noon. So does **Medi-Rays** at the Carib Arcade on Main Street (☎ **876/974-6251**), open Monday and Friday 8am to 7pm, Tuesday to Thursday 8am to 5pm, and Saturday 8:30am to 12:30pm.

Pharmacies The most central pharmacy is **Ocho Rios Pharmacy,** Shop 27 in Ocean Village Plaza (☎ **876/974-2398**), open Monday to Saturday 9am to 8pm and Sunday 9am to 7pm. Another good one nearby is **Pinegrove Pharmacy,** in Simmons Plaza (☎ **876/974-2023**), open Monday to Saturday 9am to 8pm, Sunday 10am to 3pm.

Travel Agencies The most reliable travel agent is **Trafalgar Travel Ltd.,** Shop 69, Ocean Village Shopping Centre (☎ **876/974-5130**), open Monday to Friday 8:30am to 4:30pm and Saturday 9am to 12:30pm.

WHERE TO STAY

Note that all-inclusive resorts, where guests prepay one price for all lodgings, meals, entertainment, and often drinks, are listed separately below (p. 138). Most would fall into the Expensive or Very Expensive categories. Also, many properties, such as Beaches and Sandals, can be reached via toll-free numbers. Otherwise, use a good travel agent.

VERY EXPENSIVE

Jamaica Inn 🏨🏨 Built in 1950, the gracious beachfront Jamaica Inn is a series of long, low buildings set in a U-shape near the sea, 2km (1¼ miles) east of town. Noël Coward, arriving with Katharine Hepburn or Claudette Colbert, was a regular, and Errol Flynn and Ian Fleming used to drop in from time to time. Today it's more likely to be Kate Moss. It's an elegant anachronism, a true retro hotel, and has remained little changed in 4 decades, avoiding the glitter of all-inclusives like Sandals.

Lovely patios open onto the lawns, and the bedrooms are reached along garden paths. Guest rooms are very spacious, with colonial two-poster beds, quality carved-wood period pieces, and balustraded balconies opening onto views. Bathrooms are elegant and roomy, gleaming with marble vanities, combination shower/tubs, robes, and deluxe toiletries. The beach is a wide, champagne-colored strip; close to the shore, the sea is almost too clear to make snorkeling an adventure, but farther out it's rewarding. The European-trained chef prepares both refined international and Jamaican dishes. The emphasis is on cuisine that uses fresh local produce. Men must wear a jacket and tie in the dining room at night in winter.

Main St. (P.O. Box 1), Ocho Rios. ⓒ 877/470-6975 in the U.S., or 876/974-2514. Fax 876/974-2449. www. jamaicainn.com. 54 units. Winter including all meals $440–$715 double, from $1,400 suite for 2; off season including MAP (breakfast and dinner) $340–$470 double, from $500 suite for 2. AE, MC, V. Children age 11 and under not accepted. **Amenities:** Restaurant; 2 bars; pool; 4 tennis courts; exercise room; kayaking; Sunfish sailing; 24-hr. room service; babysitting; laundry service; nonsmoking rooms; rooms for those with limited mobility. *In room:* A/C, TV, dataport, iron/board, safe, ceiling fan.

MODERATE

Crane Ridge Resort 🏝 *(Value* Overlooking Ocho Rios, this handsomely landscaped property offers one- and two-bedroom suites, each easily accommodating one to four guests. Because of the large size of the accommodations, and because each has a kitchen, this is a family favorite. The location, on 2.8 tropical hectares (7 acres) of gardens, is not on the water, but a free shuttle runs back and forth to a private beach. Each room offers a separate living area, British colonial–style furnishings, a patio, and good-size bathrooms with tubs and showers. Note that children 13 and older are charged the same full rate as adults.

17 Da Costa Dr., Ocho Rios. ⓒ 866/277-6374 or 876/974-8050. Fax 876/974-8070. www.craneridge.net. 90 units. Winter $100 double, $140 1-bedroom suite, $160 2-bedroom suite; off season $90 double, $130 1-bedroom suite, $150 2-bedroom suite. AE, MC, V. **Amenities:** Restaurant; 2 bars; outdoor pool; 2 tennis courts; Jacuzzi; limited room service; babysitting; laundry service; free beach shuttle; nonsmoking rooms; rooms for those with limited mobility. *In room:* A/C, TV, kitchenette.

Hibiscus Lodge Hotel *(Value* This intimate little inn offers more value for your money than any other resort in Ocho Rios. Perched precariously on a cliff along the shore near the Ocho Rios Mall, it has character and charm—and the golden sands of Mallards Bay Beach lie a 3- to 4-minute walk away. Medium-size bedrooms, either doubles or triples, have small, shower-only bathrooms, ceiling fans, and verandas opening onto the sea. After a day spent in a pool suspended over the cliffs, or lounging on the large sun deck, guests can enjoy a drink in the unique swinging bar or a meal at the Almond Tree (p. 144).

83 Main St. (P.O. Box 52), Ocho Rios. ⓒ 876/974-2676. Fax 876/974-1874. 26 units. Winter $115–$126 double, $157 triple; off season $103–$115 double, $140 triple. Rates include breakfast. AE, MC, V. **Amenities:** Restaurant; bar; outdoor pool; tennis court; Jacuzzi; limited room service; babysitting; laundry service; rooms for those with limited mobility. *In room:* A/C, TV, hair dryer, iron/board, safe.

High Hope Estate 🏝 Because this hotel is so intimate, whether you like it will depend on whether you click with the owner and the other guests. Basically, it's an upscale private home in the style of the British colonial world at its most rarefied that accepts paying guests. It was built for a socially prominent heiress, Kitty Spence, granddaughter of prairie-state populist William Jennings Bryan, and later served as the home and laboratory of a horticulturist who successfully bred 560 varieties of flowering hibiscus. The estate's 16 hectares (40 acres), set 165m (550 ft.) above the coast and 11km (6¾ miles) west of Ocho Rios, thrive with flowering plants as well as memories of such luminaries as Noël Coward, who used to play the grand piano that graces one of the public areas. There are absolutely no planned activities here. Bedrooms are a delight—spacious, well thought out, and exceedingly comfortable. The excellent bathrooms have shower/tub combinations. Lying only 150m (492 ft.) from the estate house, a luxurious two-bedroom villa is available. Called the Willows, it stands on .8 hectares (2 acres) of beautifully landscaped grounds, with a foundation dating back 150 years. There is a minimum stay of 5 nights. The staff is on-hand

Ocho Rios

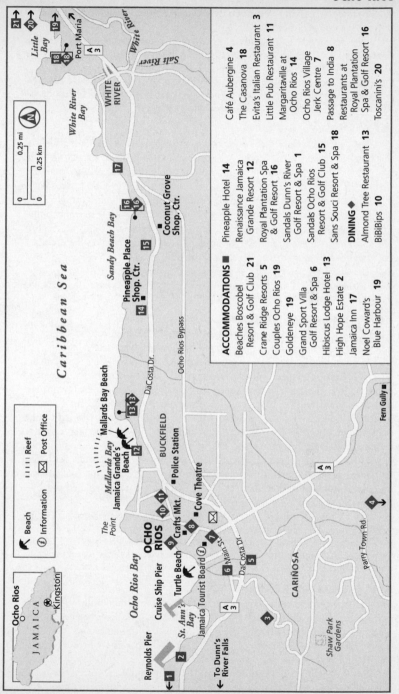

ACCOMMODATIONS ■
Beaches Boscobel
Resort & Golf Club **21**
Crane Ridge Resorts **5**
Couples Ocho Rios **19**
Goldeneye **19**
Grand Sport Villa
Golf Resort & Spa **6**
Hibiscus Lodge Hotel **13**
High Hope Estate **2**
Jamaica Inn **17**
Noel Coward's
Blue Harbour **19**
Pineapple Hotel **14**
Renaissance Jamaica
Grande Resort **12**
Royal Plantation Spa
& Golf Resort **16**
Sandals Dunn's River
Golf Resort & Spa **1**
Sandals Ocho Rios
Resort & Golf Club **15**
Sans Souci Resort & Spa **18**

DINING ◆
Almond Tree Restaurant **13**
BiBiBips **10**
Café Aubergine **4**
The Casanova **18**
Evita's Italian Restaurant **3**
Little Pub Restaurant **11**
Margaritaville at
Ocho Rios **14**
Ocho Rios Village
Jerk Centre **7**
Passage to India **8**
Restaurants at
Royal Plantation
Spa & Golf Resort **16**
Toscanini's **20**

to help supervise children, maintain the property, and prepare meals for anyone who gives advance notice

The nearest beach is a 10-minute ride away. You can rent the entire villa with a group of friends, and you can purchase all-inclusive packages.

Box 11, St. Ann's Bay, near Ocho Rios. © **876/972-2277.** Fax 876/972-1607. www.highhopeestate.com. 5 units. Year-round $125–$165 double; $500 villa. Rates include breakfast. MC, V. **Amenities:** Restaurant; outdoor pool; limited room service; babysitting; laundry service; nonsmoking rooms; rooms for those with limited mobility; TV room. *In room:* Minibar, coffeemaker, hair dryer, ceiling fan.

INEXPENSIVE

Pineapple Hotel *(Kids)* Next door to the Pineapple Place Shopping Centre, this hotel offers very basic accommodations at bargain prices. Expect no frills; stay only if you can't afford the high prices of Ocho Rios and plan to spend little time in your room. The tropically decorated quarters include private bathrooms with showers, tile floors, and air-conditioning, but if you want to make a phone call, you must do it from the front desk. TVs are available in some rooms. There's a restaurant serving Italian, American, and Jamaican food; watersports can be arranged at the front desk; and there's a swimming pool on the premises. For a seaside romp, try Turtle Beach, a short walk away.

Pineapple Place (P.O. Box 263), Ocho Rios. © **876/974-2727.** Fax 876/974-9073. 20 units. Year-round $60 double; $60 triple. Children 11 and under stay free in parent's room. AE, MC, V. **Amenities:** Fast-food restaurant; bar; pool; watersports; kids camp. *In room:* A/C, TV (in some units), iron/board, safe, no phone.

NEARBY PLACES TO STAY

Noël Coward's Blue Harbour *(★)* *(Finds)* This 1950s-aura retreat, 24km (15 miles) east of Ocho Rios, was once owned by Coward, who entertained the rich and famous of his day here. Coward dubbed the place—his first Jamaica retreat—"Coward's Folly." Today the compound is rented whole or in part to paying guests who appreciate its funky nostalgia. The compound can comfortably accommodate 10 to 12 guests, though up to 18 could squeeze in, if needed. The main house is the Villa Grande, with two bedrooms and two bathrooms with shower, plus a kitchen, dining room, and terrace. Villa Rose, a guesthouse, contains two large bedrooms, and the smaller Villa Chica is a one-bedroom, one-bathroom cottage once favored by Marlene Dietrich and Katharine Hepburn. Meals—Jamaican, vegetarian, and international—are cooked by a friendly, helpful staff. Note that the entire place is sometimes rented out by a single party, shutting out other guests.

North Coast Rd. (P.O. Box 50), Port Maria, St. Mary. © **876/725-0289** or 505/586-1244 (Questa, N.M.). Fax 505/586-1087. www.blueharb.com. 3 villas. Year-round $170 double; $1,190 weekly. Rates are all-inclusive. No credit cards. On the North Coast Rd. (A4), 129km (80 miles) west of Montego Bay and 97km (60 miles) north of Kingston. **Amenities:** Dining room; outdoor pool; limited room service; in-room massage; babysitting; laundry service. *In room:* TV, kitchenette, minibar, iron/board, safe.

ALL-INCLUSIVE RESORTS

More so than any resort in Jamaica, Ocho Rios is now firmly in the all-inclusive resort camp. Many of the older and more established inns have been swallowed up by the Sandals umbrella, reborn as all-inclusives with names like "Beaches."

Not for independent or frugal types, these all-inclusives—where things can feel scheduled and formulaic—are nevertheless the best, most luxurious lodgings at Ocho Rios (with an exception or two). Most are quite expensive as a result. The following resorts all include your room, drinks, and meals, plus often many activities, in the price. Seek detailed clarification of what's included when booking.

Noël's "Folly"

Arriving in Jamaica in 1944, the gay English playwright, songwriter, raconteur, and actor Noël Coward discovered his dream island.

He returned in 1948 and rented Goldeneye from his friend Ian Fleming, the real-life spy who later created the James Bond character at this estate. During this stopover, Coward found a "magical spot" 16km (10 miles) down the coast at St. Mary's. The land was once owned by Sir Henry Morgan, the notorious buccaneer who had built a small fortress on the property so he could spy on any stray galleon entering local waters. It was here that Coward began construction on what he called his "folly"—**Blue Harbour,** which can be rented today (see above).

Once settled in, Coward sent out invitations to his "bloody loved ones." They included Laurence Olivier, Vivien Leigh, Alfred Lunt, Lynn Fontane, Errol Flynn, Katharine Hepburn, Mary Martin, Claudette Colbert, and John Gielgud, among others. Some stayed an entire month.

Blue Harbour became so popular on the North Coast cocktail circuit that in 1956 Coward fled it and built **Firefly** on a panoramic nearby hilltop. It still stands today much as he left it (p. 149). Coward lived at Firefly with his longtime companion, Graham Payn.

In 1965 the Queen Mother came to visit Coward, who prepared a lobster mousse for her only to have it melt in the hot sun. He quickly rushed to the kitchen and opened a can of split-pea soup. She found it "divine"—perhaps because Coward had hastily laced it with sherry.

Sir Winston Churchill, who also loved Jamaica, visited Coward several times at Firefly. He told the playwright: "An Englishman has an inalienable right to live wherever he chooses."

Coward died at Firefly and is buried on the grounds. You can still see his plain, flat white marble gravestone, which is inscribed simply: "Sir Noël Coward, born December 16, 1899, died March 26, 1973."

Beaches Boscobel Resort & Golf Club ⏏ *(Kids)* Sixteen kilometers (10 miles) east of Ocho Rios on a beach, this once-tired resort looks new again after an $18-million renovation and renaming. Management has been assumed by the Sandals group, normally a couples-only chain but here especially receptive to families with children (big or small); singles and couples are welcomed, too, but might not like all the kids underfoot. There's a wide array of accommodations, from family rooms to honeymoon beach suites; each comes with a good-size private bathroom with tub/shower combination. Guests can play free at the nearby Sandals golf course. Note that this place is new, and the rates listed below may change during the life of this edition; inquire when booking.

P.O. Box 63, Boscobel Beach, Ocho Rios. © 888/BEACHES or 876/974-7777. Fax 876/975-7622. www.beaches.com. 224 units. Year-round $280–$320 per person in a double. $80 per child (2–16). Children 1 and under free. Rates are all-inclusive. AE, MC, V. **Amenities:** 5 restaurants; 7 bars; 4 outdoor pools; nearby golf; 4 tennis courts; fitness center; 3 Jacuzzis; full program of watersports (from kayaks to windsurfing); Kids Kamp program; teen disco; game center; pool tables; 24-hr. room service; babysitting; rooms for those with limited mobility; dance club; beach volleyball; kiddie pool; petting zoo. *In room:* A/C, TV, coffeemaker, hair dryer, safe.

Tips **Your Own Private Villa**

If you're looking for complete immersion in a private Jamaican community of well-maintained homes, and if you prefer a rental where you prepare your own meals, make your own bed, and do your own laundry,
consider **Ay Caramba.** A 15-minute drive east from Ocho Rios and a short
walk from James Bond Beach, this is a well-designed villa of comfortably
furnished, private, one-bedroom units. Each unit has cable TV, ceiling
fans, a washing machine, a fully equipped kitchen, a private bathroom
with shower, and a sofa bed (in addition to the bed in the bedroom). The
villa's design is based vaguely on Spanish colonial models and offers views
that sweep out over Jamaica's North Coast. Rates start at $120 per night,
and each unit can accommodate up to four people; the owner gives
excellent local advice. For more information, call © **305/532-1234** in the
U.S. or 876/975-3597 in Jamaica.

Couples Ocho Rios ℛ This is a couples-only resort (and management
defines couples as "any man and woman in love"). Most are married, and many
are on their honeymoons. Everything is in pairs, even the chairs at night by
the moon-drenched beach. Some guests slip away from the resort, which is an
18-minute drive (8km/5 miles) east of town, to Couples's private island to bask
in the buff. (A shuttle boat transports visitors offshore to this beautiful little
island with a fine sandy beach, a bar, and a pool. Security guards keep the gawk-
ers from bothering guests here.)

In general, this is a classier operation than the more mass-market Sandals (at
least the Dunn's River and the Ocho Rios versions). The bedrooms have either
a king-size bed or two doubles, pleasantly traditional furnishings, and a patio
fronting either the sea or the mountains. Good-size bathrooms have a shower/
tub combination. For a chain all-inclusive, the cuisine is above average.

Tower Isle, along Rte. A3 (P.O. Box 330), Ocho Rios. © **800/268-7537** in the U.S., or 876/975-4271. Fax 876/
975-4439. www.couples.com. 210 units. All-inclusive rates: winter $500-$540 double, $650-$750 suite; off
season $460–$515 double, $610–$725 suite. Rates include all meals, drinks, and activities. AE, MC, V. The
hotel usually accepts bookings for a minimum of any 3 nights of the week, though most guests book by the
week. No one under 18 accepted. **Amenities:** 5 restaurants; 3 bars; outdoor pool; golf; 4 tennis courts;
squash courts; health club and spa; 5 Jacuzzis; sauna; sailing; scuba diving; snorkeling; water-skiing; windsurfing; bike rental; Internet room; room service (breakfast only); nonsmoking rooms; rooms for those with
limited mobility; yoga; horseback riding;. *In room:* A/C, TV, coffeemaker, hair dryer, iron/board, safe.

Goldeneye ℛℛ Few hotels in the world manage to be so luxurious and yet
so appealingly informal as this intimate retreat. It's centered around the villa
where the most famous secret agent in the world, James Bond (007), was created in 1952 by then-owner Ian Fleming. Fleming built the imposing but simple main house in 1946, and wrote each of the 13 original James Bond books
there. In the early 1990s, music-publisher-turned-hotelier Chris Blackwell
bought and restored the by-then dilapidated property to its original modernist
dignity. Fleming's original desk remains, and the oversize Indonesian furniture
is enhanced with memorabilia from what became the most famous spy movies
in the world. The main house is usually only rented as a three-bedroom whole
for extended house parties, often to rock stars and other celebs.

You're more likely to rent one of the four additional villas that were built in
harmony with nature, on the surrounding property. Each evokes a tropical

version of a billionaire's summer camp in Maine, thanks to a juxtaposition of indoor and outdoor spaces, sofas, and well-chosen decorative pieces. Each unit has a fully equipped kitchen. All drinks, food, and most activities are included in the price. The cuisine features some Jamaican favorites as well as international dishes.

There's a pool on the premises, but it's reserved for occupants of the main house. Masonry paths lead to a nearby beach.

Oracabessa, St. Mary. © **800/688-7678** in the U.S., or 876/975-3354. Fax 876/975-3620. www.island outpost.com. 5 villas. Winter $795 1-bedroom villa, $995 2-bedroom villa, $1,195 3-bedroom villa, $3,500 Ian Fleming house; off season $595 1-bedroom villa, $795 2-bedroom villa, $995 3-bedroom villa, $2,500 Ian Fleming house. Rates include all meals, drinks, and activities. AE, DISC, MC, V. **Amenities:** Outdoor pool; watersports; limited room service; babysitting; laundry service; nonsmoking rooms; rooms for those with limited mobility. *In room:* A/C, TV, dataport, kitchenette, minibar, coffeemaker, iron/board, safe.

Grand Sport Villa Golf Resort & Spa ₰

This all-inclusive lies a 2km (1¼-mile) drive southeast of town, set on 18 hectares (45 acres) of tropical gardens on a private estate dotted with red-tile villas. A great house in the hills overlooks the Caribbean. Across from the imposing gate near the resort's entrance are the white sands of a private beach.

All but a handful of the accommodations are in one-, two-, or three-bedroom villas, each with a pool, a fully equipped kitchen, and a shaded terrace. Honeymoon villas have their own whirlpools. Thirty-six units are traditional single or double rooms on the third floor of the great house. Accommodations are high-ceilinged, roomy, and decorated in Caribbean colors. They're well furnished, with particularly fine beds, and the bathrooms with combination shower/tubs are well maintained.

Main St. (P.O. Box 728), Ocho Rios, St. Ann. © **800/BEACHES** in the U.S. and Canada, or 876/974-1027. Fax 876/974-5838. www.beaches.com. 285 units. All-inclusive rates for 3 nights per couple: winter $1,590–$1,680 double, $1,920 junior suite, $2,400–$2,640 1-bedroom villa suite, $4,170 2-bedroom villa for 4; off season $1,320–$1,560 double, $1,710 junior suite, $1,890–$2,370 1-bedroom villa suite, $3,690 2-bedroom villa for 4. AE, MC, V. Children age 15 and under not accepted. **Amenities:** 4 restaurants; 5 bars; 9 outdoor pools; 6 tennis courts; spa; 5 Jacuzzis; 2 saunas; 2 steam rooms; scuba diving; laundry service; nonsmoking rooms; rooms for those with limited mobility. *In room:* A/C, TV, dataport, kitchenette, minibar, hair dryer, iron/board, safe, beverage maker.

Renaissance Jamaica Grande Resort (Kids)

This family favorite is the largest hotel in Jamaica, a combination of two high-rise beachfront properties constructed in 1975 and 1976. In 1993 an elaborate cluster of waterfalls and swimming pools was inserted into what had been parking lots between the towers, and the entire complex was unified into a coherent whole. The place is pure theatrics and special effects, like a Hollywood production, but is short on true Jamaican style. It seems to be meant to overwhelm guests. Today the end result boasts more beachfront than any other hotel in Ocho Rios and a comfortable array of public rooms (often filled with members of tour or conference groups). The standard bedrooms are tile-floored and furnished with Caribbean furniture; each opens onto a private balcony, and contains a midsize private bathroom with tub and shower.

Main St. (P.O. Box 100), Ocho Rios, St. Ann. © **800/618-1299** or 876/974-2201. Fax 876/974-5378. www. renaissancehotels.com/ocjrt. 723 units. Year-round $191-$450 double, $367-$565 suite for 2. Rates are all-inclusive. AE, DC, MC, V. **Amenities:** 5 restaurants; 5 bars; outdoor pool; 2 tennis courts; gym; whirlpool; sauna; watersports; children's program; limited room service; babysitting; laundry service; rooms for those with limited mobility. *In room:* A/C, TV, dataport, kitchenette (in suites), minibar (in suites), coffeemaker, hair dryer, iron, safe.

Royal Plantation Spa & Golf Resort 🌟🌟   This stately inn, a rival of the Jamaica Inn, has fallen under the Sandals umbrella and become the chain's most upmarket property in Jamaica. The hotel entrance evokes the antebellum South. At any moment, you expect Scarlett O'Hara to rush out to greet Rhett. You drive up a sweeping driveway and enter through a colonnaded portico 2km (1¼ miles) east of the center. A complete renovation has brought major improvements to the rooms and public areas and added a full-service European spa. Accommodations are all suites, each opening onto the ocean views. Bedrooms are handsomely equipped with such extras as plush cotton robes, daily *New York Times*, fax service, Internet connections, CD players, and the like. Guests have full exchange privileges with the two other Sandals resorts in the area. The cuisine is far superior to that at the other Sandals properties, and the atmosphere less rowdy.

Main St., Ocho Rios. © 888/48ROYAL or 876/974-5601. Fax 876/974-5912. www.royalplantation.com. 77 units. Winter $460–$1,510 double; off season $405–$1,510 double. Children age 18 and over accepted. AE, DC, DISC, MC, V. **Amenities:** 3 restaurants; bar; golf at nearby Sandals; spa; glass-bottom boat; scuba diving; 24-hr. room service. *In room:* A/C, cable TV, VCR, minibar, safe, CD player, Internet connection.

Sandals Dunn's River Golf Resort & Spa 🌟   Located on a wide, sugary beach, this is the finest of the Sandals resorts, at least in the opinion of some guests who have sampled them all. As at all Sandals resorts, only adult male-female couples are allowed—no gays and no children. Set on the beachfront between Ocho Rios and St. Ann's Bay, the resort is very sports-oriented. It occupies 10 well-landscaped hectares (25 acres), offering attractively furnished and often quite spacious accommodations. All the rooms have an Italianate/Mediterranean motif. The elegant guest rooms are scattered among the six-story main building, two lanai buildings, and a five-story west wing. Extras include spacious balconies, walk-in closets, king-size beds, and shower/tub combinations. Before retreating to the disco or enjoying the nightly entertainment, guests can choose among several dining options, selecting from an array of restaurants that attempt variety in lieu of first-rate cuisine. The International Room is elegant, with fabric-covered walls and rosewood furniture. The Windies Restaurant serves Caribbean specialties. D'Amoré offers Italian cuisine, and Restaurant Kimonos serves Chinese, Polynesian, and Japanese dishes.

Rte. A3 (P.O. Box 51), Ocho Rios. © 800/SANDALS in the U.S. and Canada, or 876/972-1610. Fax 876/ 972-1611. www.sandals.com. 250 units. All-inclusive rates: winter $930–$1,100 double, from $1,535 suite; off season $510–$785 double, from $1,230 suite. Minimum stay of 4 days/3 nights. AE, DISC, MC, V. **Amenities:** 4 restaurants; 4 bars; snack bar/grill; 2 outdoor pools; shuttle to 18-hole golf course; pitch-and-putt golf course; 4 tennis courts; health club and spa; 3 Jacuzzis; saunas; steam rooms; watersports; limited room service (in suites only); laundry service; nonsmoking rooms; rooms for those with limited mobility. *In room:* A/C, TV, iron/board, safe.

Sandals Ocho Rios Resort & Golf Club 🌟   This resort opening onto a good sandy beach attracts a mix of unmarried and married (only male-female) couples, including honeymooners. At times the place seems like a summer camp for grown-ups (and some who didn't quite grow up). This is the most low-key of the Sandals properties. Is it romantic? Most guests think so, although we've encountered other couples whose relationship didn't survive the 3-night minimum stay.

On 5 well-landscaped hectares (13 acres) 2km (1¼ miles) west of the town center, it offers comfortably furnished but uninspired rooms with either ocean or garden views, plus some cottage units. All units are reasonably large, with king-size beds and good-size bathrooms with shower/tub combinations. You can sip drinks at an oceanside swim-up bar. Nightly theme parties and live entertainment take place in a modern amphitheater. A unique feature of the resort is an open-air disco. The resort's main dining room is Bayside, Valentino's serves standard Italian food, and the Reef Terrace Grill does above-average Jamaican cuisine and fresh seafood. A more recent addition is the Arizona Steak-house, with some sizzling good steaks and Lone Star ribs.

Main St. (P.O. Box 771), Ocho Rios. Ⓒ **800/SANDALS** in the U.S. and Canada, or 876/974-5691. Fax 876/974-5700. www.sandals.com. 237 units. All-inclusive rates per couple: winter $520–$730 double, from $1,250 suite; off season $490–$660 double, from $1,200 suite. AE, MC, V. **Amenities:** 4 restaurants; 5 bars; 3 outdoor pools; 2 tennis courts; fitness center; Jacuzzis; saunas; watersports; room service in suites only; massage; babysitting; laundry service; nonsmoking rooms; rooms for those with limited mobility. In room: A/C, TV.

Sans Souci Resort & Spa 𝕽𝕽𝕽   If a cookie-cutter Sandals is the last thing you want, head for this classier beachfront joint. Winner of four diamonds from AAA, this pink, cliff-side luxurious resort is 5km (3 miles) east of town on a forested plot of land abutting a good white-sand beach. This Grand Lido is more elegant than the one in Negril. There's a separate clothing-optional beach, a mineral bath big enough for an elephant, and a labyrinth of catwalks and bridges stretching over rocky chasms filled with surging water.

Each unit features a veranda or patio, copies of Chippendale furniture, plush upholstery, and subdued colonial elegance. Some contain Jacuzzis. Accommodations range from rather standard bedrooms to vast suites with large living and dining areas, plus kitchens. Deluxe touches include glazed tile floors, luxurious beds, and marble bathrooms with whirlpool tubs. You'll enjoy the food at the elegant Casanova restaurant.

Rte. A3 (P.O. Box 103), Ocho Rios. Ⓒ **800/448-7702** or 876/994-1206. Fax 876/994-1544. www.sanssouci jamaica.com. 146 units. All-inclusive rates: winter $500–$750 double; off season $450–$660 double. AE, DISC, MC, V. No children under 16 accepted. **Amenities:** 3 restaurants; 4 bars; 4 outdoor pools; 2 tennis courts; health club and spa; 2 Jacuzzis; sauna; watersports; 24-hr. room service; laundry service/dry cleaning; nonsmoking rooms; rooms for those with limited mobility. In room: A/C, TV, minibar, hair dryer, iron/board, safe, beverage maker.

WHERE TO DINE

Because nearly all the major hotels in Ocho Rios have gone all-inclusive, smaller, independent restaurants are struggling to survive.

VERY EXPENSIVE

The Casanova 𝕽𝕽 FRENCH   The suave Casanova is one of the most elegant enclaves along the North Coast, a super choice when you feel like dressing up. Meals are included for guests of the hotel, but nonguests who purchase a pass can also enjoy dinner and entertainment here. All drinks are included. Jazz wafting in from a lattice-roofed gazebo might accompany your meal. In the late 1960s, Harry Cipriani (of Harry's Bar fame in Venice) taught the staff some of his culinary techniques, and a little more care seems to go into the cuisine here, as opposed to the mass-market chow-downs at some of the other all-inclusives. Salads, vegetarian dishes, and soups are made fresh daily. Typical dishes include an appetizer of smoked chicken breast in a Continental berry sauce, or a small vegetable mousse with a fontina-cheese sauce. For your main course, you might prefer osso buco (braised veal shanks) or roast Cornish hen with citrus and mild spice.

In the Sans Souci Resort and Spa, along Rte. A3, 5km (3 miles) east of Ocho Rios. Ⓒ 876/994-1353. Reservations required except Tues and Fri. Nonguest evening pass (6pm–2am) of $90 per person includes dinner (beach buffet Tues and Fri), entertainment, and drinks. AE, MC, V. Mon, Wed–Thurs and Sat–Sun 6:30–9:30pm.

Restaurants at Royal Plantation Spa & Golf Resort *✿✿* JAMAICAN/
CONTINENTAL   Because this is an all-inclusive, you must purchase a pass to
enter (see below). Once inside, you can dine as lavishly as you want at any of
their trio of restaurants. You'll think you've arrived at Tara in *Gone with the
Wind:* An evening here, dining and dancing by candlelight, is one of the most
romantic experiences in Ocho Rios. You're seated at beautifully set tables with
crisp linens, either indoors or on a terrace. After the dinner plates are cleared, a
dance band plays. The Continental cuisine is spiced up a bit by Jamaican specialties; try "Fire & Spice," a chicken and beef kabob with a ginger-pimento
sauce. For the main course, we ask the chef to prepare a whole roast fish from
the catch of the day, seasoned with island herbs and spices and presented with
fresh country vegetables. Because the place attracts a lot of meat eaters, the chefs
also prepare the classics: lamb chops Provençal and the like.

Main St. *©* 876/974-5601. Reservations required. Men must wear jackets at night. Nonguest pass $130.
AE, DISC, MC, V. Daily 7:30–11am, 12:30–2:30pm, and 7–10pm.

MODERATE

Almond Tree Restaurant JAMAICAN/CONTINENTAL   The Almond
Tree is a two-tiered patio restaurant with a tree growing through the roof. Lobster thermidor is the tastiest item on the menu, but we also like the bouillabaisse
(made with conch and lobster). Other excellent choices are the roast suckling
pig, medallions of beef, and a fondue bourguignon. Jamaican plantation rice is
a local specialty. The wine list offers a variety of vintages, including Spanish and
Jamaican. Have a cocktail in the unique "swinging bar"—with swinging chairs,
that is.

In the Hibiscus Lodge Hotel, 83 Main St. *©* 876/974-2813. Reservations recommended for dinner. Main
courses $15–$26. AE, MC, V. Daily 7:30–10:30am, noon–2:30pm, and 6–9:30pm.

Café Aubergine *✿✿* *Finds* FRENCH/ITALIAN   This most intriguing
restaurant, 18km (11 miles) south of Ocho Rios (and a 40-min. drive), is an
offbeat adventure. European-trained chef Neville Anderson has converted an
18th-century tavern into a restaurant serving food as good as (or better than)
that in the best restaurants of Ocho Rios.

You're welcomed inside a gingerbread-trim house with cascading pink and red
flowers. On our last visit the cook was roasting half a cow. The dishes would pass
muster on the Left Bank: sautéed breast of chicken in a lemon caper sauce over
a bed of linguine or grilled lamb chops with a honey mustard sauce, for instance.
We're also fond of baked crab with white wine (seasoned with fresh herbs) and
the smoked marlin with pineapple sorbet.

Moneague. *©* 876/973-0527. Reservations required. Main courses $12–$25. DC, MC, V. Wed–Sun
noon–8:30pm (last seating at 8:30pm).

Evita's Italian Restaurant *✿* ITALIAN   A 5-minute drive south of the
commercial heart of Ocho Rios, in a hillside residential neighborhood that
enjoys a panoramic view over the harbor and beachfronts, this is one of the most
fun restaurants along the north coast of Jamaica. Its soul and artistic flair come
from Eva Myers, the convivial former owner of some of the most legendary bars
of Montego Bay, who established her culinary headquarters in this green and
white gingerbread Jamaican house in 1990. An outdoor terrace adds additional
seating and enhanced views. More than half the menu is devoted to pastas,
including almost every variety known to northern and southern Italy. The fish
dishes are excellent—especially the snapper stuffed with crabmeat and the

lobster and scampi in a buttery white cream sauce. Italian (or other) wines by the bottle might accompany your main course.

Eden Bower Rd. ℭ **876/974-2333.** Reservations recommended. Main courses $12–$23. AE, MC, V. Daily 11am–11pm.

Little Pub Restaurant JAMAICAN/INTERNATIONAL   Located in a red-brick courtyard with a fishpond and waterfall in the center of town, this pub is the town's most popular. No one will mind if you enjoy a drink in one of the pub's barrel chairs; if you want dinner, proceed to one of the linen-covered tables topped with cut flowers and candles. We're fond of the barbecued chicken and grilled kingfish, but you might like snapper or fresh lobster.

59 Main St. ℭ **876/974-2324.** Reservations recommended. Main courses $12–$28. MC, V. Daily 7am–10:30pm.

Margaritaville at Ocho Rios *(Kids* JAMAICAN   Lying in the new Island Village, a shopping-and-entertainment complex, this is one of the largest restaurants ever constructed on the North Coast, seating 450 diners and drinkers. A high-energy bar and grill, Margaritaville provides all-day family fun with the entertainment continuing late at night. Attractions include a rooftop whirlpool tub, a 30m-long (100-ft.) water slide, and a freshwater pool along with three bars and a Trading Post. The decor is rustic West Indian, with an Afro-Cuban aura. Of course, being a Jimmy Buffett dive, expect the world-famous tropical margaritas and those delectable "Cheeseburgers in Paradise." There's dancing here—reggae disco-style—at night.

Turtle Beach Rd. (at the cruise-ship docks). ℭ **876/675-8976.** Free admission. Main courses $12–$18; burgers and salads $7–$11. AE, MC, V. Daily 8:30am–11pm.

Toscanini's ITALIAN   The three partners behind this place all hail from Parma, Italy. Coming from a long line of restaurateurs, they bring style and a Continental sophistication to their food service and preparation. The restaurant is set in an art gallery on the coast. The menu offers many classic Italian dishes, supplemented by ever-changing specials, depending on what's fresh at the market. The best specialties include marinated marlin, various homemade pastas, carpaccio, gnocchi, and a strong emphasis on fresh lobster and seafood. The chef also caters to vegetarians. All this good food is backed up by a fine wine list.

In Harmony Hall, Tower Isles on Rte. A3, 6km (3¾ miles) east of Ocho Rios. ℭ **876/975-4785.** Main courses $12–$24; pasta dishes $10–$16. AE, MC, V. Tues–Sun noon–2pm and 7–10:30pm.

INEXPENSIVE

BiBiBips INTERNATIONAL/JAMAICAN   Set in the main tourist strip of Ocho Rios, this restaurant (whose name is the owner's nickname) occupies a sprawling open-air compound of porches and verandas. Lots of single folks come just to hang out at the bar. Drinks and flirtations sometimes segue into dinner at the adjacent restaurant, where well-prepared menu items include Red Stripe shrimp, which is deep-fried in a beer-based batter; coconut-curried chicken; vegetarian Rasta Pasta; and a combination Creole-style seafood platter. Lunches are a bit simpler, focusing mostly on sandwiches, salads, and an especially delicious jerk chicken burger. There's live entertainment, usually some kind of rap or reggae band, every Friday, Saturday, and Sunday beginning at 8pm.

93 Main St. ℭ **876/974-8759.** Lunch main courses $5.50–$21; dinner main courses $8.50–$28. AE, MC, V. Daily 11am–5:30pm and 6pm–2am.

Ocho Rios Village Jerk Centre *(Finds)* JAMAICAN   At this open-air restaurant, you can get the best jerk dishes along this part of the coast. When only a frosty Red Stripe beer can quench your thirst and your stomach is growling for the fiery taste of Jamaican jerk seasonings, head here—and don't dress up. Don't expect anything fancy: It's the food that counts, and you'll find fresh daily specials posted on a chalkboard menu on the wall. The dishes are hot and spicy, but not *too* hot; hot spices are presented on the side for those who want to go truly Jamaican. The barbecued ribs are especially good, and fresh fish is a delight, perfectly grilled—try the red snapper. Vegetarian dishes are also available on request, and if you don't drink beer, you can wash it all down with natural fruit juices.

Da Costa Dr. ℭ 876/974-2549. Jerk pork $3 ¼ lb., $10 1 lb. Whole jerk chicken $12. MC, V. Daily 10am–11pm.

Passage to India *(Finds)* INDIAN   This is the most visible and desirable Indian restaurant on the North Coast, set on the second floor of a busy shopping mall. Menu items feature a wide array of chicken, lamb, vegetable, and fish dishes. Best-selling favorites include a tandoor sizzler featuring kabobs of chicken, mutton, and vegetables; minced chicken with garlic, ginger, coriander, and cumin; and a medley of exotic mushrooms served with oregano and spices.

In Soni's Plaza, 50 Main St. ℭ 876/795-3182. Main courses J$500–J$790 (US$8.30–US$13). MC, V. Mon 10am–3pm; Tues–Sun 11:30am–10pm.

HITTING THE BEACH

The most idyllic sands are at the often-overcrowded **Mallards Beach,** in the center of Ocho Rios, and are shared by hotel guests and cruise-ship passengers. Locals may steer you to the white sands of **Turtle Beach** in the center, between the Renaissance Jamaica Grande and Club Jamaica. It's smaller, more desirable, and not as overcrowded as Mallards.

The most frequented (and to be avoided when cruise ships are in port) is **Dunn's River Beach,** located below the famous falls. Another great spot is **Jamaica Grande's Beach,** which is open to the public. Parasailing is a favorite sport here.

Many exhibitionist couples check into the famous but pricey **Couples Resort,** which is known for its private au naturel island.

Our favorite is none of the above. We always follow the trail of 007 and head for **James Bond Beach** (ℭ 876/975-3663), east of Ocho Rios at Oracabessa Beach. Entrepreneur Chris Blackwell reopened writer Ian Fleming's former home, Goldeneye. For $5 adults, $3 children, nonguests enjoy it any day except Monday.

Puerto Seco Beach lies on the eastern side of Discovery Bay, just an 8km (5-mile) drive west of Runaway Bay. On the far western side of the bay is its major attraction, Columbus Park (see below). Jamaicans who live in the hills nearby flock here on Sundays for a jivin' good time. The smoke from jerk chicken and a few ganja smokers fills the air, as do the sounds of Bob Marley and all his dozens of reggae imitators.

SPORTS & OUTDOOR PURSUITS

CALYPSO RAFTING ON THE WHITE RIVER   You can arrange to go river rafting down the White River to the east of Ocho Rios, a 45-minute drift that takes you down the largest river in the area. The trip is one of the finer ways to spend a day in Ocho Rios when you tire of the beach. You glide along the banks of the river on a 9m (30-ft.) bamboo raft built for two, experiencing the rapids and looking at the lush growth. Halfway down the river you stop at the Jungle Bar for lunch and reggae music. The cost is $40 per person, including the services of a guide. To reach the site, head east from Ocho Rios to the White River Bridge, a distance of 5km (3 miles). Rafting is possible daily from 9am to 5pm. Call © **876/974-2527** for more information.

DEEP-SEA FISHING   At the public dock at Fisherman's Point, chartered deep-sea fishing boats can be arranged. The best bet is **The Triple B** (© **876/ 975-3273**), a 11m (37-ft.) boat that takes fishermen on half-day charters for $360, or $720 for the full day. The outfitter also offers a larger boat (13m/ 42 ft.), costing $400 for a half-day or $800 for a full day.

GOLF   SuperClubs Runaway Golf Club, at Runaway Bay near Ocho Rios on the North Coast (© **876/973-7319**), charges no fee to guests who stay at any SuperClub. For nonguests, the price is $80 year-round. Carts cost $35 for 18 holes, club rentals are $14 for 18 holes, caddies are $16.

   Sandals Golf & Country Club ✦ (© **876/975-0119**), a 15-minute ride from the center of the resort, is a 5,944m (19,500-ft.) course known for its panoramic scenery. Rolling terrain, lush vegetation, and flowers and fruit trees dominate the 48-hectare (120-acre) course; a putting green and driving range are available as well. Sandals guests play free; nonguests pay $70 for 9 holes or $100 for 18 holes.

HORSEBACK RIDING   Renegade Stables, Galina, Oracabessa (© **876/ 994-0135**), is a stable that's home to about 14 horses, half of which are available for riding lessons. A trail ride lasting between 60 and 90 minutes costs $30 per person and incorporates equestrian jaunts along both forest trails and beaches.

TENNIS   Grand Sport Villa Golf Resort & Spa, Main Street, Ocho Rios (© **876/974-1027**), focuses more on tennis than any other resort in the area. It offers three clay-surface and three hard-surface courts, all lit for night play. Guests play free, day or night, but nonguests must call and make arrangements with the manager. The **Ciboney Ocho Rios** hotel (© **800/333-3333** or 876/ 974-1027; 104 Main St.) also sponsors twice-a-day clinics for both beginners and advanced players. Frequent guest tournaments are also staged, including handicapped doubles and mixed doubles.

EXPLORING THE AREA

A scenic drive south of Ocho Rios along Route A3 will take you inland through **Fern Gully** ✦, a lush gorge. This was originally a riverbed, but now the main road winds up some 210m (700 ft.) among a profusion of wild ferns, a tall rainforest, hardwood trees, and lianas. There are hundreds of varieties of ferns, and roadside stands offer fruits and vegetables, carved-wood souvenirs, and basketwork. The road runs for about 6km (3¾ miles). At Moneague, a small town, the A1 continues south into the interior of Jamaica, but the same route number (A1) also heads back north along a different route from the A3 you just took south. This A1 northerly road lies to the west of the A1 southern route to Moneague. If you take this A1 north, you'll come to the coast on the north shore again.

   Heading up A1 north, you'll pass the ruins of **Edinburgh Castle** lying 13km (8 miles) southwest of Claremont, the major town on the route back (but of no tourist interest). These ruins—not worth a detour but of passing interest if you're driving by—are a local curiosity.

This 1763 lair was the former abode of one of Jamaica's most famous murderers, a Scot named Lewis Hutchinson, who used to shoot passersby and toss their bodies into a deep pit. At his so-called "castle," really a two-story house, Hutchinson invited his victims inside. There he would wine and dine them before murdering and then robbing them.

The authorities got wind of his activities. Although he tried to escape by canoe, Hutchinson was captured and hanged at Spanish Town on March 16, 1773. Evidently proud of his achievements (evidence of at least 43 bodies was found), he left 100 British pounds and instructions for a memorial to be built in his honor. It never was.

These castle ruins can be viewed on the northern outskirts of the village of Bensonton, near the Bensonton Health Club.

Back on the A1 northern route again, you can drive to the coast, coming to it at **St. Ann's Bay,** the site of the first Spanish settlement on the island, where you can see the **statue of Christopher Columbus,** cast in his hometown of Genoa and erected near St. Ann's Hospital on the west side of town, close to the coast road. There are a number of Georgian buildings in the town—the **Court House** near the parish church, built in 1866, is the most interesting.

THE MAJOR ATTRACTIONS

Brimmer Hall Estate   Some 34km (21 miles) east of Ocho Rios, in the hills 3km (1¾ miles) from Port Maria, this 1817 estate is an ideal place to spend a day. You can swim in the pool and sample a wide variety of brews and concoctions. The Plantation Tour Eating House offers typical Jamaican dishes for lunch, and there's a souvenir shop with a good selection of ceramics, art, straw goods, woodcarvings, rums, liqueurs, and cigars. All this is on a working plantation where you're driven around in a tractor-drawn jitney to see the tropical fruit trees and coffee plants; the knowledgeable guides will explain the various processes necessary to produce the fine fruits of the island. This is a far more interesting experience than the trip to Croydon Plantation in Montego Bay, so if you're visiting both resorts and have time for only one plantation, make it Brimmer Hall.

Port Maria, St. Mary's. ℂ 876/994-2309. Tours $18. Tours Mon–Fri 9am–4pm.

Coyaba River Garden and Museum   Two kilometers (1¼ miles) from the center of Ocho Rios, at an elevation of 126m (420 ft.), this park and museum were built on the grounds of the former Shaw Park plantation. The word *coyaba* comes from the Arawak name for paradise. Coyaba is a Spanish-style museum with a river and gardens filled with native flora, a cut-stone courtyard, fountains, and a crafts shop and bar. The museum boasts a collection of artifacts from the Arawak, Spanish, and English settlements in the area.

Shaw Park Rd. ℂ 876/974-6235. Admission $5, free for children 12 and under. Daily 8am–6pm. Take the Fern Gully–Kingston road, turn left at St. John's Anglican Church, and follow the signs to Coyaba, just .4km (¼ mile) farther.

Cranbrook Flower Forest & Riverhead Adventure Trail ℛ   Centered on a much-restored water mill built by a British planter 200-odd years ago, this 53-hectare (130-acre) commercial nursery welcomes visitors on guided tours of its formal lawns, fountains, lakes, and ponds. If you're a devoted botanist, you'll appreciate the diversity of plants. Within a greenhouse, you'll see thousands of flourishing orchids and anthuriums (many shipped as cut flowers to the U.S.). Horseback riding is also available here, costing $30 for 2-hour trail rides.

Laughland's P.O. Box 8, Llandovery, near St. Ann's Bay. $©$ 876/770-8071. Admission $6, $3 children under 12. Daily 9am–5pm. From the center of Ocho Rios, take A1 west to the Chukka Cove turnoff, a distance of 29km (18 miles).

Dunn's River Falls *Overrated*   For a fee, you can relax on the beach or climb with a guide to the top of the 546m (600-ft.) falls. You can splash in the waters at the bottom of the falls or drop into the cool pools higher up between the cascades of water. The beach restaurant provides lackluster snacks and drinks, and dressing rooms are available. If you're planning to climb the falls, wear sneakers or sport sandals to protect your feet from the sharp rocks and to prevent slipping.

Climbing the falls with the crowds is a chance to experience some 183m (610 ft.) of cold but clear mountain water. In contrast to the heat swirling around you, the splashing water hitting your face and bare legs is cooling on a hot day. The problem here is slipping and falling, especially if you're joined to a chain of hands linking body to body. In spite of the slight danger, there seem to be few accidents. The falls aren't exactly a wilderness experience, with all the tour buses carrying cruise-ship passengers here. The place is always overrun.

Rte. A3. $©$ 876/974-2857. Admission $10 adults, $8 children 2–11, free for children under 2. Daily 8:30am–5pm (7am–5pm on cruise-ship arrival days). From the center of Ocho Rios, head west along Rte. A3.

Firefly *☆*   This vacation retreat was the home of Sir Noël Coward and his longtime companion, Graham Payn, who, as executor of Coward's estate, donated it to the Jamaica National Heritage Trust. The recently restored house is more or less as it was on the day Sir Noël died in 1973. His Hawaiian-print shirts still hang in the closet of his austere bedroom, with its mahogany four-poster. The library contains a collection of his books, and the living room is warm and comfortable, with big armchairs and two grand pianos (where he composed several famous tunes). Guests stayed at Blue Harbour, a villa closer to Port Maria; they included Evelyn Waugh, Winston Churchill, Errol Flynn, Lord Laurence Olivier, Vivien Leigh, Claudette Colbert, Katharine Hepburn, Mary Martin, and the Queen Mother. Paintings by the noted playwright/actor/author/composer adorn the walls. An open patio looks out over the pool and the sea. Across the lawn, Sir Noël is buried under a simple white marble gravestone.

Grants Town, in St. Mary, 32km (20 miles) east of Ocho Rios above Port Maria. $©$ 876/725-0920. Admission $10. Children under 12 free. Mon–Thurs and Sat 9am–5pm.

Green Grotto Caves *☆* *Kids*   Formed of coastal limestone, these caves were a haven for runaway slaves and pirates. The mammoth cave is full of rock formations, stalagmites, and stalactites, and has a roof of "ceiling pockets." The grotto is filled with numerous chambers and light holes, but its most dramatic feature is eerie Grotto Lake, a subterranean lake occupying its bowels.

Just off main coastal road (A3), 3km (1¾ miles) from Discovery Bay and 4km (2½ miles) west of Runaway Bay. $©$ 876/973-2841. Admission $20 adults, $10 children 4–12. Daily 9am–4pm.

Harmony Hall   This was the centerpiece of a sugar plantation in the late 19th century. Today it has been restored and is the focal point of an art gallery and restaurant that showcases the painting and sculpture of Jamaican artists as well as a tasteful array of arts and crafts. Among the featured gift items are Sharon McConnell's Starfish Oils, which contain natural additives harvested in Jamaica. The gallery shop also carries the "Reggae to Wear" line of sportswear, designed and made on Jamaica, and Anabella boxes (for jewelry).

Tower Isles on Rte. A3, 6km (3¾ miles) east of Ocho Rios. ✆ 876/975-4222. Free admission. Gallery daily 10am–6pm; restaurant/cafe Tues–Sun 10am–2:30pm and 6–11pm.

Island Village ☞   The opening in 2002 of this exotic-looking playland represents one of the largest private investments of the past decade within the touristic infrastructure of Ocho Rios. Scattered over 2 hectares (4 acres) on a beachfront within a few steps of the city's cruise-ship terminal is a replica of an idealized Jamaican village, complete with elaborate gingerbread, hundreds of feet of boardwalk, and a medley of psychedelic colors that glow, rainbow-style, in the streaming sunlight. It's not without its own theme-park, Disney-ish overtones: They include **soundstages** strategically scattered within the sightlines of **bars** that serve the kind of high-octane cocktails that could fuel a heavily loaded jetliner from here to Kingston. Music and hotel impresario Christopher Blackwell, who takes credit for the "discovery" and marketing of Bob Marley, is half-owner of this venture—thus you won't find any shame here about emphasizing reggae as both a lifestyle and an artistic venue.

Within the compound you'll find about 35 **shops** selling clothing, books, souvenirs, "reggae wear," and Bob Marley memorabilia; and four or five restaurants and bars. These include everything from a branch of **Margaritaville,** a theme-ish offspring of the Jimmy Buffett song where drinks splish splash throughout the day and night; and other eateries specializing in fast-food versions of Jamaican curries and jerk chicken or pork. There's even a movie theater and an audiovisual art gallery/minimuseum, **Reggae Explosion,** celebrating in audiovisual form the evolution of reggae from a local art to music recognized the world over. Entrance is free; hours are synchronized with the rest of the complex.

Small-scale reggae presentations occur spontaneously, often when a cruise ship is in port, and large-scale **blockbuster concerts** are scheduled about once a month, and are usually attended by hundreds, or even thousands. Except when there's a world-class concert—usually when there's no cruise ship in port—there's no admission charged for entrance to the compound, but an alert security staff ensures that "panhandlers, pickpockets, and lowlifes" (at least those residing in Jamaica) are kept off the premises. Since its opening, the place has welcomed more than a thousand visitors a day. Access to the beachfront costs $5 per person. Floating a short distance offshore is a Margaritaville trademark: a large round **trampoline** floating on pontoons. Everyone seems to jump on it a few times early in the day, but as the afternoon wears on and the heat and the rum-based cocktails take their toll, it usually evolves into a purely decorative object.

Island Village, Turtle Beach Rd. Complex open daily 9am–midnight. No central switchboard. Each establishment has its own phone.

Prospect Plantation   This working plantation adjoins the 18-hole Prospect Mini Golf Course. A visit to this property is an educational, relaxing, and enjoyable experience. On a leisurely tour by covered jitney through the scenic beauty of Prospect, you'll readily see why this section of Jamaica is called "the garden parish of the island." You can view the many trees planted by such visitors as Winston Churchill, Henry Kissinger, Charlie Chaplin, Pierre Trudeau, and Noël Coward. You'll learn about and see pimento (allspice), bananas, cassava, sugarcane, coffee, cocoa, coconut, pineapple, and the famous *leucaena* ("Tree of Life"). You'll see Jamaica's first hydroelectric plant and sample some of the exotic fruit and drinks.

Horseback riding is available on three scenic trails at Prospect. The rides are about 1 hour long. Advance booking of 1 hour is necessary.

Rte. A3, 5km (3 miles) east of Ocho Rios, in St. Ann. ℂ 876/994-1058. Tours $12 adults, $6 for children 12 and under; 1-hr. horseback ride $20. Tours Mon–Sat at 10:30am, 2pm, and 3:30pm.

Sun Valley Plantation   A real working plantation—not one gussied up as a tourist attraction—is reached by taking the A3 from Ocho Rios toward the coastal town of Oracabessa. The plantation is in the hamlet of Crescent on the B13, lying 5km (3 miles) south of Oracabessa and 29km (18 miles) from Ocho Rios. Nolly and Lorna Binns, the plantation owners, take visitors on a guided tour of the property.

Crescent, near Oracabessa. ℂ 876/995-3075. Admission $12. Tours on the hr. daily 9am–2pm.

ORGANIZED TOURS

Caribic Vacations, 1310 Providence Dr., Ironshore Estate, White Sands Beach (ℂ 876/953-9878), is the market leader. They offer a tour of Ocho Rios including Fern Gully, Dunn's River Falls, and a visit to Coyaba Museum, with shopping time scheduled in the center of Ocho Rios. The tour lasts 5 to 6 hours, costing $29 per person.

Caribic will also book a full-day tour of Port Antonio where you can drive along the coast road and go rafting on the Rio Grande. This tour includes lunch on the beach and costs $90 per person.

If you don't like being hauled around on a bus with a lot of camera-toting tourists, opt for an adventure with nature offered by **Wilderness Resorts** (ℂ 876/974-5189), south of Prospect Plantation (see above). From the coast at Prospect, you take a scenic little road along the White River Gorge to reach this 180-hectare (450-acre) compound, a fish farm and cattle ranch that's open to the public. (The scenic drive alone is worth the trip.) There are nearly 40 fishing ponds here, mainly stocked with freshwater snapper, and the plantation is riddled with hiking trials. There is also a stable full of horses, and quad bikes can be rented. You can take a general tour for 1 hour costing $65, or a 2-hour tour for $110. If you'd like to go fishing, the cost is $23; it's $35 per hour of horseback riding. One attractive package is a combination of fishing, riding, and lunch for $90.

Blue Mountain Tours, 121 Main St. (ℂ 876/974-7075), runs guided downhill bicycle tours of Jamaica's Blue Mountains. The cost is $89 per person, including transfers to the site, breakfast, and lunch. The single-gear bikes are woefully inadequate, however, for the terrain.

Red Stripe Cruises, 121 Main St. in Ocho Rios (ℂ 876/989-6759), offers a 3-hour Dunn's River trip on Tuesday, Wednesday, and Saturday at 12:30 and 3:30pm, costing $59. A special feature is its 2-hour Soca Sunset Cruise on Thursday and Saturday, costing $39 per person.

SHOPPING

For many, Ocho Rios provides an introduction to Jamaica-style shopping. After surviving the ordeal, some visitors may vow never to go shopping again. Literally hundreds of Jamaicans pour into Ocho Rios to peddle items to cruise-ship passengers and other visitors. Be prepared for aggressive vendors. Pandemonium greets many an unwary shopper, who must also be prepared for some fierce haggling. Every vendor asks too much at first, which gives them the leeway to "negotiate" until the price reaches a more realistic level. Is shopping fun in Ocho Rios? A resounding no. Do cruise-ship passengers and land visitors indulge in it anyway? A decided yes.

The Potter's Art

The largest and most visible art pottery in Jamaica is found at **Wassi Art,** Bougainvillea Drive, Great Pond (© 876/974-5044). This enterprise is often cited for its entrepreneurial courage by the country's growing core of independent business owners. Established in 1990, it developed from a personal hobby of one of its owners, Theresa Lee, an amateur potter. Today, with her husband Robert, she employs at least 50 artisans and workers in a small-scale beehive of energy about 4km (2½ miles) north of the center of Ocho Rios. They turn out wonderful pottery. You'll reach the place via a winding and impossibly rutted road.

Tours of the factory (Mon–Sat 9am–5pm) are free, last about 15 minutes, and include a brief session trying to throw a pot on an electric potter's wheel. Don't expect a high-tech operation here, as virtually every aspect of the manufacturing process, including the digging, hauling, and processing of the Blue Mountain clay, is done the old-fashioned way—by hand. All glazes used in the process are nontoxic and FDA approved.

The finished pottery comes in colors that range from the earth- and forest-toned to the bright iridescent patterns reminiscent of Jamaican music and spice. Prices of objects range from $4 to $2,000, and anything you buy can be shipped by Federal Express. There's a cafe on the premises (try their meat-stuffed patties for an insight into what a Jamaican worker's lunch might include). Part of your experience here includes dialogues with talented artisans hailing from both Jamaica and Cuba.

In general, the shopping is better in Montego Bay. If you're not going there, wander the Ocho Rios crafts markets, although much of the merchandise is repetitive.

SHOPPING CENTERS & MALLS   There are a number of shopping plazas in Ocho Rios. We've listed them because they're here, not because we heartily recommend them. Newer ones include the **New Ocho Rios Plaza,** in the center of town, with some 60 shops; opposite is the **Taj Mahal Mall,** with 26 duty-free stores. **Island Plaza** is another major shopping complex, as is the **Mutual Security Plaza** with some 30 shops.

Ocean Village Shopping Centre (© 876/974-2683) is one of the originals, with numerous boutiques, food stores, a bank, sundries purveyors, travel agencies, service facilities, and what have you. The **Ocho Rios Pharmacy** (© 876/974-2398) sells most proprietary brands, perfumes, and suntan lotions, among its many wares. Nearby is the major competitor of Ocean Village, the **Coconut Grove Shopping Plaza,** which is linked by walkways and shrubs. The merchandise here consists mainly of local craft items, and this center is often overrun with cruise-ship passengers. Ocean Village is slightly bigger and more upscale, and we prefer it.

Just east of Ocho Rios, the **Pineapple Place Shopping Centre** is a collection of shops in cedar-shingle-roofed cottages set amid tropical flowers.

The **Ocho Rios Craft Park** has 135 stalls. A vendor will weave a hat or a basket while you wait, or you can buy a ready-made hat, hamper, handbag, place mats, or lampshade. Other stands stock hand-embroidered goods and will make small items while you wait. Woodcarvers work on bowls, ashtrays, statues, and cups.

Island Plaza, right in the heart of Ocho Rios, has some of the best Jamaican art, all paintings by local artists. You can also purchase local handmade crafts (be prepared to haggle), carvings, ceramics, kitchenware, and the inevitable T-shirts.

SPECIALTY SHOPS **Swiss Stores,** in the Ocean Village Shopping Centre (© 876/974-2519), sells jewelry and all the big names in Swiss watches. The Rolex watches here are real, not those fakes touted by hustlers on the streets.

One of the best bets for shopping is **Soni's Plaza,** 50 Main St., the address of all the shops recommended below. **Casa de Oro** (© 876/974-5392) specializes in duty-free watches, fine jewelry, and classic perfumes. **Gem Palace** (© 876/974-2850) is the place to go for diamond solitaires, tennis bracelets, and 14-karat gold chains. **Mohan's** (© 876/974-9270) offers one of the best selections of 14-karat and 18-karat gold chains, rings, bracelets, and earrings. **Soni's** (© 876/974-2303) focuses strictly on souvenirs from coffee mugs to T-shirts. **Taj Gift Centre** (© 876/974-9268) has a little bit of everything: Blue Mountain coffee, film, cigars, and hand-embroidered linen tablecloths. For something different, look for Jamaican jewelry made from hematite, a mountain stone. **Diamonds Duty Free Fine Jewelry** (© 876/974-6455) beats most competition with its name-brand watches, and jewelry.

Tips **Jamaica Evaluates Its Jerks**

Jamaicans, and especially professional drivers, are passionately committed to publicizing the virtues of whatever out-of-the-way stall or kiosk that serves—in their opinion—the country's best jerk pork and chicken. Debates rage in bars and on beaches, but one site that gets consistently good reviews from jerk aficionados is **Blueberry Hill** (no phone), located on the coastal road about a .8km (½ mile) east of the North Shore community of Buff Bay, midway between Port Antonio and Ocho Rios. (It's near the junction of the North Shore Coastal highway with one of the roughest roads in the Third World—the one that runs over the Blue Mountains back to Kingston.)

Don't expect a palace. Established in 1980 and flanked by less-famous jerk stalls that have cropped up like clones, it's little more than a roadside lean-to that's caked with the carbonization of years of the slow-cooking jerk process. It serves only jerk pork and jerk chicken, both of which cost around $2 for 113 grams (¼ lb.); and $3 for .25 kilograms (½ lb.).

There's no dining room. With an engaging sense of conviviality, clients collect their bounty in aluminum-foil wrappers, and eat with their fingers while standing beside the road, or perhaps sitting on a makeshift stool. Red Stripe beer and Ting (something akin to Sprite) are the drinks of choice. Overall, it's unpretentious, delicious, friendly, and fun, and is open daily from 10am to 10pm.

Jamaica Inn Gift Shop, in the Jamaica Inn, Main Street (© **876/974-2514**), is better than most specialty shops here, selling everything from Blue Mountain coffee to Walkers Wood products, and even guava jelly and jerk seasoning. If you're lucky, you'll find marmalade from an old family recipe, plus Jamaican Reggae Rum. Local handicrafts include musical instruments for kids and brightly painted country cottages of tin. The store also sells antiques and fine old maps of the West Indies.

OCHO RIOS AFTER DARK

Far better than some tacky "nightclub," a better way to spend the early part of an evening is to take a sunset cruise before dinner. Sunsets in this part of the world often evoke the color of peach melba. In operation since 1986, and one of the largest sailboat companies on the island, the best cruises are offered by **Heave-Ho Charters,** 180 Main St. (© **876/974-5367**). These early evening cruises cost $40 per person.

The **Sports Bar** at the Little Pub Restaurant (see earlier in this chapter) is open daily from 10am to 3am. It's the main gathering place in town.

Jamaic'N Me Crazy, at the Renaissance Jamaica Grande (© **876/974-2201**), has the best lighting and sound system in Ocho Rios (and perhaps Jamaica). The crowd includes everyone from the passing yachter to the curious tourist, who may be under the mistaken impression that he or she is seeing an authentic Jamaican nightclub. Nonguests are not allowed. Hours are Wednesday to Monday 10pm to 2pm.

For more of the same without an overbearing Americanized atmosphere, try **Amnesia,** 70 Main St. (© **876/974-2633**). Rest assured that this is a lot closer to an authentic Jamaican nightclub than Jamaic'N Me Crazy. Cover is required only on nights with a live band, and it's rarely higher than J$300 (US$5).

2 Runaway Bay ⭐

Once a mere satellite of Ocho Rios, Runaway Bay, 16km (10 miles) west of Ocho Rios, has become a destination in its own right, with white-sand beaches that are much less crowded than those in Ocho Rios.

Since you're so far removed from the action such as it is in Ocho Rios, you stay at Runaway Bay mainly if you're interested in hanging out at a particular resort. It is especially recommended for those who want to escape from the hordes descending on Ocho Rios, where cruise-ship crowds and aggressive vendors can intrude on your solitude.

This part of Jamaica's north coast has several distinctions: It was the first part of the island seen by Columbus, the site of the first Spanish settlement on the island, and the point of departure of the last Spaniards leaving Jamaica following their defeat by the British.

WHERE TO STAY & DINE

Runaway Bay offers several unusual accommodations, as well as all-inclusive resorts and notable bargains.

EXPENSIVE

Chukka Cove Farm and Resort ⭐ *Finds*   Chukka Cove is an ideal center for horse lovers who'd like to live on the estate's landscaped grounds with its stables. On the estate's acreage lie six two-bedroom villas, each suitable for four guests, with a veranda, plank floors, and an architectural plan vaguely reminiscent of 18th-century models. All units come with a well-maintained private bathroom

---

Fun Fact **Nude Nuptials**

At Hedonism III Resort (p. 157), couples who want to see what they're getting before they tie the knot can be married in their birthday suits. Instead of a gown and a tuxedo, suntan lotion is recommended so that any body parts, already exposed, might not become overexposed, at least to the sun. After the "I do's" are said, the happy couple can head for the honeymoon suite at this adults-only all-inclusive.

---

with both tub and shower. A pampering staff prepares meals in your villa. Snorkeling is included.

P.O. Box 177, Richmond Llandovery, St. Ann's Bay. ℂ 876/913-4851. Fax 876/913-4783. gbascoe@cw jamaica.com. 6 villas. Winter $2,000 villa per week; off season $1,500 villa per week. Rates can be prorated for shorter stays. No credit cards. 6km (3¾ miles) east of Runaway Bay off A1. **Amenities:** Bar; outdoor pool; snorkeling; babysitting; laundry service; cooking staff. *In room:* A/C, TV, kitchenette, coffeemaker, iron/board.

MODERATE

Breezes Runaway Bay *⊛*   This stylish resort is an all-inclusive. Its clubhouse is approached by passing through a park filled with tropical trees and shrubbery. The lobby is the best re-creation of the South Seas on Jamaica, with hanging wicker chairs and totemic columns. There's a minijungle with hammocks and a nearby nude beach, in addition to the lovely stretch of sandy beach right out front. The resort lies 3km (1¾ miles) east of Paradise Beach and just next door to the town's second best beach, Cardiffall.

Guest rooms are spacious, with a light, tropical motif. They're fitted with local woods, cool tile floors, and private balconies or patios. The most elegant are the suites, with Jamaican-made four-poster beds. The good-size bathrooms have combination shower/tubs and generous marble counters.

Live music emanates from the stylish Terrace every evening at 7pm, and a nightclub offers live shows 6 nights a week at 10pm. Dine either in the beachside restaurant or in the more formal Italian restaurant, Martino's, which is the best. Breezes now has a bar on its au naturel beach. The resort's Starlight Grill has also expanded its menu to include a vegetarian cuisine. The club offers exchange and day-pass privileges with Hedonism III immediately next door.

P.O. Box 58 (10km/6¼ miles west of Ocho Rios), Runaway Bay. ℂ 800/GO-SUPER in the U.S., or 876/973-4820. Fax 876/973-6390. www.superclubs.com. 234 units. Winter $165–$209 per person per night double; off season $153–$159 per person per night double. Rates include all meals, drinks, and activities. AE, DISC, MC, V. No children under age 14 accepted. **Amenities:** 4 restaurants; 4 bars; pool; 4 tennis courts; golf and tennis schools; fitness center; 3 Jacuzzis; dive shop; sailing; scuba diving; snorkeling; windsurfing with instruction offered; limited room service; laundry service; nonsmoking rooms; rooms for those with limited mobility. *In room:* A/C, TV, minibar (in some units), coffeemaker, hair dryer, iron/board, safe.

Runaway Bay Heart Hotel *⊛* *Value*   This place wins hands-down as the bargain of the North Coast. One of Jamaica's few training and service institutions, the club and its adjacent academy are operated by the government to provide a high level of training for young Jamaicans interested in the hotel trade. The helpful staff of both professionals and trainees offers the finest service of any hotel in the area. Runaway lies a 30-minute drive east of Paradise Beach and a 5-minute drive to Cardiffall. Free shuttles are offered only to Cardiffall.

The good-size rooms are bright and airy. Bathrooms have generous shelf space and shower stalls. The accommodations open onto private balconies with views of well-manicured tropical gardens or vistas of the bay and golf course. Guests enjoy having a drink in the piano bar (ever had a cucumber daiquiri?) before heading for the dining room, the Cardiff Hall Restaurant, which serves superb Jamaican and Continental dishes.

Ricketts Ave. (P.O. Box 98), Runaway Bay, St. Ann. © 876/973-2671. Fax 876/973-4704. www.runaway heart.com.jm. 56 units. Year-round $110–$135 double. Rates include MAP (breakfast and dinner). AE, DISC, MC, V. **Amenities:** Restaurant; bar; pool; gym; limited room service; babysitting; laundry service; nonsmoking rooms; rooms for those with limited mobility. In room: A/C, TV, kitchenette, hair dryer, iron/board, safe.

Tamarind Tree Hotel 🞂 ⁄Value   More and more frugal travelers are learning about this cozy enclave a short walk from a good sandy beach at Runaway Bay. Built in 1987, its white exterior with green accents is inviting. You're lodged either in the main building or in one of three cottages, all at very affordable prices. Each cottage can sleep up to six guests. The bedrooms are simply but comfortably furnished. Five of the units are rather standard but the others are more attractively equipped and roomier. The cottages are the best deal of all, especially if you're traveling in a party or with a family. The rooms are carpeted, and 10 of them open onto their own private balconies. Each comes with a tiled bathroom with tub-and-shower combo. On-site is a little-known but good restaurant, The Bird Wing, serving international and Jamaican cuisine.

Runaway Bay. © 876/973-2678. Fax 876/973-5013. 25 units. Year-round $55–$65 double; $150 cottage. MC, V. **Amenities:** Restaurant; bar; outdoor pool; limited room service; laundry service; nonsmoking rooms. In room: A/C, TV.

INEXPENSIVE

Caribbean Isle Hotel   This small hotel, directly on a small beach 2km (1¼ miles) west of Runaway Bay, offers personalized service in an informal atmosphere. The better-known Cardiffall Beach is a 10-minute drive away. Stay here only for the affordable rates; we find the rooms somewhat tattered. But they do all have ocean views, and the superior units have private balconies. All units come with small private bathrooms containing tubs. The hotel has a TV in the bar/lounge and a dining room leading onto a sea-view patio. Dinner is rather standard fare of lobster, fish, shrimp, pork chops, chicken; local dishes are prepared on request.

P.O. Box 119, Runaway Bay. © 876/973-2364. Fax 876/973-4835. 23 units. Year-round $50 double; $65 triple. AE, MC, V. **Amenities:** Dining room; breakfast room; outdoor pool; laundry service. In room: A/C, safe, no phone.

ALL-INCLUSIVE RESORTS

The following hotels fold the cost of lodgings, meals, drinks, and most activities into one price.

Club Ambiance Jamaica   Last refurbished in 1995, this is one of the most basic of the all-inclusives, catering mainly to European travelers on a budget. Lying at the west end of Runaway Bay, it's recommended primarily for its reasonable rates—not for its somewhat bleak exterior. The shoreline near the hotel is rocky, too. Units are reasonably comfortable and clean, if not stylish. Regional art decorates the walls, and the furniture is often upholstered wicker. Accommodations come with either double or king-size beds, with balconies opening onto views of the water and private bathrooms with tub and shower.

P.O. box 20, Runaway Bay. © 800/822-3274 in the U.S., or 876/973-4705. Fax 876/973-2067. www.club ambiance.com. 90 units. Winter $115–$135 per person double or triple, $135 per person suite; off season $110–$130 per person double or triple, $115 per person suite. AE, MC, V. Children under 18 not accepted. **Amenities:** 2 restaurants; 4 bars; outdoor pool; gym; Jacuzzi; bicycles; laundry service. In room: A/C, TV, kitchenette, minibar (in suite), fridge, coffeemaker (in suite), hair dryer, iron/board (in suite), safes rented at $2 per day.

FDR (Franklyn D. Resort) *(Kids* Located on Route A1, 27km (17 miles) west of Ocho Rios, FDR is an all-inclusive that's the number-one choice if you're traveling with children. FDR lies 3km (1¾ miles) east of Paradise Beach and about .4km (¼ mile) east of Cardiffall. Its own no-name beach stretches for about 182m (600 ft.), a mixture of stone and sand. The resort, named after its Jamaican-born owner and developer, Franklyn David Rance, is on 2 hectares (6 acres) of flat, sandy land dotted with flowering shrubs and trees, on the main seaside highway. Each of the Mediterranean-inspired buildings has a terra-cotta roof, a loggia or an outdoor terrace, Spanish marble in the bathrooms, a kitchenette, and a personal attendant (called a vacation nanny), who cooks, cleans, and cares for children. Although neither the narrow beach nor the modest pools are the most desirable on the island, and most rooms lack a sea view, many visitors appreciate the spacious units and the resort's wholehearted concern for kids.

Two restaurants on the property serve free wine with lunch and dinner (and offer special children's meals), and a piano bar provides music every evening. There's live music nightly.

Main St. (P.O. Box 201), Runaway Bay, St. Ann. (② 888/FDR-KIDS in the U.S., or 876/973-4592. Fax 876/973-4600. www.fdrholidays.com. 76 units. Winter $660–$800; off season $560–$600. Rates are all-inclusive. Children 5 and under stay free in parent's suite. Children 6–15 $50 extra each. AE, MC, V. **Amenities:** 2 restaurants; 3 bars; disco; outdoor pool; tennis court; health club; dive shop; free bikes; children's center; free babysitting (9:30am–4:45pm); laundry service; nonsmoking rooms. *In room:* A/C, TV, kitchen.

Grand Lido Braco *(✿* Established in 1995, this is one of the most historically evocative all-inclusive resorts in Jamaica, lying on a prime stretch of sandy, 319m (1,050-ft.) beachfront. Set on 34 hectares (85 acres) of land near Buena Vista, a 15-minute drive west of Runaway Bay, it's a re-creation of a 19th-century Jamaican Victorian village, with charming gingerbread architecture. A copy of a courthouse hosts entertainment, and benches line the borders of the town square, where artisans display their handiwork. The old Jamaica that's portrayed here is a rather sanitized, Disney version. Yet this is not a place for children; it is a primarily adult retreat.

Accommodations are in 12 blocks of three-story buildings, each trimmed in colonial-style gingerbread and filled with wicker furniture. All the spacious units have private patios or verandas and face the ocean; blocks one through six are closer to the beachfront, and blocks five and six face a strip of sand designated as a "clothing-optional" area. Beds are very comfortable, with fine linen; the bathrooms are well maintained and have showers.

Separate dining areas serve tasty Jamaican cuisine, pizza and pasta, and blander international fare; the Piacere Restaurant offers upscale dinners and has a dress code. For variety, Munahana serves Japanese sushi and teppanyaki cuisine.

Rio Bueno, Trelawny, Jamaica. (② 877/GO-SUPER in the U.S., or 876/954-0000. Fax 876/954-0020 or 876/954-0021. www.superclubs.com. 226 units. All-inclusive rates: winter $512–$967 double, $930 suite for 2; off season $493–$729 double, $885 suite for 2. Rates include all meals, drinks, and activities. AE, MC, V. Children under age 16 not accepted. **Amenities:** 5 restaurants; 8 bars; disco; 2 outdoor pools; 9-hole golf course; 3 tennis courts; health club and spa; 4 Jacuzzis; sauna; steam room; watersports; free bikes; business center; 24-hr. room service; laundry service. *In room:* A/C, TV, coffeemaker, hair dryer, iron/board, safe, CD player, radio, beverage maker.

Hedonism III *(✿* Following a chain format established in Negril, this latest beachfront Hedonism bills itself as a "truly active (and slightly wicked!) vacation." Though this branch of Hedonism isn't as rowdy and raunchy as the

Negril branch—it's a little more serene and isolated from the action in town—it's still for the serious party person who likes to drink all night, hang out at the beach all day, and go wild at those toga parties. Set on 6 hectares (15 acres) of landscaped gardens on the eastern end of Runaway Bay, it features ocean views from all rooms and an all-inclusive package deal. Hedonism III has its own private, slightly rocky beach stretching for some 182m (600 ft.)—part of it is often nude. It lies a 15-minute drive east of Paradise Beach and a 10-minute walk west of Cardiffall.

Bedrooms are roomy and freshly decorated, with Jamaica's first-ever block of "swim-up" rooms. All swim-up rooms feature large marble tub-and-shower bathrooms with Jacuzzis and CD players. Single guests are paired up with a roommate of the same sex, or have to pay a single supplement.

The food is quite decent—everything from Italian to Japanese to Jamaican. There is even a disco with a four-story water slide! The resort also offers Jamaica's only circus workshop that features a flying trapeze, juggling, a trampoline "clinic", and various unicycle and bike-balancing acts. It's presented Monday to Saturday.

Runaway Bay. (℗ 877/GO-SUPER in the U.S., or 876/973-4100. Fax 876/973-5402. www.superclubs.com. 225 units. All-inclusive rates for 6 nights: winter $2,220–$4,029 double;. off season $1,740–$3,714 double. Rates include all meals, drinks, and activities. AE, DC, DISC, MC, V. No children under age 18. **Amenities:** 5 restaurants; 6 bars; disco; 3 large pools; 3 tennis courts; fitness center; 3 Jacuzzis; sauna; kayaking; sailing; scuba diving; water-skiing; windsurfing; nonsmoking rooms; rooms for those with limited mobility; basketball; volleyball; Circus workshop. In room: A/C, TV, dataport, iron/board, safe, beverage maker.

SPORTS & OUTDOOR PURSUITS

BEACHES & WATERSPORTS The two best beaches at Runaway Bay are **Paradise Beach** and **Cardiffall Lot Public Beach.** Both wide, white-sand strips are clean and well maintained—ideal spots for a picnic. If you're staying in Ocho Rios and want to escape the crowds, come here. You don't get a lot of facilities, however, so you'd better bring along whatever you need.

The waters are calm almost all year. Prevailing trade winds will keep you cool in the mornings and late afternoon. Because there are no lifeguards, be especially careful if you're with children.

Runaway Bay offers some of the best for **snorkeling** in Jamaica. The reefs are close to shore and extremely lively with marine life, including enormous schools of tropical fish such as blue chromis, triggerfish, small skate rays, and snapper. You can also go diving. **Jamaqua Dive Center,** at the previously recommended Club Ambiance (℗ 876/973-4845), has as its slogan: "We Be Divin'." The dive facility takes you to one of several protected reefs where the currents aren't dangerous, and where fishing boats are required to stay at least 82m (600 ft.) away from divers and snorkelers. The dive outfitter offers everything from one-tank dives to six-boat packages. All equipment needed can be rented on-site. A 1-tank dive costs $42, a 2-tank dive costs $75.

GOLF SuperClubs Runaway Golf Club (℗ 876/973-7319) charges no admission for guests staying at any of Jamaica's affiliated SuperClubs. For nonguests, the price is $80 year-round. Any player can rent carts for $35 for 18 holes; clubs are $14 for 18 holes.

HORSEBACK RIDING Jamaica's most complete equestrian center is the **Chukka Polo Club and Resort,** at Richmond Llandovery, St. Ann (℗ 876/ 972-2506), less than 6km (3¾ miles) east of Runaway Bay. A 1-hour trail ride costs $35, while a 2-hour mountain ride goes for $45. The most popular ride is a 3-hour beach jaunt that involves riding over trails to the sea, then swimming in the surf. The $65 cost includes refreshments. A 6-hour beach ride, complete with picnic lunch, goes for $130. Polo lessons are also available, costing $50 for 30 minutes. A more recent feature is a mountain-and-sea adventure on a bike (90% of which is downhill). The 3-hour bike ride, costing $50, ends in a swim and some snorkeling.

TENNIS **Grand Sport Villa Golf Resort & Spa,** Main Street, Ocho Rios (© 876/974-1027), focuses more on tennis than any other resort in the area. It offers three clay-surface and three hard-surface courts, all lit for night play. Guests play free, day or night, but nonguests must call and make arrangements with the manager. An on-site pro offers lessons for $25 an hour. Grand Sport also sponsors twice-a-day clinics for both beginners and advanced players. Guest tournaments are also frequently staged, including handicapped doubles and mixed doubles.

EXPLORING THE AREA

Columbus Park Museum ♠, on Queens Highway, Discovery Bay (© 876/973-2135), is a large, open area between the main coast road and the sea at Discovery Bay. Just pull off the road and walk among the fantastic collection of exhibits; admission is free. There's everything from a canoe made from a solid piece of cottonwood (the way Arawaks did it more than 5 centuries ago) to a stone cross that was originally placed on the Barrett Estate (14km/8¾ miles east of Montego Bay) by Edward Barrett, brother of poet Elizabeth Barrett Browning.

A Tribute to Bob Marley

Reggae fans from all over the world visit the little hamlet of Nine Mile to pay their respects at the **Bob Marley Centre & Mausoleum** (© 876/995-1763), which is open daily from 9:30am to 6:30pm, charging an admission of $12.

The village where Marley grew up and where he was buried has the unusual name of Nine Mile. It's a group of ramshackle farms, stray goats, and chickens.

You can go inside Marley's two-room shanty, filled with family memorabilia, including photographs. Marley lived here from the ages of 6 to 13. Adjoining the shack is the so-called mausoleum in which Marley was buried. He shares the gravesite with his half-brother, who was gunned down by police in Miami during a drug bust.

On-site is a vegetarian restaurant and a little shop selling Marley tapes.

The big event of the year here is Marley's birthday each February 6. Reggae fans descend on Nine Mile to listen to concerts. The performer's son, Ziggy Marley, also a reggae star, often appears to entertain.

To reach the pilgrimage site, take the B3 from Ocho Rios south to Brown's Town, a distance of 39km (24 miles). From there continue south to Alexandria for 10km (6¼ miles). Once at Alexandria, turn east (signposted ALVA), going for another 15km (9¼ miles) until you arrive at the hamlet of Nine Mile of Marley fame.

You'll see a tally, used to count bananas carried on men's heads from plantation to ship, as well as a planter's strongbox with a weighted lead base to prevent its theft. Other items are 18th-century cannons, a Spanish water cooler and calcifier, a fish pot made from bamboo, a corn husker, and a water wheel. Pimento trees, from which allspice is produced, dominate the park, which is open daily from 8am to 4pm (admission is free).

You can also visit the **Seville Great House,** Heritage Park (© **876/972-2191**). Built in 1745 by the British, it contains a collection of artifacts once used by everybody from the Amerindians to African slaves. In all, you're treated to an exhibit of 5 centuries' worth of Jamaican history. Modest for a great house, it has wattle-and-daub construction. A small theater presents a 15-minute historical film about the house. It's open daily from 9am to 5pm; admission is $4.

Port Antonio

From Ocho Rios (see chapter 6), drive east along Highway A4/A3, which will take you through some sleepy fishing villages, including Port Maria, until you reach **Port Antonio.** Situated on the coast just north of the Blue Mountains, the town is surrounded by some of the most rugged and beautiful scenery in Jamaica. Many visitors prefer to visit the mountains and highlands from a base here, rather than starting in Kingston, to avoid the capital's urban sprawl.

This is the parish of Portland. It's the rainiest, greenest parish in Jamaica, known for its many rivers and waterfalls. Once the cradle of Jamaican tourism, the region has since been eclipsed by Montego Bay, Ocho Rios, and Negril. It remains a preferred hideaway, however, for a chic and elegant crowd that comes for a handful of posh hotels.

Port Antonio itself is a verdant and sleepy seaport about 97km (60 miles) northeast of Kingston. You may have seen it in the Hollywood film *Cocktail* (still talked about here as if it were shot yesterday). Here you can still catch a glimpse of the Jamaica of old. This small, bustling town is like many in Jamaica: clean though ramshackle, its sidewalks surrounding a market filled with vendors, tin-roofed shacks compete with old Georgian and modern brick and concrete buildings. Locals busily shop, talk, and laugh, while others sit and play dominoes (loudly banging the pieces on the table, which is very much part of the game).

Go to the colorful markets to browse for local craftworks, spices, and fruits—or just to listen to conversations, negotiations, and the news of the day.

Navy Island and the long-gone Titchfield Hotel were owned for a short time by film star Errol Flynn, who was much loved and admired by Jamaicans and totally integrated into his community. Locals still talk of Flynn in Port Antonio, especially the men, who speak of his legendary womanizing and drinking in almost reverent tones.

We find Port Antonio an elite retreat, a virtual Shangri-La when compared to busier Ocho Rios or Montego Bay. It also has some of the finest beaches in Jamaica, and has long been a center for some of the Caribbean's best deep-sea fishing. Some of the most expensive yachts sailing the Caribbean can be seen here with the opening of the first-class **Megayacht Marina** ★★. It's a good place to go to get away from it all.

COMPARING RESORTS

Unlike Montego Bay, Negril, and Ocho Rios, less visited and much more remote Port Antonio is an elite retreat—long a favorite of visiting celebrities such as Bette Davis, Ginger Rogers, Harrison Ford, and Denzel Washington.

Although much of Jamaica is overbuilt, Port Antonio lies in a relatively undeveloped area. As one local vendor put it, "Ocho Rios attracts the tourist; we attract the traveler."

Fun Fact Hyperbole Through the Ages

The first "tourist," Christopher Columbus, called Port Antonio "the fairest land mine eyes have ever seen." The American poet Ella Wheeler Wilcox (1855–1919) perhaps had imbibed one too many rum punches when she exclaimed that "Port Antonio is the most exquisite place on earth." And what did swashbuckler Errol Flynn have to say? "Port Antonio is more beautiful than any woman I've ever seen."

The area's white-sand beaches are among the island's finest and least crowded. Only afew resorts here can be described as upmarket; most of this region is a haven for the frugal traveler seeking modest digs. Port Antonio lacks the all-inclusive megaresorts of Ocho Rios or Mo Bay; if that's what you need, head elsewhere. The same goes for shopping, nightlife, and deluxe dining: If they're absolutely essential to your vacation, hit the road. And if you like to run naked on the beach, your hair in braids, Negril is more your speed; Port Antonio, quite frankly, is perhaps the most staid of the major Jamaican resort towns.

Americans tend to go for Mo Bay, Ocho Rios, and Negril (in that order). In Port Antonio, by contrast, you're much more likely to encounter European visitors, especially from Germany.

The good news is that you can link up with other resorts or attractions on day trips while staying here. Port Antonio is within easy driving distance of Ocho Rios; the Blue Mountains and John Crow Mountains are at the southern edge of the town.

Hoteliers in Port Antonio know the area may never be as chic as it was in the 1950s or the early 1960s. Still, they are preparing for stiff competition in the 21st century with a push to attract a new type of traveler, the eco-sensitive hiker who wants to explore the natural beauty of the island—especially that mountain scenery to the south of Port Antonio. If you love nature, there may be no better place in Jamaica to base yourself.

And if a movie star still sneaks into town on occasion to chill out, well, that's okay with the locals, too.

1 Orientation

GETTING THERE BY PLANE If you're going to Ocho Rios first, you'll fly into the **Donald Sangster Airport** in Montego Bay (p. 50) or the **Norman Manley International Airport** in Kingston (p. 191). Some hotels, particularly the larger resorts, will arrange for airport transfers from that point. Be sure to ask when you book. You can also fly to Port Antonio's small airport, booking your connection through **International Airlink** (© 876/940-6660). This local airport, **Ken Jones Aerodrome** (© 876/913-3173), lies 10km (6¼ miles) west of the center of Port Antonio, and several taxis always meet arriving planes to take you where you want to go along the northeast coastline. There are no more direct flights from the Kingston airports into Port Antonio. The only way to reach Port Antonio from Kingston is to fly across the country to Montego Bay, board a separate flight, then fly back across the country to Port Antonio (it takes hours). The overland route from Kingston to Port Antonio is less than 2 hours.

Caribbean Sea

Woods Island

Navy Island

East Harbour

West Harbour

FOLLY ESTATE

Folly Great House

Folly Point Lighthouse

Caneside River

East Town River

Annotto River

BOUNDBROOK

Boundbrook Wharf

Ferry

Parish Church

Court House

Fort George

Titchfield

Queen St.

King St.

Valentine St.

Jamaica Tourist Board

Capitol Cinema

Market

Public Hosp.

Gideon Ave.

Harbour St.

West St.

William St.

Bridge St.

Mannings Ave.

Allen Ave.

Carder Ave.

Olivier

Smatt Rd.

Norman Rd

Park Peters Lane

East Palm Ave.

East Campbell Ave.

French Ave.

West Palm Ave.

Victor Lane

Red Hassell Lane

Cottage Lane

Ackee Lane

Jones Gate Melald Rd

Red Hassell Rd.

Bonnie View

Portland Rd.

Gale Rd.

Grossett Rd.

Army Lane

West Baptist Ave.

Hall's Ave.

Little Annotto Rd.

West Palm Ave.

Rice Piece Rd

Boundbrook Rd.

Boundbrook Ave.

Boundbrook Crescent

Boundbrook Rd

Springbank Rd.

Lighthouse Rd.

Boundbrook Cres.

Harper Lane

Eveleigh Park

Vida Lane

To Athenry Gardens & Cave of Nonsuch

To Somerset Falls

Port Antonio

Kingston

JAMAICA

0.5 mi

0.5 km

N

† Church
■ Ferry route
ⓘ Information

BY BUS   The bus from Montego Bay costs $25 one-way. We recommend the private company **Tour Wise** (℃ **876/979-1027**), whose bus will drop you off at your hotel. The trip takes about 2 hours.

BY RENTAL CAR OR TAXI   You can rent a car in Montego Bay for the 216km (134-mile) drive east along Route A1. The highway becomes A3 and then A4 before it reaches Port Antonio. Figure on at least 4 hours to make this drive safely. Expect some rough going, as the road is traffic-clogged in many spots and literally broken up in others. You also must compete with bikes, goats, gonzo Jamaican drivers, and the like. It's not much fun, but you can try it if you want to see the real Jamaica for a bit.

Officially sanctioned **JUTA taxis** (℃ **876/927-4534**), found at both the Montego Bay International Airport and Kingston's airport, will take you overland to Port Antonio, although this can be costly. From Kingston, the cost ranges from $200; from Montego Bay, its a much longer ride and costs around $220 more one-way.

VISITOR INFORMATION

The local office of the **Jamaica Tourist Board** is on the second floor of City Centre Plaza (℃ **876/993-3051**), at the west end of Harbour Street in the center of town. Hours are Monday to Friday 8:30am to 4:30pm and Saturday 9am to 1pm. If you want information about Jamaica in general, go to the **Jamaican Information Service,** 23 Harbour St. (℃ **876/993-2630**), which keeps the same hours as above.

THE TOWN LAYOUT

Separated by the Titchfield Peninsula, the heart of Port Antonio lies between two harbors. Divided only by a narrow channel, the privately owned Navy Island, still called "Errol Flynn's Island" by some old-timers, lies just offshore.

There are no clever names here, only literal ones. The western part is called "West Harbour," the eastern bay is known as "East Harbour." West Palm Avenue is the major avenue running at the southern tier of West Harbour. The larger East Harbour is bordered by Allan Avenue going east.

The town center is crisscrossed by three main roads—Gideon Avenue, Harbour Street, and William Street—each running parallel to the others. Linking up with Harbour Street, Fort George Street rises uphill along the Titchfield Peninsula. West and Harbour streets converge at a clock tower, flanked by the courthouse and the post office.

The center of Port Antonio is easy to traverse on foot, although if you get lost, asking directions can be frustrating (or amusing): Townsfolk often defy mapmakers, calling streets or roads by local nicknames. Allan Avenue, for example— which begins at the junction with Harbour Street, near Christ Church—is locally called "Folly Road" for some reason we can't discern.

GETTING AROUND   Bus transportation here is a disaster. If you don't have a private car, use a taxi. **JUTA** (℃ **876/993-2684**) runs a fleet of Toyota Corolla station wagons around the area. A typical charge, say from the heart of Port Antonio to San San Beach or the Blue Lagoon, is $15 to $20. If you're being taken to the beach and want to spend some time there before returning, you can even arrange with a driver to be picked up at a certain time.

Minibuses operate throughout the town on erratic schedules and can be waved down. They are far cheaper, costing only $2 per person. "Robot" or shared cabs are also plentiful, but these are illegal, and most of them do lack insurance.

Bligh, the Bounty & the Breadfruit

The true story of the HMS *Bounty* and its mutinous crew is the stuff of legend and film—and if you're renting videos, by the way, the Clark Gable/Charles Laughton 1930s version is far better than the 1984 Mel Gibson/Anthony Hopkins disappointment. But we digress.

Though a rich, fertile land, Jamaica in its early days did not grow enough food to support itself. Supplies were shipped down from what later became the United States, but vessels stopped sailing during the American Revolution, leading to starvation on the island. In London, Captain William Bligh was ordered to sail to Tahiti in command of the HMS *Bounty,* collect a hold of starchy, bland-tasting breadfruit, then carry it onward to feed the Jamaicans.

The *Bounty* sailed from London in 1787, rounding Cape Horn. In Tahiti breadfruit plants were duly collected. On the way back, however, the crew—led by Fletcher Christian—mutinied in protest of Bligh's harsh command. Bligh and some of his most loyal men were set adrift in the middle of the Pacific, as Christian—now the captain—sailed for Ascension Island.

Somehow Bligh survived and returned to London. He was found not guilty of wrongdoing, was made captain of the HMS *Providence,* and set sail once again to fulfill his breadfruit mission. The *Providence* sailed from London in 1791; Bligh returned to Tahiti, securing more breadfruit plants, and finally did reach the island of Jamaica in February of 1793.

The plants were sent to a little spa at Bath with its botanical gardens, where they flourished and became an important food staple on the then-starving island. If there's a statue or memorial to Bligh's remarkable persistence, though, we haven't seen it.

FACT FACTS: Port Antonio

Banks The most convenient banks are **Scotiabank,** 3 Harbour St. (© 876/ 933-2523), or at **RBTT Jamaica Ltd.,** 28 Harbour St. (© 876/993-9755), both open Monday to Thursday 9am to 2pm, Friday 9am to 4pm.

Libraries To catch up on your reading, head for the **Portland Parish Library,** Lower Fort George Street (© 876/993-2793), open Monday to Friday 9am to 6pm, Saturday 9am to 4pm.

Mail The **Port Antonio Post Office,** Harbour Street (© 876/993-2158), lies in the exact center of town by the clock. Include "Jamaica, W.I." in all island addresses. The island has no zip codes.

Medical Services The hospital is the **Port Antonio Hospital** (© 876/993-2646), which lies south of West Harbour on Naylor's Hill.

Pharmacies A trio of pharmacies is found in the center of town. They are **A&E Pharmacy,** Port Antonio Square (© 876/993-9348), open Monday to Wednesday and Friday and Saturday 9am to 6pm, Thursday 9am to 2pm;

The City Plaza Pharmacy on Harbour Street (© **876/993-2620**), open Monday to Wednesday and Friday and Saturday 9am to 6pm, Thursday 9am to 2pm; and **Square Deal Pharmacy,** 11 West St. (© **876/993-3629**), open Monday to Saturday 9am to 6pm.

Safety Generally speaking, Port Antonio is a safer destination than Montego Bay, Negril, or Ocho Rios—and much safer than Kingston. When shopping the Musgrave Market, however, pay special attention to your wallet or purse. The narrow little streets of Port Antonio, with their bad lighting at night, also invite muggers. Wander there at your own risk.

Travel Agencies The best travel agency here is **Trafalgar Travel,** 2–6 Harbour St. (© **876/993-2645**), open Monday to Friday 8:30am to 4:30pm, Saturday 10am to 1pm.

2 Where to Stay

In spite of the charms of Port Antonio, it is currently suffering from somewhat of a lack of business—resort clients are drawn to the more famous Negril, Ocho Rios, and Montego Bay resorts. Many of the hotels below are thus having to fill empty rooms with low-cost tour groups originating in anywhere from Italy to Canada. This, in turn, is causing a major (and unfortunate) deterioration in the physical condition of some of the properties, which no longer seem to be maintained in a state-of-the-art condition.

If you're booking your own accommodations in Port Antonio, you might seek information from the **Port Antonio Guest House Association** (© or fax **876/993-7118**; www.go-jam.com).

Traveling frugally? **San San Tropez** (p. 172) rents plain but very affordable rooms.

VERY EXPENSIVE

Blue Lagoon Villas 𝕽𝕽𝕽   If you see a big star rushing for the helicopter pad here, don't be surprised: This complex of villas is often favored by celebrities, who come to this resort just as they did in decades past. This is the most exclusive resort in the Port Antonio area, a pocket of posh filled with unadulterated luxury. Each of the elegantly decorated private villas comes with its own chef, housekeeper, and butler. Villas contain one, two, three, or four bedrooms, each only a 2-minute walk from the Blue Lagoon. Bedrooms are the most stylish in Port Antonio, with an emphasis on privacy and seclusion. All open onto panoramic views of the sea, and all are very spacious, with luxurious tub/shower combination bathrooms. Because the resort attracts lots of media types, each villa has a TV, VCR, and entertainment center with CD player—not to mention both indoor and outdoor dining areas, sun decks with luxe chaise lounges, and a full kitchen. These are the most photographed villas in the Caribbean, having appeared in the pages of such magazines as *Town & Country* and *Gourmet.* Note, however, that you can only rent them by the week, not the night. Nonguests may dine at the hotel's Blue Lagoon Restaurant (p. 171).

The Blue Lagoon, Fairy Hill, Port Antonio. © **800/237-3237** or 876/993-8491. Fax 876/993-7792. www.blue lagoonvillas.com. 13 villas. Winter 2-bedroom villa $7,500, 3-bedroom villa $8,500, 4-bedroom villa $9,500, 4-bedroom deluxe villa $12,500; summer 2-bedroom villa $6,500, 3-bedroom villa $7,500, 4-bedroom villa $8,500, 4-bedroom deluxe villa $11,000. Rates are by the week, and include all drinks, 1st breakfast, and pickup at the airport. MC, V. **Amenities:** Restaurant; kayaks; massage; laundry service; chef; housekeeper; butler. *In room:* A/C, TV/VCR, kitchen, private bar, safe, CD player.

Chateau en Exotica &&& *(Finds)* If you want the honeymoon retreat of all time, or else want to slip away for an illicit week, consider this oasis near San San Beach and the Blue Lagoon. It is the ultimate fantasy retreat. It's small and exclusive, standing on a 2-hectare (5-acre) private estate. On the *Million Dollar Player* show, the estate was twice chosen as the grand-prize destination. Even Jamaica's usually reserved *Daily Gleaner* has acclaimed the property as "a dream house, a place of serenity"—and so it is. Many feature films or TV shows have used the setting as a backdrop, including *Lifestyles of the Rich and Famous.* Its crystal-clear, rainbow-tiled, and fountain-fresh swimming pool is reason enough to check in. In the courtyard is a spa with thermo hydra jets and mini-waterfalls. A second spacious heated spa is set in a secluded garden gazebo hideaway. The living quarters are spacious and beautifully furnished with a certain elegance and much comfort. Breakfast in bed is a daily option. You've also got your own butler and nanny (housekeeper being the more politically correct term).

Lavish dinners can be arranged in the tented dining room, with a white-gloved butler in attendance at the candlelit setting. You can also dine alfresco by the pool with lighted Tiki torches. The tropical setting is one of fruit trees and lavish flora, with fountains and fish ponds.

San San Estate, Port Antonio. (©) and fax 561/793-7257. www.iwms.com/exotica. 3 units. Winter $395 double, $495 3–6 guests; off season $295 double, $395 3–6 guests. No credit cards. **Amenities:** Dining room; outdoor pool; 2 whirlpools; 2 spas; 5 complimentary boats; limited room service; babysitting; laundry service; basketball court. *In room:* A/C, TV, fridge, hair dryer, safe, Jacuzzi.

Trident Villas & Hotel && This luxury hideaway is located on Allan Avenue, on the coast toward Frenchman's Cove. It sits regally above jagged coral cliffs with a seaside panorama. The hotel's main building is furnished with antiques and cooled by sea breezes. Your accommodations will be a studio cottage or tower, reached by a path through the gardens. In the cottages, a large bedroom with ample sitting area opens onto a private patio with a sea view. All units have ceiling fans, plenty of storage space, and tasteful Jamaican antiques and colorful chintzes. Beds are most comfortable, while bathrooms have combination shower/tubs. Trident has a horseshoe-shape sandy beach cove at one end of its grounds, which is accessible by a path that meanders along a landscaped terrain. It's a strip of muddy bottomed seafront that's not as appealing as a dip in the hotel pool. That pool is positioned near a graceful gazebo and sits above jagged rocks where the surf crashes and churns most of the day.

Men are required to wear jackets and ties at dinner, which is a multicourse, excellent fixed-price meal; if you have dietary restrictions, make your requirements known early.

Rte. A4 (P.O. Box 119), Port Antonio. (©) 800/330-8272 in the U.S., or 876/993-2602. Fax 876/993-2960. www.tridentjamaica.com. 26 units. Winter $385 double, from $620 suite; off season $220 double, from $340 suite. Rates include MAP (breakfast and dinner). AE, MC, V. **Amenities:** Restaurant; bar; outdoor pool; deep-sea fishing; scuba diving; snorkeling; limited room service; massage; babysitting; laundry service; rooms for those with limited mobility; croquet. *In room:* A/C, minibar, hair dryer, safe, beverage maker.

Villa San Cove & This luxury property is owned by Henri Verne, who operates the swanky Chateau en Exotica as well. Both properties lie near the fabulous sands of San San Beach and the Blue Lagoon. San Cove also has its own private beach with a thatched gazebo jutting out into the water. From here, it's an easy boat ride to Princess Isle, which is owned by the Princess Nina Aga

Kahn. Whenever one of those bikini films, such as *Playmates in Paradise* or *Girls of Jamaica*, is shot, this estate is often selected as the backdrop. Bedrooms and public rooms are furnished in an elegantly refined West Indian motif, opening onto private balconies with views of the water. The cottage also has a much-photographed and very elegant spiral stairway.

San San Estate, Port Antonio. ℂ and fax 561/793-7257. www.jamaicabeachvillas.com. 2 units. Winter $395 double, $495 3–6 guests; off season $295 double, $395 3–6 guests. No credit cards. **Amenities:** Outdoor pool; babysitting; laundry service; chef/butler. *In room:* A/C, TV, iron/board, safe, Jacuzzi.

EXPENSIVE

Frenchman's Cove Resort ⚹   Lying 8km (5 miles) east of the center of Port Antonio, this resort on a 18-hectare (45-acre) private estate comes complete with its own freshwater stream running through. It opens onto a sheltered white-sand beach, one of the most idyllic along the northern coast of Jamaica. It boasts regular doubles and suites in its central core, called the great house, as well as one-, two-, or three-bedroom villas spread across a sea-bordering cliff in parklike grounds. In the great house, with its spacious bedrooms and well-maintained private bathrooms, are found the regular doubles, plus two suites with sitting areas. Rooms—and the villas, too—are attractively furnished but in a rather Caribbean minimalist style. Accommodations come in a combination of wicker and dark wood, with large walls of glass that are screened and louvered. Some villas contain bathrooms with sunken showers. The villas are actually small Jamaican stone houses opening onto views. The large three-bedroom villa (no. 18) was occupied by Queen Elizabeth and her family in the 1970s, a decade that was the heyday of this resort. One of our favorites is villa no. 7, nestled on cliffs in the midst of rainforest type shrubbery with a clear view of the beach below. On the way to the beach, you can pick a few oranges to go with your lunch.

Frenchman's Cove, Port Antonio. ℂ **876/993-7270.** Fax 987/993-7404. www.frenchmans-cove-resort.com. 12 units, 18 villas. Year-round $90 double, $100 suite, $130 1-bedroom villa, $180 2-bedroom villa, $220 3-bedroom villa. Rates include continental breakfast. MC, V. **Amenities:** Grill; 2 bars; babysitting; laundry service; rooms for those with limited mobility. *In room:* A/C, fridge (in villas), iron/board, beverage maker (in villas), phone in great house rooms only.

Goblin Hill Villas at San San ⚹   This green and sunny hillside—once said to shelter goblins—is now filled with Georgian-style vacation homes on San San Estate. The pool is surrounded by a vine-laced arbor, which lies just a stone's throw from an almost impenetrable forest. A long flight of steps leads down to the crescent-shaped sands of San San Beach. This beach is now private, but guests of the hotel receive a pass. Everything has the aura of having last been fixed up in the 1970s, but the resort is still comfortable. The accommodations are town house–style; some have ceiling fans and king-size beds (some have twin beds), but none have phones. The generally roomy units are filled with hand-made pine pieces, along with a split-level living and dining area with a fully equipped kitchen. All units have well-maintained bathrooms with shower-tub combinations. Housekeepers prepare and serve meals and attend to chores in the villas.

San San (P.O. Box 26), Port Antonio. ℂ **800/472-1148** or 876/925-8108. Fax 876/925-6248. www.goblin hill.com. 28 units. Winter $110–$195 1-bedroom villa, $185–$245 2-bedroom villa; off season $90–$165 1-bedroom villa, $145–$195 2-bedroom villa. AE, MC, V. **Amenities:** Bar; outdoor pool; 2 tennis courts; car rental; room service (8am–8pm); babysitting; laundry service; nonsmoking rooms; rooms for those with limited mobility. *In room:* A/C, TV, kitchenette, fridge, coffeemaker (in some units), no phone, chef.

MODERATE

Fern Hill Club Hotel   Airy and panoramic but showing signs of wear, Fern Hill occupies 8 forested hectares (20 acres) high above the coastline, attracting primarily British and Canadian tour-group clientele. The nearest beach is San San, a 5-minute drive east of the hotel. There's no shuttle but the reception desk can arrange for a taxi to take you there. This is a far less elegant choice than its main competitor, Goblin Hill (see above), though you can almost always get better rates here. Technically classified as a private club, it's comprised of a colonial-style clubhouse and three outlying villas, plus a comfortable annex at the bottom of the hill. The accommodations come in a wide range of configurations, including standard rooms, junior suites, spa suites, and villas with cooking facilities. All units are highly private and attract many honeymooners. Bathrooms, mainly with showers only, are adequate with plenty of shelf space.

See "Where to Dine," below, for a review of the hotel restaurant, Fern Hill Club, which offers a standard international menu.

Mile Gully Rd., San San (P.O. Box 100), Port Antonio. (C) **876/993-7374.** Fax 876/993-7373. www.fernhill clubhotel.com. 31 units. Year-round $99 double; $154 1-bedroom villa; $242 2-bedroom villa. AE, MC, V. Drive east along Allan Ave. and watch for the signs. **Amenities:** Restaurant; bar; 3 outdoor pools; tennis court; laundry service. *In room:* A/C, TV, kitchenette (in villas), iron, safe.

Jamaica Palace Hotel 🐾   This stately mansion rises from a hillock surrounded by 2 tropically landscaped hectares (5 acres). It's not on the beach, but a free shuttle will take you to one of the best sandy beaches in the area, Frenchman's Cove Beach. The public rooms are filled with furnishings and art from Europe, including a 2m (6-ft.) Baccarat crystal candelabrum and a pair of Italian ebony-and-ivory chairs from the 15th century. Outside, the Palace offers white-marble columns, sun-filled patios and balconies, and an unusual 35m (114-ft.) pool shaped like Jamaica. Most accommodations are large, with 4m (13-ft.) ceilings and oversize marble bathrooms with tub and shower. Some, however, are rather small, though still comfortably appointed. Suites are individually furnished with crystal chandeliers, Persian rugs, and original works of art. All units have excellent beds, often sleigh beds. Both Continental and Jamaican food are served in the main dining room, with its lighted "water wall" sculpted from Jamaican cave stones. There is also a poolside cafe with barbecue, live dance and calypso bands, and a boutique.

Williamsfield (8km/5 miles east of Port Antonio; P.O. Box 277). (C) **800/877-8000** in the U.S., or 876/993 7720. Fax 876/993-7759. www.jamaicapalace.com. 80 units. Winter $120–$140 double, $180–$220 suite; off season $100–$120 double, $160–$200 suite. MAP (breakfast and dinner) for 2 people $190. AE, MC, V. **Amenities:** 2 restaurants; bar; outdoor pool; free beach shuttle; limited room service; babysitting; laundry service; nonsmoking rooms; rooms for those with limited mobility. *In room:* A/C, TV ($6 extra per night), safe.

Rio Vista Resort Villas 🐾🐾 *(Finds*   Featured in *Condé Nast Traveler,* this place is ideal for a luxurious vacation, a honeymoon, or even an off-the-record weekend. Six kilometers (3¾ miles) west of Port Antonio (most of the luxe properties lie to the east), Rio Vista is only 3km (1¾ miles) from the little local airstrip, nestled between the Rio Grande and the Caribbean Sea. On a 4-hectare (10-acre) estate planted with tropical fruits, it offers handsomely furnished one- and two-bedroom cottages, plus a honeymoon villa with a river view. The setting is a garden of flowers, spices, and sweet-smelling herbs. Rooms have vaulted wooden ceilings and well-maintained tiled bathrooms, each with a shower. A housekeeper services each cottage and can assist with meals. Candlelit dinners can be arranged. Air-conditioning in summer costs $10 extra.

Fun Fact **Enter the Dragon**

The all-inclusive resort chain of **Sandals** (© 800/SANDALS; www.sandals. com) has acquired the 22-hectare (55-acre) **Dragon Bay Beach Resort** and is turning it into another one of their properties, which already exist in profusion elsewhere on the island, especially in Montego Bay, Negril, and Ocho Rios. The property will open onto Dragon Bay Beach, a little cove to the east of the more famous Blue Lagoon, a distance of 11km (6¾ miles) east of Port Antonio. This was the backdrop for the Tom Cruise bomb *Cocktail*. Remember when he performed gymnastics with a liquor bottle? That is, if you bothered to catch the flick at all. Stay tuned for future developments.

P.O. Box 4, St. Margaret's Bay. © 876/993-5444. Fax 876/993-5445. www.riovistajamaica.com. 5 villas. Year-round $110–$120 double; $120–$130 honeymoon villa; $140–$150 2-bedroom villa; $1,200 5-night honeymoon package. MC, V. **Amenities:** Restaurant; bar; outdoor pool; rafting; limited room service; massage; laundry service; nonsmoking rooms. *In room:* A/C, TV, dataport, kitchenette, fridge, hair dryer, safe, beverage maker.

INEXPENSIVE

Jamaica Heights Resort ☆ *(Finds)* The funkiest, most amusing, and hippest guesthouse in town might be full of rock stars from Düsseldorf or up-and-coming filmmakers cranking out tomorrow's indie fave. The very worldly owner, Helmut Steiner, former professor of literature and philosophy in Berlin, and his wife, Charmaine, maintain this affordable but sophisticated retreat. It's set at the top of a rutted and very steep series of roads. The resort is not on a beach but provides transportation to two of the finest beach strips of sand at Port Antonio, Frenchman's Cove and San San.

Scattered amid the wedge-shaped 3-hectare (8-acre) property are a half-dozen buildings, each white-walled with shutters, gazebos, climbing vines, and a pavilion for meditating over views of the forested terrain that cascades down to Port Antonio's harbor. The garden sports exotic palms, a stream with its own waterfalls, the most elegant Ping-Pong pavilion in the world, and dozens of botanical oddities from around the world. The minimalist accommodations are spotlessly clean. Each has a four-poster bed and funky lighting fixtures, plus shower/tub combination bathrooms. Doors can be opened or closed to create suites with between two and four bedrooms.

Spring Bank Rd., Port Antonio. © 876/993-3305. Fax 876/993-3563. www.jamaicaheights.net. 8 units. Year-round $60–$75 double. No credit cards. **Amenities:** Restaurant; outdoor pool; watersports can be arranged; laundry service; nonsmoking rooms. *In room:* No phone, beverage maker, ceiling fan.

3 Where to Dine

An array of atmospheric choices awaits you in Port Antonio. All hotels welcome outside guests for dinner, but reservations are required.

EXPENSIVE

Trident Hotel Restaurant ☆ INTERNATIONAL/JAMAICAN The elegant Trident Hotel Restaurant serves meals that evoke the Jamaica of the 1950s. The cuisine is always prepared with first-class ingredients, though the setting and the white-glove service are generally more memorable than the food. The high-pitched wooden roof set on white stone walls holds several ceiling fans that gently stir the air. The antique tables are set with old china, English silver, and Port Royal pewter. The formally dressed waiters will help you choose your wine and whisper the name of each course as they serve it. The five-course dinner menu changes daily but might include a Jamaican salad, mahimahi with may-onnaise-and-mustard sauce, steak with broccoli and sautéed potatoes, and for dessert, peach melba and Blue Mountain coffee with Tia Maria, a Jamaican liqueur.

In Trident Villas & Hotel, Rte. A4. © **876/993-2602.** Reservations required. Jackets required for men. Fixed-price dinner $44. AE, MC, V. Daily 7:30am–9:30pm. Head east on Allan Ave.

MODERATE

Blue Lagoon Restaurant ✦ JAMAICAN/JERK   There is no more romantic place in town to dine than on one of the wooden decks at this restaurant, projecting out over the lagoon made famous by the movie of the same name; trees were spared, so trees even sprout up through the decks around you. The unusual menu is devoted mostly to jerk dishes. You can order jerk pork (the most tender and most succulent of tenderloin), but even crayfish, lamb chops, chicken, and lobster are given the jerk seasoning treatment. The spicy conch, flavored with a zesty honey-garlic sauce, is another reason to dine here, and the stuffed crab back is Port Antonio's finest: The chef takes a crab shell, stuffs it with crabmeat,

The Green Gold of Port Antonio

The Spanish didn't do Jamaica much good, but they did leave an *hasta la vista* present: the banana. From the Canary Islands, their colony off the western coast of Africa, they introduced the banana to Jamaica in 1520. It had nearly the same impact that introducing the tomato had on Italy: Banana trees took to Jamaican soil at once, even better than in their native land.

At first the Caucasian residents of Jamaica refused to eat the banana, considering them food fit only for animals or slaves. Nonetheless, the banana saved many an impoverished family from starvation.

In 1873 Captain Lorenzo Dow Baker of Massachusetts loaded some bananas on his ship to take back to New England. They were an instant success there, and the future of the banana was secured, as orders came in for more and more of this tasty fruit. The Boston Fruit Company rushed to Port Antonio and began establishing banana plantations and hiring the descendants of slaves as its low-paid workers.

In time, bananas became known as "green gold." They could be picked green and would ripen in the ships carrying them back to New England.

By 1905 Captain Baker had erected the Titchfield Hotel and begun bringing in tourists. Some of the wealthiest people in America, including J. P. Morgan, came to visit at this Jamaican playground—and it all began with the banana.

In the 1920s, however, a banana blight arrived from Central America. The disease destroyed Port Antonio's banana crops. The local economy collapsed, and it has never really bounced back since, except for the tourism boom that hit—briefly—during the 1960s.

and grills it with oil and butter. Drinks are designed to amuse. Ask for a "Sex in the Lagoon," the bartender's specialty and the only XXX-rated drink in Port Antonio. (You'll have to order it for a surprise; we're not telling what's in it.) If you really want a romantic dinner, ask for your meal served on a floating raft in the middle of the lagoon.

The Blue Lagoon. © 876/993-7791. Reservations required. Fixed-price lunch $14. Dinner main courses $18–$25. MC, V. Daily 10am–10pm.

Panorama INTERNATIONAL/JAMAICAN   One of the finest dining spots in Port Antonio offers a sweeping view of the rugged coastline, with great sunsets. Specialties include jerk chicken, jerk pork, grilled lobster, and Creole fish. Depending on who's in the kitchen, the food here can be quite satisfactory, though once in a while, especially off season, the cuisine might be a bit of a letdown. The club also offers entertainment, with a calypso band during the week.

In the Fern Hill Club Hotel, Mile Gully Rd. © 876/993-7374. Reservations recommended. Main courses $8–$10 lunch, $10–$25 dinner. AE, DISC, MC, V. Daily 7:30am–10pm. Head east on Allan Ave.

San San Tropez ℛ ITALIAN   In 1994 Milan-born Fabio Favalli bought a well-located villa that had originally been conceived as the staff quarters for an upscale resort (Frenchman's Cove) that was devastated and bankrupted in the late 1980s by a hurricane. Since then, the villa has earned a well-deserved reputation as a provenance for superb Italian food. This is served at lunch and dinner, conducted in either an indoor dining room (its decor emulates that of an ancient Roman villa) or at candlelit tables beside the swimming pool. Menu items include well-prepared homemade pastas, especially linguine "Blue Lagoon" (with shellfish), lasagna, or spaghetti served either with carbonara or bolognese sauce. Any of these could be followed by portions of very fresh fish, grilled and seasoned with Italian and Jamaican herbs, and a medley of refreshing desserts. Other good choices include the staples of Italian cuisine, chicken or veal parmigiana, and osso buco.

On-site are six suites, each with ceiling fans, cable TV, air-conditioning, and a separate living room and bedroom. Depending on the season, they cost from $94 to $136, double occupancy, with breakfast included.

On San San Bay. © 876/993-7213. Reservations recommended. Pizzas $10–$18; main courses $12–$20. AE, MC, V. Daily noon–4pm and 6–10pm.

INEXPENSIVE

Anna Bananas INTERNATIONAL   Architecturally, the building that contains this open-air seafront restaurant features little more than a wooden deck with a soaring roof. There aren't even any walls to prevent storms or rain from penetrating the inside, but in light of how relaxed the place is, most clients don't seem to care. Painted a bright shade of yellow and named after the childhood nickname of the owners' daughter (who hated bananas), it was established in the late 1990s by a consortium of Texan and Jamaican entrepreneurs. Menu items, as described on a chalkboard, include cheese sandwiches, tender savory oxtail, fried fish or chicken, BLT sandwiches with avocado, and platters of zesty jerk chicken and pork (on weekends). Drinks are wide-ranging and frothy.

7 Folly Rd. © 876/715-6533. Main courses J$250–J$1,000 (US$4.15–US$17). AE, DC, MC, V. Daily 7am–11pm.

Coronation Bakery ℛ *finds*   The best bread in town emerges, steaming, from the ovens at this bakery, a landmark that the late William Chung established in June of 1953. Owned today by his son Cyril, it's set in the heart of Port

Antonio, in a 70-year-old all-wood house whose carved columns and graceful lattices support an old-fashioned zinc-roofed veranda on the second floor. Inside, for a picnic or to take back to your villa, you can buy fresh loaves of hard-crusted sourdough, perhaps with the intention of smearing it with the guava jelly that's available at any local supermarket. They also make fresh cocoa buns, a savory version of cornbread, a peppery version of Jamaican patties (dough envelopes filled with minced and heavily peppered meat), and sweet buns flavored with Jamaican allspice and nutmeg. Especially interesting are the bulla cakes, a fast-baked, unleavened bread that used to be a cheap staple for agrarian workers laboring away in the sugarcane fields. Many years ago, they were fast-baked at high temperatures (as a means of saving fuel) with very little sugar, whatever flour the homeowner had on-hand, and a small amount of bacon grease or lard. Even today they're known for their prolonged shelf life in hot, humid climes. They sell here for about 12¢ each; locals maintain they're best consumed with a thick slice of cheese, perhaps as part of a picnic at the beach.

18 West St. (© 876/993-2110. Loaf of bread J$78 ($1.25); pastries from J$7 (12¢). No credit cards. Mon–Sat 8am–8pm.

The Hub *(Finds* JAMAICAN   Set within a cement-sided, relatively nondescript building just east of the town center, this is the local restaurant most often cited by expatriates as their favorite local eatery. Lloyd Bentley, the hardworking owner, maintains a sense of humor about his restaurant's lack of a view. (It overlooks a parking lot and a side yard of the now-defunct local railroad.) But in a town loaded with seafront panoramas, patrons flock here anyway. Menu items are fresh-made and flavorful, featuring a tried-and-true blend of such dishes as pork chops, three different preparations of chicken (including a version in brown-stew sauce), stewed peas with rice, oxtail, and brown-stewed fish.

2 West Palm Ave. (© 876/715-6943. Main courses J$150–J$600 (US$2.50–US$9.95). No credit cards. Mon–Sat 8:30am–midnight; Sun noon–8pm.

A NEARBY PLACE TO DINE

Mille Fleurs *(R&R* CARIBBEAN   This restaurant is terraced into a verdant hillside about 180m (600 ft.) above sea level with sweeping views over the Jamaican coastline and the faraway harbor of Port Antonio. Sheltered from the frequent rains, but open on the side for maximum access to cooling breezes, it features candlelit dinners, well-prepared food, and lots of New Age charm. Lunches include sandwiches, salads, grilled-fish platters, and soups. At night, you might feast on fresh lobster or tender lamb and beef dishes, even savory rabbit or smoked marlin. The restaurant has been praised by *Gourmet* magazine for its dishes. You may want to try the coconut-and-garlic soup, and the fish with spicy mango-shrimp sauce is a specialty. Breads and most jams are made on the premises. Two dishes are vegetarian.

In the Hotel Mocking Bird Hill, North Coast Hwy. (© 876/993-7267. Reservations recommended. Lunch platters $10–$30; main courses $19–$40. AE, MC, V. Daily 8:30–10am, noon–2pm, and 7–9:30pm.

4 Beaches & Outdoor Pursuits

BEACHES

Although local waters can be turbulent at times, and it rains a lot, the white-sand beaches in and around Port Antonio put it on the tourist map. Invariably, they are far less crowded than those of Montego Bay and Ocho Rios. The best of these white sandy strips follow.

Fun Fact **The Blue Lagoon**
_____

Remember 14-year-old Brooke Shields, way back before she tried to become a TV star? She made the film *The Blue Lagoon* in the calm waters of this protected cove, playing a teen castaway who swam naked with now-forgotten Christopher Atkins.

Lying about 2km (1¼ miles) east of San San Beach, the Blue Lagoon 🏖🏖🏖 is not on a beach. But when you see these beautiful waters, you'll forget all about sands and take the plunge. The lagoon isn't always cerulean blue: Throughout the day, reflections can turn it jade or sapphire. Once we noticed a rainy sky turning it a shade of mauve. The water is 56m (185 ft.) deep at its deepest point, although the Arawak Indians believed it was bottomless. It was once the lair of the pirate Tom Mallard, when it was called Mallard's Hole—before the name was changed to something more romantic, that is.

Tales spin about the Blue Lagoon. One concerns Errol Flynn, who is said to have dived to the bottom of the lagoon aided only by snorkeling gear. Some say he did it once; others maintain he performed this feat every day. That's dubious, but it *is* true that Robin Moore, author of *The French Connection,* once owned most of the land opening onto the lagoon.

Islanders also maintain that if you swim in the lagoon with your mouth open, drinking in the water, it will "turn a man into a bull." Hundreds of people make this claim about the aphrodisiac powers of these waters. "In America," a caretaker told us, "men take Viagra. Here all we need is one cup from the Blue Lagoon, and we're fit as a fiddle all night."

On-site is a small restaurant with changing rooms, along with a little mineral spring bath. Many visitors flock here for a Saturday night bash, when live reggae is played.

During the day someone at one of the little makeshift kiosks is on-hand to rent you a paddleboat or snorkeling equipment. The Blue Lagoon teems with marine life, including schools of rainbow-hued fish, and even on occasion a squid gliding by and, less welcome, a barracuda giving you the fish eye.

This beauty spot, one of the finest on the island, is open daily from 9am to 10pm, charging an admission of $4. Call ☎ **876/993-7791** for more information.

FOLLY & JAMAICAN REEF BEACHES   In the center of town on the northern border are two beaches, Jamaican Reef Beach and Folly Beach, both lying at the northern coast of the Titchfield Peninsula. Neither is worth bothering with unless you're staying in town at a guesthouse and don't have a car. Either beach can be walked to from the center of town. Opening onto East Harbour, Jamaican Reef Beach has darkish sand and looks unattractive; it is always littered with debris. The nearby Folly Beach is only a little strip of sand with a grassy knoll. Instead of swimming, you might stop by at its little bar serving plain "I-tal" (unsalted, vegetarian) meals and good tropical punches, which costs $3 to enter daily from 9am to 5pm. There are showers on the beach to wash away the sand.

SAN SAN BEACH   Not as tidily kept as Frenchman's Cove, San San is a private beach that has a longer strip of sand than the cove and is narrower. The beach is often frequented by wealthy owners of second homes built along a small peninsula called Alligator Head.

Guests who check into such hotels as Jamaica Palace, Goblin Hill, and Fern Hill (see "Where to Stay," earlier in this chapter) can use this beach for free, and it's open to anyone else willing to shell out $8 between 10am and 4pm. The beach has watersports equipment, lifeguards, showers, and a picnic area with grills. In winter, waves washing ashore make this one of the best places along the northeast coast for windsurfing.

The little island you see offshore goes by various names: Monkey Island, Woods Island, Pellow Island, and Princess Island. Many visitors swim to the islet from San San Beach; if you try it, watch for spiny sea urchins as you step ashore. The island also has a good reef for snorkeling.

WINNIFRED BEACH   This is not the name of your spinster aunt, but the best public beach east of Port Antonio. It lies just to the east of Dragon Bay Beach, en route to Boston Bay Beach (see below). The half-moon-shaped strip of sand attracts more islanders than visitors. Offshore is a dramatic reef of living

The Jerk Center of the Universe

Boston Beach is the most famous jerk center in Jamaica, with pit after smoky barbecue pit lining the beach. This is where you come to find the ultimate in this food form. Sometimes residents of Kingston drive all the way up here just to stock up on these tasty bits of meat.

Jerking, of course, is the spicy slow barbecuing of meats such as pork, chicken, or sausage. The technique was said to have originated with the Windward Maroons, who hunted wild pigs in the Rio Grande Valley and cooked their meat over green pimento wood.

The jerk sauce is made from little rounds of crenellated red and yellow peppers grown in the countryside. After sampling one of these sauces, you'll surely agree that your favorite Texas red-hot sauce tastes like a cool glass of V8; the hot sauce is so hot that many visitors claim it's hallucinogenic. You can also purchase cans of the sauce from various vendors.

More adventurous jerk fans go for the pig or goat heads, cow feet, or chitlins. All parts of the animal are cooked here—and, really, after enough of that hot sauce, you won't know what you're eating anyway.

All the stands are good, but if hard-pressed to name our favorite jerk stand here, we'd give the curiously named **Sir G HQ** our vote. You'll recognize the place by the rows of wooden skewers cooking pork and chicken over huge barbecue pits. Fish is also smoked here. You can also order "sides" of roast baked yams or roasted breadfruit.

The downing of this peppery food will give you a reason "to put out the fire," as the locals say, and that means downing one Red Stripe beer after another.

coral teeming with marine life, attracting snorkelers to this beach, which has foul toilets and changing rooms. Locals sometimes stage reggae parties here on a Saturday night. During the day a boatman or two will take you out on a bamboo raft or one of their small craft to a secluded little beach just around the headland; escape with a loved one if you find Winnifred too crowded. No admission fee is charged, and for lunch a number of jerk huts line the shore. Many of the Rasta men here will also serve you i-Tal food.

BOSTON BAY BEACH   Another public beach, Boston Bay is more famous for its jerk-pork stands (see box on p. 175) than it is for its sands. Lying 18km (11 miles) east of Port Antonio, and .8km (½ mile) to the east of Winnifred Beach, it is a strand of golden sands opening onto turquoise waters that aren't always tranquil. The waves have made Boston Beach among the finest in Jamaica for windsurfing. Hidden away on a secluded cove, this beach was once owned by the writer Robin Moore. You'll find lots of picnic tables where you can enjoy your recently purchased lunch of jerk pork, chicken, or whatever.

DEEP-SEA FISHING   Northern Jamaican waters are world-renowned for their game fish, including dolphin fish (mahimahi), wahoo, blue and white marlin, sailfish, tarpon, barracuda, and bonito. The Jamaica International Fishing Tournament and Jamaica International Blue Marlin Team Tournaments run concurrently at Port Antonio every September or October. Most major hotels from Port Antonio to Montego Bay have deep-sea-fishing facilities, and there are many charter boats.

A 12m-long (40-ft.) **sportfishing boat** (© 876/993-3209) with a tournament rig is available for charter rental. Taking out up to six passengers at a time, it charges $950 per half-day or $1,600 per day, with crew, bait, tackle, and soft drinks included. It docks at Port Antonio's Marina, off West Palm Avenue, in the center of town. Call for bookings.

GOLF   Port Antonio may never rival Montego Bay as a golfing mecca, but there is the 9-hole **San San Golf Course & Bird Sanctuary** (© 876/993-7645) lying 6km (3¾ miles) east of San San Beach. A course existed here in Port Antonio's heyday in the 1960s. In 1998 the course was reopened. Its setting offers dramatic scenery, with a backdrop of lush vegetation on one side and the ocean on the other. A round of 9 holes costs $50. You can also play the course twice for $70. Caddies cost $12, with pull carts going for $5. Clubs are rented at the pro shop for $10. Birders often flock to the area to see the many species here.

HIKING   The Rio Grande Valley (see below) is one of the lushest places in the Caribbean to go on hiking jaunts. Hiking trails often follow paths blazed decades ago by hunters seeking wild pigs.

If you're not a serious hiker and want only an easy preview of this luxuriant valley, you can take the 30-minute hike to the **Scatter Water Falls** from Barridale, 10km (6¼ miles) southwest of Port Antonio. Here bamboo rafts will transport you across the Rio Grande, where you can walk in about 20 minutes to the falls. There you'll find pools for cooling off and a little bar serving fresh tropical punches.

Most other hikes are far more strenuous. One of the most difficult is the 19km (12-mile), 2-day hike to **Nanny Town,** named after Queen Nanny, the Amazon-like warrior goddess of the Maroons. One of the most remote places in all of Jamaica, this was the legendary hideout of the Maroons in the 1700s, who came here to escape from the British and went undiscovered for years.

The Rise & Fall of Navy Island

When the movie swashbuckler Errol Flynn arrived in Port Antonio in 1947, his career had peaked and was rapidly heading downhill. But Flynn was still a legend, especially among the local men who spread tales of his womanizing. That was years before his reputation declined dangerously with the publication of Charles Higman's *Errol Flynn: The Untold Story,* which labeled him a Nazi spy, an international criminal, a thief, an addict, a smuggler of guns, drugs, and gold—not to mention a bisexual who liked very young boys.

Sailing from Kingston in his yacht, *Zaca,* one day the Australian actor came ashore at Port Antonio and thought he'd found paradise. Flynn decided to stay, purchasing a ranch near Boston Bay in the John Crow Mountains with his wife Patrice Wymore, the 1950s movie actress. He also purchased the old Titchfield Hotel (now gone) and Navy Island, just offshore.

His wild parties at the Titchfield became the stuff of legend. Everyone old enough to remember Flynn (and dozens who were too young) recount Flynn episodes to this day. Ms. Wymore stayed at the plantation most of the time, raising coconuts, cattle, bananas, and pimento, while Flynn could be found on Navy Island—spending many of those declining years in the arms of an underage bombshell.

Flynn died in 1959, his dreams of turning Port Antonio into a tourist mecca never realized. He was said to have lost Navy Island on a "bad poker night," though that isn't documented; to this day, grandiose plans for reopening the island as a resort have never really materialized. At one point, the actor Louis Gossett Jr. was said to be prepared to pay $3 million for the island, but that deal collapsed; subsequent deals for smaller sums of money have also broken down. The Jamaican government is today the owner of the island, still seeking outside investors to restore the place to something like its former glory.

It is currently off-limits to visitors, its hotel rotting in the sun, a single caretaker patrolling its empty grounds.

A campsite can be found along the Makunnu River. This hike is only for the stout of heart, and it takes you along the steep slopes of the Blue Mountains.

Less difficult is the 5-hour hike to **Watch Hill,** a former lookout point for the Maroons. You'll pass miles of banana groves and the decaying ruins of an 18th-century sugar plantation. This hike is graded moderate.

Our favorite trail is the 6km (3¾-mile), 7-hour **White River Falls** ⟨⟩ hike starting at Millbank, a hamlet south of the Maroon stronghold of Moore Town (p. 183). This hike takes you along the White River, and you can also go upstream to the Seven Falls. After a swim in the first one or two falls, you may decide not to press on, as the going gets rough and the trail is slippery. If you're lucky, you'll see colonies of the rare swallowtail butterfly. These beautiful insects are enormous, and make for one of the most memorable sights nature has to offer in Jamaica.

Shorter and easier hikes in the Lower River Valley can also be arranged, including a 4-hour hike, rated medium grade, along the **Darley Trail.**

One final trail, also difficult, is the 7-hour, 11km (6¾-mile) **Guava River Trail,** starting in the hamlet of Bellevue. The trail goes along the Guava River in the heart of the Blue Mountains. You can swim in the river and continue upstream until you come to some hot springs.

The best and most professional outfitter for arranging tours is listed in the "Eco-Cultural Tours" box on p. 180.

SNORKELING & SCUBA DIVING   At a depth range of 24 to 27m (80–90 ft.), **Alligator Long** is one of the most visited dive sites east of Port Antonio. Advanced divers come here. Divers go along a narrow coral ridge 9m (30 ft.) high and peppered with sea fans, sponges such as the azure vase sponge, soft gorgonians, and many coral heads. Marine life includes the pork fish and several species of hamlets (the indigo hamlet, for example). You'll see squirrelfish darting about, along with stingrays, triggerfish, and spadefish.

The best outfitter is **Lady Godiva's Dive Shop** in Blue Lagoon (© 876/993-8988), 11km (6¾ miles) from Port Antonio. Full dive equipment is available. Technically, you can snorkel off most of the beaches in Port Antonio, but you're likely to see much more further offshore. The best spot is Winnifred on the other side of Dragon Bay. The reef is extremely active and full of a lot of exciting marine life. Lady Godiva offers two excursions daily to this spot for $21 per person including snorkeling equipment for the day.

RAFTING   Although it's not exactly adventurous (it's a tame and safe outing), rafting the Rio Grande is the best rafting experience on the island, and the most fun. Rafting started on the river as a means of transporting bananas from plantations to waiting freighters. In 1871 a Yankee skipper named Lorenzo Dow Baker decided that a seat on one of the rafts was better than walking, but it was not until actor Errol Flynn arrived that the rafts became popular as a tourist attraction. Flynn used to hire the rafts for his friends, and he encouraged the rafters to race down the Rio Grande against one another, betting on winners. Now that bananas are transported by road, the raft skipper makes perhaps one or two trips a day down the waterway. If you want to take a trip, contact **Rio Grande Tours,** Berrydale (© 876/913-5434).

The rafts, some 10m (33 ft.) long and only 6m (4 ft.) wide, are propelled by stout bamboo poles. There's a raised double seat about two-thirds of the way back. The skipper stands in the front, trousers rolled up to his knees, the water washing his feet, and guides the craft down the lively river, about 13km (8 miles) between steep hills covered with coconut palms, banana plantations, and

---

(*Fun Fact* **How *Not* to Raft a River**

Local legend tells of the day the noted author Truman Capote visited to try rafting the Rio Grande. He'd had a brief, abortive affair in New York with Errol Flynn, who had invited him down to Port Antonio. Like Flynn, Capote was a heavy drinker.

As though playing a part in some madcap comedy, Capote's unfortunate raft tipped over right in the middle of the river, and it was all local guides could do to rescue the drunken author. They still chuckle about it today.

flowers, through limestone cliffs pitted with caves, through the "Tunnel of Love," a narrow cleft in the rocks, then on to wider, gentler water.

Trips last 2 to 2½ hours and are offered from 9am to 4pm daily at a cost of $52 per raft, which holds two passengers. A fully insured driver will take you in your rented car to the starting point at Berrydale, where you board your raft. If you feel like it, take a picnic lunch, but bring enough for the skipper, too, who will regale you with lively stories of life on the river.

5 Exploring the Area

You need spend no more than an hour touring the center of raffish Port Antonio—there's not that much to see. Another hour can be spent visiting the markets (see "Shopping," later in this chapter). After that, it's either back to your resort to lie on the beach or, if you're adventurous, you can drive along the coast or dip into the hinterlands south of Port Antonio.

A WALKING TOUR OF PORT ANTONIO

The **Central Square** of Port Antonio is dominated by an old clock tower (though no one remembers when it was last in working order). It stands in front of the two-story **Port Antonio Courthouse,** constructed in the 1890s in the Georgian style. The cast-iron balcony adorning it was a gift from a foundry in Glasgow, Scotland. This is also the site of the post office, the busiest place in town besides the market.

You, too, can join the shoppers here by going across the street and into the **Village of St. George Shopping Mall,** perhaps the strangest, most bastardized bit of architecture in all of Jamaica.

From the square, walk north along Harbour Street, which will become Fort George Street as it takes you to the tiny **Titchfield Peninsula** and **Folly Beach.** The peninsula splits East Harbour from West Harbour. At the end of the peninsula, you'll come to Titchfield High School, erected on the grounds of **Fort George** by the British. The old cannons and some decaying walls of the former fort can still be seen. To defend West Harbour, the British erected the fort here in 1729, with walls 3m (10 ft.) thick. A total of 22 cannons were turned toward the sea against a possible invasion.

Along Fort George Street once stood the **Titchfield Hotel,** bought in later years by Errol Flynn (see box on p. 177). It has since been torn down, but in its heyday was the most fashionable hotel in the West Indies, drawing the likes of Rudyard Kipling and William Randolph Hearst.

On the way back to the Central Square, you can stop off at the **De Montevin Lodge** (see "Where to Dine," p. 170). De Montevin can be entered at 21 Fort George St. This lodge is the best example of late Victorian gingerbread architecture in town. From its terrace, take in the town's best view of its two harbors.

After leaving the lodge, continue down from Fort George Street until it empties into Harbour Street. Walk southeast on this street until you come to **Christ Church,** a redbrick Anglican church that is vaguely Romanesque in architecture. The church (© **876/993-2600**) dates from 1840 and was designed by Annesley Voysey, who adorned it with a large stained-glass window and wooden pews. At the turn of the 20th century, the Boston Fruit Company—growing rich on the bananas being shipped out of Port Antonio—donated the church's eagle lectern.

Leaving the church, you can walk back up Harbour Street, cutting west at the intersection with West Street. As you walk down this street, on your right you

Eco-Cultural Tours

Unique Destinations has designed a series of eco-cultural packages for travelers who want to discover offbeat Jamaica. These "Discover Jamaica Naturally" packages include accommodations in a hotel or villa in Port Antonio, welcome drinks, selected meals, hotel taxes/service charges, and a variety of excursions, such as bamboo rafting and hiking trips to remote waterfalls, scuba diving, snorkeling, and horseback riding. Packages for 3 nights/4 days start at $300 per person (double occupancy). A variety of other packages is also available, including the Birding Adventures package, which journeys into the Rio Grande Valley, John Crow Mountains, and Blue Mountains (to observe Jamaica's exotic birds and butterflies); the Maroons of the Rio Grande package, which includes a trip to historic Moore Town to meet the "Colonel" of the Maroons and a hike to the sacred Nanny Falls; and the Hike and Heal Retreat, which includes a visit to a Maroon herbalist for a special garden tour and presentation, followed by a relaxing herbal bath or essential-oil massage. For more information, contact Unique Destinations at © **401/647-4730.** You can also visit the Unique Destinations website at **www.portantoniojamaica.com**.

will see **Musgrave Market,** the most famous market in northeast Jamaica (see "Shopping," later in this chapter).

If you continue past this market, West Street becomes West Palm Avenue. To your immediate right, jutting into West Harbour, is the **Port Antonio Marina** and then **Boundbrook Wharf** immediately to the west. Back when bananas were more important to the local economy than they are now, Boundbrook Wharf was the busiest loading dock in the West Indies. It inspired a famous, backbreaking song about day labor (see box on p. 182). Today, however, loading machines have replaced the sweaty laborers of yesteryear.

From the marina or the wharf, you can walk east, retracing your steps back to Central Square where our walk began. Taxis are found here waiting to take you where you want to go next.

EAST OF PORT ANTONIO 🐠🐠

The east coast from Port Antonio wins our beauty contest for one of the most beautiful shorelines in the Caribbean, and most definitely in Jamaica. There's a nostalgic aura to it, too, as if it yearns to return to the glamorous 1950s and 1960s when celebrities haunted its coves and villas much more often than they do today.

If some of the coast looks like a movie set, know that more films have been shot here than anywhere else in the Caribbean—none of them really very good, however.

The northeastern coastline of Jamaica is sometimes called "Errol Flynn country" because the actor created a plantation along its shore. The A4 highway goes by the **Errol Flynn Estates** at Fair Prospect and Priestman's River. Flynn's aging, elegant widow, the film star of the 1950s, Patrice Wymore Flynn, still lives here on these 809 hectares (2,000 acres) of pastureland and coconut groves.

The first stopover is at:

THE FOLLY GREAT HOUSE   Come here only if you don't have a lot to do that day, and expect to see a roofless structure with weeds growing up through the foundations. Perhaps it'll inspire you to write a Gothic novel. This house was built in 1905 by Arthur Mitchell, an American millionaire, for his wife Annie—the daughter of Charles Tiffany (founder of the famous New York jewelry store). Seawater was used in the concrete mixtures of its foundations and in the mortar, and the house began to collapse only 11 years after the couple moved in. Because of the beautiful location, it's easy to see what a fine great house it must have been.

The desecrated ruins lie on Folly Peninsula in the East Harbour, right on the outskirts of Port Antonio. Broken bottles and graffiti have replaced the luxurious appointments of yesterday.

If you drive out to the end of Folly Peninsula, you'll see the **Folly Point Lighthouse,** which makes a good spot for a picnic overlooking Woods Island or Monkey Island (among its other names), where Mitchell kept a monkey zoo.

TURTLE CRAWLE BAY   At a point 3km (1¾ miles) east of Port Antonio, you blink and then blink again. Your eyes aren't deceiving you. On a headland jutting out into the sea stands **Trident Castle** , all gleaming white and looking like something Walt Disney might have created in an off-moment. Locals sometimes call it "Folly II" (after The Folly Great House; see above), because the faux castle lay unfinished for many years for lack of money.

Originally this Austrian baroque fantasy with its rococo stonework was the creation of Baroness Fahmi, Port Antonio's most flamboyant resident. She sold it to the architect, Earl Levy, scion of one of the most prominent Jamaican families. Their long-standing feud has often provided fodder for the press; Levy, who had his own architectural ideas, is now in charge and allowed scenes from *Clara's Heart* to be shot at the castle. That wasn't its only starring role. Remember *The Mighty Quinn,* starring Denzel Washington? Mimi Rogers, a "hotel guest" in the film, seduced Denzel here.

The castle is not open to the public—unless you want to rent it, that is. It is indeed possible to book the entire castle as part of a family (or group) vacation package. The manager of the adjacent Trident Hotel will have full details.

The baroness struck back by erecting the faux Grecian Jamaica Palace in 1989, on the eastern shore of Turtle Crawle Bay. Her palace, standing almost in defiance of Trident Castle, was used as a backdrop for *Playmates in Paradise,* bringing in those lecherous boys from *Playboy* magazine in pursuit of "bunnies." Her hotel is now a rival of Levy's Trident Hotel.

LONG BAY   From Boston Bay Beach, the A4 highway continues its southeasterly descent along the coast until it reaches Long Bay and its "half moon" of sandy beach. The expression "the deep blue sea" could be used to describe the waters offshore. The distance is 8km (5 miles) from Boston Bay.

This beach is not the greatest place for a swim because of a dangerous undertow, but it's ideal for a picnic. We like to buy jerk pork and jerk chicken from the vendors in Boston Bay and enjoy it here on this beach.

Many locals still make their living from the sea, and their fishing boats, evocative of canoes, can be seen along the shore. You can usually persuade one of these fishermen, for a fee to be negotiated, to guide an impromptu little tour of the bay in their boat.

Fun Fact **Loading Dem Bananas on Dat Barge**

"Work all night for a drink of rum, daylight come and me wanna go home." Everyone knows that simple song, "Day O"; Boundbrook Wharf (see above) inspired it, the classic banana-boat song still played and sung throughout the Caribbean—and elsewhere.

In recent years, Long Bay has become something of a destination for frugal travelers, especially backpackers. In winter we've often encountered young people. Windsurfers also flock to Long Bay in winter, viewing it as one of the most reliable places for surfing along the northern shore. Bring your own equipment, however.

If you didn't bring lunch from Boston Bay, you can go to the jerk stand at Fishermen's Park. There, a Rasta man will feed you well right in the heart of the settlement.

MANCHIONEAL   Eleven kilometers (6¾ miles) from the coast along A4 from Long Bay, you come to the sea town of Manchioneal, the most venomously named of any town in Jamaica. The fishing village is named for the poisonous manchineel tree (a different spelling from the town). Those dangerous trees have been cut down, but the name remains. This tree is still found throughout the Caribbean, often near beaches. Any innocent who has sought shelter under it in a rainstorm can testify to its poisonous acid—that is, if they are still around.

The small fishing village drowses in the hot sun against the backdrop of a scallop-shaped bay of sapphire blue waters. The sandy beach here is wide, and many lobster fishermen sail out in their boats from the village. For lunch you can patronize one of the little jerk shacks along the shore. One of the savory delicacies sold here is roast conch, which is spicily seasoned and delectable (as long as you don't mind its slightly rubbery consistency).

Manchioneal has a reputation for being the least friendly town along the northern coast. Under no circumstances should you take someone's picture without asking their permission, which is rarely granted. Locals are very suspicious of foreigners. "Why?" we asked one of the vendors along the shore. "We figure you're up to no good or you wouldn't be here," he enigmatically replied.

The best retreat from Manchioneal is to head inland for 3km (1¾ miles) until you come to **Reach Falls** 👁👁, one of the most beautiful spots in all of Jamaica. For years the Jamaica Tourist Board featured Reach Falls in its brochures advertising their island. But few people ever came here because it is so remote.

All that changed after the release of the film *Cocktail.* Tom Cruise and his film girlfriend indulged in some aquatic hanky-panky beneath these waterfalls, and soon the falls were on every local's and visitor's itinerary, attracting tour buses from as far away as Ocho Rios.

There's usually someone on-site trying to extract money from you, often $4, though it could be less. You're allowed to go into the falls, fed by Driver's River, to cool off. No one objects if you drop your swimsuit here and flaunt your wares, either. The cascades tumble over tiers of limestone into a pool that has the color of a jade ring.

If you want to take a hike for .8km (½ mile) up the river, with its lush foliage, you'll come to **Mandingo Cave.** The cave has a whirlpool and can be explored, but be warned: It has quite deep pools, and isn't completely safe.

RIO GRANDE VALLEY   One of the lushest and most dramatic valleys in the Caribbean lies directly south of Port Antonio. The river itself is fed from drainage from the John Crow Mountains, creating luxuriant growth along with waterfalls, a tropical rainforest, and roaring rivers. One of its beauty spots is Nonsuch Caves and the Athenry Gardens (see below).

Most visitors flock here to go rafting on the Rio Grande (see "Beaches & Outdoor Pursuits," beginning on p. 173). For the serious adventurer, this country invites deeper exploration, especially those willing to hike through it and put up with some hardships along the way.

For some recommended hikes, see "Hiking," also under "Beaches & Outdoor Pursuits," earlier in this chapter.

The Rio Grande Valley is also the home of the Windward Maroons, a formerly hostile, warlike people who fought the British and refused to become docile slaves. They believed in freedom or death. The descendants of these once-fierce people still live in the area, practicing bush medicine and following ancient rites little changed from the days when their ancestors lived in Africa.

It is recommended that you always explore this valley in the company of an experienced guide. If you'd like to discuss a number of tour options, you can consult a specialist. See the box, "Eco-Cultural Tours," on p. 180.

Here are some highlights of the valley:

Athenry Gardens and Cave of Nonsuch   Six kilometers (3¾ miles) south of Port Antonio, it's an easy drive and an easy walk to see the stalagmites, stalactites, fossilized marine life, and evidence of Arawak civilization in Nonsuch, lying at the gateway to the Rio Grande Valley. The cave is 1.5 million years old, and you can explore its underground beauty by following railed stairways and concrete walkways on a 30-minute walk. The place is dramatically lit. Although the United States and Europe have far greater cave experiences, this is as good as it gets in Jamaica. From the Athenry Gardens, there are panoramic views over the island and the sea. The gardens are filled with coconut palms, flowers, and trees, and complete guided tours are given.

Portland. (C) **876/779-7144.** Admission (including guide for gardens and cave) $6 adults, $3 children age 11 and under. Daily 10am–4pm. From Harbour St. in Port Antonio, turn south in front of the Anglican church onto Red Hassel Rd. and proceed approximately 1.6km (1 mile) to Breastworks community (fork in road); take the left fork, cross a narrow bridge, go immediately left after the bridge, and proceed approximately 6km (3¾ miles) to Athenry Estates.

MOORE TOWN   Eighteen kilometers (11 miles) south of Port Antonio, a long-forgotten world unfolds. This is the largest surviving village of the Windward Maroons, who held off British soldiers for years, refusing enslavement.

Fun Fact **Bush Medicine**

Have a headache? Forget aspirin as you travel through the Rio Grande Valley; bush medicine is still commonly practiced here. You can take a "headache-no-more" powder, made from the cowfoot leaf, and chances are your headache will go away—though we're not doctors and can't give medical advice, some of this medicine actually does seem to work. One elderly woman told our party that the cowfoot leaf powder "not only cure the headache, but take care of your piles [hemorrhoids] too." The jury's still out on that one.

The Windward Maroons

Known often as the Blue Mountain Maroons, the Windward Maroons fled into the hills to escape slavery and British soldiers who were hunting them down. In the remote hinterlands of Jamaica, they survived for years before the British found and destroyed their settlements.

The descendants of those Maroons live in the Rio Grande Valley today, although their young men and women have a tendency to drift off to seek a better life in Kingston once they grow up.

It wasn't until 1739 that Quao, the Blue Mountain Maroon leader, bowed to Cudjoe, the Maroon leader in the west of Jamaica, and signed a peace treaty with the British, granting the Maroons some form of independence, which they still enjoy today.

The most legendary of the Maroons was Queen Nanny, although not much is known about her. She was said to possess magical powers. According to tall tales, she kept a cauldron bubbling day and night without benefit of fire, to boil alive any British soldier who tracked her down.

At the Maroon center of Moore Town (see below), the locals are still staunchly independent and still suspicious of foreigners.

Moore Town consists of just one dirt road running along the Wildcane River. It was founded in 1739 when the peace treaty with the British was signed (see box above); a Council of Maroons, with 24 members, is the governing body. The council is led by a "colonel." If he's spotted and pointed out by your guide, you should ask him permission to visit the town, which is usually granted. Of course, you don't have to ask permission, but it's considered polite to do so, in recognition of the colonel's sovereignty.

At the southern end of town lies **Bump Grave,** the burial site of Queen Nanny, the fierce leader of the Windward Maroons (see box above). The grave is inevitably marked with flying flags and often with fresh flowers from the Blue Mountains.

The traditional dances and ceremonies here, imported directly from Africa, have changed little over the years. They include the Kromanti Drum Dance, its name that of an infamous slave market on Africa's Ivory Coast. Sometimes the Maroon dancers continue for hours in a ritual of communication with ancestral spirits, climaxing with the sacrifice of an animal. These ceremonies are not open to the public, however—the Maroons, in general, still seem very distrustful of outsiders, and toting a camera into their inner enclaves isn't recommended.

Directly south of Moore Town is another little hamlet, **Cornwell Barracks,** yet another Maroon settlement.

WEST OF PORT ANTONIO

With far less attractions than the east of Port Antonio, the western coastline is worth a day of your time if you can spare it.

As you leave Port Antonio heading west along Route A4, you come first to:

ST MARGARET'S BAY   At this point the Rio Grande empties into the ocean, 8km (5 miles) from Port Antonio. The river rushes under an iron bridge, built in 1890, on its way to the sea.

HOPE BAY   This fishing town, with its unattractive beach of grayish sand, need not occupy much of your time. There are some jerk stands, tropical punch bars, and several crafts shops hawking their wares, but not much else.

The adventurous should instead head south along a secondary road, where it's easy to spot several places to go swimming on the upper reaches of the fast-flowing and aptly named Swift River. South of Hope Bay, a beautiful drive takes you through lush valleys surrounded by mountains and groves of bananas and cocoa.

Watch for an unusual drink served at roadside stands called a "chocolate tea ball." The bartender grates a cocoa ball into a mixture of hot water and milk, then adds plenty of rum—a kind of local toddy.

There's a hamlet called Swift River where you can cross a tiny bridge over the river and follow it to some intoxicatingly cool, deep pools good for swimming.

At a point just over 3km (approx. 2 miles) from Hope Bay on the A4 highway, you come to:

SOMERSET FALLS   Here, the waters of the Daniels River pour down a deep gorge through a rainforest, with waterfalls and foaming cascades. You can take a short ride in an electric gondola to the hidden falls. A stop on the daily Grand Jamaica Tour from Ocho Rios, this is one of Jamaica's most historic sites; the falls were used by the Spanish before the British captured the island. At the falls, you can change into a swimsuit and enjoy the deep rock pools. You can also buy sandwiches, light meals, soft drinks, beer, and liquor at the snack bar. The guided tour includes the gondola ride and a visit to both a cave and a fresh-water fish farm. On certain days, the site is likely to be overrun with camera-toting tourists. For $4, tours are conducted daily from 9am to 5pm.

En route to Buff Bay you can stop off at a fairly good beach of golden sand at **Orange Bay** for a quick dip.

The A4 highway then continues into:

BUFF BAY   This little seafront hamlet is where farmers from the Blue Mountains bring their produce to market. If you're not really interested in a walk through this market, continue for another 16km (10 miles) or so along the A4 highway to:

ANNOTTO BAY   This town's heyday has come and gone. Back in the 19th century it was a center for banana exports. It owed its success to a Scottish doctor, John Pringle (1848–1923), who came here, purchased 18th-century sugar plantations going to ruin, and converted them into banana plantations, which became a quick cash crop.

The banana business went belly-up, as did the sugar factory—the town's chief employer. Hurricane Gilbert in 1988 almost completely killed Annotto, yet it struggles on. Nothing much remains of the British-built Fort George that guarded the harbor, however.

From Annotto, continue along Route 4 until you come to A3 cutting south. Follow this route along the Wag River Valley until you come to:

CASTLETON BOTANICAL GARDENS ✿   Midway between Kingston and Annotto Bay, this is one of the most remote botanical gardens in the West Indies. The gardens grow lush here because of heavy mountain rains on the western periphery of the Blue Mountains.

On 6 luxuriant hectares (15 acres) you'll see mahogany trees, tree ferns, teak, calabash, cannonball trees, coffee, ebony, cocoa, azaleas—you name it. Nothing is state of the art, however. You are out in the wilderness in "unknown Jamaica" if you visit here.

Begun in 1862 with plants shipped from England's Kew Gardens, these botanical gardens are far more accessible than the once-famous ones at Bath. The gardens are known for introducing many trees to Jamaica, including the Poinciana. The gardens aren't what they used to be, after nature and lack of care have taken their toll. But they still make for a fascinating visit.

The flora is mammoth, including the junglelike ferns. In 1897 some 180 species of palms were planted here, some of whose "children" still survive. On the banks of the river, under a big shady tree, a picnic table awaits you. You might be offered a fruit to taste, perhaps the exotic African velvet apple. This is also a habitat of the streamer tail hummingbird (called a doctor bird), the national bird of Jamaica. We've also seen the tiny bee hummingbird here, one of the smallest birds on the planet.

The gardens (no phone) are open daily from 9am to 5pm; admission is free but tips are appreciated.

ORGANIZED TOURS

Valley Hikes (© 876/993-3881) arranges the best hikes through the Rio Grande Valley (see above). The hikes are conducted in a lush area between the Blue Mountains and the John Crow Mountains, with experienced local guides. Many tours are available, one of the most popular and best being a 1- to 2-hour waterfall tour costing $35 per person. A 6.5km (4-mile) hike into the Blue Mountains, seeking its flora and fauna, also can be arranged.

Attractions Link (© 876/833-4108) is a worthy competitor. It offers one of the best bus tours into the Blue Mountains, with a visit to a coffee plantation and a picnic in Holywell National Park at 1,518m (5,060 ft.) above sea level. Including lunch, the cost is $75 per person.

Another trip takes you to Reach Falls and Long Bay Beach, east along the coast, where you can go for a dip. Go with someone else who loves and enjoys a cooling dip: The cost is $65 per couple.

6 Shopping

Port Antonio is not a shopping bazaar like Mo Bay and Ocho Rios. Most activity centers around **Musgrave Market** ⊛, on West Street, in the center of town. This is one of our favorite markets in all of Jamaica. It evokes a movie set on which the director is about to call, "Lights, camera, action!" The most active market day is Saturday. To see the market at its most frenzied, go any day of the week from 8am to noon.

The sprawling **Fort George Village Shopping Arcade,** which opened in 1997 to immediate denunciations, is not a mirage. What would that architectural critic, Prince Charles, think? To call it an architectural monstrosity would be too kind; this three-floor structure looks like some of the world's major

---

⌒ Fun Fact Better Than What the Snake Gave Eve

If you want to taste one of the most luscious fruits grown in the West Indies, go into Musgrave Market (above) and ask one of the fruit-and-vegetable vendors to sell you a juicy ripe plum called a "June." Some of the old-timers refer to the fruit as "Jew." After you bite into this succulent fruit, which locals will tell you came from the Garden of Eden, you'll become addicted to it.

architectural ideas, thrown into a blender—baroque, English Tudor, French Gothic, with hints of Syria and Iraq thrown in for spice—and spit out. In theory, at least, the arcade was designed to represent various architectures from around the world.

Regardless of what you think of its design, the arcade is fun for a shopping jaunt. You'll find everything from a first-class art gallery to a bookstore, a shoe emporium, and even a hawker of tires (yes, tires). Many of the shops found no one willing to sign a lease. The market can be seen in the center of town across from the courthouse, en route to Titchfield Hill.

On Harbour Street, you'll come to the **City Centre Plaza,** but it's rather dull. As for its crafts, we've seen better. Still, it might come in handy for souvenirs and those things visitors always need: postcards for the ones you left behind, suntan lotion, and that Nora Roberts paperback for the beach.

If you've already perused the shopping possibilities of the native markets, you might scout out the craft and gift stores of the resort hotels.

At the **Gallery Carriacou** 🔥 on the grounds of Hotel Mocking Bird Hill, on Mocking Bird Hill (✆ **876/993-7267**), you can view the sensuous paintings and sculptures of Barbara Walker, who is one of the partners in the hotel. Her works, and those of other noted Jamaican artists, make up the finest collection of art for sale in the area. Walker also conducts classes in sculpture and papermaking.

7 Port Antonio After Dark

Drawing a fashionable crowd, the **Tree Bar,** on the grounds of Goblin Hill Villas at San San (✆ **876/925-8108**), stands high on a hill commanding a panoramic view of 4.8 hectares (12 acres). The aptly named bar is wrapped around huge ficus trees, whose mammoth aerial roots dangle over the drinking area. Giant-leafed pothos climb down the trunks. It's the sort of eco-adventure place that should prove increasingly popular.

Go at your own risk to the infamous **Roof Club,** 11 West St. (no phone). The most crowded and animated nightclub in Port Antonio, it lies one floor above street level in a boxy-looking industrial building in the heart of town. Inside, the venue is earthy, raunchy, crowded, and boozy, with enough secondhand ganja smoke to get virtually anyone high. Recorded (and more rarely, live) reggae and soca music blares at high volumes—so loud, in fact, that first-timers might not immediately understand the blandishments of other clients, male and female, to buy them a drink.

Expect a neo-psychedelic decor of mirrors, UV lighting, and free-form Day-Glo artwork. A visit here is not for the squeamish or the faint-hearted, and it's a good idea to come with a friend and/or ally. Try to stay relatively sober, keep your wits about you, and enjoy the slow-moving gyrations of ordinary folks who—sometimes with the help of a spliff or two—get involved in the beat of the music and groove accordingly. Beers cost around $3 each. It's open nightly from around 6pm, but most of the genuine hanging out and crowding happens after 11pm, especially from Thursday through Sunday.

8 Side Trips: A Coastal Drive to Kingston

If you're going on to Kingston after time spent in Port Antonio, and are driving, we suggest a visit to one of the most forgotten areas of the Caribbean. The neglected and impoverished parish of St. Thomas lies in the far east of Jamaica to the immediate east of the capital at Kingston.

The only tourists in the area are likely to be Kingstonians, who flock to its fishing villages and coastal hamlets on the weekends "to get down low."

To reach Kingston via the coastal route, you can travel the A4 southeast to Manchioneal (see "East of Port Antonio," p. 180). Once here, we suggest you continue past Manchioneal—going through the town of Hectors River—until you come to the turnoff for the old spa at Bath. The road swings west at this point.

If you don't want to visit Bath, stay on the A4 highway as it heads south to the coast and the overgrown village of Port Morant. But Bath will be a journey into nostalgia.

BATH Thirteen kilometers (8 miles) to the north of Port Morant, the largely abandoned spa of Bath is one of the most nostalgic settings in Jamaica, as if it existed in a time capsule. A decay hangs over the town, but there is evidence of its former celebrity, too.

Known for its Bath Fountain and its still functioning Bath Fountain Hotel, the little spa struggles on. On the banks of the Garden River, Bath lies in the heart of an agricultural region devoted to sugarcane and banana trees. According to legend, a miraculous fountain was discovered here in 1609 by an injured runaway slave. Wounded by a British soldier who shot him, the slave was said to have stumbled onto the spring and fell in. The next morning his wounds were cured.

Word of the miraculous healing power of the spring spread across the island, and in time wealthy British plantation owners arrived here to take the cure, complaining of everything from gout to syphilis.

By the mid–18th century a building had grown up around the mineral spring, followed by a hospital. Some landowners erected summer homes here, and the spa flourished for a time. However, disputes among the landowners divided them, and the upheavals became so violent that by the early 19th century, Bath was deserted, all its fine summer homes abandoned. Just 10 residents remained. Its moment of glory had come and gone quickly, and Bath would never recover.

During its brief moment in the sun, however, the **Bath Botanical Gardens** were opened, the oldest such gardens in Jamaica. They lie at the eastern end of the spa town. Hurricanes and neglect have done their damage here, but there is still something left even though the gardens are unkempt. The breadfruit trees growing here are said to be the descendants of those plants brought by Captain Bligh in an attempt to introduce a new foodstuff to starving Jamaica (see box on p. 165). Many plants that now flourish across Jamaica were introduced here, including the jacaranda, jackfruit, bougainvillea, and mango. Guava trees, bamboos, tropical crotons, and royal palms still grace the grounds. If a caretaker is around, a tip would be expected.

Tattered and worn, **Bath Fountain** is still running. Sometimes vacationers from Kingston come to use these baths, which are radioactive (although no more so than those at a European spa). The temperature of the springs can reach 128°F (53°C). You usually give an attendant J$300 (US$5) plus a tip for a 20-minute soak; any longer is dangerous. The spa is open daily from 7am to 11pm, and an attendant on-hand also gives massages and facials.

If you must spend the night, a dubious choice is the **Bath Fountain Hotel & Spa** (© 876/703-4345), a pink colonial-style hotel that dates from the mid–18th century—the spa baths (see above) are located on the ground floor of the hotel. Rooms are modesty itself, if clean and very plainly furnished;

you wouldn't want to linger here for a spa holiday. Rates are $30 in a double without bathroom, $40 to $50 in a double with bathroom. There are 16 units in all, each with a wall fan, but no air-conditioning, phones, or TV. Hot mineral water, direct from the springs, is pumped into your private bathroom for about 30 minutes each morning. On-site is a little restaurant that hardly merits a mention.

After leaving Bath you can follow the Port Morant Road to the coast, linking up again with A4 and heading west to:

MORANT BAY   This small town is the capital of the remote and rarely publicized parish of St. Thomas, "Jamaica's forgotten parish."

The setting for the 1865 Morant Bay Rebellion, lead by national hero Paul Bogle, it had an infamous moment in history before fading into obscurity once again. Bogle, with a contingent of angry men, all freed slaves, led a protest to the local courthouse, violently objecting to what was viewed as an unfair incarceration of another freed slave. The protest led to a riot, in which more than two dozen men were killed and the courthouse torched. The British authorities reacted swiftly; Bogle was hanged in front of the burnt courthouse, while some 600 freed slaves were also rounded up and put to death. Many others were tortured.

In front of the present Morant Bay Courthouse stands a monument to Bogle. Across from the courthouse you can see some cannons that once belonged to the now-gone Morant Bay Fort, which guarded the harbor.

The best beach in the area lies to the immediate east. It's open to the public, and contains picnic tables, changing rooms, and wretched toilets. If you break the drive for a swim here, make sure your car is firmly locked and within your sight or you could get robbed.

WHERE TO STAY

Whispering Bamboo Cove Resort *Finds*   This undiscovered little oasis lies at Morant Bay east of Port Antonio on the scenic south coast of Jamaica. If you stay here, you'll be escaping from the world. It is within easy proximity to the Botanical Gardens and Mineral Springs in Bath, Reach Falls, and the Blue Lagoon in Portland. You can select a room opening onto the sea or a view of the Blue Mountains in the distance. Bedrooms are simply but comfortably decorated, most often with hardwood mahogany. The better accommodations open onto spacious balconies. You're given a choice of king-size beds or twins. A treat every morning is the generous Jamaican breakfast served in the main dining room. If you wish, lunch or dinner, most often seafood, can also be served to you here. A private beach borders the resort, offering good swimming in a reef-protected area.

105 Crystal Dr., Morant Bay, St. Thomas. © **876/982-1788.** Fax 876/734-1049. www.discoverjamaica. com/gleaner/inns/whisper.html. 14 units. Year-round $55–$80 double; $90 suite. Children under 12 stay free in parent's room. DC, MC, V. **Amenities:** Breakfast room; meals on request; bar; laundry service; rooms for those with limited mobility. *In room:* A/C (in some units), TV, fridge.

YALLAHS   Along the A4 highway, beyond Port Morant, is Yallahs—the largest little town you'll pass through before arriving in Kingston. This lackluster little town is sited near two good beaches: Bailey's Beach to the east and Flemarie Beach to the immediate west.

If you like butterflies, you've come to the right place. The town is bordered by a large salt pond, home to thousands of yellow butterflies.

If you'd like to break for lunch between Morant Bay and Yallahs, the seaside hamlet of **White Horses** is the best place. The beach here is rocky, but you'll find shack after shack of little huts frying fish caught fresh that morning by local fishermen.

ELEVEN MILE After leaving Yallahs and before arriving in Kingston, you pass through the hamlet of Eleven Mile. Here a marker keeps alive the memory of Jack Mansong—"Three-Finger Jack," as he was called. A runaway slave, he became a bandit and a menace to the countryside, a sort of Jamaican Robin Hood said (in legend) to have stood 2m (7 ft.) tall.

After he tried to kill a slave trader, Mansong was captured, jailed, and sentenced to death. On the night before his execution, however, he escaped and kidnapped the trader, imprisoning him in a cave somewhere deep within the parish.

The British put a reward of £300 ($495) on Mansong's head, a virtual fortune in those days. Tempted by the money, the Maroon leader named Quashie tracked down Three-Finger Jack and shot him. Three-Finger Jack was gone, but his legend still excites Jamaican schoolchildren today.

Kingston & the Blue Mountains

Kingston, the largest English-speaking city in the Caribbean, is the capital of Jamaica and its cultural, industrial, and financial center. It's home to more than 750,000 people, including those living on the plains between the Blue Mountains and the sea. The buildings here are a mixture of modern, graceful, old, and just plain ramshackle. The bustling port is evocative of one in Africa, with a natural harbor that's among the largest in the world. The University of the West Indies has its campus on the edge of the city.

Few other cities in the Caribbean carry as many negative connotations as Kingston, thanks to widely publicized reports of violent crime, congestion, bad roads, and difficult-to-decipher traffic signs.

But it is also here that you find Jamaica at its most urban and confident, most witty and exciting, most challenging. No other place in Jamaica offers so many bars, clubs, or cultural outlets. And no other place in Jamaica

has such a concentration of creative artists and opinions.

We've carefully screened the recommendations contained within this guidebook, eliminating any that lie within the most dangerous neighborhoods. Keep an open mind about Kingston—it can be a lot of fun if you keep your guard up, but isn't for the faint of heart.

When you've had enough of the city, escape to the **Blue Mountains** at the northern edge of the city. There is no more beautiful mountain chain in the West Indies. The hills are at their most stunning and evocative when a blue mist hovers over them. The Blue Mountains are most famously associated with a celebrated coffee bean, but they're also full of trails, rivers, waterfalls, bird life, fruit, and even marijuana.

Don't expect superhighways: The roads are terrible. Luckily, the best way to appreciate this amazing scenery is by foot—though only if you're very fit.

1 Orientation

ARRIVING BY PLANE International arrivals are at **Norman Manley International Airport,** while domestic flights—say, from Montego Bay—fly into the smaller **Tinson Pen Airport.**

Norman Manley Airport lies 27km (17 miles) southeast of the center of Kingston. Guard your luggage carefully, as there have been many reports of theft—sometimes involving baggage handlers.

GETTING FROM THE AIRPORTS INTO THE CITY If you're driving in a rented car, do not stop even if someone is flagging you down. That person appearing to be in distress might actually be an armed robber.

The best way to get into town is aboard an officially sanctioned **JUTA** taxi (© **876/927-4534**). The cost of a ride is about $22 from Norman Manley airport, $14 from Tinson Pen airport.

VISITOR INFORMATION   The main office of the **Jamaica Tourist Board** is at 64 Knutsford Blvd. (© 876/929-9200), open Monday to Friday 8:30am to 4:30pm. A branch office is found at the Norman Manley International Airport (© 876/924-8023), and is usually open to meet international flights.

CITY LAYOUT

Downtown Kingston is its historic core, rising just north of the waterfront and harbor. The "main street" of Kingston is **King Street,** heading north from the water to the Parade. King Street begins at **Ocean Boulevard** and runs north to **Sir William Grant Park.**

Parallel to Ocean Boulevard run two more arteries—**Port Royal Street** and **Harbour Street,** bordered by North and South Parade.

GETTING AROUND   Driving around Kingston is a journey into hysteria. The public bus transportation is horrendous, and foreigners are often pickpocketed. Thus, the taxi is the most reliable form of transportation. Official taxis with red license plates fall under the **JUTA** umbrella, the government-sanctioned taxi agency (© 876/927-4534). Your hotel will call one (unless one is parked out front). Taxis meet arriving planes, and are also plentiful in the shopping district.

Fares are charged per car, not per passenger. Because most of the taxis aren't metered, tell the driver where you are going and agree on the rate before getting in. Make sure you and the cabbie agree on which dollars you are talking about—American or Jamaican.

FAST FACTS: Kingston

Banks The best and most convenient bank is **Scotiabank,** at Duke and Royal streets (© 876/922-1000), open Monday, Thursday, and Friday 8:15am to 4pm and Tuesday and Wednesday 8:15am to 3pm. Another convenient choice is **Citibank,** 63–67 Knutsford Blvd. (© 876/926-3270), open Monday to Thursday 9am to 2pm and Friday 9am to 3pm.

Bookstores There are no great bookstores in all of Kingston, but if you want some light reading, try **Bookland,** 53 Knutsford Blvd. (© 876/926-4035), open Monday to Friday 9am to 6pm and Saturday 10am to 5pm.

Internet Access In Kingston you can generally use your hotel phone line to get online with a laptop. Otherwise, you can go to **Hilton Kingston Jamaica Cyber,** 77 Knutsford Blvd. (© 876/926-5430), open daily 7am to 10pm, charging $7.50 per hour. Six computers are available.

Mail The main **Kingston Post Office** is at South Camp Road (© 876/922-9430), open Monday to Friday 8am to 5pm. Keeping the same hours is another branch at 115 Hope Rd. (© 876/927-7258). Many savvy visitors skip the inefficient postal systems in Jamaica and deal directly with **FedEx** at 40 Half Way Tree Rd. (© 876/960-9192), open Monday to Friday 8:30am to 5pm and Saturday 9am to noon. Another option for fast service is **DHL,** 60 Knutsford Blvd. (© 876/929-2554), open Monday to Friday 8:30am to 5pm and Saturday 9am to 1pm. Include "Jamaica, W.I." in all island addresses. The island has no zip codes.

Medical Services Most of the medical facilities of Jamaica are found in Kingston. A private facility that's best for visitors is **Medical Associates**

Hospital, 18 Tangerine Place (© **876/929-2991**), with an emergency ambulance service as well. **St. John's Ambulance,** 2E Camp Rd. (© **876/926-7656**), offers ambulance service in Kingston. The **Deluxe Ambulance Service,** 54 Molynes Rd. (© **876/923-7415**), is on 24-hour call.

Pharmacies The most convenient in New Kingston (where virtually everybody stays) is **Moodies Pharmacy** in the New Kingston Shopping Centre at 30 Dominica Dr. (© **876/926-4174**), open Monday to Saturday 8:30am to 7pm. There's another good pharmacy, the **Manor Park Pharmacy,** 186 Constant Spring Rd. (© **876/924-1424**), open daily 8:30am to 10:30pm.

Safety Kingston is the most dangerous city in the Caribbean. Take more precautions here than you would elsewhere. The major problem facing most foreigners is mugging: Robbery is commonplace.

New Kingston is the safest place to be. The downtown area is far more dangerous—in fact, some Jamaican taxi drivers have refused to take us there on business. Two readers from Kansas City wrote that their car broke down in downtown Kingston. They locked it and went to get help—and by the time they returned, their luggage and all their possessions had been stolen. The car was also completely stripped, from the radio down to the tires.

The downtown is not without its attractions, but should be visited carefully, and almost never at night. Some of the most dangerous districts, Six Miles and Riverton City, should be avoided at all times. Finally, if you hear Kingstonians talking about what parts of their city they won't go to, take heed.

Travel Agents The best one is **Great Vacations,** New Kingston Shopping Centre, 30 Dominica Dr. (© **876/929-6290**), open Monday to Friday 7am to 7pm and Saturday 10am to 2pm. It is the local representative of Thomas Cook.

2 Where to Stay

The best accommodation, Strawberry Hill, and the reason many people visit the Kingston area in the first place, is not in the city but within the Blue Mountains. The rates listed below are year-round. All leading hotels in security-conscious Kingston have guards.

EXPENSIVE

The Jamaica Pegasus 𝒜 A favorite with business travelers, the Jamaica Pegasus barely outclasses its nearest rival, the Hilton, in a close race. It's located in the banking area of Kingston, which is also a fine residential area. After a major renovation, the hotel is now better than ever and is the site of many conventions and social events. The hotel combines British style with Jamaican warmth, arranging watersports and sightseeing. Each of the well-furnished bedrooms is of moderate size and contains bathrooms with combination tubs and showers and balconies opening onto mountain, sea, or cityscapes. The decorating, in dark tones, often brown, makes you yearn for the lighter pastel look of most Caribbean hotel bedrooms. Several floors of luxuriously appointed suites form the Knutsford Club, which offers special executive services.

Kingston Area

ATTRACTIONS ●
Bob Marley Museum **20**
Devon House **15**
Gordon House **31**
Headquarters House **31**
Hope Botanical Gardens & Zoo **25**
Institute of Jamaica **32**
Jamaica House **17**
The Jewish Synagogue **30**
King's House **18**
Mico College **3**
National Arena **28**
National Gallery **33**
National Heroes Park **2**
National Library **32**
National Museum **32**
National Stadium **27**
St. Andrews Scots Kirk **14**
St. William Grant Park **1**
University of the West Indies **26**

ACCOMMODATIONS ■
Altamont Court Hotel **11**
The Courtleigh **8**
Hotel Four Seasons **10**
Indies Hotel **13**
The Jamaica Pegasus **5**
Kingston Hilton Hotel **7**
Strawberry Hill **24**
Terra Nova Hotel **16**

DINING ◆
Akbar **29**
Alexander's **8**
Boon Hill Oasis **19**
Chelsea Jerk Centre **9**
The Columbus Restaurant **5**
Heather's **4**
The Hot Pot **6**
Indies Pub and Grill **12**
Jade Garden **21**
Norma's on the Terrace **15**
Palm Court **7**
Redbones the Blues Café **22**
The Restaurant at the
  Hotel Four Seasons **10**
Strawberry Hill **24**
Thai Gardens **29**
The Upper Crust (Guilt Trip) **23**

LIGUANEA

Hope Rd.

Hopefield Ave.

Donhead Ave.

Wellington Dr.

Old Hope Rd.

Hope Botanical Gardens

Braemar Ave.

MONA HEIGHTS

Mona Rd.

BEVERLEY HILLS

University of the West Indies

Mona Reservoir

Seymour Ave.

L O N G   M O U N T A I N

Gibraltar Camp Rd.

Hermitage Rd.

Tom Redcam Ave.

Arthur Wint Dr.

National Arena

National Stadium

Mountain View Rd.

Long Mountain Rd.

VINEYARD TOWN

DOWNTOWN KINGSTON

Jubilee Market

Heywood St.

Ward Theatre

Sulton St.

Darling St.

Salt La.

Young St.

N. Parade

St. William Grant Park

Coke Church

E. Queen St.

W. Queen St.

S. Parade

Camp Rd.

Marcus Garvey Ave.

Beckford St.

Luke La.

Temple La.

Church La.

Mark La.

Duke St.

Johns La.

East St.

Laws St.

Georges La.

Barry St.

Parish Church

Barry St.

Sabina Park

Railway Station

Marcus Garvey Dr.

Tower St.

Pechon St.

West St.

Mathews La.

Princess

Orange St.

Peters La.

King St.

Post Office

Institute of Jamaica/ National Library

Hanover St.

Rum La.

Rosemary La.

Maiden La.

Melbourne Park

Water La.

Water La.

Harbour St.

Port Royal St.

Port Royal St.

Crafts Market

National Gallery

Nethersole Dr.

Victoria Ave.

Lower Elleston Rd.

Pier No. 1

Kingston Mall

Kingston Harbour

Ocean Blvd.

Conference Center

Cruise Ship Piers

Tower St.

BOURNEMOUTH GARDENS

SPRINGFIELD

Kingston Harbour

To Airport

0   0.5 mi

0   0.5 km

N

195

A Calypso Lament

Oh, I'm sad to say, farewell today,
I'll be back to Kingston town bay,
My heart is down, my thoughts are spinning around,
Because the girl I love is here in Kingston town.

—Jamaica farewell

The 4pm tea service is a bit of a social event among some residents. The premier restaurant is The Talk of the Town. The Brasserie is the hotel's informal restaurant that opens onto the swimming pool, where a splashing fountain cools the air. It adjoins a circular bar near the pool, at which occasional barbecues are prepared.

81 Knutsford Blvd., Kingston 5. ℂ **876/926-3690.** Fax 876/929-5855. www.jamaicapegasus.com. 300 units. Year-round $140–$220 double; $250 junior suite; $300 royal suite. AE, DC, MC, V. **Amenities:** 3 restaurants; 2 bars; outdoor pool; 2 tennis courts; gym; business center; 24-hr. room service; laundry service/dry cleaning; nonsmoking rooms; rooms for those with limited mobility. *In room:* A/C, TV, dataport, minibar, hair dryer, safe.

Kingston Hilton Hotel ℛ   The Hilton is an imposing mass of pink stucco pierced with oversize sheets of tinted glass. It is an almost peas-in-the-pod version of the Pegasus (see above): If you were to wake up in the middle of the night at either hotel, it would take a minute to discern which hotel you're sleeping in. The main core of the hotel is a 16-floor tower, containing 220 guest rooms. There are also some poolside units. Completely refurbished bedrooms feature up-to-date appointments, and midsize tiled bathrooms come with combination tubs and showers. For a view of the city and the Blue Mountains, go for a tower room; otherwise, book one of the plush accommodations around the "swimming hole."

Fine cuisine is offered at the Terrace Café, providing a la carte Jamaican and international food. The Rendezvous Bar and Palm Court Restaurant offer more elegant dining and fine wines.

77 Knutsford Blvd. (P.O. Box 112), Kingston 5. ℂ **876/926-5430.** Fax 876/929-7439. www.hilton.com. 303 units. $160–$180 double; $225–$265 suite. Children under 12 stay free in parent's room. AE, DC, MC, V. In the center of New Kingston. **Amenities:** 3 restaurants; bar; nightclub; pool; 2 tennis courts; gym; sauna; business center; limited room service; laundry service/dry cleaning; nonsmoking rooms; rooms for those with limited mobility. *In room:* A/C, TV, hair dryer, safe.

MODERATE

The Courtleigh ℛℛ   We often prefer the Courtleigh to the Hilton or Pegasus because it's a warmer, friendlier place, and has a more personal atmosphere. The prices are affordable as well. The six-floor hotel is the filling in the "sandwich" between the Hilton and the Pegasus, standing at the core of the business district. The well-furnished bedrooms live up to the standards of its two neighbors. We like the mahogany furnishings, evocative of the West Indies, and always request one of the units with a four-poster bed. The suites are particularly notable here, including such extras as big desks, two TVs, a dining table, a kitchenette, and a walk-in closet. Each comes with a midsize, tiled private bathroom with a tub/shower combination. The rectangular pool is often a rendezvous for business clients, and Alexander's (p. 199), the hotel restaurant, is worth a visit even if you're not a guest.

85 Knutsford Blvd., Kingston 5. ℂ **876/929-9000.** Fax 876/926-7744. www.courtleigh.com. 127 units. Year-round $125–$145 double; $200–$420 suite. AE, MC, V. Rates include continental breakfast. **Amenities:**

Restaurant; 2 bars; outdoor pool; gym; limited room service; laundry service/dry cleaning; coin-operated laundry; nonsmoking rooms; rooms for those with limited mobility. *In room:* A/C, TV, dataport, kitchenette (in some units), coffeemaker, hair dryer, iron/board, safe.

Terra Nova Hotel 𝄞 *Finds*   This house is on the western edge of New Kingston, near West Kings House Road. Built in 1924 for a young bride, it was converted into a hotel in 1959. At one time it was the birthplace of the well-known hotelier and Island Records mogul Chris Blackwell. Set in 1 hectare (2½ acres) of gardens with a backdrop of greenery and mountains, it's now one of the best small Jamaican hotels, although the rooms are rather basic and not at all suited for those who want a resort ambience. Most of the bedrooms are in a new wing. All units have neatly kept bathrooms with shower units. The Spanish-style El Dorado Room, with a marble floor and wide windows, serves local and international food.

17 Waterloo Rd., Kingston 10. © 876/926-2211. Fax 876/929-4933. 35 units. Year-round $120–$135 double. AE, MC, V. **Amenities:** Restaurant; coffee shop; bar; outdoor pool; exercise room; limited room service; nonsmoking rooms; rooms for those with limited mobility. *In room:* A/C, TV, dataport, minibar (in some units), hair dryer, iron/board, safe, beverage maker.

INEXPENSIVE

Altamont Court Hotel   This hotel offers a less-expensive alternative to larger competitors such as the Hilton and Meridien. It might remind you of a motel, thanks to exterior hallways and furniture like you might expect within a well-kept roadside inn in Florida. The staff here is less alert and well informed than you might hope for, but rooms are comfortable and there's a sense of well-ordered decency and thrift. Each of the rooms has either two double beds or one king-size bed, and all units contain a small private bathroom with tub/shower combination. The hotel's most alluring feature is its large swimming pool.

1–5 Altamont Terrace, New Kingston, Kingston. © 876/929-4497. Fax 876/929-2118. www.cariboutpost. com/altamont. 55 units. Year-round $95 double; $120 suite. AE, DC, MC, V. **Amenities:** Restaurant; bar; outdoor pool; Jacuzzi; limited room service; babysitting; laundry service/dry cleaning; nonsmoking rooms; rooms for those with limited mobility. *In room:* A/C, TV, dataport, coffeemaker, hair dryer, safe.

Hotel Four Seasons 𝄞 *Value*   Small-scale, well maintained, and respectable, this is one of the most appealing hotels in Kingston, thanks to a sophisticated design that combines a once-private home with a rambling series of modern wings, courtyards, gardens, and fountains. Rooms are cozy and comfortable, but the spiritual core of the place is the Elizabethan-inspired bar and restaurant (see "Where to Dine," below). Owned by two German sisters, this place enjoys something approaching cult status in Germany. Guest rooms evoke the furnishings of a well-maintained, upscale motel, and are usually decorated in wicker or plantation-style furniture. Most rooms have French doors opening onto private balconies or patios, overlooking either the garden or the pool. Each unit comes with a small private bathroom. Oh, and don't be confused by the name: It has absolutely no association with the big Four Seasons hotel chain.

18 Ruthven Rd. (near Halfway Tree Rd.), Kingston 10. © 876/929-7655. Fax 876/929-5964. 76 units. Year-round $76–$90 double. AE, DC, MC, V. **Amenities:** Restaurant; 2 bars; outdoor pool; gym; limited room service; laundry service/dry cleaning; nonsmoking rooms. *In room:* A/C, TV, dataport, fridge (in some units), iron/board, safe.

Indies Hotel   On a small side street in the heart of New Kingston, opening onto a flower garden, this half-timbered building with double gables features a small reception area decorated with potted plants. The adequate and reasonably comfortable bedrooms, restaurant, and bar are grouped around a patio. Each unit is furnished with a small bathroom with a shower. There's a friendly atmosphere and good-quality budget meals. The fish and chips are good, and they also bake pizzas, serve steak with all the trimmings, and sometimes cook lobster thermidor.

5 Holborn Rd., Kingston 10. ℂ **876/926-2952.** Fax 876/926-2879. http://indieshotel.com. 15 units. Year-round $57–$64 double; $77 triple. AE, MC, V. Near the intersection of Trafalgar Rd. **Amenities:** Restaurant; bar; limited room service; laundry service; dry cleaning. *In room:* A/C, TV, iron/board, safe.

3 Where to Dine

Kingston has a good range of places to eat, whether you're seeking stately meals in plantation houses, hotel buffets, or fast-food shops.

EXPENSIVE

The Columbus Restaurant ⋇ ITALIAN   The finest Italian cuisine in Jamaica is served at this hotel restaurant, a favorite with business travelers. The elegantly furnished restaurant offers good service and quality ingredients. Chefs tempt you with penne pasta with chicken, vegetables, and a white-wine sauce, and tender and flavorful sautéed beef loin with a spicy sauce. Another specialty that's a worthy dish is breast of chicken sautéed with herbs and spices, glacé, and ham and cheese. Members of Kingston's fashionable set often come here for a festive occasion, which is made all the more so if they order the Amaretto cheesecake.

The Jamaica Pegasus Hotel, 81 Knutsford Blvd. ℂ **876/926-3690.** Reservations required. Main courses J$650–J$1,050 (US$11–US$17). AE, MC, V. Daily 6–10pm. In New Kingston, off Oxford Rd.

Norma's on the Terrace ⋇⋇ JAMAICAN/INTERNATIONAL   This is the creation of Jamaica's most famous businesswoman, Norma Shirley, purveyor of food to stylish audiences as far away as Miami. It's housed beneath the wide porticos of the gallery surrounding Kingston's most famous monument, Devon House. Ms. Shirley has taken the old, woefully dusty gardens and transformed them into something you'd find on a manicured English estate. Menus change with the season, but usually reflect Ms. Shirley's penchant for creative adaptations of her native Jamaican cuisine. Stellar examples include Jamaican chowder with crabmeat, shrimp, conch, and lobster; grilled whole red snapper encrusted with herbs and served with a thyme-and-caper sauce; and grilled smoked pork loin in a teriyaki/ginger sauce, served with caramelized apples.

In Devon House, 26 Hope Rd. ℂ **876/968-5488.** Reservations recommended. Main courses $30–$80. AE, DISC, MC, V. Mon–Sat 10am–10pm.

Palm Court ⋇ INTERNATIONAL   One of the best hotel restaurants in New Kingston is this one, on the Kingston Hilton Hotel's mezzanine floor. In a formal, intimate setting, you can dine on a refined cuisine beneath paintings by prominent Kingston artists. The chef's specialty is "Port Royal," a plate of snapper, salmon, jumbo shrimp, and lobster sautéed just right in a white-wine sauce before being served with a saffron sauce. Snapper often appears as a separate main course in either a butter sauce or a sauce sprinkled with slivered almonds. Imported meats, such as a rack of lamb or steaks from the United States, are also served here.

In the Kingston Hilton Hotel, 77 Knutsford Blvd. ℂ **876/926-5430.** Reservations recommended. Main courses J$638–J$1,913 (US$11–US$32). AE, DC, MC, V. Mon–Fri 11:30am–11pm; Sat 6:30–11pm.

Redbones the Blues Café ⋇⋇ *Finds* JAMAICAN   The name alone lured us to this elegant place, which is the only restaurant in Kingston with cuisine as good as Norma's on the Terrace. All aglow in yellow and peach hues, Redbones is in a former Spanish colonial house. You're greeted with pictures of jazz greats on the wall, everybody from Billie Holiday to Louis Armstrong. A cozy bar, its ceiling studded with records, is installed in someone's former bedroom. Owners Evan and Betsy Williams give standard Jamaican dishes a new twist. Ask for "bammy," a cassava dish crowned with sautéed shrimp, or a platter of stuffed crab backs, a delectable selection on a tri-color salad. A spinach callaloo with cream cheese is encased in a divine strudel. Seafood pasta is laden with shrimp, lobster, and salmon in a creamy coconut sauce. The best item on the menu is spicy lamb chops in a guava glaze. Live jazz or something is always going on.

21 Braemar Ave. ℃ 876/978-6091. Reservations required. Main courses J$750–J$1,500 (US$16–US$33). AE, MC, V. Mon–Fri 1–11pm; Mon–Sat 6:30–10pm.

MODERATE

Alexander's JAMAICAN/INTERNATIONAL   This is the showplace dining room of one of Kingston's top hotels, and as such, it often attracts business meetings, government delegations, and international travelers who appreciate its good service and culinary savvy. Within a setting inspired by the Jamaican sugar plantations of the 1800s, with muted tropical colors and a view that overlooks the hotel's swimming pool, you can order such starters as smoked marlin or Caribbean crab backs, then move to sirloin steaks; medallions of beef with grilled tomatoes; or filets of pork with brandy, mustard, and cream sauce. After your dinner, consider a drink in the hotel's bar/lounge, Mingles.

In the Courtleigh Hotel, 85 Knutsford Blvd. ℃ 876/968-6339. Reservations recommended. Lunch main courses J$385–J$620 (US$6.40–US$10); dinner main courses J$460–J$1,200 (US$7.65–US$20). AE, MC, V. Daily noon–3pm and 6–10:30pm.

Jade Garden ⚔ CHINESE   The best Chinese restaurant in Kingston, Jade Garden serves well-prepared food in an elegant, formal setting. Chow mein and chop suey dishes are here, but ignore them to concentrate on the more challenging offerings. Beef with oyster sauce is delectable, as is the pork with ham choy. For unusual flavors, try Pi Paw bean curd with chopped Chinese sausage, shrimp, black mushrooms, and water chestnuts. Also excellent is Subgum War Bar, a combination of meats sautéed with Chinese vegetables and served on a sizzling-hot platter. Deep-fried prawns stuffed with prawn mousse and served in a garlic-butter sauce are excellent as well.

106 Hope Rd., in Sovereign Centre. ℃ 876/978-3476. Reservations recommended. Main courses J$600–J$3,700 (US$9.95–US$61). AE, MC, V. Daily noon–10pm. North of the town center, west of National Stadium.

The Restaurant at the Hotel Four Seasons (Value GERMAN/JAMAICAN/ INTERNATIONAL   This hotel restaurant (see "Where to Stay," above) offers one of the most consistently reliable luncheon buffets in Jamaica. It's supervised by a pair of hardworking East German–born sisters whose unfailing standards

A Call to Action

You're gonna lively up yourself and don't be no drag,
You're gonna lively up yourself because reggae is another bag.
You lively up yourself and don't say no,
You're gonna lively up yourself 'cause I said so.

—Bob Marley, "Lively Up Yourself"

have made it a staple on the capital's restaurant scene. Menu items are freshly made and succulent, with everything from Jamaican pepper-pot soup to goulash, jerk chicken or pork, schnitzels and sauerbraten, and roulades of pork or veal.

18 Ruthven Rd. ⓒ **876/929-7655.** Reservations recommended. Set-price buffet lunch J$750 ($12); lunch and dinner main courses J$480–J$1,600 (US$7.95–US$27). AE, MC, V. Daily noon–3pm and 6–10pm. Near Half Way Tree Rd.

INEXPENSIVE

Akbar ⓡ (Finds) NORTHERN INDIAN   This is the best Indian restaurant in Kingston. It consists of four dining rooms, each outfitted in earth tones with touches of mint green. Don't overlook the possibility of a meal in the Moghul-style garden, within earshot of a splashing fountain. Menu items are rich with the seasonings of the East, with seafood, vegetarian, lamb, beef, and chicken dishes, as well as a selection of exotic breads. Specific and stellar examples include Chicken Moghlai cooked in cream sauce with nuts and egg butter; mutton in a spicy sauce; and beef Akbar—one of the most justifiably popular house specialties, skewered and flavored with herbs.

11 Holborn Rd. ⓒ **876/926-3480.** Reservations recommended. Main courses J$595–J$1,200 (US$9.90–US$20). AE, MC, V. Daily noon–4pm and 6–11pm.

Boon Hall Oasis ⓡ (Finds) JAMAICAN   Down a series of pathways and steps carved into a remote hillside outside the city, this place serves Sunday brunch only beneath galvanized metal roofs in a series of dining pavilions, all within a garden. Well-prepared menu items include filet of red snapper with brown sauce or a vinegar-based *escoveitch* (marinated fish); three different preparations of shrimp (including one flambéed in honey-flavored rum sauce); and three different preparations of chicken. Art exhibitions and poetry readings sometimes take place here.

Stony Hill, St. Andrew. ⓒ **876/942-3064.** Reservations recommended. Sun brunch J$800 (US$13). No credit cards. Sun 11am–3pm (last order). Take a taxi from Kingston, or turn on Seaview Rd. (opposite Petcom Gas Station—Stony Hill Sq.). Take the 3rd left onto Airy Castle Rd., then look out for the signs pointing to Boon Hall Oasis.

Chelsea Jerk Centre ⓡ (Value) JAMAICAN   This is the city's most popular purveyor of jerked meats. Set in a low-slung angular concrete building, it offers food to take out or eat in a comfortably battered dining area. Although no formal appetizers are served, you might order a side portion of what the scrawled-on chalkboard refers to as "festival" (fried cornmeal dumplings). The best bargain is Chelsea's Special: rice, peas, and vegetables, plus jerked pork or chicken. Remember to order the various components of your meal at different kiosks in the huge hall; oxtail, stewed fish, and beer are also available.

7 Chelsea Ave. ⓒ **876/926-6322.** Reservations not accepted. Jerk half-chicken J$300 (US$5); .5kg (1 lb.) jerk pork J$500 (US$8.30). MC, V. Mon–Thurs 10am–10pm; Fri–Sat 10am–1am; Sun noon–10pm. Near the New Kingston Shopping Centre.

Heather's JAMAICAN/SYRIAN   Loud, convivial, and sometimes boisterous, this establishment combines a popular singles bar with a somewhat more sedate restaurant. There's a massive mango tree thrusting its way skyward through a hole in the roof. Tasty menu items include grilled fish kabobs, sweet-and-sour fish, Cajun-style blackened fish, Heather's crab cakes, and Heather's special shrimp.

9 Haining Rd., New Kingston. ⓒ **876/926-2826.** Reservations recommended. Main courses J$600–J$1,300 (US$9.95–US$22). AE, DC, MC, V. Mon–Sat noon–4pm and 5pm–midnight.

The Hot Pot JAMAICAN   Set within a short walk of both the Pegasus and Hilton hotels, this is a simple local restaurant with an animated crowd of regulars and straightforward, unfussy cuisine. Within a green-and-white interior, near a view of a modest garden, you can drink Red Stripe beer or rum drinks. The chefs are so good you'll want to hire them to cook for you, especially after you've tasted their garlic chicken, their ackee with salt fish, and their sweet-and-sour fish. The place stays open throughout the day, serving breakfast, lunch, and dinner without interruption. The food is what you'd be served in a typical Jamaican home—nothing fancy, but satisfying and filling—and the prices are astonishingly low.

2 Altamont Terrace. ℂ **876/929-3906.** Main courses J$200–J$300 (US$3.30–US$5). AE, MC, V. Daily 7am–8pm.

Indies Pub and Grill JAMAICAN   Indies, an informal neighborhood restaurant across the street from the Indies Hotel, was designed around a garden terrace. You can also dine in the inner rooms, haphazardly but pleasantly decorated with caribou horns, tortoise shells, half-timbered walls, an aquarium sometimes stocked with baby sharks, and even a Canadian moose head. There's a full sandwich menu at lunchtime. In the evening you can enjoy grilled lobster, fish and chips, barbecued chicken or pork, chicken Kiev, or roast beef. It's a little better than standard pub grub. Pizza is a specialty. A bottle of Red Stripe, the Jamaican national beer, is the beverage of choice here.

8 Holborn Rd. (in New Kingston, off Hope Rd.). ℂ **876/920-5913.** Main courses J$300–J$1,255 (US$5–US$21); pizzas J$470–J$700 (US$7.80–US$12). AE, DISC, MC, V. Mon–Fri 11am–11pm; Sat 11am–1am.

Thai Gardens ⭐ *Finds* THAI   The chefs here come directly from Bangkok, and the flavors are authentic, achieved with imported ingredients. The place is filled with artifacts sent over from Thailand. We recommend it as a change of pace from too much Jamaican cuisine. Specialties include fried noodles with Thai shrimp wrapped in an eggshell, and a good steamed snapper served with chili-laced lemon sauce.

10 Holborn Rd. ℂ **876/906-3237.** Reservations recommended. Main courses J$695–J$1,595 (US$12–US$27). Daily noon–3pm and 6–11pm.

The Upper Crust (Guilt Trip) JAMAICAN/INTERNATIONAL   About 2km (1¼ mile) north of New Kingston, this open-air restaurant originated as a small-scale pastry shop that eventually expanded into a neighborhood institution. In addition to the pastries, which are made on the premises and displayed behind a glass-fronted case, menu items include crab-back salads, curried snapper, jerk chicken lasagna, grilled lamb chops with ratatouille, and an especially good grilled filet of snapper with dried-pepper shrimp in a curry sauce.

20 Barbican Rd., Liguanea. ℂ **876/977-5130.** Lunch main courses J$225–J$1,150 (US$3.75–US$19); dinner main courses J$650–J$1,250 (US$11–US$21). MC, V. Daily noon–3pm and 6–10:45pm.

4 Beaches & Other Outdoor Pursuits

BEACHES   You don't really come to Kingston for beaches, but there are some here. To the southwest of the sprawling city are the black-sanded **Hellshire Beach, Gunboat Beach,** and **Fort Clarence.** These beaches are very popular with the locals on weekends, and all have changing rooms, heavy security, and numerous food stands. The reggae concerts at Fort Clarence are legendary on the island.

Just past Fort Clarence, the fisherman's beach at **Naggo Head** is an even hipper destination, or so Kingston beach buffs claim. After a swim in the refreshing waters, opt for one of the food stands selling "fry fish" and bammy (cassava bread).

The closest beach to the city is **Lime Cay** 𝕮, a little island on the outskirts of Kingston Harbour, reached by a short boat ride from Morgan's Harbour at Port Royal. This is one of the best spots we've found in Kingston for a picnic. Weekend cookouts are commonplace, and the swimming is good in unpolluted waters. To get a boat ride to the beach, check with the reception desk at Morgan's Harbour Hotel (p. 208).

CRICKET This is the national pastime of Jamaica. The best cricket games are played in Kingston at **Sabina Park** on South Camp Road. For information about matches, contact the tourist office (p. 192).

GOLF   Caymanas Golf Course, Spanish Town (© **876/922-3386**), lies 10km (6¼ miles) west of Kingston and is open to the general public. This is an 18-hole, par-70, 6,268m (20,565 ft.) course. Golfers praise this course for its elevated tees and its uphill shots. It costs $36 for a round of golf here on weekdays, $44 on weekends, plus $22 for the cart rental, and another $15 for the club rental.

A course closer to town, **Constant Spring** at Constant Spring (© **876/924-1610**), dates from the 1920s. A mentor of Robert Trent Jones Sr., Stanley Thompson, laid out this par-70, 5,666m (18,588-ft.), 18-hole golf course at the foot of the Blue Mountains. A round costs $35 on weekdays, $41 on weekends, and club rentals are available. There's also a small pro shop, restaurant, and bar.

SCUBA DIVING Some of the best-known dive sites in the area include **Windward Edge,** with a depth range of 21 to 27m (70–90 ft.). Reached after a 30-minute boat ride, this site lies 11km (6¾ miles) outside of Kingston Cays. There are great photo opportunities here.

Suitable for all levels of divers, the *Cayman Trader* wreck has a depth range of 9 to 15m (30–50 ft.). A Norwegian cargo ship, the *Trader* caught on fire in 1977. It was later towed to this site and sunk. The wreck is scattered over a large area. Another stunning wreck that an outfitter can take you to is the *Texas,* a U.S. Navy ship that went down in 1944. Advanced divers seek out this site, at a depth of 30m (100 ft.). It is particularly known to divers for its stunning black coral.

TENNIS The best tennis courts are at two hotels in New Kingston. **The Jamaica Pegasus,** 81 Knutsford Blvd. (© **876/926-3690**), offers two hardsurface courts, each lit for night play. Courts are open to the public, costing $15 per hour during the day or night. Two hard-surface courts are also at the **Kingston Hilton Hotel,** 77 Knutsford Blvd. (© **876/926-5430**), charging $10 during the day or $13 at night. These courts are also open to nonguests.

5 Seeing the Sights

Even if you're staying at Ocho Rios or Port Antonio, you may want to visit Kingston, Port Royal, and Spanish Town to sightsee.

IN TOWN

The most important art collection in Jamaica is housed at the **National Gallery** 𝕮𝕮, Roy West Building, Kingston Mall (© **876/922-1561**). This gallery is a showcase for the nation's most talented artists. On the ground floor you're greeted with the controversial bronze statue of the late Bob Marley, the reggae great. A work by Christopher Gonzalez, the statue originally was meant to stand in Celebrity Park, but aroused opposition among Marley fans, who felt it portrayed their hero in an unflattering light. You be the art critic here.

The Jamaican School of Art is best highlighted by Edna Manley, a well-known sculptor who was married to Norman Manley, the former prime minister. She was also the mother of another prime minister, Michael Manley. Locals refer to her as the "Barbara Bush of Jamaica." She died in 1876 at the age of 86. One of her most celebrated sculptures is *Ghetto Mother,* located in the main lobby.

Also attracting a lot of attention locally are the mahogany figurines and other works by Mallica Reynolds, better known as Kapo. His religious themes have made him a household word in Kingston. Some art critics have called his sculpture "the work of a modern genius."

Entrance is $1.50 for adults and $1 for children, and hours are Tuesday to Thursday 10am to 4:30pm, Friday 10am to 4pm, and Saturday 10am to 3pm. You'll better understand what you're seeing if you hire a guide, which costs J$800 (US$13) for a tour.

One of the major attractions, **Devon House** *✿*, 26 Hope Rd. (℗ **876/929-6602**), was built in 1881 by George Stiebel, a Jamaican who made his fortune mining in Latin America—becoming one of the first black millionaires in the Caribbean. A striking classical building, the house has been restored to its original beauty by the Jamaican National Trust. The grounds contain crafts shops, boutiques, two restaurants, shops that sell the best ice cream in Jamaica (in exotic fruit flavors), and a bakery and pastry shop with Jamaican puddings and desserts. Admission to the main house is $6; hours are Monday to Saturday from 9:30am to 5pm. Admission to shops and restaurants is free.

At the **Hope Botanical Gardens & Zoo** *✿✿*, Hope Road (℗ **876/927-1257**), you can visit a Jamaican Shangri-La, a 20-hectare (50-acre) plot of beauty and the largest botanical garden in the West Indies. It is adjacent to the Mona campus of the University of the West Indies. The "Hope" in the name comes from Richard Hope, a British Army commander who lived here in the mid–17th century. After the grime of downtown Kingston, it's a lovely place for a tranquil stroll; attractions include a cactus garden, sago palms, an orchid house, various greenhouses, an ornamental pond, and a "forest garden," with an aviary for the "birdie" in you. There's also a little zoo on-site.

The admission-free gardens are open daily from 6am (we like to go very early in the morning) to 6pm. The zoo is open daily from 10:30am to 5pm, charging an admission of J$20 (US35¢) for adults or J$10 (US15¢) for children 4 to 12. There's also a cafe offering cold drinks and light snacks.

Between Old Hope and Mona roads, on the eastern outskirts, a short distance from the Botanical Gardens, is the **University of the West Indies** *✿* (℗ **876/927-1660**), built in 1948 on the Mona Sugar Estate. Ruins of old mills, store-houses, and aqueducts are juxtaposed with modern buildings on what must be the most beautifully situated campus in the world. The chapel, an old sugar-factory building, was transported stone by stone from Trelawny and rebuilt. The remains of the original sugar factory here are well preserved and give a good idea of how sugar was made in slave days. Organized tours are available. You are also allowed to stroll around the campus Monday to Saturday from 9am to 5pm. You must see the Public Relations office first.

The **National Library of Jamaica** at the Institute of Jamaica, 12 East St. (© 876/967-2494), a storehouse of the history, culture, and traditions of Jamaica and the Caribbean, is the finest working library for West Indian studies in the world. It has the most comprehensive, up-to-date, and balanced collection of materials on the region, including books, newspapers, photographs, maps, and prints. It's open Monday to Thursday from 9am to 5pm, Friday from 9am to 4pm.

Bob Marley Museum, 56 Hope Rd. (© 876/927-9152), is the most-visited sight in Kingston, but if you're not a Marley fan, it may not mean much to you. The clapboard house with its garden and high surrounding wall was the famous reggae singer's home and recording studio until his death on May 11, 1981, in a Miami hospital. You can tour the house and view assorted Marley memorabilia, and you may even catch a glimpse of his children, who often visit the grounds. Hours are Monday to Saturday from 9:30am to 4pm. Admission is J$500 (US$8.30) for adults, J$400 (US$6.65) for children 13 to 18, and J$200 (US$3.30) for children 4 to 12. It's reached by bus no. 70 or 75 from Halfway Tree, but take a cab to save yourself the hassle of dealing with Kingston public transportation.

ORGANIZED TOURS

The best tours, the most personal, and the most comfortable are operated by **Island Car Rentals** (© 876/926-8861), which will make arrangements to pick you up at your hotel. A minimum of two people is required for a tour. One of the most requested tours is the **Bob Marley Tour,** taking in the Kingston sights associated with the reggae star. The cost is $48 per person. The rental agency also conducts a cultural and historic tour of the highlights of Kingston for $58 per person. If you'd like a tour of what's left of Port Royal, the charge is $54 per person.

6 Shopping

To protect you from the sun, covered arcades lead off King Street, but everywhere are many people going about their business. There are some beggars and the inevitable peddlers who sidle up and offer "hot stuff, *mon*"—which frequently means highly polished brass lightly dipped in gold and fraudulently offered at high prices as real gold.

There is no more typical or evocative city market in all of Jamaica than **Jubilee Market,** overflowing onto Orange Street on the west side of the Parade (Sir William Grant Park), under a roof and in the heart of Kingston. This market was named to honor Queen Victoria's Jubilee. A haven for pickpockets, it is nonetheless filled with all the flamboyant color and drama of Jamaica. Virtually "everything is for sale," one vendor told us, "from Jamaican babies to the most exotic fruits to possessions of Bob Marley." All the Marley mementos are fake, of course.

Kingston Crafts Market, at the west end of Harbour Street (reached via Straw Ave., Drummer's Lane, or Cheapside), is a large, covered area of small stalls, selling all kinds of island crafts: wooden plates and bowls; pepper pots made from mahoe (the national wood of the island); straw hats, mats, and baskets; batik shirts; banners for wall decoration, inscribed with the Jamaican coat of arms; and wood masks with elaborately carved faces. You should bargain a bit and vendors will take something off the price, but not very much.

One of the most modern shopping centers in Jamaica, the **New Kingston Shopping Centre,** 30 Dominica Dr., is known for the range of merchandise rather than for a particular merchant. It's sleek and contemporary, centered around a Maya-style pyramid. This is where to head if you're looking for the highest quality goods, including local items that might not readily be available in your hometown.

The **Shops at Devon House,** 26 Hope Rd. (© 876/929-6602), ring the borders of a 200-year-old courtyard once used by slaves and servants. It's one of the most beautiful and historic mansions on Jamaica. Four of the shops are operated by Things Jamaican (see below), a nationwide emporium dedicated to the enhancement of the country's handicrafts. Shops include the Cookery, offering island-made sauces and spices, and the Pottery, selling crockery and stoneware.

Things Jamaican, 26 Hope Rd. (© 876/926-1961), is affiliated with the government and set up to encourage the development of Jamaican Arts and Crafts. There is an array of products, including rums, liqueurs, jerk seasonings, and jellies such as orange pepper. Look for Busha Brown's fine Jamaica sauces, especially their spicy chutneys such as banana, and their spicy "love apple" sauce (it's actually tomato). Many items are carved from wood—not only sculptures, but salad bowls and trays as well. You'll also find hand-woven baskets and women's handbags made of bark (in Jamaica, these are known, unflatteringly, as "old lady bags").

Wassi Art Gallery and Collectibles, 26 Hope Rd. (© 876/906-5016), is one of the most interesting shops in Devon House. All the merchandise is made by Wassi Art, a labor-intensive, low-tech Jamaican method. Look for functional, durable kitchenware prized by Jamaican homeowners for its eco-sensitive, earthy appeal. Anything you buy can be shipped via FedEx. Items cost from $5 to $2,000.

Frame Centre Gallery, 10 Tangerine Place (© 876/926-4644), is one of the most important art galleries in Jamaica. Its founder and guiding force, Guy McIntosh, is widely respected as a patron of the Jamaican arts. There are three viewing areas and more than 300 works.

The **Mutual Life Gallery,** Mutual Life Centre, 2 Oxford Rd. (© 876/929-4302), is one of Jamaica's most prominent art galleries. This center offers an insight into the changing face of Jamaican art. The gallery's exhibitions are organized by Gilou Bauer, who encourages unknowns as well as showcasing established artists with flair. Exhibitions change once a month, but there are usually long-term exhibits as well. The gallery is a not-for-profit institution.

Tuff Gong Recording Studios, 220 Marcus Garvey Dr. (© 876/923-9383), can be both a shopping expedition and an attraction. South of Denham Town, this is the headquarters of the late Bob Marley's family business. You might even run into his son, Ziggy Marley, coming out of a recording session; his Melody Makers have their headquarters here. Sometimes you can persuade someone to let you in for a tour. If not, settle for a visit to their gift shop, filled with reggae CDs and tapes, records, T-shirts, handicrafts, and other mementos.

Loaded with a wider variety of medications than any other pharmacy in Kingston, the **Dick Kinkead Pharmacy, Ltd.,** 72–76 Harbour St. (© 876/922-6525), has been compared to a civic institution. Local residents sometimes head here for advice before seeing a doctor. All substances are made on the premises, including a medicinal toothpaste made from tropical roots and herbs called Chew Dent; it's made from chew stick *(gouania lupuliodes),* in the tradition of West Africans.

7 Kingston After Dark

Kingston offers a variety of nighttime entertainment. Most events are listed in the daily press, along with a host of other attractions, including colorful carnivals and festivals that are held island-wide throughout the year. In nearly all the after-dark establishments of Kingston, foreign visitors are only about 3% of those in attendance. Most Kingston places, except for the bars in first-class hotels, are patronized mainly by locals.

Caution: The city is very unsafe at night. Take taxis everywhere.

THE PERFORMING ARTS

Kingston is a leading cultural center of the West Indies. Notable theaters include **Ward Theatre** on North Parade Road (℃ **876/922-0453**), and the **Little Theatre** on Tom Redcam Drive near the National Stadium (℃ **876/926-6129**). Both stage local and imported plays and musicals, light opera, revues, Jamaican dance and choral groups, and pop concerts. Ticket prices vary. From downtown Kingston (Parade and Cross roads), buses 90A and 90B run here.

THE CLUB & BAR SCENE

Within the relatively sedate premises of one of Kingston's best-established hotels, **Mingles** (in the Courtleigh Hotel, 85 Knutsford Blvd.; ℃ **876/929-9000**) is a rich-looking—and richly popular—bar and disco. Sheathed with full-grained mahogany panels, with uniformed bartenders whose look might remind you of Jamaica during the era of Noël Coward, it's a clubby-looking but often rocking site known for a revolving combination of reggae, pop, soca (a danceable form of reggae), and Latino meringue. Folk here tend to flirt, talk, and gossip on Friday night, and dance, dance, dance on Saturday night. The bar here is open Monday through Friday 5pm to midnight and Saturday 5pm to 3am. There is no cover charge except on Saturday, when it's J$200 (US$3.30).

One of the hottest new venues after dark is **Asylum,** 69 Knutsford Blvd. (℃ **876/929-4386**), where the program changes nightly. Some nights are devoted only to reggae music, other nights to various contests, sometimes to the old hits of the 1970s and 1980s. A crowd, mainly of locals in their twenties or thirties, flocks here to enjoy the music, the dance, the entertainment, and even karaoke. It's very tropical and very happening, Tuesday to Sunday from 10pm to 4am, charging a cover ranging from J$200 to J$300 (US$3.30–US$5).

The open-air **Carlos Café,** 22 Belmont Rd. (℃ **876/926-4186**), is all the rage with its flamingo-colored tones and Caribbean decor. There's a whimsical feel here, attracting a crowd of men and women in their twenties and thirties. You can also dine here—on Monday, crab is featured on the menu. On Friday it's a fish fry and karaoke. On any night something is happening, perhaps a show by Cuban salsa dancers. There's no cover, with a Red Stripe beer costing J$100 (US$1.65). Hours are Monday to Friday 5pm to 2am, Saturday 3pm to 2am.

8 Side Trips to Spanish Town & Port Royal

Historic Spanish Town and Port Royal can both be reached easily from Kingston and are well worth a visit.

SPANISH TOWN ☞

Spanish Town, some 16km (10 miles) west of Kingston, was the capital of Jamaica from 1662 to 1872 and was founded by the Spanish.

Spanish Town

0.25 mi
0.25 km

FERNDENE PEN

FELSTEAD PEN

Brunswick St.

Cross Pen Rd.

Kent St.

Waterloo Ln.

Grove Ave.

Monk St.

Smith's Ln.

RAVENSWORTH

Rio Cobre

Hanover St.

Young St.

William St.

Trinity Church

Martin St.

Nugent St.

King St.

THOMPSON PEN

Thompson Park

Cumberland St.

Old Market St.

Old French St.

Manchester St.

Adelaide St.

Beckford St.

Constitution St.

Red Church St.

White Church St.

Monk St.

Barrett St.

Bishop's Ln.

Burial Ground

Wellington St.

Chambers Ln.

Oxford Rd.

Ellis St.

Melbourne Ln.

Bullocks Ln.

Wellington St.

Barrack St.

King St.

Prison Oval (Cricket Ground)

Railway Ln.

Bourkes Rd.

Condrans Ave.

Morrison St.

Bourkes Rd.

Salt Pond Rd.

Port Henderson Rd.

A 2

Railway Station

ELLERSLIE

Salt Island Rd.

Spanish Town Bypass

Parochial Rd.

CORLETTS

March Pen Rd.

A 1

† Church
✉ Post Office

JAMAICA
Spanish Town ○ ✈
            Kingston

The English cathedral, surprisingly retaining its Spanish name, **San Jago de la Vega** ✈, was built in 1666 and rebuilt in 1712. Because the cathedral was built on the foundation and remains of the old Spanish church, it is half English, half Spanish, and shows two definite styles—one Romanesque, the other Gothic. It's one of the most interesting historical buildings in Jamaica. The black-and-white marble stones of the aisles are interspersed with ancient tombstones, and the walls are heavy with marble memorials that almost form a chronicle of Jamaica's history, dating back as far as 1662.

After visiting the cathedral, walk 3 blocks north along White Church Street to Constitution Street and the **Town Square.** Graceful royal palms surround this little square. On the west side is **Old King's House,** residence of Jamaica's British governors until 1872, when the capital was transferred to Kingston. It hosted many celebrated guests—among them Lord Nelson, Admiral Rodney, Captain Bligh of HMS *Bounty* fame, and King William IV. Gutted by fire in 1925, its facade has been restored.

Jamaica People's Museum of Craft & Technology, Old King's House, Constitution Square (© 876/922-0620), is open Monday to Friday from 9am to 4pm. Admission is J$100 (US$1.65) for adults, J$40 (US65¢) for children. The garden contains examples of old farm machinery, an old water-mill wheel, a hand-turned sugar mill, a fire engine, and more. An outbuilding houses a museum of crafts and technology, together with a number of smaller agricultural implements. In the small archaeological museum are old prints, models, and maps of the town's grid layout from the 1700s.

The streets around the old Town Square contain many fine Georgian town houses intermixed with tin-roofed shacks. Nearby is the **market,** so busy in the morning that you'll find it difficult, almost dangerous, to drive through. It does provide, however, a bustling scene of Jamaican life.

On the north side of the square is the **Rodney Memorial,** the most dramatic building on the square, commissioned by a grateful assembly to commemorate the 1782 victory of British admiral Baron George Rodney over a French fleet, saving the island from invasion.

The remaining side of the square, the east, contains the most attractive building, the **House of Assembly,** with a shady brick colonnade running the length of the ground floor, above which is a wooden-pillared balcony. This was the stormy center of the bitter debates of Jamaica's governing body. Now the ground floor is the parish library.

PORT ROYAL ✦

From West Beach Dock, Kingston, a ferry ride of 20 to 30 minutes will take you to Port Royal, subject of a hundred adventure novels that conjure up visions of swashbuckling pirates, led by Henry Morgan, swilling grog in harbor taverns. This was once one of the largest trading centers of the New World, with a reputation for being the "wickedest city on earth." Blackbeard stopped here regularly on his Caribbean trips. But it all came to an end on June 7, 1692, when a third of the town disappeared underwater during a devastating earthquake.

Today Port Royal, derelict and rundown, is a small fishing village. Some 2,000 residents—and a lot of ghosts—live here. A seafaring tradition continues, and the town is famous for both fresh seafood and quaint architecture. Once there were six forts here with a total of 145 guns; some of the guns remain today, but only Fort Charles still stands.

SEEING THE SIGHTS

As you drive along the Palisades, you arrive first at **St. Peter's Church.** It's usually closed, but you may persuade the caretaker, who lives opposite, to open it if you want to see the silver plate, said to be spoils captured by Henry Morgan from the cathedral in Panama. In the ill-kept graveyard is the tomb of Lewis Galdy, a Frenchman swallowed up and subsequently regurgitated by the 1692 earthquake.

Fort Charles (© 876/967-8438), the only one remaining of Port Royal's six forts, has withstood attack, earthquake, fire, and hurricane. Built in 1656 and later strengthened by Henry Morgan himself for his own purposes, the fort displays scale models of ships from past eras. It's open daily from 9am to 5pm; admission is J$100 (US$1.65) for adults, J$50 (US85¢) for children.

WHERE TO STAY

Morgan's Harbour Hotel & Beach Club   On the premises of this yachtie favorite is a 200-year-old redbrick building once used to melt pitch for His

Majesty's navy, a swimming area defined by docks and buoys, and a series of wings whose eaves are accented with hints of gingerbread. Set on 9 hectares (22 acres) of flat and rocky seashore, the resort contains the largest marina in Kingston, plus a breezy waterfront restaurant and a popular bar (where ghost stories about the old Port Royal seem especially lurid as the liquor flows on Fri night). Longtime residents claim that the ghosts of soldiers killed by a long-ago earthquake are especially visible on hot and very calm days, when British formations seem to march out of the sea.

The well-furnished bedrooms are laid out in an 18th-century Chippendale-Jamaican style. Medium-size bathrooms are tidily maintained, each with a shower in the bathroom. The Buccaneer Scuba Club organizes dives to some of the 170-odd wrecks lying close to shore (see "Cays & Mangroves" box in this section).

Port Royal, Kingston 1. ℭ 800/44-UTELL in the U.S., or 876/967-8030. Fax 876/967-8073. www.hotelbook. com. 50 units. Year-round $160 double; $184 suite. AE, DISC, MC, V. Take the public ferryboat that departs every 2 hr. from near Victoria Pier on Ocean Blvd.; many visitors arrive by car or taxi. **Amenities:** Restaurant; bar; 2 outdoor pools; limited room service; laundry service; nonsmoking rooms; rooms for those with limited mobility. *In room:* A/C, TV, dataport, minibar, hair dryer, iron/board, safe, beverage maker.

WHERE TO DINE
Sir Henry Morgan's Restaurant INTERNATIONAL/JAMAICAN   The bar and restaurant offer guests panoramic views of Kingston Bay and the Blue

The Wickedest City on Earth

As the notorious pirate Henry Morgan made his way through the streets in the late 17th century, the prostitutes hustled customers, the rum flowed, and buccaneers were growing rich and sassy. The town was Port Royal, at the entrance to the world's seventh largest natural harbor. It was filled with drinking parlors, gambling dens, billiard rooms, brothels, and joints offering entertainment such as cock fights, target shoots, and bear baiting. Buccaneers not only got drunk—they fought duels and pursued "foul vices" after long months at sea. All this earned Port Royal the title of "The Wickedest City on Earth."

All this came to a thundering end on the hot morning of June 7, 1692. Without warning, a severe earthquake sunk most of the town, killing some 2,000 people. The skies turned copper over this once-vibrant pirate city. To this day it is known as the famous "Sunken City" of Port Royal.

Today Port Royal is a small fishing village at the end of the Palisades strip. Some 2,000 residents—and a lot of ghosts—live here. Its seafaring traditions continue, and the town is famous for both its fresh seafood and quaint architecture of old days. Once there were six forts here with a total of 145 guns; some of the guns remain today, but only Fort Charles still stands.

Actually, the 1692 earthquake was only one of nine that descended upon Port Royal. And that's not all: 16 of the worst hurricanes to hit the Caribbean and three devastating fires ravaged the town. It's a wonder anything is still standing today.

Norman Manley International Airport shares the same thin peninsula with Port Royal, but otherwise, all is quiet in the town today. It's easy to conjure up images not only of Morgan but of another buccaneer, Roche Brasiliano, who liked to roast Spaniards alive. To celebrate, he'd break out a keg of wine on the streets of Port Royal; whether they wanted to or not, he forced passersby to have a drink with him at gunpoint.

What happened to Henry Morgan after piracy was outlawed here in 1681? He was knighted in England and sent back to arrest his old hell-raising mateys.

Mountains. Except for the elegant lobster or seafood salad, lunch is a relatively simple affair. You can order various sandwiches and desserts, along with a daily luncheon special—a traditional Jamaican dish. The catch of the day is steamed or fried. You get more of a choice at dinner; your best bet is either the fresh Jamaican lobster, which can be prepared in a number of ways—everything from thermidor to grilled with garlic butter. The traditional Jamaican pepper steak, with hot and sweet peppers, is excellent, as is the selection of homemade ice creams to finish your meal.

In Morgan's Harbour Hotel & Beach Club, Port Royal. ℂ 876/967-8075. Main courses J$400–J$1,500 (US$6.65–US$25). AE, MC, V. Daily 7am–10:30pm.

Cays & Mangroves

Although close to the urban sprawl of Kingston, you can return to nature by taking a boat tour leaving from **Morgans Harbour Hotel Marina** in Port Royal. The nearby mangroves are a natural habitat for Jamaica's bird life, especially pelicans and frigates, which use the area as a breeding ground. Entirely surrounded by water, it is also an important haven for other water-loving birds and wildlife.

Close to Morgan's Harbour and the Kingston airport, the mangroves have survived hurricanes and earthquakes. Jamaican officials created a waterway, allowing small boats to enter. During this trip you can see oyster beds, fish-breeding grounds, and a wide assortment of mangroves, along with boat wrecks. If you're lucky, you may even spot a pod of dolphins.

After the mangroves you're taken on a tour of some of Jamaica's most famous cays, including Lime Cay and Maiden Cay. Close to them is Gun Cay, so aptly named for the remains of cannons and large guns. Many a "bloody war" among notorious pirates was fought here.

Regrettably, there aren't any organized tours anymore, but the staff at Morgans Harbour Hotel & Beach Club can generally hook you up with a local boatman.

9 Exploring the Blue Mountains ★★★

Jamaica has some of the most varied and unusual topography in the Caribbean, including a mountain range laced with rough rivers, streams, and waterfalls. The 77,699-hectare (192,000-acre) **Blue Mountain–John Crow Mountain National Park** is maintained by the Jamaican government. The mountainsides are covered with coffee fields, producing a blended brew that's among the leading exports of Jamaica. But for the nature enthusiast, the mountains reveal an astonishingly complex series of ecosystems that change radically as you climb from sea level to the fog-shrouded peaks.

The Blue Mountains, Jamaica's highest peaks, form a virtual botanical Garden of Eden. Steep and exhausting, and invariably hot and muggy, the trails and hikes are nonetheless not as hazardous—or frightening—as, say, the Alpine peaks of Switzerland and Austria. The foothills of the Blue Mountains begin on the outskirts of Kingston.

To the east of the Blue Mountains, moving toward the sea, are the **John Crow Mountains** ★★, another vast area of scenic beauty, although the trails here are more overgrown than the more trodden paths of the Blue Mountains. The most dedicated hikers have, in 3 days, gone from the Grand Ridge of the Blue Mountains to Port Antonio on the coast. But they had to take a machete to hack their way and blaze a trail.

GETTING AROUND If you're not a hiker, the easiest way to tour the Blue Mountains is by car, although you can't visit the most remote or difficult-to-reach beauty spots that way. You can, however, get quite a dramatic preview via the road. The main route into the Blue Mountains is the B1, which begins on the western outskirts of Kingston. Follow signposts to the hamlet of The Cooperage, the gateway to the mountains.

Though improved, this narrow road is still difficult; landslides do occur during the rainy season. Many drivers prefer a four-wheel-drive vehicle. Also watch for oncoming trucks—the macho drivers won't give an inch. And remember that the last gas station (called "petrol" here) is on the outskirts of Papine, in northeast Kingston. You'll need to fill up there.

Public transport in the mountains is hopelessly unreliable.

ORGANIZED TOURS

Cycling is a good option when touring the Blue Mountains. **Blue Mountain Bike Tours** (✆ 876/974-7075 in Kingston) offers all-downhill bike tours through the Blue Mountains—you peddle only about a half-dozen times on this several-mile trip. Visitors are driven to the highest navigable point, then cruise most of the way down. Lunch, snacks, and lots of information about coffee, local foliage, and history are provided. The cost is about $89 per person.

You can opt to head out alone into the Jamaican wilderness, but considering the dangers of such an undertaking, and a possible mugging you might encounter en route, it isn't advisable. A better bet involves engaging one of Kingston's best-known specialists in eco-sensitive tours, **Sunventure Tours,** 30 Balmoral Ave., Kingston 10 (✆ 876/960-6685).

The staff offers lots of tour choices. The Blue Mountain Sunrise Tour involves a camp-style overnight in one of the most remote and inaccessible areas of Jamaica. For a fee of $110 per person, participants are retrieved at their Kingston hotels, driven to an isolated ranger station accessible only via four-wheel-drive vehicle, and guided on a two-stage hike that begins at 2pm. A simple mountaineer's supper is served at 6pm around a campfire; late, at 3am, climbers hike by moonlight and flashlight to a mountaintop aerie selected for its view of the sunrise. You stay aloft until around noon, then head back down to Kingston. There's also a shorter 4-hour trek offered, costing $25 to $30 per person.

HIKING

Most visitors come to the Blue Mountains for hiking. Because of rains, the worst months for hiking are May, June, September, and October. There are more than 30 known trails in the Blue Mountains, but only two-thirds are likely to be passable at any given time.

At no point do we recommend that you hike alone in the Blue Mountains. Weather conditions can change rapidly, and hiking maps are, in general, very poor; it is easy to lose your direction. Security is also a major concern for the unaccompanied hiker on the Kingston side of the mountain. A guide will not only clear an overgrown path for you, but may keep you out of harm's way. (To retain the services of a guide, ask at the tourist office.)

The most popular and scenic hike begins at **Whitfield Hall** ★★ (✆ 876/927-0986), a high-altitude hostel and coffee estate about 10km (6¼ miles) north of the hamlet of Mavis Bank (see below). Reaching the summit of Blue Mountain Peak requires between 4 and 5 hours from here each way. You can also take much shorter hikes if you don't want to see everything. En route, hikers pass through acres of coffee plantations and forest, with temperatures cooler than one might expect and high humidity encouraging lush vegetation. Along the way, watch for bird life such as hummingbirds, many species of warblers, rufous-throated solitaires, yellow-bellied sapsuckers, and Greater Antillean pewees.

Dress in layers and bring bottled water. If you opt for a 2am departure to watch the sunrise from atop the peak, carry a flashlight as well. Sneakers are usually adequate, though many climbers bring hiking boots. Be aware that even during the "dry" season (Dec–Mar), rainfall is common; during the "rainy" season (the rest of the year), rain, fog, and mist are all frequent.

EXPLORING THE BLUE MOUNTAINS

IRISH TOWN   From the hamlet at Papine on the northern tier of Kingston, you can continue on the winding road north to Irish Town, going via **The Cooperage** 3km (1¾ miles) to the north, a tiny hamlet taking its name from the Irish coopers who lived and worked here in the 19th century. They made wooden barrels to hold the Blue Mountain coffee that was transported to Kingston, where it was later shipped to the ports of New York, Boston, and London.

From here, you can continue north to Irish Town, also named for the coopers who lived here, or swing east toward Mavis Bank.

For this route, however, we'll continue north to Irish Town, home to Chris Blackwell's magnificent **Strawberry Hill.** This is the premier place for food and lodging in the Blue Mountains; Bob Marley was brought to this site to recover in 1976 after an attempt on his life by a gunman. In later years other visitors have included Mick Jagger and the Rolling Stones, and U2.

Nearby is a hamlet called **Redlight** that was once one of the most notorious villages in the West Indies, filled with whorehouses catering to the soldiers stationed in barracks at Newcastle.

After Redlight, the winding B1 takes you to:

NEWCASTLE   This village has one of the best views of Kingston from any vantage point in the Blue Mountains.

Towering over Newcastle is the 1,542m (5,060-ft.) **Catherine's Peak** 🏔🏔, named for Lady Catherine Long, the first woman to scale it—in 1760! It's the highest point in the parish of St. Andrew. A little road off the B1 just north of here takes you to the summit, often shrouded in mist.

WHERE TO STAY

Strawberry Hill 🏔🏔 *(Finds*   Music-industry-mogul-turned-hotelier-extraordinaire Chris Blackwell worked here to re-create an idealized version of Jamaica that he remembered from his childhood. The setting is a former coffee plantation in the Blue Mountains, on precariously sloping rainforest terrain 930m (3,100 ft.) above the sea. Views from its terraces overlook the capital's twinkling lights. Eco-sensitive and fully contained, it has its own power and water-purification system, a small-scale spa, and elaborate botanical gardens. One former guest described this exclusive resort as a "home away from home for five-star Robinson Crusoes." Maps and/or guides are provided for tours of nearby coffee plantations, hiking and mountain biking through the Blue Mountains, and tours by night or by day of the urban attractions of nearby Kingston.

Accommodations are lavishly nostalgic, draped in bougainvillea and Victorian-inspired gingerbread, and outfitted with gracious mahogany furniture like that of a 19th-century Jamaican great house. Local craftspeople fashioned the cottages and furnished them with canopied four-poster beds and louvered mahogany windows. The elegant bathrooms, each designed in an artfully old-fashioned motif, come with shower/tub combinations. The food served in the hotel's glamorous restaurant is good enough to draw foodies from throughout eastern Jamaica.

Irish Town, Blue Mountains. ℂ 800/OUTPOST in the U.S., or 876/944-8400. Fax 876/944-8408. www.strawberryhillresort.com. 12 units. Winter $335 double, $385 junior suite, $675 1-bedroom villa, $775 2-bedroom villa; off season $275 double, $355 junior suite, $575 1-bedroom villa, $675 2-bedroom villa. AE, DISC, MC, V. Guests are personally escorted to the hotel in a customized van or via a 7-min. helicopter ride. It's a 50-min. drive from the Kingston airport or 30 min. via mountain roads from the center of the city. **Amenities:** Restaurant; bar; pool; spa with hydrotherapy facilities and massage; sauna; bike rental; limited room service; babysitting; laundry service; nonsmoking rooms; rooms for those with limited mobility. *In room:* TV (on request), kitchenette, minibar, coffeemaker, hair dryer, iron/board, safe.

WHERE TO DINE

Strawberry Hill 🦀🦀🦀 MODERN JAMAICAN   The most charming restaurant in the Jamaican capital involves a taxi ride up a meandering Blue Mountain road to the hotel of the same name (see "Where to Stay," above). Dining is within an interconnected series of catwalks, verandas, and gazebo-style pavilions that were meticulously re-created along 19th-century patterns. Each manages to seem simultaneously upscale yet unpretentious. The delectable menu items change with the season, but are likely to include such Jamaican dishes as grilled shrimp with fresh cilantro, fresh grilled fish with jerk mango and sweet-pepper salsa, or rotis stuffed with curried goat and fresh herbs. It's called "new Jamaican cuisine," and it is. Sunday brunches here are enduringly popular, thanks partly to a lavish array of more than 40 dishes, each arranged in a separate gazebo-like pavilion like a temple to fine gastronomy.

Irish Town, Blue Mountains. ℂ 876/944-8400. Reservations recommended. Lunch main courses $20–$25; set-price Sun brunch $45; 3-course set-price dinner $49. AE, MC, V. Daily noon–3pm and 6–10pm; Sun brunch 11:30am–3pm. From Kingston, drive 11km (6¾ miles) north, following Old Hope Rd. to the northern suburb of Papin. When you get to Papin, turn left onto Gordon Town Rd., cross a bridge, and turn left onto Newcastle Rd., where you go left. From there, follow the steep uphill road for another 11km (6¾ miles) along dramatic and winding mountain roads, following the signs to Strawberry Hill.

Three kilometers (1¾ miles) past Newcastle the road continues to:

HARDWAR GAP   This hamlet at the crest of Grand Ridge is a famous stopover point for those doing the tour of the Blue Mountains. Visitors drop by the restaurant described below for a welcome bite.

WHERE TO DINE

The Gap Cafe & Gift Shoppe 🦀 *Finds* JAMAICAN   The location is 1,260m (4,200 ft.) above sea level in the mountains overlooking Newcastle, with vistas of Kingston and the surrounding hills; Ian Fleming wrote parts of *Dr. No* in the house. The Blue Mountain coffee alone is worth the visit, and it's individually ground and brewed as you sit back taking in the scenery. You can also partake of curry or sautéed shrimp, and our favorite dish, pasta with jerk chicken. The chef is quite proud—and rightly so—of his crab backs, as well.

Main Rd., Hardwar Gap in the Blue Mountains, John Crow Mountain National Park. ℂ 876/997-3032. Main courses J$550–J$700 (US$9.15–US$12). AE, MC, V. Mon–Fri 10am–5pm; Sat–Sun 10am–6pm.

Just 183m (600 ft.) above the Gap Cafe you arrive at the:

HOLYWELL NATIONAL RECREATION PARK 🦀🦀   This 121-hectare (300-acre) park, part of the greater Blue Mountain park, is the end of the line for most visitors who want to have a glimpse of the Blue Mountains but don't want to venture forth on any arduous hikes into unknown terrain. If you brought the makings of a picnic lunch, it is also an ideal spot.

The enveloping forest covers **Oatley Mountain,** a sanctuary for wildlife, mainly tropical birds, which are seen in abundance here. For those who'd like short hikes to sample the mountain scenery without having to do much difficult hiking, this is the place to go. The main trails, and also the most scenic, have been outlined on bulletin boards in the area. The ranger station here ((C) **876/997-8044**) will provide more details, and perhaps a ranger may even accompany visitors on short hikes.

Our favorite is the 3km (1¾-mile) **Oatley Mountain Trail,** which goes into an almost junglelike interior. There are also lookout points where you can enjoy panoramic views. Another trail, the **Cascade Water Trail,** is only 2km (1¼ miles) or so and takes you to a beauty spot where you can plunge into the chilly waters to cool off.

The **Jamaican Conservation and Development Trust,** 29 Dunbarton Ave. in Kingston ((C) **876/960-2848**), rents a trio of cabins in the area for those who book in advance. Six people can fit comfortably into the bigger cabin, four overnighters in a smaller cabin. The cost of a cabin for the night ranges from J$2,500 to J$3,500 (US$42–US$58). Tent sites are J$200 (US$3.30).

The cost of entering Holywell Park is $5 for adults and $2 for children ages 4 to 12. The park is open Tuesday to Sunday 10am to 5pm.

SECTION   After leaving Holywell, and after another 5km (3 miles), you arrive at the hamlet of **Section,** the heart of the coffee-growing district. The road to the left takes you all the way to the coast and Buff Bay if you're going on to Port Antonio (see chapter 7), a distance of 29km (18 miles).

Other than the gorgeous scenery, the attraction at Section is the **Old Tavern Coffee Estate** ⨏ ((C) **876/999-7070**), which can be toured for free. You should, however, call in advance. A British fellow, Alex Twyman, started this estate when he arrived some 3 decades ago; his coffee is the finest in the Blue Mountains. Caffeine aficionados pay $35 for a .5kg (1-lb.) bag, and it's worth it—ask Martha Stewart. Visitors are allowed to tour the 52 hillside hectares (130 acres) and learn more about coffee than they ever wanted to know. There's even a waterfall where you can take a dip.

Back at the Cooperage (see above), if you had driven north instead of east, you would arrive in the hamlet of:

GORDON TOWN   En route east to Gordon Town, you pass through the riverside village of **Industry.** In spite of its unattractive name, this is a good spot for river swimming. Gordon Town is the only settlement in the Blue Mountains that could be called an actual town. It takes its name from the Gordon High-landers of Scotland, who were once billeted here.

There's little to see, but hikers come to take the winding **Gordon Town Trail** ⨏ above Industry and Redlight until they reach the Sugar Loaf, at 2,100m (7,000 ft.). This 21km (13-mile) trail (called a "track" here) is one of the most scenic and rewarding in the Blue Mountains.

Continuing east from Gordon Town, the road takes you to the hamlet of **Guava Ridge,** from which you can head north for 5km (3 miles) to explore **Content Gap,** another center of coffee production. Many hikes are possible from here, including one that goes back to Gordon Town. There are only a few meager hostels and campsites for sleeping, however.

CLYDESDALE   This hamlet is filled with evocative memories, as it was once the site of a well-known coffee plantation that went belly-up in 1937. Today the Jamaica Forestry Department runs it. This is the only commercial tree planta-tion in the Blue Mountains, with picnic spots and a waterhole where you can jump in buck-naked if you wish.

Towering over Clydesdale is the spectacular **Cinchona Botanical Gardens** ⨏⨏ at 1,500m (5,000 ft.). You can only go with a car about 2km

(1¼ miles) from the gardens. You'll have to follow a signpost the rest of the way. The admission-free gardens keep no set hours, but it's best to show up any day of the week between 9am and 4pm. This 4-hectare (10-acre) site was once planted with cinchona trees for producing quinine used to treat malaria in the old days. The slopes are also covered with wild coffee plants. If a gardener is free, he might take you on a **Panoramic Walk** where he'll point out some of the rarer botanical species. A tip would be nice.

Hikers strike out from here for a 10km (6¼-mile) bit of trailblazing down to Mavis Bank (see below).

Back south at Guava Ridge, the road continues directly east and into:

MAVIS BANK In the Yallahs River Valley, you come upon this mountain hamlet, the last true settlement on the trail to the Blue Mountain Peak. If you're driving into the Blue Mountains, this is the end of the road for vehicles; there's a parking lot close to the police station. Some Land Rovers go beyond, but we find the roads disastrous.

There's one attraction in town worth a visit: the **Jablum Coffee Company** ⚜ (© **876/977-8015**), open for tours by appointment, costing $8. Hours are Monday to Friday 9 to 11am and 1 to 3pm. This century-old enterprise, one of the most famous coffee factories in Jamaica, produces from 75,000 bushels of Blue Mountain coffee a year. At the start of a tour you're offered a cup of the delectable brew, then led through the entire process of production "from the coffee bean to the steaming cup." This is very much a working factory, not something gussied up for visitors. Afterward, you may want to purchase some bags of coffee—it's far cheaper here than in Kingston.

WHERE TO STAY
Forres Park This is part of a working coffee farm with very basic accommodations in either the main house or in a cabin on the grounds. Floors are concrete, and furnishings are made of pine. Tiers of coffee bushes cascade down the hillside. The staff will also arrange hikes to the Blue Mountain Peak and the Cinchona Botanical Gardens. It's quite simple here, but each unit comes with a tub/shower combination.

Mavis Bank. © **876/927-8275.** Fax 876/978-6942. mlyn@cwjamaica.com. 14 units. Year-round $60 double. No credit cards. *In room:* No phone.

ABBEY GREEN Although some hikers begin at Mavis Bank, others prefer to go all the way to Abbey Green 8km (5 miles) to the northeast in order to begin their long trek to the Blue Mountain Peak. This is an almost magical part of Jamaica, some 1,350m (4,500 ft.) above sea level.

WHERE TO STAY
Whitfield Hall ⚜ One of the most isolated places in Jamaica, this hostel is located more than halfway up Blue Mountain. The main draw is the opportunity to see the mountains from a hill climber's point of view. Whitfield Hall is a coffee plantation dating from 1776, the last inhabited house from that colonial period. It provides basic accommodation for 30 guests in rooms containing two or more beds. Blankets and linens are provided, but personal items such as towels and soap are not. There is no official restaurant, but for a small fee all three meals can be provided. All water comes from a spring, and lighting is by kerosene pressure lamps called *tilleys*. A wood fire warms the hostel and its guests—it gets cold in the mountains at night. Most guests request a pickup in Kingston by the hostel's Land Rover, which costs $40 each way for up to six passengers; you can

also drive yourself via Old Hope Road to the Kingston suburb of Papine, then to Gordon Town, turning right over the bridge near the police station and continuing into the hills another 16km (10 miles) to Mavis Bank.

c/o John Allgrove, 8 Armon Jones Crescent, Kingston 6. ℂ **876/927-0986.** 8 units (none with bathroom), 1 2-bedroom cottage. Year-round J$850 (US$14) per person; J$3,800 (US$63) cottage for up to 4 occupants. No credit cards.

BLUE MOUNTAIN PEAK ✿✿✿   The ultimate goal of the adventurous hiker, this mountain, at 2,220m (7,400 ft.), is the tallest in Jamaica. The first time we visited, our Jamaican guide told us, "This is where God takes you when he wants a compliment about how wonderful he created the world." You wander into a lush Eden filled with orchids, bromeliads, ginger lilies, cheesebury, and lichens.

Many hikers prefer to come here very early to watch the sun rise. The climb from Abbey Green is about 13km (8 miles), and you'll need a guide to take this trail to the top. See above for details of a good tour company.

The first part of the trail, called Jacob's Ladder, is the most difficult. After walking for about 2 hours, a distance of more than 6km (3¾ miles), you come to the **Portland Gap Ranger Station.** It's wise to stop in here and alert the ranger on duty that you're taking this trail. Leave your name and that of a contact person. At the station you'll find potable water, foul pit toilets, and a trio of basic cabins where you can crash on the floor for $10 a night. Bookings can be made through the **Jamaican Conservation and Development Trust,** 29 Dunbarton Ave. (ℂ **876/960-2848**) in Kingston.

Beyond the ranger station, it's still another 5km or more (3 or more miles) to the panoramic peak. Some hikers give up when they reach aptly named **Lazy Man's Peak** at 2,100m (7,000 ft.). There's a good view of the main peak here. But if you're determined, it's another 30 minutes to reach the summit. There is no more spectacular panorama in all the West Indies: You feel you're standing at the top of the world.

The downside? You have to get back down that mountain—and return to civilization.

Appendix:
Jamaica in Depth

1 History 101

IN THE BEGINNING Jamaica was settled around 6000 B.C. by Stone Age people about whom little is known. They were displaced around A.D. 600 by the Arawak, Indians who originated in northern South America (probably in the area of modern Guyana). Skillful fishers and crafters of pottery and bead items, they had copper-colored skin and lived in thatch-covered huts similar to those used in parts of Jamaica today. The Arawak made flint knives and spears tipped with sharks' teeth, but they never developed the bow and arrow. They lived mainly on a diet of fish and turtle steak. The Arawak were completely unprepared for the horrors brought by the Spanish conquest.

CRUEL COLONY In 1494, during his second voyage to the New World, Christopher Columbus visited Jamaica and claimed the island for the Spanish monarchy. Although he quickly departed to search for gold and treasure elsewhere, he returned accidentally in 1503 to 1504, when he was stranded with a group of Spanish sailors for many months off Jamaica's northern coastline while they repaired their worm-eaten ships.

Beginning in 1509, Spaniards from the nearby colony of Santo Domingo established two settlements on Jamaica: one in the north (Nueva Sevilla, later abandoned) in modern St. Ann Parish; and another in the south, San Jago de

Dateline

- **ca. 6000 B.C.** Indian groups settle Jamaica.
- **ca. A.D. 600** Arawak Indians come to the island.
- **1494** Columbus visits Jamaica.
- **1503–1504** Columbus is stranded on the North Coast.
- **1509** Spain establishes colony at St. Ann's Bay.
- **1513** First enslaved Africans arrive.
- **1520** Sugarcane cultivation introduced.
- **1655** British troops overrun Jamaica.
- **1658** British repel Spanish invaders.
- **1661** Major British colonization begins.
- **1670** Hundreds of privateers given royal protection in Jamaica.
- **1692** Earthquake destroys Port Royal.
- **1739** Rebellious Maroons sign treaty with British.
- **1800** Census reveals huge majority of blacks in Jamaica.
- **1808** Slave trade abolished by Great Britain.
- **1838** Slavery ended.
- **1866** Jamaica becomes a British Crown Colony.
- **1930** Jamaicans push for autonomy.
- **1943** Bauxite mining begins.
- **1944** Universal adult suffrage instituted.
- **1960s** Tourist industry grows.
- **1962** Jamaica achieves independence on August 6.
- **1970s** Bob Marley and reggae gain world fame.
- **1972** Michael Manley, a socialist, becomes prime minister.

la Vega (St. James of the Plain), on the site of present-day Spanish Town. Pirates estimated the Arawak population in Jamaica at the time to be about 60,000.

In 1513 the first African slaves reached Jamaica, and in 1520 sugarcane cultivation was introduced. In the 1540s the Spanish Crown grudgingly offered the entire island to Columbus's family as a reward for his service to Spain. Columbus's descendants did nothing to develop the island's vast potential, however. Angered by the lack of immediate profit (abundantly available from gold and silver mines in Mexico and Peru), the Spanish colonists accomplished very little other than to wipe out the entire Arawak population. Forced into slavery, every last Arawak was either executed or died of disease, overwork, or malnutrition.

- **1980** Edward Seaga, a moderate, succeeds Manley.
- **1980s** High unemployment spreads, though tourism thrives.
- **1988** Hurricane Gilbert devastates Jamaica.
- **1989** Manley, now moderate, returns to power.
- **1992** P. J. Patterson becomes prime minister.
- **1997** Patriarch Michael Manley dies; elections retain Patterson and People's National Party.
- **2001** Violence erupts in Kingston; 40 are killed.
- **2002** Queen Elizabeth's visit rekindles emotions about the British role in modern Jamaica.

RAISING THE UNION JACK   After 146 years as a badly and cruelly administered backwater of the Spanish Empire, Jamaica met with a change of fortune when a British armada arrived at Kingston Harbour in 1655. The fleet sailed on orders from Oliver Cromwell, but it had failed in its mission to conquer the well-fortified Spanish colony of Santo Domingo. Almost as an afterthought, it went on to Jamaica. Within a day, the Spaniards surrendered the whole island to the British, who allowed them to escape. Most of the Spaniards emigrated to nearby Cuba, although a handful remained secretly on the island's North Coast.

Six months later, British colonists arrived, but many died. In 1657 Spaniards based in Cuba initiated a last-ditch effort to recapture Jamaica. Two of the fiercest and biggest battles in Jamaican history pitted the Spanish against the British. The defection from the Spanish army by some Maroons (escaped slaves and their descendants living in the Jamaican mountains) led to the permanent exit in 1660 of Spanish troops from Jamaica. Humiliated, these soldiers escaped to Cuba in canoes.

In 1661 the British began to colonize Jamaica in earnest. They appointed a governor directly responsible to the Crown, with orders to create a governing council elected by the colonists. All children born of British subjects in Jamaica became free citizens of England. Within 2 years the population of Jamaica had grown to more than 4,000. Hostilities between England and Spain continued, with skirmishes and raids by the British on Spanish colonies in Cuba and Central America.

EARTHQUAKES, FIRES & PROSPERITY   British interest in Jamaica grew as opportunities for adding profit and territory increased. In 1687 Sir Hans Sloane, physician to powerful British aristocrats and namesake of London's Sloane Square, wrote two influential scholarly books on the geography, flora, fauna, and people of Jamaica. The volumes helped convince Britain to continue its investments in the island.

In 1690 a slave rebellion was crushed by the British, who executed its leaders. Some participants escaped to the mountains, where they joined the independent Maroons.

Jamaica Natural

Jamaica and the rest of the Caribbean archipelago are summits of a submarine string of mountains, which in prehistoric times probably formed a land bridge between modern Mexico and Venezuela. Covering about 10,982 sq. km (4,240 sq. miles), the island is approximately the size of Connecticut, yet offers a diverse landscape. It is 235km (146 miles) long; its width ranges from 35 to 93km (22–58 miles).

Millions of years ago, volcanoes thrust up from the ocean floor, forming Jamaica's mountains, which reach to 2,221m (7,402 ft.) high (loftier than any along the eastern seaboard of North America). These mountains, located in an east-to-west line in central Jamaica, contain more than 120 rivers and many waterfalls, as well as thermal springs. In the high mountains of the east, the landscape features semitropical rainforest and copses of mist-covered pines. The mountains are bordered on the north and east by a narrow coastal plain fringed with beaches. The flat, arid southern coastline reminds visitors of African savanna or Indian plains, whereas the moist, fertile North Coast slopes steeply from hills down to excellent beaches. Much of Jamaica is underlaid by limestone, dotted with dozens of caves that store large reservoirs of naturally filtered drinking water.

Almost everything grows in Jamaica, as proved by colonial British botanists who imported flowers and fruits from Asia, the Pacific, Africa, and Canada. The island contains unique orchids, ferns, bromeliads, and varieties of fruit, like the Bombay mango, that don't flourish elsewhere in the Western Hemisphere. Birds, insects, and other animals are also abundant.

Framing the capital of Kingston, the Blue Mountains dominate the eastern third of the island. This is the country's most panoramic area, and it's split by a network of paths, trails, and bad roads—a paradise for hikers. From this region comes Blue Mountain coffee, the most expensive in the world. Younger than the Blue Mountains, the John Crow Mountains rise at the northeastern end of the island. Only the most skilled mountain climbers or advanced hikers should attempt this rugged karstic terrain. It rains here almost daily, creating a rainforest effect.

Jamaica's longest river is called Black River, and it's bordered by marshes, swamps, and mangroves where bird and animal life, including reptiles, flourish. Black River, which is also the name of a small port, is in the southwestern section, lying east of Savanna-la-Mar and reached by Route A2.

On June 7, 1692, just before noon, one of the most violent earthquakes in history struck the city of Port Royal. In less than 20 minutes the three shocks, ascending in intensity, caused the sea to recede and then rush back with terrible force, drowning the virtuous and wicked alike. Much of the city actually dropped into the sea. A handful of survivors attempted to rebuild parts of the city, but in 1704 a great fire destroyed every building except a stone-sided fort.

Although the centerpiece of Jamaica had disappeared, the countryside was fast becoming one of the world's great producers of sugar—mostly to sweeten the flood of tea being imported by Great Britain from Asia.

POWER STRUGGLES & EMANCIPATION   The struggle for control of Jamaica intensified over the next 50 years as the island became one of the most profitable outposts of the British Empire, despite hurricanes, pirate raids, and slave rebellions. For ease of government, it was divided into 13 parishes, whose boundaries remain today.

Most troublesome for the British were the Maroons, who escaped control by fleeing into the mountains and forests. In 1734, in one of many dramatic battles, the British captured the Maroon stronghold of Nanny Town, destroying its buildings and killing many of its inhabitants. The survivors committed suicide by jumping off a cliff, preferring death to enslavement.

By 1739, however, both the British and the Maroons recognized the virtues of mutual cooperation, and signed a series of peace agreements. The Maroons were given tax-free land in different parts of the island and were allowed to govern themselves. In return, the Maroons also agreed to hunt down runaway slaves and return them to their masters.

By the time of the American Revolution, the population of Jamaica had reached almost 210,000, some 193,000 of whom were slaves. After 1776 it increased further as Loyalist residents of the United States moved south to Jamaica. An official census in 1800 revealed a Jamaican population of 300,000 blacks and 20,000 whites. This disparity was not lost upon either the powers in London or the leaders of the increasingly politicized blacks.

However, the boom times—dependent on a supply of slave labor—would not last. The importation of forced laborers from Africa was outlawed in 1807, and in 1838 slavery itself was made illegal in all British dependencies, including Jamaica. The sugar industry began to decline.

A MODERN AGE DAWNS   Still, progress marched forward on other fronts, ushering in a more modern Jamaica less dependent on a plantation economy. Telegraph communication with Europe was established in 1869; nickel coins—guaranteed by the Bank of England—were issued for the first time. The educational system was improved, irrigation projects were initiated, and British tourism began to revive fortunes in the 1890s. A Lands Department was organized to sell government land to local farmers cheaply. Island teachers organized themselves into unions, and the railroad was extended to Jamaica's northeast tip at Port Antonio. New bridges and improved roads also helped open the island. Jamaican planters began investing heavily in the production of bananas.

On January 14, 1907, another great earthquake shattered much of Kingston, destroying or damaging nearly every building. More than 800 lives were lost, and total damage was estimated at £2 million. But Parliament and the Church of England spent massive funds to rebuild Kingston; the new street plan they created remains the basis for the city's layout to this day.

During World War I, Jamaica sent about 10,000 men to fight with British forces in Palestine, where they battled heroically against the Ottoman Empire. The war effort was complicated by hurricanes that devastated the island's banana crop, but progress was still made: In May 1917, for instance, Jamaican women were given the right to vote.

In 1938 Alexander Bustamante organized Jamaica's first officially recognized labor union. At first imprisoned but later freed and knighted by the British, he is today regarded as the founder of modern Jamaica.

At the outbreak of World War II in 1939, Jamaica was placed under rigid control, as the governor set prices and censored the press, the telephones, the telegraph, and international mail. By 1943 many Jamaicans were moving north to the United States to work in munitions factories. During that same year, bauxite, the raw material for aluminum, was mined for the first time in St. Ann Parish. The next year, a new constitution provided for universal adult suffrage.

FREEDOM ARRIVES   In 1957 Jamaica attained full internal self-government under a system based on well-established British models. Lengthy celebrations marked the event. Montego Bay airport opened 2 years later, and Kingston airport was expanded to handle the flood of visitors. Despite economic growth, however, large-scale emigration to Great Britain continued.

On August 6, 1962, Jamaica finally achieved its independence (though it still recognizes the British monarch as the formal head of state). Sir Alexander Bustamante, head of the Jamaica Labour Party (JLP), became the country's first prime minister. And the last British troops in Jamaica departed the island, officially ending a colonial era begun in 1655.

RECENT TIMES   In 1966 Haile Selassie I, emperor of Ethiopia, came to Jamaica on a 3-day state visit. The stay sparked national interest in the emperor's life, and as a result there was a notable increase in Jamaican converts to Rastafarianism, a religion that venerates the late emperor, known earlier as Ras Tafari (see "Rastafarianism," below). During the 1970s the popularity of Rastafarian musician Bob Marley and other Jamaican reggae performers spread worldwide, carving a place for Jamaica on the international music stage.

Fun Fact **Did You Know?**

- Jamaica is the third largest of the 51 inhabited islands in the Caribbean—only Cuba and Hispaniola are bigger.
- Ackee, though cooked and used as a vegetable, is actually a fruit that is poisonous until it bursts open and its gases escape. It is part of Jamaica's national dish, ackee and salt fish.
- Blue Mountain coffee, grown on the slopes of Jamaica's loftiest mountain, is among the tastiest and most sought-after coffees in the world.
- From 1503 to 1504, Christopher Columbus spent about a year off the North Coast of Jamaica because his worm-eaten vessels weren't seaworthy.
- In the 17th century, the notorious privateer Henry Morgan presided over Jamaica's Port Royal, known as the "wickedest city on earth."
- On August 6, 1962, England's Princess Margaret and U.S. Vice President Lyndon B. Johnson watched as the British Union Jack was lowered and a new flag raised as Jamaica attained independence. The new flag featured a gold cross on a black-and-green background.
- Rastafarians, a Jamaican religious group, venerate the late Ethiopian emperor, Haile Selassie.
- Some Jamaicans regard ganja (marijuana) as a sacred plant and testify to its healing power.

In 1972 Michael Manley, a trade unionist who headed the left-wing People's National Party (PNP), was sworn in for the first of what would eventually be several terms as prime minister. Jamaicans began arguing vehemently about whether the nation should embrace socialism, and about its relationship with the United States. In 1977 Cuban President Fidel Castro paid a 6-day official visit, which led to a perception in Washington that Jamaican politics were increasingly shifting leftward.

Despite Manley's political prowess, Edward Seaga of the moderate JLP defeated him and became prime minister. Shortly afterward, Jamaica broke diplomatic ties with Cuba. Seaga's mandate was solidified during the 1983 elections. Seaga attempted to promote economic growth and cut inflation, but with little success. Unemployment rose, as did violent crime. Then, in September 1988, the island was devastated by Hurricane Gilbert, which destroyed 100,000 homes and affected a number of resort properties.

A more moderate Manley returned to power as prime minister in 1989, retiring in 1992 due to ill health; he was succeeded by Percival J. Patterson, also a moderate. In 1998 Patterson launched a crackdown on those who badgered tourists to buy or barter for drugs, sex, or merchandise. Jamaica also established night courts, making it possible for law-enforcement officers to appear in court without having to abandon their beats.

Still, in 2001 Jamaica saw yet another eruption of violence; gun battles between police and government opponents caused at least 40 deaths. To quell the violence, Patterson ordered out the entire Jamaican army of 3,000 soldiers. What sparked this violence wasn't clear.

In early 2002, the "queen of Jamaica"—Queen Elizabeth II—paid a royal visit. She came to show good will but also stirred up controversy about why an independent nation still retained a European monarch as head of state—a throwback to colonialism that many still resented. For his part, Patterson assured Jamaicans he would work to create a national identity more distinct than ever from the former days of British rule.

Jamaica faced a dim financial year in 2003, with a budget deficit of about 11%. High interest rates kept inflation in the single figures but the Jamaican dollar weakened.

2 Jamaican Style

ART

The bulk of Jamaican artwork has been executed since 1940, when the yearning for independence and a sense of national destiny colored many aspects of the country's life. Whereas reggae, the national musical form, is strongly influenced by a subculture (the Rastafarians), Jamaican painting is much wider-ranging and diverse.

The most easily accessible Jamaican artwork is "yard art," which rises from the concrete, litter, and poverty of the island's cities. Punctuated with solid blocks of vivid color, and sometimes interspersed with graffiti, these murals are often viewed as an authentic reflection of the Jamaican soul. Subjects include political satire, naive (or intuitive) depictions of an artist's friends and family, idealized Jamaican landscapes, and kaleidoscopic visions of heaven and hell. Examples of yard art seem to increase, along with graffiti and political slogans, before each election. Predictably, however, a flood of uninspired woodcarvings, handicrafts, and banal painting has appeared in recent years because of worldwide commercial and sociological interest in yard art. *Caveat emptor.*

Jamaica's leading painters include Carl Abrahams, whose recurrent theme is the Last Supper; Barrington Watson, known for a romanticized, charming view of the Jamaican people; Eugene Hyde, one of the country's first modern abstract artists; and British-born Jonathan Routh, whose illustrations of Queen Victoria during elaborate state visits to Jamaica—none of which really occurred—provoke laughter as far away as London. Also noteworthy are Christopher Gonzalez, who won a commission from the Jamaican government for a statue of reggae superstar Bob Marley; David Boxer, one of the first Jamaican surrealists; and Osmond Watson, known for his sharp-angled and absorbing depictions of the human face.

ARCHITECTURE

The obsession of Jamaican planters with contemporary British taste helped create an architectural elegance rivaled by only a handful of other British colonies, notably Pennsylvania, Massachusetts, and Barbados. Although the island style began with an allegiance to Georgian models, concessions were made to the heat, humidity, bugs, hurricanes, and earthquakes of the tropics. Later, after Jamaica became recognized as the leading outpost of British military power and agrarian skill in the West Indies, Jamaican architectural principles spread to other parts of the Caribbean.

Georgian-type design, manifest in Jamaica's port facilities, Customs houses, and civic buildings, was most graceful in the island's many Great Houses. Intended as centerpieces for enormous sugar plantations, these buildings include some of the finest examples of domestic architecture in the West Indies. Among common design elements are wide verandas on at least two sides, balustrades, intricate fretwork, sophisticated applications of contrasting types of lattice, deep and sometimes ornate fascia boards, and a prevalence of pineapple-shaped finials above cornices and rooflines. The first floors of Jamaican buildings were usually elevated by low stilts or pilings to allow air to circulate. This prevented rot, cooled the ground floor, and helped keep insects, rodents, and scorpions out of living quarters.

Not all of Jamaica's 18th-century buildings were designed along Georgian lines. Smaller, less pretentious houses were built in styles appropriate to the income of the owners and the demands of the sites. Jamaican vernacular architectural style was developed by tenant farms and indentured servants, many from Scotland, and by the children of freed enslaved persons. These houses usually received the prevailing trade winds, and typically were angled to prevent smoke from the kitchen from blowing into living quarters. Known for the pleasing proportions of their inner spaces, the buildings continue to surprise contemporary architectural critics by their appropriate placement and convenient interior traffic patterns.

Since the end of World War II, architecture in Jamaica has followed two distinct variations on colonial themes. Banks, civic buildings, and commercial structures have generally been inspired by the thick walls, small windows, and massive dignity of the island's 18th- and 19th-century British forts. Hotels and private dwellings, on the other hand, typically trace their inspiration to the island's Great Houses or the unpretentious wooden cottages that still dot the landscape.

3 The Jamaican People & Their Culture

Jamaica's 2.5 million people form a spectrum of types that bespeak the island's heritage. Most Jamaicans are black, but there are also people of Chinese, Asian Indian, Middle Eastern, and European background. About 75% of the people are classified as black African and about 15% as Afro-European.

Jamaicans are generally friendly, funny, opinionated, talented, and nearly impossible to forget. Their sense of humor is dry and understated, yet robust. National pride is specific—beating the British at cricket, winning gold medals in the Olympics, or attaining world boxing titles.

And Jamaica is more diverse than one might imagine. The British brought slaves from the west coast of Africa, notably the area of modern Ghana, who belonged to the Fanti and Ashanti ethnic groups. Others are descended from the Ibo and Yoruba people of present-day Nigeria. When the forced laborers were freed in 1838, most deserted the plantations and settled in the hills to cultivate small plots of land. They founded a peasantry that is still regarded as the backbone of Jamaica.

After slavery was abolished, the British brought in Chinese and East Indians to work the plantations. You can still see pockets of these immigrants here and there.

Jews are among the oldest residents of Jamaica. Jewish families have been here since the time of the earliest Spanish settlements. Though small in number (about 400), the Jewish community has been influential in government and commerce.

In 2003 the birthrate in Jamaica was about 17 per 1,000 persons, the death rate 5 per 1,000. Life expectancy at birth was 78 years for females, 76 years for males. There was a net out-migration of 6 persons per 1,000 inhabitants. The annual population growth rate was .61%.

RASTAFARIANISM

Although relatively small in number (there were about 14,000 firm adherents in the early 1980s), Rastafarians have had a wide-ranging influence on Jamaican culture. Their identifying dreadlocks (long, sometimes braided, hair) can be seen at virtually every level of society. In 2003, there were 265,000 Rastafarians.

Stressing the continuity of black African culture throughout history, Rastas believe in their direct spiritual descent from King Solomon's liaison with the Queen of Sheba. Rastafarianism, according to some, is based on an intuitive interpretation of history and scripture—sometimes with broad brush strokes—with special emphasis on the reading of Old Testament prophecies. Rastafarians stress contemplation, meditation, a willingness to work inwardly to the "I" (inner divinity), and an abstractly political bent.

Their beliefs are enhanced through sacramental rites of ganja (marijuana) smoking, Bible reading (with particular stress on references to Ethiopia), music, physical exercise, art, poetry, and cottage industries like handicrafts and broom making. Reggae music developed from Rasta circles has produced such international stars as the fervently religious Bob Marley. Jamaica's politicians, aware of the allure of Rastafarianism, often pay homage to its beliefs.

A male Rastafarian's beard is a sign of his pact with God (Jah or Jehovah), and his Bible is his source of knowledge. His dreadlocks are a symbol of his link with the Lion of Judah and Elect of God, the late Emperor of Ethiopia Haile Selassie, who, while a prince, was known as Ras Tafari (hence the religion's name). During the emperor's 1966 visit to Jamaica, more than 100,000 visitors greeted his airplane in something approaching religious ecstasy. The visit almost completely eclipsed Queen Elizabeth's a few months earlier.

LANGUAGE

The official language of Jamaica is English, but the unofficial language is a patois. Linguists and a handful of Jamaican novelists have recently transformed this oral language into written form, although for most Jamaicans it remains solely

Ganja

Marijuana use is the island's biggest open secret, and you'll no doubt encounter it during your vacation. (To be honest, it's the big draw for some visitors.) Vendors seem to hawk it at random, often through the chain-link fences surrounding popular resorts.

Ganja is viewed with differing degrees of severity in Jamaican society, but it's still officially illegal. We should warn you that being caught by the authorities with marijuana in your possession could lead to immediate imprisonment or deportation.

Marijuana and Jamaica have long endured a love-hate relationship. The plant was brought here by indentured servants from India in the mid–19th century. Revered by them as a medicinal and sacred plant, and referred to by the British as "Indian hemp," it quickly attracted the attention of the island's plantation owners because its use significantly reduced the productivity of those who ingested it. Legislation against its use quickly followed—not for moral or ethical reasons, but because it was bad for business.

During the 1930s the slow rise of Rastafarianism (whose adherents believe marijuana use is an essential part of their religion) and the occasional use of marijuana by U.S. bohemians, artists, and jazz musicians, led to growing exports of the plant to the United States. A massive increase in U.S. consumption occurred during the 1960s. Since the mid–1970s, after more stringent patrols were instituted along the U.S.–Mexico border, drug trafficking has slowed. Still, today between 75% and 95% of all marijuana grown in Jamaica is consumed in the United States.

Cultivation of the crop, when conducted on the typical large scale, is as meticulous and thorough as that of any horticulturist raising a prize species of tomato or rose. Seeds, sold illegally by the quart, must first be coaxed into seedlings in a greenhouse, then transplanted into fields at 60-centimeter (2-ft.) intervals. Popular lore claims that the most prolific seedlings are raised in Jamaica's red, bauxite-rich soil and nurtured with

spoken—and richly nuanced. Experts say more than 90% of its vocabulary is derived from English, with the remaining words largely borrowed from African languages. There are also words taken from Spanish, Arawak, French, Chinese, Portuguese, and East Indian languages.

Although pronounced similar to Standard English, the patois preserves many 17th- and 18th-century expressions in common use during the early British colonial settlement of Jamaica. This archaic and simplified structure, coupled with African accents and special intonation, can make the language difficult to understand. Some linguists consider it a separate language, whereas others view it as an alternate form of English. Some of the most interesting anecdotes and fables in the Caribbean are usually told in the patois, so understanding its structure can add to your insight into Jamaican culture.

Proverbs and place names express some of the vitality of Jamaican language. For "Mind your own business," there is "Cockroach no business in fowl-yard."

all-organic fertilizers such as bat dung or goat droppings. As the plants mature, tattered scarecrows, loud reggae music, fluttering strips of reel-to-reel recording tape, and slingshots manned by local laborers are used to fend off the birds that feed on the seeds.

Even more feared than natural predators, however, are the Jamaican police. The constables periodically raid fields and destroy the crop by burning it or spraying it with herbicide.

Marijuana plants reach maturity 5 to 6 months after transplanting, often with a height of about 3m (9½ ft.). Stalks and stems are then pressed for hash oil; leaves are dried for smoking, baking into pastries, or use in herbal teas. Most seeds are saved for the next planting.

Various types of ganja can be grown in a single field, each identified by names like McConey, Cotton, Burr, Bush, Goat's Horn, Lamb's Breath, and Mad. Bush and Mad are the least potent of the crop, while the strongest are acknowledged to be Lamb's Breath, Cotton, and Burr. The last three are marketed in the United States under the name *sinsemilla* (Spanish for "without seeds"). Rastafarians typically prefer specific types of marijuana, much the way a gastronome might prefer specific types of caviar or red wine. To each his own.

Smuggling the dried and packaged final product is disconcertingly efficient. A small plane lands at any of the country's hundreds of out-law airstrips, which are sometimes disguised immediately before and after use by huts and shacks moved into place by crews of strong-armed men. The planes then whisk away the crop, much of it to Florida. Undoubtedly, in a country with chronically low wages and constant fear of unemployment, the temptation to accept bribes runs high among government officials in both high and low positions.

Despite its widespread presence, marijuana is illegal in Jamaica and drug-sniffing dogs are employed at all airports. Our advice? Don't end your vacation in jail.

For being corrupted by bad companions, "You lay wid dawg, you get wid fleas." And for the pretentious, "The higher monkey climb, the more him expose."

Both British and biblical place-names abound in Jamaica. Examples include Somerset and Siloah, Highgate and Horeb. One also sees Arawak names like Linguanea, Spanish ones like Oracabessa, Scottish names like Rest-and-Be-Thankful, and entirely Jamaican names like Red Gal Ring.

A final note: The patois has been embellished and altered with the growth of Rastafarianism. Rastas have injected several grammatical concepts, one of the most apparent being the repeated use of "I"—a reminder of their reverence of Ras Tafari. "I" is almost always substituted for the pronoun "me." It is also sub-stituted for many prefixes or initial syllables. Thus, "all right," becomes "I're," "brethren" becomes "Idren," and "praises" becomes "Ises." The Rastafarian changes of Jamaica's patois are a recent phenomenon and have not always been adopted by non-Rastas.

FOLKLORE

Nothing shaped the modern culture of the Caribbean more than the arrival of slaves from various parts of Africa. They brought gods, beliefs, superstitions, and fears with them. Although later converted to Christianity, they kept their traditions vibrant in fairs and festivals. Jamaican cultural and social life revolved mostly around the church, which was instrumental in molding a sense of community. Storytellers helped maintain ties to the past for each new generation, since little was written down until the 20th century.

Some folk beliefs are expressed in music, notably in the lyrics of reggae. Others are expressed in rhythmic chanting, whose stresses and moods once accompanied both hard labor and dancing. Other beliefs can be found in fairy tales and legends about the island's slaves and their owners. The telling of oral narrations is a highly nuanced art form. Repetition and an inspired use of patois are important features.

Healing arts make use of Jamaican tradition, especially in the "balm yard," an herb-garden-cum-healing place where a mixture of religion and magic is applied by a doctor or "balmist" of either sex. Some medicines brewed, distilled, or fermented in the yard are derived from recipes handed down for many generations and can be effective against ailments ranging from infertility to skin disease. A balm yard is usually encircled by a half-dozen thatch-covered huts, which house supplicants (patients). Bright-red flags fly above each hut to chase away evil spirits. Ceremonies resembling revival meetings are held nightly, with a "mother" and a "father" urging the crowd to groan ecstatically and in unison. The threat of damnation in hellfire may be mentioned as punishment for anyone who doesn't groan loudly enough or believe fervently enough. It is believed that prayer and supplications to Jesus and various good and evil spirits will help relieve the sick of their ailments.

The two most famous spirits of Jamaica are Obeah and the jumbie. Originating in the southern Caribbean, Obeah is a superstitious force that believers hold responsible for both good and evil. It is prudent not to tangle with this force, which might make trouble for you. Because of a long-established awareness of Obeah, and an unwillingness to tempt it with too positive an answer, a Jamaican is likely to answer "Not too bad" if asked about his or her health.

There's no agreement on the nature of a jumbie. It's been suggested that it is the spirit of a dead person that didn't go where it belonged. Some islanders, however, say that "they're the souls of live people, who live in the bodies of the dead." Jumbies are said to inhabit households and to possess equal capacities for good and evil. Most prominent are Mocko Jumbies, carnival stilt-walkers seen in parades.

One folk tradition that can while away hours of a Jamaican's time is reciting Anansi stories. A notorious trickster—with a distinctly Jamaican sense of humor—Anansi manipulates those around him and eventually acquires whatever spoils happen to be available. In one well-known story, Anansi steals sheep from a nearby plantation; in another, he pilfers half of every other person's plantain. Among the funniest are episodes in which Anansi exposes the indiscretions of an Anglican priest. Anansi's traits include a lisp, a potent sense of greed, and a tendency to be wicked.

These stories are sometimes funny, sometimes poignant, sometimes sexually suggestive. They often are parables, teaching a basic lesson about life. Each narrative has a well-defined and often charming ending, which tends to be followed by an explosion of laughter from the storyteller. Several collections of Anansi stories have been published.

DANCE & DRAMA

A sense of drama and theatrics is innate to most Jamaicans, as shown in the easy laughter, irreverent humor, and loose-limbed style that are the island's pride and joy. In Kingston in particular, everyone is a star, if only for a moment, during one or another of any day's interpersonal exchanges.

The natural flair of Jamaicans has been channeled into many different drama and dance groups. One of the most visible is the **National Dance Theatre Company (NDTC)**, whose goal is to assemble a body of dancers, actors, and singers to express and explore the Jamaican sense of stylized movement. Applauded by audiences around the world, the company offers abstract interpretations of the Jamaican experience, going far beyond the parameters of a purely folkloric dance troupe. Members are mostly volunteers (lawyers, secretaries, laborers, and nurses by day, highly motivated performers by night), and the troupe has usually refused to accept funds from the government. Among the troupe's most famous performers are Rex Nettleford, a dancer and cofounder, and Louise Bennett, pantomime artist, storyteller, and an early proponent of Jamaican patois as a literary language. Established in 1962, NDTC holds a season running from July to December, with most performances in August. It performs at several locations, so you'll need to inquire about where to attend on a particular day.

4 Calypso, Reggae & Rap: The Rhythms of Jamaica

Many people visit Jamaica just to hear its authentic **reggae**. Reggae is now known around the world and is recognized in the annual Grammy Awards run by the U.S. music industry.

The roots of Jamaica's unique reggae music can be found in an early form of Jamaican music called **mento**. This music was brought to the island by African slaves, who played it to help forget their anguish. Mento is reminiscent of the rhythm and blues that, in the mid–20th century, swept across North America. It is usually accompanied by hip-rolling dances known as dubbing, with highly suggestive lyrics to match. Famous Jamaican mento groups reaching their prime in the 1950s included the Ticklers and the Pork Chops Rhumba Box Band of Montego Bay.

In the late 1950s, Jamaican musicians combined boogie-woogie with rhythm and blues to form a short-lived but vibrant music named **ska**. Jamaican artists in this form included Don Drummond, Roland Alphanso, Lloyd Knibbs, Theophilus Beckford, and Cluet Johnson. The five often played together during a vital chapter in Jamaica's musical history. It was the politicization of ska by Rastafarians that led to the creation of reggae.

CALYPSO

No analysis of Jamaican music would be complete without the inclusion of Jamaican-born musician, actor, and political activist Harry Belafonte. Recognizable to more North American and British listeners than any other Jamaican singer in the 1950s and early 1960s, he became famous for his version of the island's unofficial anthem, "Jamaica Farewell," in which the singer leaves a little girl in Kingston Town. Although he worked in other musical forms, Belafonte is particularly known for his smooth and infectious calypsos. *Note:* Some purists in the crowd will point out that calypso is really a product of Trinidad, but it remains very popular in Jamaica (and Barbados).

REGGAE

The heartbeat of Jamaica, reggae is the island's most distinctive musical form, as closely linked to Jamaica as soul is to Detroit, jazz to New Orleans, and blues to Chicago. The term *reggae* is best defined as "coming from the people." It is taken from a song written and performed in the late 1960s by Jamaica-born "Toots" Hibbert and the Maytals ("Do the Reggay").

With a beat some fans claim is narcotic, it has crossed political and racial lines and temporarily drained the hostilities of thousands of listeners, injecting a new kind of life into their pelvises, knees, fingertips, and buttocks. It has influenced the music of international stars like the Rolling Stones, Eric Clapton, Paul Simon, the B-52s, Stevie Wonder, Elton John, and Third World, as well as lesser-known acts like Black Uhuru, Chicago's Blue Riddim Band, and many rap groups. Most notably, it propelled onto the world scene a street-smart kid from Kingston named Bob Marley. Today the recording studios of Kingston, sometimes called "the Nashville of the Third World," churn out hundreds of reggae albums every year, many snapped up by danceaholics in Los Angeles, Italy, and Japan.

Reggae's earliest roots lie in the African musical tradition of mento. Later, the rhythms and body movements of mento were combined with an improvised interpretation of the then-fashionable French quadrille to create the distinctive hip-rolling and lower-body contact known as dubbing. Lyrics became increasingly suggestive (some say salacious) and playful as the musical form gained confidence and a body of devoted adherents.

In the 1950s calypso entered Jamaica from the southern Caribbean, especially Trinidad, while rhythm and blues and rock 'n' roll were imported from the United States. Both melded with mento into a danceable mixture that drew islanders into beer and dance halls throughout Jamaica. This music led to the powerful but short-lived form called ska, made famous by the Skatalites, who peaked in the mid-1960s. When their leader and trombonist, Don Drummond, became a highly politicized convert to Rastafarianism, other musicians followed and altered their rhythms to reflect the African drumbeats known as **kumina** and **burru.** This fertile musical tradition, when fused with ripening political movements around 1968, became reggae.

One of the most recent adaptations of reggae is **soca,** which is more upbeat and less political. Aficionados say that reggae makes you think, but soca makes you dance. The music is fun, infectious, and spontaneous—perfect for partying—and is often imbued with the humor and wry attitudes of Jamaican urban dwellers. Soca's most visible artists include Byron Lee and the Dragonaires. A skillful entrepreneur and organizer, Lee is the force behind the growing annual Jamaica Carnival (first week of April), which draws more than 15,000 foreign visitors to Kingston, Ocho Rios, and Montego Bay.

Leading early reggae musicians included Anton Ellis and Delroy Wilson. Later, Bob Marley and (to a lesser degree) Jimmy Cliff propelled reggae to world prominence. Marley's band, the Wailers, included his Kingston friends Peter MacIntosh (later known as Peter Tosh), Junior Brathwaite, and Bunny Livingston (now known as Bunny Wailer). Since the death of Marley in 1981, other famous reggae musicians have included his son Ziggy Marley, Roy Parkes, Winston "Yellowman" Foster, and Roy Shirley. Among noteworthy bands are Third World and The Mighty Diamonds.

RAP

After 1965 the influx of Jamaican immigrants to North America's ghettos had a profound (and profitable) influence on popular music. Such Jamaican-born stars as Clive Campbell, combining the Jamaican gift for the spoken word with reggae rhythms and high electronic amplification, developed the roots of what eventually became known as rap. Taking on a street-smart adaptation of rhyming couplets, some of which were influenced by Jamaica's rich appreciation of word games and speech patterns, he organized street parties where the music of his groups—Cool DJ Herc, Nigger Twins, and the Herculords—was broadcast to thousands of listeners from van-mounted amplifiers.

Designed to electrify rather than soothe, and reflecting the restlessness of a new generation of Jamaicans bored with the sometimes mind-numbing rhythms of reggae, popular Jamaican music became less awestruck by Rastafarian dogmas, less Afro-centric, and more focused on the urban experiences of ghetto life in New York. Music became harder, simpler, more urban, and more conscious of profit-searching market trends. Dubbed dance-hall music, the sounds seemed inspired by the hard edge of the survival-related facts of life ("girls, guns, drugs, and crime") on urban streets.

One of the major exponents of the new form is Super Cat (William Maragh), who wears his hair cut short ("bald-head") in deliberate contrast to the dreadlocks sported by the disciples of Marley. The sounds are hard and spare, the lyrics as brutal and cruel as the ghetto that inspires them. Whereas Marley, during the peak of his reggae appeal, sold mainly to young whites, the new sounds appeal mostly to young black audiences who relate to the sense of raw danger evoked by dance-hall music's rhythms and lyrics. During some of Shabba Ranks's concerts, audiences in Jamaica have shown their approval by firing gunshots into the air—known locally as a "salute of honor."

RECOMMENDED RECORDINGS

Jamaica's culture is indicative of and certainly can be defined by its main musical export—reggae. The undisputed king of reggae, the late Bob Marley, popularized the genre, which is musically stylized by percussive guitar riffs and lyrically peppered with political and social activism.

Legend (Best of Bob Marley and the Wailers) (Tuff Gong/Island Records, 422846210-2) chronicles the late artist's body of work. Termed a poet and a prophet, Marley brought reggae into the American conscience and mainstream. The album features a collection of hits such as "Get Up, Stand Up," "Jamming," "One Love," and perhaps his biggest hit, "Stir It Up." *Legend* was released in 1984 and has already outsold such megahits as The Beatles' *Sgt. Pepper's Lonely Hearts Club Band*, and Pink Floyd's *Dark Side of the Moon*.

Honorary Citizen (Columbia/Legacy, C3H 65064), a three-CD boxed set, covers the career of Marley's contemporary, Peter Tosh, a reggae legend in his own right and also termed a poet, prophet, preacher, and philosopher. *Honorary Citizen* features the best of Tosh's work, including some unreleased and live tracks with artists such as Marley, Bunny Wailer (of the Wailers), Mick Jagger, and Keith Richards. Tracks include "Fire Fire," "Arise Blackman," and "Legalize It" (Columbia/Legacy, C3H 65064).

Liberation (Shanachie Records, 43059) by Bunny Wailer is another important album of the reggae movement. When *Newsweek* selected the three most important musicians in the Third World, Bunny Wailer was among them. He has controlled his artistic development, despite tragedies in his career, while avoiding any compromise of his vision.

One Love (Heartbeat Records, CDH111/112) by Bunny Wailer, Bob Marley, and Peter Tosh (Three Greats) offers the three biggest legends of reggae together on one album—a "Three Tenors" of reggae. This compilation is the first chronological and definitive study of Bob Marley and the Wailers and Peter Tosh in their formative years. The music, the cornerstone of the ska era, includes previously unreleased alternate takes and rarely recorded Jamaican singers.

Ziggy Marley and the Melody Makers, Best of 1988–1993 (Virgin, 724384490821) spans the successful and ongoing career of one of Bob's many children. Ziggy is largely responsible for reggae's 1990s mainstream acceptance, penning such crossover hits as "One Bright Day," "Joy and Blues," and "Brothers and Sisters," which are contained in this collection. His debut album, *Conscious Party,* is still his best work.

Liberation—The Island Anthology (Island Records, 314518282-2) by Black Uhuru is a boxed set of collected works from the band's 1980s Island Records catalog. The 1980s were still dominated by the Marley sound, and Black Uhuru was the band that passed the reggae torch along to Ziggy Marley.

The Lee "Scratch" Perry Arkology (Island/Jamaica, 61524 3792) is another recent boxed set release of another "old skool" reggae artist from "back in the day." Covering Perry's entire career, it contains recordings from the many different bands he formed, as well as solo works, including two never-before-released tracks.

In Concert—Best of Jimmy Cliff (Reprise, 2256-2) is a recording with a legendary pedigree. Produced by legends Andrew Loog Oldham and Cliff, this album features Ernest Ranglin on lead guitar and Earl "Baga" Walker on bass. It includes the classic "Many Rivers to Cross" and "The Harder They Come."

Jah King Don (Mango/Island Records, 162539915-2) by Burning Spear is known for its strongly political lyrics. This record could serve as a definition for hard-core reggae. It includes "World Power" and "Land of My Birth."

Too Long in Slavery (Virgin, CDFL9011) is an album by one of Ziggy Marley's contemporaries, Culture. All songs were written and performed by J. Hill, K. Daley, and A. Walker.

The recordings by the Marleys, Tosh, and the Wailers are considered to be purist reggae, defined as such today because of reggae's splintering into many different forms, such as dance/house music and rap.

Best Sellers (Rykodisc Records, 20178) by Mikey Dread is a compilation album spanning the career of Dread, Jamaica's best-known DJ. With material ranging from 1979 to 1990, it was Dread (along with the band Maxi Priest) who ushered reggae into the new dance movement.

Many Moods of Moses (VP Records, VPCD1513-2) by Beenie Man is the latest release by an artist whose political lyrics maintain all the criteria for purist reggae, but he adds a dance beat heard only from the likes of Dread before the 1990s. Tracks from this album include "Who I Am (Zim Zamma)" and "Oysters and Conch."

Sawuri (Dom Records, CD 1067), the self-titled release by Sawuri, offers a Creole taste to the Jamaican sound. It features the Caribbean artists Marcel Komba and Georges Marie.

Militant (Ras Records, ML 81811-2), released by Andrew Bees in 1995, is a signal that the purist reggae will always remain en vogue in Jamaica. Tracks such as "Struggle and Strive," "Militant," and "Life in the Ghetto" evoke modern realizations of the same themes Marley, Tosh, and Wailer sang about in the past—except now with the mounting frustrations of citizens from a Third World society.

5 Jamaican Food & Drink

A visit to Jamaica doesn't mean a diet of just local cuisine. The island's eating establishments employ some of the best chefs in the Caribbean, hailing from the

United States and Europe, and they can prepare a sumptuous meal of elegant French, Continental, and American dishes.

When dining in Jamaica, try some fish, which is often delectable, especially dolphin (the game fish, not the mammal), wahoo, yellowtail, grouper, and red snapper. These fish, when broiled with hot lime sauce as an accompaniment, may represent your most memorable island meals. Sweet-tasting Caribbean lobster is different from the Maine variety.

Elaborate buffets are often a feature at the major resort hotels. These buffets display a variety of local dishes along with other, more-standard fare, and they are almost always reasonably priced. Entertainment is often a reggae band. Even if you are not staying at a particular hotel, you can call on any given night and make a reservation to partake of a buffet.

Before booking a hotel, it's wise to have a clear understanding of what is included in the various meal plans offered.

To save money, many visitors prefer the Modified American Plan (MAP), which includes room, breakfast, and one main meal per day, nearly always dinner. The visitor is then free to take lunch somewhere else. If the hotel has a beach, guests often will order a light a la carte lunch at their hotel, which is added to the bill. The American Plan (AP), on the other hand, includes all three meals per day. Drinks, including wine, are usually extra.

If you want to eat your main meals outside the hotel, book a Continental Plan (CP), which includes only breakfast. To go one step further, choose the European Plan (EP), which includes no meals.

APPETIZERS

Except for soup, appetizers don't loom large in the Jamaican kitchen. The most popular appetizer is **stamp and go,** or salt-fish cakes. **Solomon Gundy** is made with pickled shad, herring, and mackerel, and seasoned with onions, hot peppers, and pimento berries. Many Jamaicans begin their meal by enjoying **plantain and banana chips** with their drinks.

The most famous soup, **pepper pot,** is an old Arawak recipe. It is often made with callaloo, okra, kale, pig's tail (or salt beef), coconut meat, yams, scallions, and hot peppers. Another favorite, **ackee soup,** is made from ackee (usually from a dozen ripe open pods), flavored with a shin of beef or a salted pig's tail. **Pumpkin soup** is seasoned with salted beef or a salted pig's tail. **Red-pea soup** is also delicious (note that it's actually made with red beans).

Tea in Jamaica can mean any nonalcoholic drink, and **fish tea,** a legacy of plantation days, is made with fish heads or bony fish, along with green bananas, tomatoes, scallions, hot peppers, and other spices.

MAIN COURSES & SIDE DISHES

Because Jamaica is an island, there is great emphasis on seafood, but many other tasty dishes are also offered. **Rock lobster** is a regular dish on every menu, presented grilled, thermidor, cold, or hot. **Salt fish and ackee** is the national dish, a mixture of salt cod and a brightly colored vegetable-like fruit that tastes something like scrambled eggs. *Escoveitch* (marinated fish) is usually fried and then simmered in vinegar with onions and peppers.

Among meat dishes, **curried mutton** and **goat** are popular, each highly seasoned and likely to affect your body temperature. **Jerk pork** is characteristic of rural areas, where it is barbecued slowly over wood fires until crisp and brown.

Apart from rice and peas (usually red beans), usually served as a sort of risotto with added onions, spices, and salt pork, some vegetables may be new to you.

They include **breadfruit,** imported by Captain Bligh in 1723 when he arrived aboard HMS *Bounty;* **callaloo,** rather like spinach, used in pepper-pot soup (not to be confused with the stew of the same name); **cho-cho,** served boiled and buttered or stuffed; and **green bananas** and **plantains,** fried or boiled and served with almost everything. Then there is **pumpkin,** which goes into soup, as mentioned, or is served on the side, boiled and mashed with butter. **Sweet potatoes** are part of main courses, and there is also a sweet-potato pudding made with sugar and coconut milk, flavored with cinnamon, nutmeg, and vanilla.

You'll also come across intriguing **dip and fall back,** a salty stew with bananas and dumplings, and **rundown,** mackerel cooked in coconut milk and often eaten for breakfast. The really adventurous can try **manish water,** a soup made from goat offal and tripe said to increase virility. **Patties** (meat pies) are a staple snack; the best are sold in Montego Bay. Boiled corn, roast yams, roast salt fish, fried fish, soups, and fruits are available at roadside stands.

DRINKS

Tea, as mentioned above, is a word used in Jamaica to describe any nonalcoholic drink, a tradition dating back to plantation days. Fish tea (see "Appetizers," above) is often consumed as a refreshing pick-me-up and is sometimes sold along the side of the road. **Skyjuice** is a favorite Jamaican treat for a hot afternoon. It's sold by street vendors from not-always-sanitary carts. It consists of shaved ice with sugar-laden fruit syrup and is offered in small plastic bags with a straw. **Coconut water** is refreshing, especially when a roadside vendor chops the top off a fruit straight from a tree.

Rum punches are available everywhere, and the local beer is **Red Stripe.** The island produces many liqueurs, the most famous being **Tía María,** made from coffee beans. **Rumona** is another good one to bring back home with you. **Bellywash,** the local name for limeade, will supply the extra liquid you may need to counteract the tropical heat. **Blue Mountain coffee** is considered among the world's best coffees—it's also very expensive. Tea, cocoa, and milk are also usually available.

6 Jamaican Films

More than any other island in the Caribbean, Jamaica has offered itself to the movie industry as a site for fabricating celluloid dreams. Partly the result of savvy marketing, partly the result of a landscape varied enough to offer diverse filmmaking settings, the island might at any time during your visit host crews for filming movies, documentaries, or TV shows and commercials.

This is to some extent the heritage of 1940s and 1950s film star Errol Flynn, whose parties and personal shenanigans added a Hollywood gloss to Port Antonio and other areas of Jamaica. The actor owned both a hotel and a house in Port Antonio for years, and the town is still the home of his widow, ex–film actor Patrice Wymore. Hollywood filmmakers first visited the island in 1941 to shoot exteriors for the George Brent and Ann Sheridan comedy *Honeymoon for Three,* and again in 1954 to shoot the climax of *20,000 Leagues Under the Sea.* Altogether, more than 50 motion pictures and dozens of documentaries, music videos, and TV commercials have been filmed amid the shantytowns, Great Houses, Spanish and English colonial forts, deserts, beaches, and seascapes of Jamaica.

The best-selling novels of the 20th century include the James Bond spy series written by Ian Fleming at his house on Jamaica's northeast shore. The movie versions of some, such as *Dr. No* and *Live and Let Die,* were partly filmed in Jamaica.

The filming of other, even larger, adventure films followed shortly after the first Bond films. Although its story is set mostly on Devil's Island off French Guiana, *Papillon,* starring Steve McQueen, was largely filmed in Jamaica, near the crowded North Shore town of Falmouth. A make-believe French colonial prison was constructed, using British overseers and an army of Jamaican carpenters and masons.

During the 1970s, when Jamaican politics took an abrupt turn to the left, foreign filmmakers (as well as investors in other industries) stayed away from the island. In 1984, however, the newly elected centrist prime minister, Edward Seaga, relaxed import-export laws and enacted tax incentives for the film industry, making Jamaica again an important site for international films. The government also cut red tape. Filmmakers were lured in addition by Jamaica's trained technicians and actors (all nonunion, offering services priced much lower than their U.S. or British counterparts), and occasional access to army and navy facilities. Because of the various advantages, Jamaica snared the location rights for Tom Cruise's *Cocktail,* Whoopi Goldberg's *Clara's Heart,* Bill Murray and Peter O'Toole's *Club Paradise,* and a 1990 remake of *Lord of the Flies.* Each was filmed near Errol Flynn's old stamping ground, Port Antonio.

Documentaries have been filmed in Jamaica as well. Heritage Films chose the Blue Mountains as a cost-effective substitute for Kenya and Tanzania when producing a biography of zoologist Dian Fossey. Entitled *The Strange Life and Death of Dian Fossey,* this film should not be confused with Sigourney Weaver's *Gorillas in the Mist,* which was shot in Africa. Several films dealing with reggae have also been produced in Jamaica.

For the 26-episode remake of the *Flipper* TV series, which presented the adventures of two young brothers with a herd of tame dolphins, the locale was shifted from the Florida Keys to Jamaica, and the script was updated to include a Jamaican actor as one of the young protagonists.

Even in films not requiring a Caribbean setting, Jamaica retains a strong pull on the imaginations and budgets of Hollywood filmmakers. One such example is the humorous horror movie *Popcorn,* which a viewer might easily believe had been filmed in Los Angeles. Actually, the film was shot with English and American actors in Kingston, and has nothing to do with swaying palms and coral reefs. Most challenging to the film's art directors was the creation of a giant mosquito poised menacingly atop the protagonists' car.

The Lunatic, released in 1992, is a ribald comedy. Set in a tiny Jamaican hamlet, it tells the madcap story of a vagabond with a good heart, a "randy" German visitor, and a butcher of many talents. The film has been called "a Caribbean fantasy."

Wide Sargasso Sea (1993), an adaptation of the Jean Rhys novel of 1966, received good critical notices. Rich in imagery of 19th-century Jamaica, it tells the story of a young English aristocrat named Rochester (played by Nathaniel Parker) who arrives in Jamaica and marries a Creole sugar-plantation heiress (played by Karina Lombard). Rochester turns out to be *the* Rochester—that is, the brooding man of *Jane Eyre* by Charlotte Brontë. In her novel, Rhys attempted to "fill in" the doomed saga of Rochester's first marriage as a prelude to *Jane Eyre.*

Stepping Razor—Red X (1993) has been called a "reggae *Malcolm X.*" This politically galvanizing portrait tells the tragic story of reggae legend Peter Tosh, who was murdered in 1988. The voice in the film is that of Tosh himself, culled from the "Red X" tapes he was working on for a planned autobiography. Much vintage footage of life in Jamaica in the 1960s is shown in the film, along with re-creations of Tosh's childhood.

Cool Running (1993) is loosely based on the story of a Jamaica bobsled team that achieved massive publicity at the 1988 Winter Olympics. The team had practiced without every having seen snow. The film was shot not only in Calgary (site of the Olympics) but in Ocho Rios and Montego Bay. One critic suggested it was a snowbound *Chariots of Fire* with reggae music.

How Stella Got Her Groove Back (1998) is an effective commercial for the island, starring Angela Bassett as a vacationing San Francisco stockbroker who dallies with Taye Diggs amongst lush scenery. The Jamaica tourism board says that travelers still call to ask where the movie was shot. The answer: mostly in and around Mo Bay, at Half Moon Beach and the Round Hill Hotel, where Diggs returned for his off-screen wedding.

Several less flattering films focus on the lives of gangsters ("shottas") and drug traffickers in Kingston. *Belly* (1998) features rappers DMX, Nas, Method Man, and TLC's T-Boz; popular Jamaican actor Paul Campbell stars in *Third World Cop* (1999); and Wyclef Jean appears in *Shottas* (2002).

Instinct (1999) stars Cuba Gooding, Jr. as a psychologist studying a disturbed anthropologist, played by Anthony Hopkins, who's been living with a pack of gorillas in the African jungle. The movie is another example of the Jamaican landscape's scenic versatility, with the Roaring River and rainforests outside of St. Ann plausibly standing in for the wilds of Rwanda.

Index

Falmouth, 83–85
Falmouth Courthouse (Falmouth), 83
Families with children
best resorts for, 7–8
information and resources, 28
Fern Gully, 147
Festivals and special events, 23
Film, flying with, 32
Films, Jamaican, 234–236
Firefly (Grants Town), 149
Fishing
Negril, 113
Ocho Rios, 147
Port Antonio, 176
special events, 23
Flynn, Errol, 135, 161, 162, 164, 174, 177–180, 234, 235
Folklore, 228
Folly Beach (Port Antonio), 174–175, 179
The Folly Great House (near Port Antonio), 181
Folly Point Lighthouse (near Port Antonio), 181
Font Hill Beach, 121
Font Hill Wildlife Sanctuary, 121
Fort Charles (Spanish Town), 208
Fort Clarence (Kingston), 201
Fort George (Port Antonio), 179
Fort George Village Shopping Arcade (Port Antonio), 186–187
Fort Montego (Montego Bay), 76
Frame Centre Gallery (Kingston), 205
Frenchman's Cove (Port Antonio), 174
Frommers.com, 30

Gallery Carriacou (Port Antonio), 187
Ganja (marijuana), 44, 226–227
Gardens
Athenry Gardens and Cave of Nonsuch (near Port Antonio), 183
Bath Botanical Gardens, 188
Castleton Botanical Gardens, 185–186
Cinchona Botanical Gardens (Clydesdale), 215–216
Coyaba River Garden and Museum, 148

Hope Botanical Gardens & Zoo (Kingston), 203
Mrs. Stephenson's Garden (Mandeville), 132
Gay and lesbian travelers, 27
Georgian House (Montego Bay), 76
Gloucester Avenue (Montego Bay), 76
Goldeneye (Oracabessa), 10
Golf, 37
best courses, 4–5
Kingston, 202
Montego Bay, 74–75
Negril, 112
Ocho Rios, 147
Port Antonio, 176
Runaway Bay, 158
Gordon Town, 215
Gordon Town Trail, 215
Gosse, Philip, 120
The Great Morass, 122–128
Green Grotto Caves (near Discovery Bay), 6, 149
Green Island, 114
Greenwood Great House (Montego Bay), 78–79
Grove Court (Mandeville), 132
Guava Ridge, 215
Guava River Trail, 178
Guesthouses, 43
Gunboat Beach (Kingston), 201

Half Moon, golf, 75
Half Moon Beach (Green Island), 114
Half Moon Golf, Tennis & Beach Club (Montego Bay)
golf, 5
tennis, 5, 38, 75
Half Moon Plaza (Montego Bay), 81
Half Moon Resort, swimming with the dolphins, 75
Handcrafts, 11
Negril, 115
Ocho Rios, 153
Hardwar Gap, 214
Harmony Hall (near Ocho Rios), 149–150
Health concerns, 25–26
Health insurance, 24–25
Hedonism II (Negril), nightlife, 11–12, 116–117
Hedonism III Resort (Runaway Bay), nude weddings at, 155
Hellshire Beach (Kingston), 201
Hendricks Building (Black River), 122

High season, 21
Hiking, 37
Abbey Green, 216
Blue Mountain Peak, 217
Blue Mountains, 211, 212–213
Cinchona Botanical Gardens (Clydesdale), 216
Holywell National Recreation Park, 214–215
Port Antonio, 176–178
Rio Grande Valley, 186
Hilton High Day Tour (Montego Bay), 77–78
History of Jamaica, 218–223
Holidays, 22
Holland America Line-Westours, 39
Holywell National Recreation Park, 214–215
Honeymoon resorts, best, 6–7
Hope Bay, 185
Hope Botanical Gardens & Zoo (Kingston), 203
Horseback riding, 38
Montego Bay, 75
Negril, 112
Ocho Rios, 147
Prospect Plantation (St. Ann), 151
Rhodes Hall Plantation (near Negril), 114
Riverhead Adventure Trail, 148–149
Runaway Bay, 158–159
House of Assembly (Spanish Town), 208
Hurricane season, 22

Industry, 215
Insurance, 24–25
Internet access, 31–32
Kingston, 192
Mandeville, 129
Montego Bay, 54
Negril, 92
Irish Town, 213
Ironshore Golf & Country Club (Montego Bay), 75
Island Plaza (Ocho Rios), 152, 153
Island Village (Ocho Rios), 150

Jablum Coffee Company (Mavis Bank), 216
Jamaica Grande's Beach (Ocho Rios), 146
Jamaican people and Culture, 224–229
Jamaican Reef Beach (Port Antonio), 174–175

Frommer's® Complete Travel Guides

Alaska
Alaska Cruises & Ports of Call
American Southwest
Amsterdam
Argentina & Chile
Arizona
Atlanta
Australia
Austria
Bahamas
Barcelona, Madrid & Seville
Beijing
Belgium, Holland & Luxembourg
Bermuda
Boston
Brazil
British Columbia & the Canadian Rockies
Brussels & Bruges
Budapest & the Best of Hungary
Calgary
California
Canada
Cancún, Cozumel & the Yucatán
Cape Cod, Nantucket & Martha's Vineyard
Caribbean
Caribbean Cruises & Ports of Call
Caribbean Ports of Call
Carolinas & Georgia
Chicago
China
Colorado
Costa Rica
Cuba
Denmark
Denver, Boulder & Colorado Springs
England
Europe
Europe by Rail
European Cruises & Ports of Call

Florence, Tuscany & Umbria
Florida
France
Germany
Great Britain
Greece
Greek Islands
Halifax
Hawaii
Hong Kong
Honolulu, Waikiki & Oahu
India
Ireland
Israel
Italy
Jamaica
Japan
Kauai
Las Vegas
London
Los Angeles
Maryland & Delaware
Maui
Mexico
Montana & Wyoming
Montréal & Québec City
Munich & the Bavarian Alps
Nashville & Memphis
Newfoundland & Labrador
New England
New Mexico
New Orleans
New York City
New York State
New Zealand
Northern Italy
Norway
Nova Scotia, New Brunswick & Prince Edward Island
Oregon
Ottawa
Paris

Peru
Philadelphia & the Amish Country
Portugal
Prague & the Best of the Czech Republic
Provence & the Riviera
Puerto Rico
Rome
San Antonio & Austin
San Diego
San Francisco
Santa Fe, Taos & Albuquerque
Scandinavia
Scotland
Seattle
Shanghai
Sicily
Singapore & Malaysia
South Africa
South America
South Florida
South Pacific
Southeast Asia
Spain
Sweden
Switzerland
Texas
Thailand
Tokyo
Toronto
USA
Utah
Vancouver & Victoria
Vermont, New Hampshire & Maine
Vienna & the Danube Valley
Virgin Islands
Virginia
Walt Disney World® & Orlando
Washington, D.C.
Washington State

Frommer's® Dollar-a-Day Guides

Australia from $50 a Day
California from $70 a Day
England from $75 a Day
Europe from $70 a Day
Florida from $70 a Day
Hawaii from $80 a Day

Ireland from $80 a Day
Italy from $70 a Day
London from $90 a Day
New York from $90 a Day
Paris from $90 a Day
San Francisco from $70 a Day

Washington, D.C. from $80 a Day
Portable London from $90 a Day
Portable New York City from $90 a Day
Portable Paris from $90 a Day

Frommer's® Portable Guides

Acapulco, Ixtapa & Zihuatanejo
Amsterdam
Aruba
Australia's Great Barrier Reef
Bahamas
Berlin
Big Island of Hawaii
Boston
California Wine Country
Cancún
Cayman Islands
Charleston
Chicago
Disneyland®
Dominican Republic
Dublin

Florence
Frankfurt
Hong Kong
Las Vegas
Las Vegas for Non-Gamblers
London
Los Angeles
Los Cabos & Baja
Maine Coast
Maui
Miami
Nantucket & Martha's Vineyard
New Orleans
New York City
Paris

Phoenix & Scottsdale
Portland
Puerto Rico
Puerto Vallarta, Manzanillo & Guadalajara
Rio de Janeiro
San Diego
San Francisco
Savannah
Vancouver
Vancouver Island
Venice
Virgin Islands
Washington, D.C.
Whistler

FROMMER'S® NATIONAL PARK GUIDES

Algonquin Provincial Park
Banff & Jasper
Family Vacations in the National
  Parks

Grand Canyon
National Parks of the American
  West
Rocky Mountain

Yellowstone & Grand Teton
Yosemite & Sequoia/Kings
  Canyon
Zion & Bryce Canyon

FROMMER'S® MEMORABLE WALKS

Chicago
London

New York
Paris

San Francisco

FROMMER'S® WITH KIDS GUIDES

Chicago
Las Vegas
New York City

Ottawa
San Francisco
Toronto

Vancouver
Walt Disney World® & Orlando
Washington, D.C.

SUZY GERSHMAN'S BORN TO SHOP GUIDES

Born to Shop: France
Born to Shop: Hong Kong,
  Shanghai & Beijing

Born to Shop: Italy
Born to Shop: London

Born to Shop: New York
Born to Shop: Paris

FROMMER'S® IRREVERENT GUIDES

Amsterdam
Boston
Chicago
Las Vegas
London

Los Angeles
Manhattan
New Orleans
Paris
Rome

San Francisco
Seattle & Portland
Vancouver
Walt Disney World®
Washington, D.C.

FROMMER'S® BEST-LOVED DRIVING TOURS

Austria
Britain
California
France

Germany
Ireland
Italy
New England

Northern Italy
Scotland
Spain
Tuscany & Umbria

THE UNOFFICIAL GUIDES®

Beyond Disney
Central Italy
Chicago
Cruises
Disneyland®
England
Florida
Florida with Kids
Inside Disney

Hawaii
Las Vegas
London
Maui
Mexico's Best Beach Resorts
Mini Las Vegas
Mini-Mickey
New Orleans
New York City

Paris
San Francisco
Skiing & Snowboarding in the
  West
Walt Disney World®
Walt Disney World® for
  Grown-ups
Walt Disney World® with Kids
Washington, D.C.

SPECIAL-INTEREST TITLES

Athens Past & Present
Cities Ranked & Rated
Frommer's Best Day Trips from London
Frommer's Caribbean Hideaways
Frommer's China: The 50 Most Memorable Trips
Frommer's Exploring America by RV
Frommer's Gay & Lesbian Europe
Frommer's Best RV and Tent Campgrounds
  in the U.S.A.

Frommer's Road Atlas Europe
Frommer's Road Atlas France
Frommer's Road Atlas Ireland
Frommer's Wonderful Weekends from
  New York City
The New York Times' Guide to Unforgettable
  Weekends
Retirement Places Rated
Rome Past & Present

Travel Tip: He who finds the best hotel deal has more to spend on facials involving knobbly vegetables.

Hello, the Roaming Gnome here. I've been nabbed from the garden and taken round the world. The people who took me are so terribly clever. They find the best offerings on Travelocity. For very little cha-ching. And that means I get to be pampered and exfoliated till I'm pink as a bunny's doodah.

travelocity

1-888-TRAVELOCITY / travelocity.com / America Online Keyword: Travel

Travel Tip: Make sure there's customer service for any change of plans — involving friendly natives, for example.

One can plan and plan, but if you don't book with the right people you can't seize le moment and canoodle with the poodle named Pansy. I, for one, am all for fraternizing with the locals. Better yet, if I need to extend my stay and my gnome nappers are willing, it can all be arranged through the 800 number at, oh look, how convenient, the lovely company coat of arms.